Does the Church Know How to Teach?

DOES THE CHURCH KNOW HOW TO TEACH?

An Ecumenical Inquiry

EDITED BY

KENDIG BRUBAKER CULLY

THE MACMILLAN COMPANY
COLLIER-MACMILLAN LTD., LONDON

ACKNOWLEDGMENTS

Permission to reprint the following is gratefully acknowledged:

"Some Bases of Common Concern in Education," by James J. Megivern, C.M., copyright © 1968 by *St. John's University Alumni Magazine*.

Excerpts (quoted in Chapter VI) from *Credibility of the Church Today*, by Gregory Baum, copyright ©1968 by Herder & Herder, Inc., and from *The Church*, by Hans Küng, copyright © 1968 by Sheed & Ward.

Library of Congress Catalog Card Number: 79-90872

FIRST PRINTING

The Macmillan Company
866 Third Avenue, New York, N.Y. 10022

Collier-Macmillan Canada Ltd., Toronto, Ontario

Printed in the United States of America

CONTENTS

PREFACE   vii

I   *Historical Perspectives on Religion and Education in the American Scene*

     A.   JAMES MICHAEL LEE   3

     B.   D. CAMPBELL WYCKOFF   22

II   *Understanding the Psychology of Religious Learning*

     A.   ROBERT P. O'NEIL   41

     B.   ROY S. LEE   55

III   *Education in the Sociological Situation, U.S.A.*

     A.   ROSEMARY R. RUETHER   79

     B.   MARTIN E. MARTY   101

IV   *Attitudes Toward an Ecumenical Orientation for Religious Education*

     A.   SISTER ANN PATRICK WARE, S.L.   127

     B.   HOWARD GRIMES   150

V   *Some Bases of Common Concern in Education*

     A.   JAMES J. MEGIVERN, C.M.   177

     B.   GERALD E. KNOFF   187

VI   *The Church's Worship as Formative of the Christian Community*

        A.   GEOFFREY I. KEATING, S.S.E.   215

        B.   IRIS V. CULLY   235

VII   *The Discipline of Theology—Seminary and University*

        A.   BENEDICT M. ASHLEY, O.P.   261

        B.   RANDOLPH CRUMP MILLER   289

VIII   *Implications of Catholic-Protestant Educational Dialogue*

        EDITOR'S NOTE   317

        A.   THE DECLARATION ON CHRISTIAN EDUCATION   319

        B.   DIALOGUE WITH NON-BELIEVERS   331

        C.   KENDIG BRUBAKER CULLY   342

NOTES   353

CONTRIBUTORS   373

INDEX   375

PREFACE

In RECENT YEARS, especially since Vatican Council II, the "great dialogue" has been proceeding apace. Copious studies and books have dealt with various aspects of the dialogue among Christians. Notably lacking, however, until now has been any substantial exploration into the realm of education, except for some materials that have appeared in the journal of the Religious Education Association, *Religious Education*, through the ecumenical vision of its editor, Randolph Crump Miller.

The present book is designed to further the ecumenical dialogue insofar as its educational aspects are concerned. The editor is deeply grateful to the outstanding—and very busy—religious education theorists and practitioners who consented to expand a conversation that until now has barely begun as far as published materials are concerned. The writers of this book have been exploring an area not yet fully understood, yet certainly better documented than those astral spaces into which cosmonauts have lately been venturing. It is hoped that the conversations initiated here may continue happily and productively into the decades ahead.

Although "Catholic" and "Protestant" writers have spoken here, it must be clearly understood that none of them speaks "officially" for his own ecclesial body. (Only the documents in the first two parts of Chapter Eight can be labeled "official.") The writers have spoken as individual scholars and believers, variously rooted in the church families in which they are situated. Since all scholars have access to objective sources of information, it will be noted that there are many areas of common agreement. Likewise, since each scholar looks at data from his personal stance, there are bound to be many expressions of opinion which some would call subjective.

A word may be in order as to the origin of the conversation. It grew out of a luncheon conversation among three persons at a Louisville, Kentucky, hotel, during a meeting of the Professors and Research Section of the Division of Christian Education, National Council of the Churches of Christ in the U.S.A. The conversationalists were Iris V. Cully, Gerard S. Sloyan, and myself. Since Father Sloyan was the only Roman Catholic speaker attending the meeting, we chatted about the unfortunate lack of ecumenical dialogue vis-à-vis education. He was most helpful, later on, in another conversation, when he and I outlined together what might appear in such a work as this, and who the potential contributors might be. Our later conversation, also, was at luncheon, that time in a sidewalk restaurant in Washington, D.C. Perhaps there is something symbolic in the fact that a book about common Christian concern and enterprise in education should have had its genesis in the breaking of bread, albeit non-sacramentally! Out of a common sharing of a mutual educational task, perchance there may emerge an affirmative answer—in the future, if not completely now—to the question stated in the title of this volume.

KENDIG BRUBAKER CULLY

New York City

ONE

Historical Perspectives on Religion and Education in the American Scene

A. by JAMES MICHAEL LEE

B. by D. CAMPBELL WYCKOFF

A. *by* JAMES MICHAEL LEE

T HE TITLE OF this volume reads *Does the Church Know How to Teach?* To answer this question, we must first look at the educational mission of the church.

The church's educational mission does not live in the past, but the past surely lives in the church's educational mission. Indeed, it might be argued that too much of the past lives in the church's present educational mission. What I am suggesting is that many of the problems facing the church's present educational mission are not so much problems arising from the essence of this mission to the modern world, but rather from problems which are historically conditioned. It is the aim of this chapter to examine three major problems facing the Roman Catholic Church's present educational mission, and to ascertain the extent to which these problems are problems in themselves as contrasted with the extent to which the inheritance of past structures and modes of being have in fact caused the present problems in the first place.

Problem: Should Catholic Schools Continue to Exist?

The American Roman Catholic school system as it presently exists is unique in the church, both in the modern world and throughout all of ecclesiastical history. As Jerome Diffley has commented, there is no precedent in church history for establishing

3

such a system of church-related schools as American Catholics did for the general education of *all* children regardless of vocational destination.[1] Unique in the history of the church, the American Catholic school enterprise is a *total* school effort, ranging from kindergarten through elementary school, secondary school, college and university, professional schools such as medical school, and special education. The war cry of the Third Plenary Council of Baltimore (1884) was "every Catholic child in a Catholic school." In the Catholic school, in theory at least, religion is supposed to pervade every subject. Thus in 1937 James Burns and Bernard Kohlbrenner could write: "The ideal Catholic school calls for Catholic textbooks to serve as the basis for teaching."[2] To be sure, the Catholic textbook historically has tended to be rather typical in Catholic schools, not only in the obvious areas of history, literature, and religion, but also in spelling, arithmetic, reading, and even in penmanship.[3]

The underlying assumption made by American Catholicism is that a total Catholic school system is necessary if the church is to survive and to be strong. Indeed, it not infrequently happens in new suburbs that the Catholic school is erected before the church building itself—with liturgical services being conducted temporarily in the school gymnasium. So strong is the feeling on the part of the hierarchy that the Catholic school is necessary for the survival of the American church that in 1967 when I published a book suggesting that Catholic elementary schools be abandoned because the empirical evidence indicates that an educational institution cannot inculcate deeper values into children between the ages of six and twelve, a Midwestern cardinal issued a pastoral letter to be read from every pulpit in his archdiocese denouncing me and this view.

Catholic schools did not exist in any form for several centuries after Jesus—an indication of how those closest in time to Jesus viewed the importance of the total Christian school in the educational mission of the church. Why then should the American church, nineteen hundred years later, view the Catholic school as such an integral and necessary part of the church's educational mission? American history can furnish a clue.

In the colonial period, there were basically three patterns of school development: the New England, the Middle Atlantic, and the Southern. The one which eventually provided the dominant pattern for public education down to the present time was the New England pattern. The New England pattern had as its avowed purpose the preservation and inculcation of Protestantism. Indeed, the first educational legislation passed in what is now the United States, the Massachusetts 1642 act, directed parents and town officials to see to the education of children under their jurisdiction, notably to insure that these children could read the Bible and understand the principles of religion. The Protestant character of the schools was established by a Massachusetts act passed five years later, and remained more or less typical of the nation's schools until at least World War I.

Hand-in-hand with the Protestant character of the nation's public schools was the strong Protestant flavor of the colonies and later of the republic—a Protestantism which was marked, among other things, by a strong feeling of anti-Catholicism. In 1642 Virginia passed an act against "Catholics and priests." In 1654 Maryland disenfranchised Catholics; in 1700 Massachusetts enacted legislation against "Jesuits and popish priests." Maryland's 1704 "Act to Prevent the Growth of Popery" had as one of its key provisions the penalty of deportation from the colony of any Catholic who operated a school or otherwise formally instructed children. The mid-nineteenth century constituted a heyday for militant anti-Catholicism. In 1835 the Native American Party was established, and in 1842 the American Protestant Association was formed with the twin aim of promoting Protestantism and of uniting in order to defend Protestant interests against "popery." The *Baptist Record* endorsed the advice of the *Protestant Banner* concerning the alleged Catholic threat to public schools in the early 1840s: "If the priests succeed in erecting the cross of antichrist over our common school houses, they will have gained a triumph which every Christian and philanthropist will deplore."[4]

The "Rum, Romanism, and Rebellion" issue in the presidential campaign of 1884 reflected much of the Protestant sentiment of that time, a sentiment which spilled over into the school questions as evidenced in such publications as the 1888 one by Daniel Dorchester entitled *Romanism Versus the Public School System.*[5] The modern Ku Klux Klan, founded in Georgia in 1915, was quite militant in its anti-Catholicism. The 1928 presidential election contained sizable elements of anti-Catholicism, and as late as the 1960 presidential campaign, John F. Kennedy had to face considerable national opposition from conservative and liberal Protestants, an opposition which culminated in his famous confrontation with a group of Protestant ministers in Houston to defend himself from charges that a Catholic President implied dictation of national policy by the American hierarchy and the Vatican.[6]

It was not surprising, therefore, that the latent or manifest anti-Catholicism which up until very recent times has typified much of American life, combined with the Protestant cast of the American public school which perdured at least until World War I, caused Catholic leaders to erect their own defense system to preserve and encourage the Catholic religion in America. This defense system was the total Catholic school enterprise, a venture which was given strong sanction in ecclesiastical law. The first American ecclesiastical legislation emanated from the First Provincial Council of Baltimore (1829), which stated that ". . . we judge it absolutely necessary that [Catholic] schools should be established in which the young may be taught the principles of faith and morality, while being instructed in letters."[7] This legislation, which technically was exhortatory rather than binding under pain of sin, was restricted to the ecclesiastical province of Baltimore. Stronger legislation which was binding on the entire country had to wait for the three plenary councils of Baltimore, attended by bishops from the entire United States. The First and Second Plenary Councils of Baltimore (1852 and 1866 respectively) officially exhorted all Catholic parents to send their children to Catholic schools at all levels. Although these exhortations were promulgated with vigor, they technically remained at the legal level of exhortation as contrasted with formally binding law.

It was the Third Plenary Council of Baltimore (1884) which enacted the binding legislation on Catholic schools which remains technically in force down to the present day. The two key educational enactments of this Council were those (1) requiring all Catholic parents, under pain of sin, to send their children to Catholic schools at all levels, unless specifically exempted by their bishop for serious reasons; (2) requiring all parishes to erect and maintain *in perpetuum* Catholic elementary schools attached to their parishes. For many years these regulations, particularly the first, were strongly enforced. However, in recent years, because of the fact that there have been far more Catholic children than Catholic school classrooms and teachers to accommodate them, the legislation has not been zealously enforced. One of the last cases to attract national attention occurred in 1941 when Thomas Toolen, bishop of Mobile (Alabama), forbade the sacraments to those Catholic parents who sent their children to public schools.

The American ecclesiastical legislation requiring attendance of Catholic children in Catholic schools has been quite consistent with —if indeed sometimes more mild than—similar legislation emanating from the Vatican. Pius IX's celebrated Syllabus of Errors (1864), especially Numbers 15, 17, and 18, condemned as grave errors against. the Catholic religion: (1) a belief that the entire system of public schools belongs to the state, and (2) a belief that Catholics may approve any system of education "severed from the Catholic faith and the power of the Church." Three years later, the Vatican's Sacred Congregation of the Propagation of the Faith observed that "in general, no sufficient reason can be conceived for entrusting Catholic young people to non-Catholic universities." In 1875 this same sacred congregation, with the approval and the confirmation of the pope himself, issued the "Instruction to the Bishops of the United States Concerning the Public Schools." This *instructio* laid down the general principle that both natural and divine law forbids Catholic students to attend non-Catholic schools unless such attendance is absolutely necessary. This *instructio*, incidentally, exerted significant impact on the educational legislation of the Third Plenary Council of Baltimore. Canon 1374 of the Code of Canon Law (*Codex Juris Canonicis*, 1917), the statutory legal system presently governing the Roman Church, specifically forbids Catholics from attending secular schools. Only in exceptional circumstances can the local bishop grant a Catholic student permission for such attendance. In his famous encyclical on Christian education, *Divini Illius Magistri* (1929), Pius XI states ". . . it follows that the so-called 'neutral' or 'lay' school from which religion is excluded is contrary to the fundamental principles of education. Such a school, moreover, cannot exist in practice; it is bound to become irreligious."[8]

In this same encyclical, Pius XI also condemns "mixed schools" in which "students are provided with separate religious instruction, but receive other lessons in common with non-Catholic pupils from non-Catholic teachers."[9] The Second Vatican Council's "Declaration on Christian Education" (1965) states: "As for Catholic parents, the Council calls to mind their duty to entrust their children to Catholic schools, when and where this is possible."[10]

But all of these events—even Vatican II—are now in the past. Times have changed, and people and attitudes have changed with them. In the increased clarity generated by the new enlightenment, a fresh re-examination of the current situation in public schools and the current needs of the church's educational mission perhaps might prove fruitful.

Are the public schools really "godless"? Do the public schools consciously neglect moral and spiritual formation in their students? Is religion really excluded from the public schools?

A careful examination by Cleo Berry of nine educational thinkers and statesmen who were most influential in shaping the prevailing concept of the place of religion in the nation's public schools revealed that eight of the nine believed that the constitutional principle of separation of church and state did not mean the complete elimination of the teaching about religion in the public schools.[11] Neil G. McCluskey, a careful student of the career of Horace Mann (the so-called founder of the American public school) has shown that Mann felt that the clerically dominated secular education in Massachusetts was a miserable failure, "from which he argued that the only agency left for properly inculcating moral training was that of the 'nonsectarian' public school."[12] Mann held this view despite the fact that he wished the teaching of Christianity, according to his own understanding of Christianity, to be included in the public schools.

In 1951 the Educational Policies Commission, the most influential component of the National Education Association in terms of shaping both polices and theoretical orientations which condition the thrust of America's public schools, published its report, *Moral and Spiritual Values in the Public Schools.* This report urged home, school, and community actively to co-operate in instilling moral and spiritual values into the pupils.[13] The ten moral and spiritual values which the Educational Policies Commission urged should pervade the public school curriculum were human personality, moral responsibility, institutions as the servants of men, common consent, devotion to truth, respect for excellence, moral equality, brotherhood, the pursuit of happiness, and spiritual enrichment. In terms of specifics, the Educational Policies Commission urged the following: Moral and spiritual values should be stated as aims of the public school; initiative by individual teachers in promoting moral and spiritual values in the students should be encouraged by the authorities; the education of teachers should deal with moral and spiritual values; the teaching of values should permeate the entire educational process; all the school's resources should be used to teach moral and spiritual values; the public schools can and should teach about religion. Religion is such an important aspect of both the heritage of American people and also their present life that to exclude religion from the curriculum, in the view of the Educational Policies Commission, is to provide students with an incomplete and inadequate education for fruitful living.

This important and seminal statement of the Educational Policies Commission is no mere empty exhortation; its influences have been felt in actual practice. For example, Alcuin Walker's careful analysis of 115 content selections, chosen at random from upper public elementary school readers, revealing that approximately one half of these selections were found to contain one or more of the ten moral and spiritual values enunciated by the Educational Policies Commission. Of interest is the fact that the value of "spiritual enrichment" occurred most frequently; "human personality" ranked second, with "moral responsibility" third.[14] By way of parenthesis, one might observe that the newer religion textbooks and audiovisual media used in Roman Catholic schools are emphasizing much the same kinds of moral and spiritual values, and indeed in a much less directly denominational fashion than in the old days.

Historically, the Educational Policies Commission's statement is really a basic affirmation of the traditional belief and practice in American public schools, as has been previously shown. Neil McCluskey also has observed that the three most influential figures in American public education in terms of charting its basic course —Horace Mann, William Torrey Harris, and John Dewey—believed that the public schools have a highly significant function in teaching moral and spiritual values.[15]

There is a definite movement in public education today by educators, educationists, and administrators in the direction of factual "teaching about" religion at every level in the public schools.[16] The American Association of Colleges of Teacher Education, through a special commission, has explored ways in which teacher-preparation institutions can effectively prepare future public school teachers to teach about religion and properly to introduce the religious dimension into various subject-matter areas.[17] The American Association of School Administrators, through its Commission on Teaching Religion in the Public Schools, has warmly endorsed teaching about religion in the public schools and bringing the religious dimension—as distinguished from the purely sectarian or proselytizing dimension—into appropriate curricular areas.[18]

Public school educators and educationists are increasingly recognizing that religion constitutes an area of positive human development, a personality-fulfilling aspect of life, and consequently an area which perforce must be included in the curriculum and the work of the public school. Education for democratic living requires that American civilization be explored in all its facets, in order that students are able to elicit its universal values, and also in order that they can be educated to enhance its universal quality by their own personal interaction with it. Jack Cohen's remarks are cogent in this connection:

> If the American public school is to teach about religion, its task then, is to teach children how to think about religion—not to observe it as a religious ritual and worship. Religious observance of American religion no more belongs in the public school than does the observance of sectarian religion. It would be dangerous to try to create an American religion which would follow too closely the patterns of the historical religions of those of other or established religions. . . . I believe religion should be part of the curriculum of the [public] school. If it is to be taught, however, the school cannot compromise on free inquiry and on its objective of training free and tolerant minds. It is necessary, therefore, for educators to clarify for themselves whether their first responsibility in the school is to the traditions of democratic education or to the notion that religion as a subject or a quality of the curriculum is in a class by itself. This is an area of decision that has

been almost completely overlooked by defenders of public education against the encroachment of sectarian religion. . . . Educators, therefore, must themselves learn to see religion as it is involved in the very educational process itself. . . . Education, and religion as quality, mean alike the dedication of the entire self to the pursuit of ideal values, the expansion of the scope of one's community until it takes in all humanity and all history; they are the promotion of the spirit of freedom and equality which are the hallmarks of American education.[19]

In terms of the church's educational mission, it should not be overlooked that in recent years, notably since Vatican II, there has been an increasing recognition by theologians and religious educators of the interaction, and indeed in many sectors a convergence, of the Catholic religion with the broad areas of moral-spiritual values such as those enunciated by the Educational Policies Commission. As I observed previously, the newer Catholic religious textbooks illustrate this growing awareness of interaction and frequent convergence. Thus the question can be legitimately posed to Catholics: In light of this growing convergence, is there today still a need for the church's educational mission in America to maintain a separate, total-school system apart from a public school enterprise which wishes to and indeed does inculcate into its pupils moral and spiritual values which the Roman Church so dearly prizes? Would not a revitalized Confraternity of Christian Doctrine program, one which would deliberately co-operate with and augment the moral-spiritual value thrust of the public school, and which would subsequently erect special programs tending to develop these values into their fuller expansion in terms of inculcation of Christian faith and charity, be more beneficial to the church's educational mission in our contemporary pluralist society?

The total-school system of the American church is basically a protest school system; it is an institutional form of protest whereby the church is protesting that the government is not providing the type of schools which it deems essential for its children. As I have written elsewhere,[20] unless the private Catholic protest school serves an educational purpose essentially distinctive from that of the government public school, which enrolls approximately 85 percent of school-age persons, then it has no legitimate basis for existence. There are two elements in this statement. First, the Catholic school must be radically and essentially distinctive in its purpose. The foundation for this conclusion is the familiar philosophical principle of Ockham's razor: "Beings should not be multiplied without necessity." Public schools exist in abundance. New—and in one sense "competing" schools—should not be set up side by side with the public schools unless these "competing schools" are truly distinctive and essentially different. Also adduced in support of this conclusion is the hallowed principle of subsidiarity: the church, being ontologically higher, should not do what the state, being ontologically lower, can do as well. The second element is that the church school must be actually fulfilling both its own distinctive purpose as well as those purposes which it shares with the public school.

In pondering the place of the total Catholic school in the church's educational mission, it might be well to ask certain questions: How "Catholic" are classes in spelling, reading, mathematics, chemistry, medicine, athletics, and even English or history? Are these learning situations fulfilling in a significant degree the educational mission of the church? Could not the church's resources—financial and personnel—be directed to other areas whose "payoff" is more profitable in terms of the goal of the church's educational mission? Is the present Catholic school system basically a carry-over from the historical past, or is it a meaningful, fruitful, and optimally efficient response to the pressing problems confronting the contemporary church's educational mission?

In the updated church, there is renewed emphasis on the family as the prime mover and most influential factor in the Christian education of the offspring. The mutual, deep love relationship between husband and wife seems to have more impact on the self-system of the young child than does his later education.[21] There are many segments within the church—notably in the area of religious education—which are tending to discard what they believe to be the excessive reliance placed by the American church on the Catholic school's role in the moral-spiritual formation of youth in favor of strengthening that most natural and most effective educational agency for deep Christian learning, the family. To be sure, empirical research clearly shows that the most formative period in a person's life with respect to forging his deeper attitudes, values, and beliefs is the period from birth to six years of age—before the child enrolls in a Catholic school.[22] The carefully conducted, large-scale research investigation undertaken by Andrew Greeley and Peter Rossi on Catholic adults who attended Catholic schools and those who had attended government schools indicated that the family is a vastly more significant force than is Catholic schooling in affecting the person's future religious behavior. Indeed, this study concluded that by far the most significant factor in providing Catholic education for the child is his family.[23]

What do the arguments given thus far in this chapter suggest? They suggest that the church's educational mission to the modern world would best be served by shifting away from the exclusive commitment to total Catholic schooling and toward the broader and more fecund approach of Catholic education. The continued total identification of Catholic education with Catholic schooling would appear to be deleterious to the best interests of the church as teacher of all men, as well as of the church as teacher of all Catholics.

At the outset of this chapter, it was noted that the assumption upon which the present structure of the total Catholic school system rests is that such a system is necessary for the survival and the power of the contemporary American Catholic church. I believe that this chapter has already cast some doubt on the validity of this assumption. The previously cited Greeley–Rossi study also indicated that there was no evidence from its findings that this assumption is true.[24]

What Is the Stance of Catholic Schooling to the Church as a Whole?

The church's educational enterprise from the early days of the republic until the present day has paralleled the growth of the church itself; where the church was strong and active, so also was there a flourishing Catholic school system. This is a natural outgrowth of the basic educational thesis of the Roman Church in America—Catholic schools in this country are viewed as a direct pastoral arm of the church, particularly of the hierarchy and to a lesser extent of the lower clergy and the religious. Thus at the 1967 meeting of the Executive Board of Directors of the National Catholic Educational Association, the formal suggestion was made that "it would be of great benefit if the bishops at one of their meetings would issue a statement clarifying the fact that Catholic schools still represent the first line of activity for the teaching magisterium of the Church."[25] It is this stance of Catholic schooling toward the church as a whole that has produced many of the current tensions within the Catholic educational enterprise.

Because the Catholic school system was viewed as the pastoral arm of the church, various segments comprising the ruling classes in the church entered the educational apostolate. The result was not infrequently an intersection of various power-groups, an intersection which did not work for the best educational interests of the church's schools. For example, in a Catholic elementary school, there are a variety of conflicting forces at work. First there is the pastor, who juridically controls his parish school, and the sister-principal, who must conduct the school. The sister-principal in turn is subject to her local religious superior, who quite often is a nun teaching in that same school. The religious institute operating this school and the diocese in which the school is located are autonomous entities and are not subject to either one—the result being either lack of co-ordination or outright friction. Another example of the conflicting forces at work is the strife which took place in the 1920s and 1930s between administrators in the private Catholic high schools and those in the then strongly emerging diocesan Catholic high schools. Still another example can be found in the unplanned development of the Catholic educational enterprise. Thus seemingly every religious institute for women believed that it had an inherent pastoral mandate, albeit vague and amorphous, to erect its own Catholic college, with the result that there exists today a proliferation of small, mediocre Catholic colleges, often clustered meaninglessly in the same geographical region. (Erie, Pennsylvania, for example, with a population of 130,000 has three Catholic colleges.)

A second result of the Catholic educational enterprise being regarded as a pastoral arm of the church is that the Catholic school system at every level is regarded as the exclusive province of the hierarchy, the clergy, and the religious. The Catholic school is not the domain of all the people of God, for, after all, the people of God are not typically considered as *pastores*. Catholic schooling is still today basically a clerical affair, not primarily a lay activity. The National Catholic Educational Association, the appropriate professional association, is heavily dominated by clerics. In 1968–69, for example, the president of the Association was a bishop, all twenty members of the general executive board were clerics and religious, the executive secretary was a cleric, and six of the seven vice-presidents were clerics. Superintendents of Catholic schools are all clerics. It is the hierarchy or clergy which have (on their own initiative over the years) become the exclusive spokesmen for Catholic schools. In the 1920s it was the totally clerical and religious ruling body of the NCEA, of the National Welfare Conference, and of the Jesuit magazine *America* who represented the American Catholic school position on federal aid.[26] Again, it was the American bishops through NCWC who in the early 1960s, speaking for the American Catholic school interests, came out in favor of federal financial assistance to Catholic schools.

Particularly among traditional Catholics and non-Catholics, the public perception of a "typical" Catholic schoolteacher or school administrator is that of a priest or a nun, despite the fact that more and more laymen have entered the teaching ranks of Catholic schools at all levels.[27] However, administrative posts in Catholic schools are still by and large reserved for clergy and religious. There are very few laymen to be found as presidents of Catholic universities, or as principals of Catholic elementary or secondary schools. An unpublished NCEA investigation made in 1965 revealed that 84 percent of all Catholic secondary schools surveyed have no provision whereby a layman can become principal.[28]

Perhaps the fact that Catholic education is viewed as a pastoral arm of the church explains why, despite extraordinarily strong statements from several popes on the primacy of the family in education, parents have been greatly neglected in the Catholic school enterprise. Fund-raising and school support seem to constitute the chief role of parents. Until 1960 there was no national Catholic parent-teachers association. In that year the National Home and School Service was established; it is estimated that only about 50 percent of all Catholic elementary and secondary schools have affiliated chapters.[29] Unlike its influential counterpart in the public school system, the NHSS specifically excludes from the basic purposes of the organization any role of the parents in making or helping to form school policy.

To be a pastor or shepherd means in one sense to control the flock, and the clergy and religious certainly seem to have been thoroughly pastoral in this sense with Catholic schools. Very few Catholic elementary or secondary schools are owned or controlled by lay persons; only a handful of Catholic institutions of higher learning, notably Webster, St. Louis, Portland, and Notre Dame, are now governed by laymen. Again, there are historical reasons for this phenomenon, notably lay trusteeism, which John Tracy Ellis has termed "the most serious trouble that confronted the Catholic Church in the United States after the Revolution."[30] Ellis adduced many causes for the problem of lay trusteeism, including an imperfect knowledge on the part of both clergy and laity of the canonical provisions pertaining to the administration and holding of church property.

A third result of the Catholic educational enterprise being regarded as a pastoral arm of the church is that until very recently there has not been an appropriate measure of professionalism characterizing Catholic school activity. Pastoral dedication, rather than professional technical competence, was traditionally the quality most emphasized in Catholic school personnel at the elementary and secondary levels. Also, until recently, Catholic school teachers typically did not hold teaching licenses from the state, nor were most Catholic schools accredited by appropriate regional accrediting associations. Bishops, clergy, and religious frowned on (and often forbade) Catholic lay teachers at the subcollegiate level from establishing institutional chapters of either of the two major secular professional educational associations, the National Education Association or the American Federation of Teachers. Nor has the Catholic professional educational association, the National Catholic Educational Association, yet achieved that measure of professionalization which should characterize a professional group.

A fourth result of the Catholic educational enterprise being regarded as a pastoral arm of the church is that Catholic schools seem to be divisive in terms of the local parish or diocese. In discussions

I have had with certain Catholic school officials from various parts of the country, it would appear that families whose offspring attend non-Catholic schools are regarded somehow as second-class Catholics compared with those whose children go to the Catholic school. This feeling has apparently led to a less than ideal Catholic community consciousness in some parishes and dioceses across the land.

A fifth result of the Catholic educational enterprise's being regarded as a pastoral arm of the church is that academic freedom in Catholic educational institutions has taken long in coming and in developing. Bishops and other ecclesiastical officials frequently intervene in Catholic schools at all levels to silence or remove a person who speaks or acts in a way other than that in which the bishop or ecclesiastical official believes a Catholic school person should comport himself. The celebrated 1967 Catholic University of America debacle is one case where such curtailment of academic freedom on the part of the hierarchy became the focus of national attention; yet there have been innumerable instances on all levels of Catholic schooling where the ruling classes in the church have removed or silenced a teacher without attracting any widespread notice.

The history of the Catholic educational effort in the United States indicates that there was a time in which Catholic schools benefited significantly from being a part of the church's pastoral arm. But this time has since disappeared, and it would seem that in the interests both of Catholic education itself and of the church's wider pastoral ministry, there should be a divorce between Catholic educational institutions and the pastoral arm of the church. Autonomy of Catholic schools—in whatever form or non-form they will eventually assume—does not imply that they will be less effective agents of the church's educational mission. In fact, it might be successfully argued that such autonomy will make Catholic schools more effective agents of the church's educational mission. Education, if it is to be effective, must be reflective of the temper of the times; and the temper of the times is to disassociate schools from any control which emanates from outside that of professional enterprise. A church educational enterprise of whatever sort which is the province of all the people of God, which is highly professional and proficient, which is characterized by a climate of freedom from outside control, and which is unifying rather than devisive in the local church community, will surely yield a more fruitful pastoral harvest in the modern world than will a continuance of the old, antiquated system.

What Is the Stance of Catholic Schooling to Religious Education?

The church's basic teaching mission to the modern world is not education in the arts or in the sciences, but in the religious domain. Yet it is ironic that despite this basic principle, and despite the fact that a vast network of Catholic schools has been erected to provide a milieu in which more effective religious learning is intended to take place, there has not yet been developed a clear set of goals of religious instruction. Nor has there been developed any taxonomy of educational objectives for the religious domain comparable to the taxonomies of the cognitive domain and the affective domain developed by secular educationists.[31] Parenthetically, it might be noted that there are no clear-cut goals enunciated for all of Catholic schooling.[32]

Xavier Harris has observed that from the Council of Trent (1545) until the end of the eighteenth century, religious instruction for minor children was still considered by the church to be a parental responsibility, except for preparation for the reception of the appropriate sacraments; what secondary schools there were provided for a review of the catechism, but religious instruction was not regarded as the real business of the school. Hence in those times religious instruction (or more properly, catechism instruction) did not occupy a distinct place in the curriculum and was not regarded as a regular school subject.[33] Even in 1920 in American Catholic secondary schools "no definite policy had been developed as to the place of religion in the school curriculum. In general, the older schools tended to regard religion as extra-curricular. The newer schools included religion in the regular curriculum."[34] In 1947 a national study of Catholic secondary schools concluded that religion was still not highly regarded as an important subject in many Catholic high schools' curricula:

The regulation [concerning required courses] is sometimes stated [by Catholic high schools] in terms of the "solid" and "light" subjects. A not uncommon statement is the following: "We require twelve units in the solid subjects, and four in the light ones." The statements are not without their provocative features: "We require twelve in solid subjects, and four in light subjects such as religion and the arts."[35]

On the secondary school level, Catholic schools from the 1920s until the mid-1930s placed great emphasis on adapting the religion course to the psychological condition of the students—probably due to the influence of progressive education, which enjoyed its heyday during this period. The 1950s and early 1960s witnessed stress on doctrinal content.[36] The post-Vatican II religion courses both at the elementary and secondary levels appear to be centering around the interrelationship of human development, doctrinal content, and the social gospel approach. Of interest, however, is that throughout this century in American Catholic school religion courses, particularly in the secondary schools, teaching methodology did not receive a proportionate development.[37] The didactic, verbal, lecture type of instruction prevailed.

The selection of religion teachers, particularly at the secondary level, has been a legendary scandal in the history of American Catholic education. Any priest or religious in the old days was *ipso facto* deemed capable of teaching religion. Indeed, teaching religion was not infrequently the last refuge for priests and religious who previously had failed at other, so-called more important tasks. However, in recent years, especially in the 1960s, there has been a considerable impetus on the part of Catholic school officials to select outstanding teachers as their religion instructors, and to send them to graduate school for professional preparation in religious instruction. Regretfully, however, most of these teachers pursue graduate work in summer school only, thus severely short-shrifting their own professional development. (After all, seminarians do not pursue their prepriestly formation only during summer school.)

While some in-service teachers of religion are pursuing graduate work in theology, there appears to have been a definite recognition that studies in religious education provide more appropriate professional preparation. Catholic universities—and even some of the smaller Catholic colleges—have eagerly responded to the demand,

and introduced graduate programs in religious education. With one exception, these graduate programs have followed the traditional theological model in which religious education is regarded as a mode of pastoral theology. The program at the Catholic University of America has served as somewhat of an exemplar for other Catholic institutions of higher learning which subsequently have inaugurated religious education programs. The one exception to this theological thrust of religious instruction preparation programs is that instituted by the graduate department of education at the University of Notre Dame. The Notre Dame program is unique in that it revolves around the social science model, and views religious instruction not so much as a mode of pastoral theology but rather as a specialization in the teaching-learning process of effecting behavioral changes in the students' lives.[38]

Patrick Rooney has contended that the milieu of the Catholic school is such that it tends to extinguish the lessons learned in the religion class.[39] Gerard S. Sloyan has suggested that probably the best way of improving the quality of religion classes in Catholic education is to remove these classes from the Catholic school curriculum, and teach them in another, out-of-school milieu.[40] The suggestions made by Rooney and Sloyan have significant bearing on the premise that the Catholic school is essential for the church's educational mission, and that religion can be most effectively learned only in a Catholic school milieu.

More Catholic students are enrolled in non-Catholic schools than in Catholic schools. It is generally conceded by specialists in religious education that neither the Confraternity of Christian Doctrine nor the Newman Clubs have been highly successful in their programs of religious education. The United States Catholic Conference (formerly the national Catholic Welfare Conference) in the late 1960s divested itself of most of its former activities in Catholic education in order to concentrate on religious education. Prominent in the USCC's projected plans are a thorough revitalization of religious education programs and strategies for Catholic students in non-Catholic educational institutions.

Conclusion

There is a fourth major problem but limitations of space preclude its treatment. This problem concerns the stance of Catholic schooling in relation to American society in general. Indeed, this is a pressing problem, especially when it is realized that the church's educational mission is not only to its own membership, formally speaking, but also to the outreach. Indeed, with the newer theology's infusing the church, it is being appreciated that the outreach is really not the outreach at all, but rather an integral segment of the church per se. Perhaps as the church examines its own educational mission anew, both to its inner core and to its outreach, the result will be an in-search into its role as a pivotal perpetuator of Jesus' commission to teach all nations. Until such an in-search comes to pass, I believe that the educationist, or at least this educationist, will have to hold in abeyance the answer to the question: "Does the church really know how to teach—now, in the United States?"

B. *by* D. CAMPBELL WYCKOFF

CONTROVERSY surrounds the question of how to write the history of education. The broadest context for the history of education is to begin with the oral tradition and the apprentice system of learning and to show how various systems of learning and forms of schooling emerged and developed as societies became more complex or faced troublesome periods of social change.[1] A much narrower view sees the history of education as the recounting and interpretation of the rise of the school and its formal functions in the modern state.[2]

In this chapter I propose that the history of education focus on schools of various kinds—public schools, church schools, independent schools, colleges and universities, and professional schools—but that education also be seen as a function of other social institutions like the family and informal community agencies. Further, in a short chapter, the aim of surveying the history of the educational scene must be limited to looking over the history of education in America in the light of key problems, and discussing the events and trends that illuminate those problems.

On the American scene this means keeping in mind how education responded to the expansion and consolidation of the nation: the colonial period, the founding of the nation, continental expansion, industrialization, and emergence into world responsibility and leadership. Subtle changes in the national purpose have taken place at various times: the early aim of providing a liberal education for the elite, the democratic and humanitarian thrust toward universal public education, the use of the schools as the primary means of assimilating immigrants of various ethnic and cultural backgrounds, the gradual assumption by the state of responsibility for the education of children and young people at all levels from preschool through higher education regardless of abilities, and the taking on by the schools of some responsibility for community leadership and change. These changes in aim must be kept in mind. So must certain dominant themes in American life: humanitarianism, the rural-urban and farm-labor tensions, the reinterpretations of the meaning of democracy, and the sharpening of nationalism and internationalism. At the same time, the varieties of institutional interests in education must not be forgotten: the schools themselves, the institutions of higher education, teacher training schools, organized education movements, the family, the church, youth-serving character-building agencies, and adult education movements.

"A Protestant perspective" can mean a number of things. A history of Protestant education in America could be worked out. Such a study has not been attempted recently, although it is needed. Yet, while it will cite events from this area, the primary purpose of this chapter is not to trace this history. A theological critique of American education from a Protestant standpoint would be possible. This would be made difficult, of course, by the lack of a well-defined Protestant theology of education, not to mention the lack of a well-defined Protestant theology as such. However, Protestantism in America can be thought of as an influential socio-religious movement, beginning in the earliest period of the colonization of the eastern seaboard, and continuing to the present time, in which Protestantism has been deeply involved both innovatively, in furthering integrated education, for instance, and conservatively, in resisting certain directions of social change.

From this perspective, a critical survey of education on the American scene is possible. There are four key problems in light of which this survey is to be done. What have been the contributions of Protestantism to American education? How have American education and Protestantism been related to each other? What problems has American education presented to Protestantism? What are the prospects of future relationships between Protestantism and American education?

Protestant Contributions to Education

What have been the contributions of Protestantism to the American educational scene? Its greatest contributions have been in parish education. The Sunday school, which began as a missionary and evangelistic agency of the church, designed to give the rudiments of learning and morality to children and young people outside the church, as well as to convert them, soon became the church's major agency for the education of its own children, young people and adults. During the period of westward expansion, the Sunday school, being non-denominational in character, could be used as the vanguard of the church in providing for the religious needs of newly founded communities.

A concomitant of the Sunday school was its huge coterie of lay workers, persons who assumed on a voluntary basis the responsibilities of organizing and managing the schools, providing the teaching force and providing the leadership for the movement as well. These persons had to be trained to carry out their duties. A system of leadership training was instituted which in time led to the launching of the Chautauqua Institution movement. Chautauqua in turn broadened its scope to the total leisure-time liberal education of adults and became a prototype for the American adult education movement.[3]

The success of the Sunday school's approach to children encouraged Protestant educational leaders to expand this type of work in other directions. Summer vacations provided an ideal time for this expansion, and all over the country ever since the early years of the twentieth century, Protestant churches have held vacation church schools. These schools are generally held during the morning hours, Monday through Friday, sometimes for as long as four or six weeks at a time, a setup that has distinct advantages over the shorter and more infrequent sessions of the Sunday school. Further expansion took place at about the same time into after-school hours. The weekday church school allowed, as did the vacation church school, for much more use of systematic instruction, arts and crafts, and recreation.

Concern for young people became active in the years of heavy industrialization that preceded and followed the Civil War. Young, unattached urban men were served by the Protestant-oriented Young Men's Christian Association, an organization that provided them with guidance, a place to live and eat, religious services, study opportunities, recreation, and social activities. Later its counterpart for women, the Young Women's Christian Association, came into existence. More oriented to the parish, although independent ecclesiastically, was the Christian Endeavor Union with its Sunday evening meetings, service activities, and social activities. While the YMCA and the YWCA have maintained a vigorous independent life, denominationally sponsored youth programs have largely supplanted the Christian Endeavor Union in the parish.

Protestants have long maintained a summer outdoor program for older children and young people. Customarily, certain forms of leadership education took place in resort areas in spots like those that had been developed for evangelistic camp meetings. It was only a step to setting up conference centers for young people and camps for children and junior highs. Some Protestant denominations aim to have a developed campsite for every parish, so that it may be available at all times for children's camping, youth activities, parish activities, family camping, and retreats. Others provide such facilities on a district or area basis.

A recent addition to the educational services provided by the Protestant parish is the preschool nursery. This is often a half-day, five-days-a-week program, staffed by fully trained nursery school teachers and financed through tuition charges. In areas where such services are needed, some churches also provide day care centers for the children of working mothers.

The earliest Protestant educational contribution of note to the American scene was the college. Protestant churches and groups of Protestant ministers and laymen in colonial America saw the need for higher education and mobilized their resources to provide for it. Calvinists, Anglicans, Quakers, Baptists, and Lutherans were among the first to do so. Even Bishop Berkeley's abortive attempt to provide for American higher education through a college in

Bermuda strengthened Yale by the personal advice and assistance he gave while resident near Newport. Later the churches vigorously worked to the end that no section of the enlarging country would be without a college. These remain distinguished periods in American education even though the greatest of the schools are no longer church-affiliated, and state-sponsored higher education has far outstripped the church schools in the numbers served. As higher education has increasingly been conducted under secular auspices, the phenomenon of the "campus ministry" has arisen, whereby the churches maintain clergy to conduct religious services and perform other functions on the campus.

In the mid-nineteenth century the churches threw great energy into the movement to found and maintain local academies at the high school level. Many such schools were begun and flourished for a time. A historian like Bernard Bailyn holds that at one time the academy movement was a viable alternative to public secondary education, and that this contribution to American education is largely forgotten only because the proponents of the public high school won the day.[4]

Certain Protestant denominations, notably of conservative Calvinist and Lutheran persuasion, have consistently built and maintained school systems of their own. A distinctive feature of Calvinist schools is that they are parent-controlled.[5] The Lutheran Church–Missouri Synod, outstanding among Protestants for this kind of education work, maintains elementary schools, high schools, colleges, teachers colleges, and theological seminaries in a closely integrated system.[6]

Responsive to critical social needs as they emerged in American life, Protestant churches through their home mission boards have sought to provide appropriate educational services. The first such service was a system of schools and colleges for the American Indians, some of which still flourish. After the Civil War, the Protestant educational focus moved toward providing education at every level for Southern Negroes. Over the years, this need has not diminished, although it has changed, and the advent of integration has only accentuated the unfulfilled character of the education of the American blacks. In turn, educational provision has been made for the Spanish-speaking people of the Southwest and the West

Indies, Oriental peoples on the West Coast, and people in Appalachia and Alaska. More recently, a few educational experiments have been begun in the urban ghetto. Mission schooling has been a continuing enterprise, yet individual institutions have had a somewhat temporary character. Established policy has been to maintain these schools only as long as critical need exists and cannot be met through the resources of government or private agencies.

The provision of Protestant leadership had occasioned the rise of an extensive system of professional education. The key institution in this system is the theological seminary, a postgraduate school sometimes interdenominational in character, sometimes a school within a university complex, but most often a denominationally sponsored and controlled enterprise. Until recently the seminary system was considered fairly stable. But questions about the nature of the ministry and appropriate ministerial education, together with misgivings occasioned by small enrollments and financial problems, have begun to result in the closing or merging of some seminaries.

The training of unordained church members was at one time largely a matter of small and rather ill-equipped training schools. These have gradually disappeared, or have been absorbed into seminaries, or have in a few cases become largely accredited schools. The functions now performed by the seminaries and these specialized schools are chiefly those of training professional religious educators, church social workers, and missionaries.

A unique phenomenon on the American scene is the Bible school or Bible college. Established and supported by conservative theological forces, these schools at first were intended to provide a type of church leadership training for laymen, and a Bible-centered training for an evangelistic clergy. Most often these schools were for post-high school work, but some had no set entrance level. Of late, however, these schools have self-consciously grown into full-fledged colleges and have added scientific and liberal courses, playing down to some extent the almost exclusively biblical emphasis that formerly dominated their curriculum and program.[7]

Perhaps accidentally, or simply because of the problems raised in the process of preparing and disseminating the materials involved, Protestant religious publishing has loomed large on the

American scene. Over the last century a great variety of educational books have poured from the church presses, including an increasingly substantial line of books for children and young people. Every church periodical has some avowed educational purpose, and some have achieved wide circulation among clergy and church members. The backbone of Protestant educational publishing, however, has been curriculum production, which has been the occasion of intensive theological and educational inquiry and debate over the years. A special phase of church publishing—the books and study materials produced in support of missionary education—has had the effect of in-depth interpretation of national and international problems.

Strangely enough, Protestantism has produced few educational thinkers who have captured the public attention. Only two men, writing as Protestants, have been widely studied. One was Horace Bushnell, whose *Christian Nurture* (1846)[8] stirred both educational and religious controversy in its day. The other was George Albert Coe, whose *A Social Theory of Religious Education* (1917)[9] was in some ways a religious commentary on and extension of the world of educational thought dominated by John Dewey. There has been no American Protestant educational counterpart of John Henry Newman.

Protestantism's contributions to education on the American scene, have been quite functional, and responsive to particular needs and opportunities that have arisen from time to time in American life. There has been no overall strategy or plan, either in terms of contributions to the total American educational scene, or in terms of Protestant work as such.

American Education and Protestantism

How have American education and Protestantism been related to each other? Having surveyed the major contributions of Protestantism to the American scene, attention now turns to the underlying relationships in the concern of Protestantism for the whole of American education. Here the situation is quite different, since Protestantism in America finds itself in a secular, pluralistic society in which its educational concerns for the whole society, even if they

could be formulated, could not be directly implemented. This ultimately undefined relationship, however, does not mean that practical and theoretical relationships do not exist. It is this state of affairs
that is now surveyed.

The focus here is on schools for the general public, although a bit
will be said later about the church school in particular. The official
relationship of church sponsorship and control (predominantly
Protestant) over schooling for the general public lasted only into
the early nineteenth century. From then on sponsorship and control went into the hands of local, nonsectarian boards of education,
supervised in turn by secular state boards.

However, Protestant influence persisted in many aspects of the
general school scene. A case could be made for the persistence of
Protestant cultural values in the aims of education, reflected in
character education, citizenship education, and education for patriotism. In the curriculum of the schools, religious exercises, invaria-
bly Protestant in tone, continued until the recent Supreme Court
decision banning prayer and devotional Bible reading. Music, art,
and literature must inevitably draw from sources that are religiously inspired, and Protestant artists, composers, and writers
were and are widely studied. Until fairly recent decades the adult
personnel in the schools were predominantly Protestant in most
sections of the country, and their motivations for being in education
often stemmed from "culture Protestant" convictions. This was
true of teachers, administrators, and members of boards of education.

An outstanding example of such a person is Horace Mann, who,
although sincerely disavowing any sectarian interest in his educational work and actually propounding the principle of separation of
church and state in education, nevertheless built into his educational theories and recommendations a set of value assumptions that
directly represented the views of the Unitarians of his time. Intellectual freedom, for instance, was chiefly to be prized, and a basic
biblical moral education was to be at the heart of the curriculum.[10]

Culture Protestantism continued as an influence in the public
schools partly because it was never seriously challenged. The Roman Catholic parochial school system drained off much of the
potential tension from that quarter. Church schools were available

to most of those who actively disliked the watering down of theological orientation in the public schools. Jewish groups simply kept quiet and did their distinctive educational work (language training, biblical and Talmudic studies, and liturgical training) in after-school hours. Occasionally a Protestant prejudice, as in the Tennessee evolution case, won out and temporarily became school policy. But most Americans were satisfied with the substitution of moralism for theology and patriotism for religion.

The defined relationship, of course, was that of separation of church and state. This cherished American political doctrine was established by the founding fathers in order to keep either institution from dominating the other. Freedom of operation and freedom from interference were guaranteed to each. The realities of American religious pluralism could be said to have dictated this policy, and there is obviously much to support this view. Yet the doctrine rests on much more universal historical ground as a reflection of the unsatisfactory and problematical relationship between church and state in Europe.

No one quite seemed to notice, however, when education slipped out from under church control in America and became a public state function. Pluralism again entered the picture, combined with the ideal of universal education. Universal education could hardly be achieved in a pluralistic country if education was left under church control. The one agency capable of achieving this end under the circumstances was the community at large, and for all practical purposes this meant developing the schools under some new governmental structure, with the support of the community's powers of taxation. The unrecognized problem remained: Can a viable educational system be built which assumes that separation of church and state is to be interpreted as separation of religion and education?

Institutional separation of church and state is essential to American life. But this does not argue that a functional separation of religion and education is possible. Religion is a basic human process by which truth and value are put in symbolic form and become the objects of personal and community commitment and the basis for individual and social behavior and action. The American experience indicates that when established religions are removed from the educational scene, other views and values are quickly sub-stituted. These new views and values (perhaps mimicking a popular understanding of the older aims but in secularized language) are put in the form of new symbols and become new objects of personal and community commitment and new basis for individual and social behavior and action.[11]

That education cannot fulfill its ends without the engendering of a religious quality in life is illustrated by much of American educational theory, notably in the case of John Dewey. In *A Common Faith* (1934),[12] Dewey distinguished between the "religious," a quality of personal and social commitment to the highest human values, and the "religions," which he thought of as outward vestiges of previous commitments contaminated by the attribution of value to the supernatural. A religious quality, non-supernaturalistic in orientation, was essential to the education of the general public and was appropriate to the public schools. This view was developed with great appeal and in detail by Ward Madden in his *Religious Values in Education* (1951).[13]

If education requires experience that attains religious quality in order that it may be fulfilled as education, the question for a pluralistic America is: What shall be the content of this religious quality? Does pluralism mean that a new common religion will spring up and be used in the schools, while the historic religions are prevented from gaining a hearing?

Protestant bodies have generally gone out of their way to be supportive of the American public schools. During the last twelve years, pronouncements have been issued declaring that the public schools are to be backed because they provide the basis for equal opportunity for all in American life and because attendance at public schools brings children and young people of different religions, ethnic backgrounds, and social strata into vital contact with one another as Americans.[14]

There are specific relationships that Protestants share with other religious faiths in America. "Released time" is the plan by which a period of school time each week is devoted to religious instruction by the various religious faiths for their children. While released time has been the subject of great debate and legal maneuvering, it is now well accepted that it is legal provided the instruction is given off school property and is not administered by school officials.

"Shared time" has been widely suggested, and less widely tried, as an attempt to have the church and the school share together in the educational process without violating the principle of separation. This plan maintains that some subjects in the curriculum have religious implications, and that others do not. Those with religious overtones would be taught under church auspices and on church property for part of the school day. Those without religious significance would occupy the rest of the day and would be conducted on school property by public school teachers.

The Supreme Court has banned devotional practices in the schools, and has indicated that there is to be no teaching of specific sectarian ends. At the same time, the Court has advised that the public schools have a responsibility for teaching about religion as part of the life, culture, and heritage of the people. Protestants are participating with members of other faiths, at the invitation of public school bodies, in exploring the implications of this possible development in the curriculum.

To turn briefly to church schools, a few specific relationships must be mentioned. Private church schools are often assisted by the state by being given some of the same services that public schools enjoy: bussing, textbooks, and health services. These are construed as services to the child and not to the school. The church college receives a great deal of help from governmental agencies in building construction, research grants, and supervisory services. At the same time, the church actively maintains chaplaincies, and in many cases participates in institutions in the field of religion, on the campuses of state-supported colleges and universities.

Problems for Protestantism

What problems has American education presented to Protestantism? American education, in the public school system and the college and university system, has become a major force in our national life. In a complex technological society, the day of education via the oral tradition and apprenticeship appears to be far behind us. Instead, the American people are building and supporting multimillion-dollar institutions to accomplish purposes that cannot be handled by less adequate forms of education.

In the process, the schools have tried to be responsive to needs and opportunities as they have emerged. Subject matter has proliferated; vocational education has burgeoned; competitive athletic programs dominate the student mind; other extracurricular activities (music, drama, and the like) have developed into major operations; outdoor and summer education are on the increase. In many instances this creates a simple problem of time for Protestantism, dependent as it has been on after-school time, Sundays, and summers for its program. Community conflicts of some proportions have developed in situations where school activities, in order to fulfill their own plans, have moved into traditional "church time." In some cases local treatylike agreements have had to be hammered out to guarantee the church the time it needs for its work with children and young people. At the present time church summer programs may be in some jeopardy because of the school's tendency to move toward full utilization of the summer.

More important have been the problems created by uncritical Protestant acceptance of models developed for public education. Chief among these has been the system of grouping and grading (kindergarten to twelfth grade, with its subgroupings such as junior high and senior high). Indicative of the problem is the prompt shift in grouping and grading in church education that follows any shift in the system of grouping and grading in the public school. Is religious education actually so much of a piece with other forms of education that it can make use of their decisions in these matters without raising questions of its own?

But process models have also been uncritically accepted. School curriculum patterns have suggested patterns for Christian education; the educational year being worked out in quarters or semesters, and the institution being organized into units. Little thought has been given to the essential difference between the pattern of an educational enterprise that occupies a good part of the week and an educational enterprise that meets as a rule for little more than one hour per week. Likewise, religion has been assumed to be a subject that can be studied and organized for study like other school subjects, with textbooks, class recitations, and homework. Even those who have held that the Christian faith differs radically from any human discipline have been seduced into organizing this kind of education in the biblical, theological, and historical fields. Further, moral education in the schools, character education in youth-serving agencies, and religious education in the church have become so intertwined in the popular mind that religious education has tended to lose any distinctiveness except for the story and music materials used and the overt utilization of prayer.

So pervasive have patterns of school administration and supervisory services become that Protestantism in America has never even tried to develop for itself a theory for the guidance of educational operations. "Directors" and "superintendents" share with "boards" and "committees" the duties of planning, organization, management, and supervision. No attempt has been made in the direction of a language for Protestant educational operations, to say nothing of a set of theological concepts in this area. When Protestant educators attempt to prepare themselves for an effective ministry as church leaders, they have nothing to consult except the literature of education, social work, and business. No one has delineated the special character of the relationships of educational leadership in the community of faith—the worshiping, witnessing, working community of persons in Christ.

Furthermore, the theoretical models for Protestant educational thought have been the same as those of general American education. As American public and private education has looked for its theory to Pestalozzi, Froebel, Herbart, Dewey, Charters, and Brunner, so has Protestant religious education. Strangely, even when distinctively Protestant concerns have motivated theorists like Pestalozzi, Froebel, and Herbart, and have provided key concepts for their educational systems, these particular concerns have dropped out of American Protestant educational thought as their theories have been mediated to the American Protestant educator via secular channels. The exception to this is W. W. Charters, a public education theorist whose personal commitments led him to provide direct leadership for Protestant curriculum developments in the 1920s.[15]

Even school buildings have provided models for Protestant religious education. Church school "plants" (an interesting adoption of industrial terminology) are often built to conform to the classroom-auditorium-gymnasium pattern of the public school. Ironically, some of the new plans for utilization of electronic educational media call for school buildings essentially similar to the church's long-abandoned "Akron plan," while there is a growing group of public school advocates of non-graded education to take place in large "open space" educational areas.

But the problems created for Protestantism by American education have not been limited to scheduling and patterns of education. As acute as any problem has been that of the level and quality of instruction. When a child or young person spends his school week in a well-equipped setup under the guidance of well-trained teachers, high standards of educational excellence and quality of program are inevitably built into his thinking. In such situations he is held to high levels of achievement under conditions designed to foster such achievement. Follow him into a church school that is ill-equipped, with materials of lesser quality, teachers who are untrained volunteers holding to no observable standards of pupil achievement, and the contrast is clear. The normal result is a lack of seriousness on the pupil's part, and a tendency to discount the religious education enterprise.

At the heart of the problems created for Protestantism by American education are, of course, matters of conflicts in values. Where family, school, college, and church differ in their fundamental values, a condition of competition for the mind of the child and young person is created. Such competition can only result in frustration for the institutions involved, unsatisfactorily hammered-out compromises by the rising generation, or a sense of indifference or malaise. To mention only a few typical conflicts in values: the adoption by the schools of a predominantly scientific point of view, dominant stress on athletics and athletic competition, vocational emphasis geared almost exclusively to the needs of a technological era, and the assumption that education is an end in itself and is to be pursued for its own sake.

A key problem in the field of higher education has been the elimination of theology from the curriculum and its relegation to special schools which in themselves are professionally oriented and thus not ideally suited to the pursuit of theological scholarship. In church colleges, "Bible and religion" have been substituted for theology, while in state schools, departments of philosophy have replaced it. The result is generations of Protestants largely unacquainted with theology or theological method; thus the continuing scandal of Protestant "religiosity"—uninformed, undirected, sentimental religion. Vigorous steps have been taken recently to correct this situation with the introduction of courses in theology taught by competent scholars in private and state colleges and universities. Unaccountably, church colleges have tended to lag behind in this matter.[16]

In the American situation, the secularizing process in education has had a further peculiar result. In Catholic education and in Protestant-controlled education, worship has characteristically been a central activity. Secular American education has substituted for this various types of mass meetings and patriotic observances. Occasionally clergy are invited to pray at the beginning or end of such meetings. The result is that worship becomes a "strange" activity to the American Protestant child or young person. When he comes to worship, some forms are like the mass meetings with which he is familiar, and he may fail to see any essential difference; other forms are surrounded with peculiarities and mysteries. In any case, worship becomes something different, on the side, and not a central act around which all of his life is organized.

This same sense of peculiarity surrounds the whole phenomenon of denominationalism in the mind of the American public school pupil. In the sense of American unity which the schools seek to foster, there is little place for serious consideration of denominational differences. Current American ecumenism may not be so much a genuine seeking of unity out of the integrity of diversity as an impatience to get rid of already meaningless institutional fragmentation.

These problems of scheduling, educational models, quality of education, conflicts in values, the role of theology in education, the strangeness of worship, and the erosion of denominationalism have gradually increased over the years. There is no question but that a secularized education in America has contributed to their becoming acute problems for Protestantism. Some are on the way to being solved, but most of them fester and become more acute.

Prospects of Future Relationships

What are the prospects of future relationships between Protestantism and American education? The results of historical reflection can produce only impressions about the future. One has a clear impression, however, of substantial change in American Protestantism in the near future. Part of that change will be in organization and structure, part in function. The organizational and structural changes will be in the direction of consolidation and closer ecumenical ties. The functional change will be toward more effectively meeting the challenge of American urbanization. Clearly, American Protestant thought is in ferment; the realities of the contemporary social and intellectual world are breaking down older theological formulations and bringing new insights and thought-forms into existence. In the process there will inevitably be a new sense of task and a new sense of ecumenical partnership in that task.

Assuming no radical break with the past, it is possible to see the Protestantism of the future in a fourfold relationship with American education. First, Protestantism may be able to undertake (as it has not been able to do in the past) basic criticism of the American educational scene, to the end of assisting in the attainment of a viable American system. The American Protestant theologian can, as an American, put his critical theological tools, particularly those of Christian ethics and practical theology, to work in diagnosing and prescribing for the whole American educational enterprise. To some extent, this has already been done for higher education, and to good effect. It remains to be done for other forms and levels of education.

Second, Protestantism will need to put its brains to work to discover the distinctiveness of its own religious education enterprise. What really is an education that is genuinely Protestant in character? What would be the shape of the educational enterprises that would adequately implement this vision? This is an inquiry for the whole intellectual and practical energy of the church.

Third, as insight into Protestantism's genuinely distinctive educational enterprises grows, experimental projects will have to be undertaken to test the viability of that insight. These experimental projects may be new forms of schooling, parish education, and paraparochial educational ministry. When thorough theological reflection on the nature of education takes place, there is no telling what forms, shapes, and functions new educational ministries could take.

Fourth, the understanding and reconstruction of American education and the discovering and testing of genuinely Protestant educational enterprises will provide the groundwork upon which serious planning for co-ordinated supplementary education may proceed. Protestantism is not about to take over American education; it is not even seriously interested in having its slice of American education in the sense of being responsible for the full education of the Protestant population. Its strategy will remain that of providing an education supplementary to that of the public schools, colleges, and universities. But the future may bring opportunity for more carefully planned co-ordination of that supplementary education with the mainstream of secular schooling, so that the educational enterprises of the Protestant churches will provide adequately for the genuine religious fulfillment of their people and for the fullest contribution of Protestant thought and energy to the whole American educational scene.

TWO

Understanding the Psychology of Religious Learning

A. by ROBERT P. O'NEIL

B. by ROY S. LEE

A. *by ROBERT P. O'NEIL*

RATHER THAN TRY to grapple with this problem as a complex whole, it may help to make several distinctions among forms of learning that could be classified as religious.

First, there is the formal, conceptual learning of doctrine, dogma, Scripture, and other facets of theology. This type of learning is pursued in seminaries by means of classes and lectures aimed at a thorough, expert knowledge at a professional level. Although the problem of changing the curricula of seminaries is most topical,[1] this does not seem to be a central issue for this chapter.

Second, there is the preverbal, primitive learning to act in accord with parentally imposed commands and prohibitions. This learning may well be reinforced later by religious sanctions, but most of the behavior is dictated by the superego, the unconscious conscience. This type of learning is relevant to this discussion in so far as it affects the person's later view of such basic religious concepts as God, sin, punishment, and salvation.

Third, and somewhat opposed to the second form, there is the more or less conscious learning and integration of moral concepts into the person's value system. They are religious in that they derive from a religious frame of reference rather than a humanistic-ethical or superego framework. These moral concepts are translated into developmentally mature moral judgments and acts. Obviously, this type of learning is part of our discussion.

Finally, there is the developmental internalization in the home of religious beliefs, attitudes, and practices that is usually followed by some formal learning of their history, aim, substantiation, and interrelationships. This is probably what most people refer to when they speak of religious education—the teaching of religion to children. It is rarely divorced from the teaching of moral principles; thus in pactice the third and last forms of religious learning overlap a great deal. The above scheme is not intended to be an authoritative division of religious learning, nor an exhaustive classification, but rather a helpful way to make the discussion manageable. An even more useful division of forms of religious learning is to separate them according to certain dimensions such as cognitive-emotional and conscious-unconscious. This allows us to examine the role played by such factors as habit, attitude, conflict, defense, and other psychologically important aspects of the personality. These will be discussed later.

It is the fourth form of religious learning that should be discussed first. The Catholic parochial school system and the Confraternity of Christian Doctrine exist for the religious education of Catholic children. This form of religious learning is certainly first in financial expense, first in manpower use, and foremost in controversy today. Our task is not to present a historical overview of Catholic education. There are many excellent works available in this area,[2] and One A in this book has examined it. However, it seems that a presentation of psychological facts relative to learning or even to religious learning in particular would be somewhat sterile without a cursory examination of some of the current dimensions of Catholic education. An understanding of some of the successes and failures of the past may aid in structuring the current controversy over the religious education of the young.

The Past

The obvious source for assessing the impact of Catholic education upon today's adults and parents is the famous study by Greeley and Rossi.[3] The basic aim of the survey was to determine to what extent attendance at a Catholic school influenced the adult religious behavior of Catholics. The study did not answer, nor did it intend to, the question of whether or not to keep Catholic schools. Interestingly enough, it provided ammunition for both sides to use. Some of their conclusions are relevant to this discussion. The major across-the-board conclusion was that religious education had an impact only on those children who came from a family in which at least one parent received Communion weekly. These were classified as "devout" families. With these children, the effects were very good. Without this type of home environment, it was found that Catholic schools had no discernible effect upon religious behavior.[4]

Although this brief statement cannot begin to do justice to the many interesting comparisons found in the study, the principal conclusion says much for the psychology of religious learning operative in Catholic schools during the school years of today's adults. It reinforced and encouraged attitudes, beliefs, and practices already fostered within the home, and the two forces acted multiplicatively upon the behavior of the developing child.

The measures of religious behavior used in the study can be described as relatively traditional indices of religious participation and belief: frequency of church attendance and reception of the sacraments, doctrinal orthodoxy, acknowledgment of the teaching authority of the church, and so forth. It does not seem unduly speculative to assert that a primary goal of Catholic education was the inculcation of these very practices, attitudes, and beliefs. It is also a fair generalization to assert that there was general agreement, perhaps more implicit than explicit, among parents, teachers, and the Catholic hierarchy as to the goals and methods of Catholic religious education.

The psychological atmosphere in Catholic education prior to the Second Vatican Council may be described by some generalizations. They obviously do not fit all schools in all areas, but are rather meant to represent a broad viewpoint that held sway for many years. First, there was a decided and unequivocal emphasis upon the *preservation of the faith.* Translated into pedagogy, this meant an unquestioning acceptance of the doctrines of Catholicism. The twelve-year curriculum of religion as a subject in the schools was most frequently a three-time repetition of a four-year cycle (each of the four years devoted to the life of Christ or to the sacraments,

for example). In the next cycle, four years later, the same topic
would be explored in greater detail and with more conceptual
material. Stress was laid upon the *one* and *true* church. Fraternization with non-Catholics was discouraged as a likely first step in the
erosion of the faith. Some unfortunate psychological effects of this
approach were the creation of suspicion of non-Catholics and especially of non-believers (with a preconscious certainty that if *they*
were to truly seek and inquire, they would believe), a firm sense of
being right and an almost unshakable conviction in the rightness of
the church and the Catholic faith.

Second, there was an emphasis placed upon *act-morality* as the
vehicle of salvation or punishment. Much attention was paid to the
distinction between mortal and venial sins. A computerlike concept
of God often resulted from this overvaluation of each behavioral
pseudoevent. Acts and even fantasies were elevated to the status of
decision makers, and it was made quite clear that one could irrevo-
cably choose salvation or damnation in the time it took to say either
word.

A third factor, much dependent upon these two, was the well-
deserved reputation of the Catholic schools for *discipline.* There is
no question but that this was the case. Courtesy, respect, and obedience were prized virtues, and the students from Catholic schools
were generally respectful toward authority and well-behaved.

A close look at the model of Catholic education in the past reveals
that in some ways it resembled the second and fourth forms
of religious learning mentioned above. There was a strong emphasis upon the non-cognitive internalization of moral laws, and
their control of behavior through guilt. There was also a focus
upon an unquestioning acceptance of the various parts of Catholic
doctrine.

The Turmoil

The winds of change blowing through the church are at gale
strength in the area of religious education. Vatican II was in large
part responsible for the questioning, the criticism, and the desire
for change in the areas of religious and moral training. However,
Vatican II was in itself a response to many forces and pressures.

Our concern is with the impact made by the burgeoning body of knowledge in the behavioral and social sciences. It was and is clear that the old methods and philosophies were neither equipping students to function as mature Christians, nor adequately conveying the truths of the faith. Moral and religious crises were no longer isolated, individual problems, but social realities. A sense of the extent and depth of the problem can be gathered from recent books such as *The Restless Believers* by John Kirvan, chaplain to the Catholic students at Wayne State University.[5]

The somewhat frenetic reactions to the realization of the system's inadequacies have produced a state of goal diffusion and text suffusion. It is not our task to assess the relative merits of the different texts nor the philosophies behind them, but it is important to realize that each major series of parochial school and CCD texts has a different emphasis. Some lean heavily on Scripture—"salvation history"; others stress liturgy; still others emphasize the brotherhood of man and social consciousness.[6] In brief, no one seems to have the answer as to what should be taught and how it should be taught.

With this somewhat tangential introduction out of the way, it is time to examine the psychological facts, research, and conclusions that are relevant to religious learning.

Cognitive Development

The formal religious education of children and adolescents is dependent upon, among other factors, the level of cognitive development of the individual. That is, topics are introduced when the child is intellectually capable of comprehending and dealing with them. In this respect, it does not differ from other disciplines. Religion, however, unlike grammar, mathematics, or science, is extremely difficult to translate into concrete concepts without the risk of misunderstanding. Religion deals with very abstract, conceptual matters. Its application to moral behavior may be made quite concrete, but to explain God, original sin, salvation, or other basic ideas of religion to children is at best a frustrating task. It is only recently that certain assumptions about the intellectual development and capacities of children have been tested. The results of this research have led to modifications of goals and expectations in religious education. A brief review of the current state of knowledge concerning cognitive development will illustrate these changes.

The most respected name in developmental psychology is that of Jean Piaget. His work spans several decades and has resulted in numerous books and articles. Of particular relevance is his work on the stages of cognitive development. He proposed four levels of development in the area of understanding the world of reality through concepts. The first two levels occur prior to approximately seven years of age and are not of great concern to formal education. However, beginning at about seven years of age and lasting until about eleven is a stage that Piaget labels the "subperiod of concrete operations." John H. Flavell describes this period as one in which the child " . . . seems to have at his command a coherent and integrated cognitive *system* with which he organizes and manipulates the world around him . . . [and] with which he can structure the present in terms of the past without undue strain or dislocation."[7]

This level, the elementary grades, is distinctly different and superior to the preschool capacity of the child. New areas are introduced into his life in formal terms: mathematics, science, syntax, and so forth. He is capable of many complex mental operations. There begins to be a well-functioning sense of reflective criticism, as when he corrects errors in speech immediately, rather than, as in the preschool years, only after external correction. Despite this appearance of a capacity to deal with, produce, and reproduce concepts, Flavell points out several crucial limitations: "Concrete operations are concrete, relatively speaking; their structure and organizing activity is oriented toward concrete things and events in the present. . . . The starting point is always the real, not the potential."[8]

In a review which was a critical survey and integration of over a hundred articles, both theoretical and empirical, in the area of concept attainment, I.S. Sigel concluded: "Introduction of concepts into an inadequately mature cognitive organization can result in a hollow core of concept acquisition."[9] In practical terms, both authors quoted above make the point that although a child during the years of seven to eleven is *apparently* able to manage quite well in dealing with abstract concepts, the appearance may be deceiving. The implications for the formal learning of religious concepts are obvious and will be taken up later.

More data on the growth of the ability to deal with abstract symbols and concepts come from the most widely used individual intelligence tests for children, the Stanford-Binet Intelligence Scale and the Wechsler Intelligence Scale for Children (WISC). Neither of these tests assumes any real competence on the part of the child of seven to eleven years to handle true abstractions comfortably. The correct answers at this age are primarily in the domain of concrete operations. The shift in emphasis both of question content and of response scoring occurs at about eleven or twelve years of age. The focus then turns to the conceptual and abstract.

One compilation of psychological research in the area of cognitive development related the findings to religion in this way. (1) The "age of reason," defined in terms of cognitive development sufficient to enable the child to comprehend concepts, grasp relationships, and understand distinctions, occurs at the onset of adolescence, that is, between eleven and thirteen years of age in almost all children. (2) Prior to this developmental level, children's thinking is egocentric, syncretic, non-logical, concrete, and non-relational; children's judgments are heteronomous, rigid, authoritarian, and inconsistent. (3) The development of thinking and judgment in moral matters follows a developmental sequence determined primarily by cognitive development and age-related experience. (4) Although manifestations of mature thinking and judgment may occur prior to the onset of adolescence, these are precursors of developing abilities, not evidence of consistent and sustained capacity.[10]

Although much more research could be cited to buttress the point,[11] it is not a matter of intense debate or disagreement. Certain details of Piaget's theory may be in dispute, for example, but there is little quarrel with the overall conclusions regarding high-level thinking and understanding in childhood. The issue is not a matter of dispute in education or even in religious education. The problem is rather one of translating an insight from the behavioral sciences into religious pedagogy.

Emotional Development

Equally important to the goal of religious education is the child's level of emotional development.[12] It has far greater impact in this area than in mathematics or in other relatively neutral subjects. The child is being introduced to a formal knowledge of beliefs, attitudes, and practices that until now he had learned in an informal manner within his family. Questions are asked and issues raised which may engage powerful feelings. A common example is a conflict between the real or perceived meaning of something explained by the teacher and an opposing position taken by the parents, either overtly or by implication. The conflict between brotherly love and bigotry is an issue which has led to a change of texts at the insistence of parents in certain dioceses. Current accepted interpretations of scriptural references often run counter to those held by parents from their education of ten or twenty years ago. The type of conflict described above, although often a problem to resolve, is fortunately most often experienced by the child at the conscious, verbal level. As such, it is infinitely more amenable to intervention than a conflict that remains at the level of feelings and emotions, inarticulate but powerful.

The child of six to ten years of age is still highly motivated by a desire to win parental approval and praise from teachers. In addition, there is an immaturity of perceptual development such that his ability to discriminate certain classes of reality objects is still shaky. Combining these two elements, we see the child's uncritical acceptance of all that the teacher says or implies adds to a strong need to conform to the teacher's expectations. Children are not capable of asking the kind of question that might clarify a religious concept in their minds because they have no previous experience in dealing with this level of concept. Religious concepts are often presented as analogous to situations in the child's life or to common myths of childhood. The child of six to ten cannot, as a rule, perceive the subtle differences or focus upon the central part of the analogy. Parents can testify to the fantastic tales brought home by wide-eyed children and defended by "But the teacher said so!"

The whole area of authority and power is a vast intellectual vacuum for the child at this age, and it is most often filled in by fantasy. His ideas about hierarchies of power, chain of command, or the relationship between crime and punishment are primarily determined by his emotions. Research has shown how extreme is the child's view of bad acts, the role of intention, punishment, and so forth.[13] He is brutally harsh in his view of punishment, authoritarian and rigid in his interpretation of law, and all but devoid of the ability to put himself in another's place. Therefore, when he hears stories from Scripture involving massive retaliation, he is unable emotionally to make the intellectual leap to the intended theme, whether it be later forgiveness or the contrast between Old Testament justice and New Testament love. The net result of the cognitive and emotional immaturity is very often a potpourri of distorted, semiunderstood, concrete ideas.

Some of the modifications in religious pedagogy are directly due to the impact of recent research in child development. The basic questions, however, have not been asked with much vigor. That is, what is the child capable of understanding in terms of religious and moral concepts? Is there any evidence that children understand such concepts as God, salvation, sin, redemption, punishment, or forgiveness before the age of twelve or thirteen? Does the previously cited research in the area of cognitive development apply to religious concepts? These basic religious concepts are of the highest level of abstraction. The research, facts, and conclusions all point to the critical limitations placed upon a child's understanding by his level of development, which is very highly correlated with chronological age. Apparently, there is a very basic contradiction between what religious learning demands of the child and what the facts indicate the child is capable of learning. Modification of techniques and dilution of the concepts are evasions of this basic contradiction.

When we turn to the area of moral training as part of religious learning, it is again worthwhile to make some distinctions. In this area, the cognitive is less important than the emotional, for behavior is more controlled by moral habits than by cognitive decisions. This aspect of religious education is particularly important in that later moral behavior may well depend upon the individual's perception of the adequacy and relevance of moral principles first learned in his youth.

Moral Training and Education

The second and third forms of religious learning mentioned earlier were both forms of moral learning—one primitive and superego-based, the other mature and principle-oriented. Religion and religious education can, unfortunately, reinforce both of these forms. To consider the obvious first, it is easy to see how, in the elementary grades, religion presented in terms of sin, punishment, responsibility, and the all-just God can totally warp a child's concept of his relationship with God. The equation of God and parental authority not so subtly encourages this attitude. Many parents and teachers unconsciously reinforce an attitude most children have that any misfortune or calamity is punishment for some past misdeed. Fixation can too easily occur, and the child carries this idea with him into adulthood.

Current changing catechetical and sacramental practices reflect the growing awareness of the child's vulnerability in the early grades. Confession is being postponed until the child reaches the fourth or fifth grade, a decided improvement over the practice of initiating confession in the second grade. Sin as a concept is not emphasized in the early grades, and when it is mentioned, the approach is increasingly indirect and gentle. More and more teacher manuals include brief summaries of the age-grade characteristics of the developing child, as well as admonitions regarding the presentation of particularly sensitive areas of doctrine.

Although these changes are praiseworthy, there yet remain many conflicts between catechetical practice and psychological insights. There is a sizable amount of substantiated research and conclusions which supports the statement that "moral" behavior appears long before behavior based upon moral judgments. To illustrate, a child will sometimes tell the painful truth, share his toys, or refrain from aggression long before he can produce reasons for doing so. It is worth noting in this regard that a white rat can be conditioned into "moral" behavior such as food sharing or the inhibition of aggression. The child is acting on the basis of his learning experiences within the home, reinforced by the factors of praise and punishment, love and its withdrawal.

The research can be summarized in several statements. Morality of behavior in the preadolescent child is dependent primarily upon external sanctions rather than the operation of internal, principle-directed judgments. The development of this moral judgment capacity is not related to social class, religion, or nationality, but is conditional upon intellectual development. This developmental process increases with age regularly, and it is not until early adolescence that true moral judgments appear. During the preadolescent years of seven to twelve or thirteen, there are severe limitations imposed upon a child's ability to perceive situations, apply principles, reflect upon the implications, or even to make up his mind.[14] Kohlberg summarized it best when he stated: "The research findings on the slow age development of moral judgment, ego strength, and self-criticism suggest the wisdom of a gradualistic view of the child as morally accountable."[15]

Before moving on to a consideration of developmental morality, some of the facts, principles, and well-accepted hypotheses to which we have appealed may be summarized.

Psychological Principles in Religious Education

By far the most general and important principle is that of *readiness*. That is, there must be an intellectual and emotional fit between the child's capacities at a given age level and the material to be presented. Much work needs to be done in this area, inasmuch as many of the assumptions that have guided religious education in the past were wholly untested against data.

Specifically, there are several areas of development that need to be emphasized. There are limitations placed upon the comprehension of the seven- to eleven-year-old by the concreteness of his orientation. To hope for higher-level, abstract, relational, or critical thinking at this age is unrealistic. The preadolescent child is highly motivated by a need for adult approval. This can often blur the distinction between comprehension of concept and its mere reproduction. At this age, the child is easily impressed by mythological characters and fairy tales. His enthusiasm for this ought not to be mistaken for religious zeal. A child often has difficulty grasping the essential and ignoring the accidental; he is likely to focus upon a peripheral aspect of an idea which has some emotional or fantasy appeal. A child before twelve or fourteen is susceptible to grave distortions of concepts. His tendency is to overdramatize and particularly to exaggerate power and authority. The ideas of law, responsibility, and intention are especially muddied by his lack of experience in living. Morality to the youth is a black and white phenomenon with little room for relativism of judgment or extenuating circumstances.

There are other principles that need to be applied in the area of morality, both conceptually and behaviorally. The child before adolescence has a vulnerability to emotional conditioning of behavior. A perceived threat of loss of love or approval is a strong deterrent to behavior, but this is no evidence of the internalization of principles. A perception of God as a vigilant observer of wrongdoing can easily lead to later scrupulosity if it is unwittingly reinforced by teachers. A moral precept that is not subject to later critical examination is most likely learned in an atmosphere of high emotion and low cognition, that is, in the preschool stage. The task of formal education would seem to be to provide some substance to a moral principle, focusing upon the conscious and cognitive aspects.

In the area of moral learning, it appears that a basic question has not been asked. Is there any evidence to justify the formal introduction of moral concepts such as sin or personal responsibility to God in the preadolescent years? To phrase it another way, does the formal presentation of moral concepts at the preadolescent level make a significant difference in the moral behavior of religiously educated children as contrasted to children reared in a non-religious environment? The answer to the latter question cannot easily be given, although a conclusion of Greeley and Rossi is pertinent and provocative: "With our admittedly limited tools, we could not discover any relationship between Catholic school attendance and disposition to help others."[16] The answer to the first question is, from one point of view, a qualified no. This rests on the evidence that moral development, like other parts of the personality, is age-related and sequential.

Developmental Levels of Morality

The fundamental and universal quality of childhood morality is obedience. The child is subject to others—parents, teachers, group leaders. He is neither allowed nor expected to make major decisions. In important areas such as education and money, he is protected by law from making long-range decisions that might turn out to be harmful. The child prior to adolescence is in all ways but one a minor. The exception is in moral matters. Although he is considered "in training" for every other aspect of his life, he is made responsible for his moral welfare long before he is responsible for his health.

Here, lest there be misunderstanding, a brief clarification must be inserted. None of the statements made nor evidence presented is aimed at freeing the child from responsibility. The critical issue has to do with the extent of his moral responsibility, and just as importantly, who the agent of moral training is. The assumption has been made that formal education and the teacher are important variables in a child's moral training. This remains to be demonstrated, or even justified. Parents are the agents of moral training and cannot share the responsibility. The pressure to share it has resulted in large part from a misunderstanding of the first question —the extent of the child's moral responsibility.

The child's moral responsibility is terminal with his parents. It is not until adolescence that he is capable of developing the awareness, understanding, judgment, and self-control necessary for moral responsibility to God. Because of this immaturity, the child is responsible to his parents. The parents are responsible to God. It is theologically and psychologically valid to recognize that habits learned during these years are likely to continue, and therefore to emphasize the development of good moral habits. This is the accepted view in other areas of personality development such as emotional control, social skills, attitudes toward learning, authority, or achievement, and even personal hygiene. In all such matters, however, we recognize the limitations of poor impulse control, short attention span, and the lack of sustained motivation. A child is given an allowance; he may be indulged or strictly controlled, but he is not expected to understand economic theory until college.

If one were to ask almost any friend who is not a theologian (and some who are) to explain his concept of a personal God, grace, or the soul, what would be the result? Yet we expect children to achieve some understanding of the intelligible. Children are assumed to be able to comprehend the brotherhood of man when research demonstrates the inability of a ten-year-old to grasp the concept of society or of the continuity of the community beyond the life of the individual.[17] Virtually every concept taught in religion courses or applied to moral education can be subjected to this type of criticism.

It is not until just before puberty that the child begins to achieve a level of development which is appropriate to the introduction of moral and religious concepts. Moral and religious training, however, has been taking place in the home, within the family, every day of the child's life. It would seem more in line with what is known about child and parent to concentrate upon increasing the adequacy of the training given by parents.

Conclusion

In what may appear to be an abrupt reversal of field, it must be stated that there are many grounds for optimism in the area of religious and moral education. Some critical statements have been made and some challenging issues have been raised in this chapter. However, it is evident that many efforts are being made to improve not just the content, but the structure of religious and moral education. Some firm evidence of this is the changes made thus far— changes that five or ten years ago were undreamed of. As the behavioral and social sciences come to be more acceptable to those in decision-making positions, there will be even more changes. It is to be hoped that anthropology, psychology, and sociology will aid in producing changes that are both progressive in effectiveness and conservative in respect for the contributions of the past.

B. *by ROY S. LEE*

A NY CHURCH, or subgroup within a church, or any individual undertaking the task of religious education, has to make a choice between two principles which will govern how he proceeds. The two principles are not necessarily incompatible, in theory at least, but in practice they tend to exclude each other. The question at issue is which of them is to be regarded as the dominating one. On the one hand Christian education may be seen as essentially aimed at procuring belief in a set of doctrines carrying the authority of the church, acceptance of and conformity to a code of moral conduct more or less precisely defined, and observance of disciplines and habits of worship laid down as essential by the church in question. This is the authoritarian principle. The ultimate authority of course is God, but in this view the church is regarded as his mouthpiece or at least as the appointed guardian of truths revealed by God and of the commandments he has given. In another form of this authoritarian principle it is not the church but the Bible which is seen as the medium of God's authority, but the aim is the same—to procure the adoption of whatever the authority is believed to prescribe.

On the other hand lies the empirical principle. According to this the basic aim of religious education should be the development of the individual. According to this principle it is more important, more Christian, that the individual be helped to think for himself and arrive at his own ideas rather than accept doctrines presented to him as true simply on the authority of the church or Bible. Similarly, conformity to an imposed code of conduct is regarded as less valuable, less desired by God, than that the individual should develop his own moral judgment. In other words, this view lays primary stress on nurturing persons, whereas the other view stresses the inculcation of doctrines and commandments. For the latter view, the authoritarian, religious education means first of all religious instruction, and the effort it makes to procure the development of children is for the purpose of bringing them to accept what is already held by the teachers to be true or right beyond question. For the empirical view religious education has a wider connotation. It will imply instruction, of course, because persons must be educated to think and given material to think about, but however convinced the teachers may be that what they teach is true, the most important thing is that the children should be stimulated to think for themselves, to be critical, in the best sense of the word, of what they are taught, and to develop inward standards of conduct. They can be helped in this by being taught what the church has come to accept as true and right, but it must not be imposed upon them by any kind of social, moral, or spiritual pressure. It is this view which is accepted in this chapter.

Both views make use of psychology. The authoritarian is interested in the psychology of learning, so that the right methods may be used for inculcating what it wants to teach. The empirical view is also ready to learn from the psychology of learning, but this is part of and subsidiary to a wider interest, the psychology of the development of the human person. Right beliefs, right attitudes are seen as emerging from right growth and the emphasis is laid on procuring right growth. It is the aim of this chapter to examine some of the main lines of growth.

Before we can do that there is one matter which must be cleared up. It is not intended to suggest by the title of the chapter that there are fundamental differences between religious learning, that is, learning religion, and the learning of any other kind of knowledge or behavior. Religious learning obeys the same laws as other kinds of learning, if we may dignify by the name "laws" the psychological processes discovered as the way the human mind works. What differences there are arise from the nature of religion, not from the learning processes, for it involves the various functions of the mind in different degrees of intensity and completeness than the learning of something else, say mathematics. But the same processes are present in both, in spite of the variation of degree to which they are involved.

Theological and Psychological Explanation

It is essential to establish this from the beginning if we are to understand the proper place of a psychology of religion. The processes of learning religion will be made clear as we proceed, but there can be no valid psychology of religion unless we make the fundamental assumption as our starting point that *all* religious behavior is explicable in psychological terms. We cannot resort to non-psychological concepts as a substitute for psychological ones. This does not deny the validity of attempts to use theological or metaphysical concepts to explain our experiences; it simply denies that they can be interchanged with psychological ones. For instance, "grace" is a theological concept, used to describe aspects of behavior which point to a dependence upon God; but the psychologist has to give an account of the mental processes which constitute that behavior, and his description of it will be in terms of perceptions, images, ideas, ideals, integration of the personality, and so on. He can only deal in "natural" processes.

An example may make this clearer. If a man sees an angel, it is because an angel is present to him in such a form that he perceives the angel in the same manner as he would perceive, say, a table; that is, because light reflected from the angel (or perhaps radiating from him) stimulates the optic nerve; or else his vision of the angel is a hallucination, because he has projected upon the outside world the form of an angel constructed in the recesses of his mind and, not aware that it is a projection, mistakes his subjective vision for the perception of an objective reality. But even if the angel is present to be seen (I am not arguing for or against the objective reality of angels, but reflecting over a hypothetical case) his perception of the angel is strictly conditioned by what his previous experience has conditioned him to perceive; that is, by the myriads of perceptions

which have become built into an ordered system of a world of
objects structured in light, color, shape, feel, sound, and so on; by
the images and ideals of the world in general, by stories of angels
he has read or heard or representations of them that he has seen,
by his expectation of or emotional need for some visible communication from God. His mind is not a blank to receive a complete
perception from outside, but actively meets the sensations coming
to it from outer or inner stimuli and fits them into the slots which
previous experience has formed and interprets them accordingly.
A friend of mine who was color-blind from early infancy recently
had color vision restored to her by an operation. She now finds
herself in a bewildering world in which she is hard put to recognize
objects with which she was perfectly familiar when she saw them
only in shades of gray. She has to learn by experience to perceive
the new world into which she has been plunged at a stroke. This
can be done only gradually; there are so many things to be learned
about colors and their relation to form and light. She has to arrange
her new experience into an ordered and consistent pattern, the
pattern which we assume to be the "real" world.

We need not doubt the existence of a world beyond our experience—though that may not be the best way of describing it—a
world which is the source of the given element in our experience,
a world which is the context of our existence, which impinges upon
us in an infinite variety of ways, a world of which we ourselves are
a part. But when we say that we perceive the world, or know the
world, we are using a kind of mental shorthand. We are referring
to the world we have constructed out of our experience, not the
world as it is in itself. This leaves us open to error when we try to
think about that world, for we can only think in terms of our
experience. The error lies in assuming that the world in itself exists
in the mode in which we think about it, whereas we are thinking
about our apprehension of it.

God—an Interpretative Myth

The importance of making the distinction becomes obvious if we
substitute God for the angel I used in the illustration I gave just
now. In what sense, if any, can we be said to know God? Clearly,

if angels exist, there are situations possible in which we could perceive them, for they would be objects, like ourselves, within the totality of existing things. To say that God *is* affirms a different order of existence, for God cannot be within the totality of things as we are. His "withinness" also is different. As with his existence, so with his action. God cannot be regarded as sending from a distance an angel to speak to us or Jesus to die for us, for God is not distant from us. We must be, in some sense, within his being, as also are the angel and Jesus. The truth is that any language that we use in talking about the existence of God, or the action of God, which implies that he has separated objective existence over against us, cannot be anything but metaphorical. To take it as literal inevitably reduces God to the status of a created being and contradicts what we mean by calling him Creator. God is not God if he is an object within the totality. Our apprehension of him must be mediated through our experience of the universe and "God" is an interpretative idea of that experience, in its emotional as well as its cognitive aspects. Our immediate experience is of "ourselves in the universe" and what we call "God" is the pattern of order and unity in which we arrange the totality of our experiences. The pattern may be a good one or a bad one, adequate or inadequate to the experiences, but there is no way of getting outside them to test it. And the pattern is not merely one of intellectual or conceptual order; it must integrate our sentiments, values, ideals, and relationships, the whole gamut of our experiences. The language of theology or metaphysics may introduce terms like absolute, ultimate, eternal, transcendent, immanent, revelation, etc., and in practice these obscure our dependence upon experience of our environment, but when they are examined closely they are all a confession of our inability to comprehend God within the categories of thinking to which we are confined by our nature as human beings.

Nevertheless, if we are to think and talk about God, as we must, it is the common language that we must use, for it constitutes the tools of thought and of communication, however much it lays us open to self-deception or misunderstanding. In religious education in particular this is essential. Children are unable to think in abstract conceptions in religion before the age of ten at least.[1] It is better, therefore, in talking to them about God, to use more concrete terms adapted to their way of thinking, terms such as Heavenly Father, Loving Father, Maker and Giver of all things, Protector, provided that we ourselves are aware that we are using metaphors or analogies, or using "evocative" language,[2] and provided also that we do not try to rivet them into the minds of the children as final and unquestionable truths, but encourage the children as they grow to seek fuller understanding of the teaching, understanding that is appropriate to the successive stages of their development. The older child should not be expected to think and feel about God in the way a young one does.

Once we have grasped the fact that there are stages in the apprehension of God, the place of psychology in religious education becomes clearer. Its first task is to explore the nature of the growth which takes place within the personality of the child. This growth, which I will examine in more detail presently, is far more complex than is commonly assumed. Growth in intellectual understanding is one of the strands in it, but unfortunately this has often been taken to be the chief area of religious education. I say "unfortunately," because overemphasis on it has tended to create a false idea of what religion is. Nevertheless, it is an important part; thus one of the tasks of psychology is to discover the processes of learning. Having discovered them, we can make our religious education more effective. Another strand which also tends to be overemphasized, or stressed out of context, is the moral element in religious behavior. It has too often been assumed that we know how the moral outlook is formed, what it should be, and how to inculcate it. Modern psychology has made great advances in the study of the development of the moral aspect of personality and has shown the falseness of much that used to seem self-evident. Similarly, other elements of religion have been subjected to scrutiny and as a result it would seem almost as though we have to start from scratch again to understand what is religious learning. And the first lesson we learn is that it cannot be treated in isolation but must be seen as inextricably bound up in the general development of the personality. The second lesson is that the individual person cannot be separated from the context of persons and things which constitute his environment and that he only becomes what he is because of action and reaction within the context as he grows. Thus the study of the phenomena of religion throws us back into general psychology. The idea of God and attitudes toward God are reached by the same kind of processes as any other ideas and attitudes. We must therefore study the nature of human growth and development.

Stages of Development

Let us take for granted that there is something we can call maturity, even if we find it difficult to define precisely what we mean by it, and even if, in the end, it proves to be an ever receding ideal rather than a state we actually attain. Little is gained by trying to define it *a priori.* It is more profitable to examine how people grow and what arrests in growth may occur. When we adopt this procedure we observe that each individual passes through a number of stages in approaching what may tentatively be called maturity. The various stages are fairly clearly marked off from each other by the characteristics they display. We can classify the stages according to different criteria, such as intellectual development, physical attainments, emotional attitudes, social attitudes, adjustment to the real world, dependence or independence of personality, and so on.[3] The stages might be listed differently according to the criteria taken. One division that proves fruitful is that which is commonly adopted by psychoanalysts. It gives four stages on the way to maturity: infancy, childhood, adolescence, adulthood. It is this that I shall adopt.

Infancy lasts from birth to about the age of six. It is a period of physical and mental dependence, in which the effective environment of the infant is almost entirely the family. In the first two years the mother-child relationship is overwhelmingly important in his mental growth, since everything that he experiences is associated with her in the images of her which he gradually forms. In the second part of infancy the father emerges as a recognized other person, and that period sees the rise of the emotional complexities of the triangular relationship. Freud called this the Oedipus complex. Infancy is marked by the rapid emotional, instinctive, and intellectual developments which take place in it. It is a period of inner turbulence and instability in which the personality is struggling to take shape, partly under the pressure of innate constitutional drives, partly under the pressures and demands the social environment and his own mental and physical helplessness put upon him. He is struggling to find a *modus vivendi* and an identity which enables him to cope with his own inner conflicts and the world as he comes to know it.

Infancy is brought to an end by the resolution of the Oedipus complex. The emotional conflicts which constitute it are brought to a stable state, and childhood ensues. This period is marked by three outstanding characteristics. First, emotional development or change becomes quiescent; no new forms and no new conflicts emerge, and in particular the sexual instincts (in the psychoanalytical sense of "sexual"), which were very active in infancy, pass into latency, from which they emerge again at the end of childhood. Secondly, the interests of the child turn away from the family to the world around him; the family becomes a base from which he explores the world. Thirdly, he feels the need to distinguish sharply between fantasy and reality; he seeks to separate fact from non-fact, "truth" from what is imaginary. It is also a period of action rather than of feeling.

The onset of puberty brings childhood to an end and ushers in adolescence. Its great increase of instinctive energy cannot be contained by the barriers erected at the end of infancy and enduring through childhood, nor are the channels established then adequate to provide satisfactory outlet. A fresh period of growth sets in. The adolescent is plunged into a renewed struggle, analogous to that of infancy, to bring his divergent and sometimes contradictory urges under control and to find adequate ways of expressing himself. Hence adolescence is a second period of turmoil in which there is rapid growth of the personality. The adolescent is driven to search for a consistent identity and a meaningful role in society. And as well as having to struggle to become himself, he is compelled to look at the world in new ways and to find deeper values by which to live. It is a period of criticism and rebellion against the past, represented by the adult world, as well as one of idealism and romanticism about the new world which he is going to help create.

By the time adulthood has been reached the individual has gained a fair measure of stability. He has found an identity, or several partial identities; he is able to adjust to the world, accepting the limits it imposes on him; and he can be a person among other persons. He has found a meaning and purpose to live for. In adulthood these developments are consolidated and once again his energies flow outward, as in childhood, toward achievement in the world of reality.

Aspects of Growth

Not only have we to consider the stages of development, we have also to take into account the aspects of development, the lines of growth which seem to be most important in the formation of the mature personality. Examined in this way the individual is seen to have five major tasks to fulfill in his growth toward maturity. He has (1) to develop the tools of his mind; (2) to integrate his experiences; (3) to become a unified person; (4) to adjust to the world beyond himself; (5) to become a moral being. It scarcely needs to be said that these strands of the developing personality are interwoven and interdependent, that failure in one may render the others impossible of full attainment, and that to understand one requires knowledge of the others. This complexity makes the task of psychology difficult, but it is necessary to isolate them for the sake of understanding what is involved in human growth. I shall examine them one by one in their significance for religious learning, but their interdependence in the living person must never be forgotten.

The Tools of the Mind

The most obvious of these, perhaps too often taken for granted, is language. By means of language we are able to arrange our experience systematically, relate diverse experiences to each other, separate different modes of experience into categories represented by nouns, adjectives, verbs, adverbs, prepositions, tenses, and so on. By language we can make the effort of communicating our experience to other people and share in theirs. Language is the means by which we form concepts and by which we reason, that is, it is the most advanced tool that man has evolved to enable him to deal with himself, his fellows, and the world. Without it he cannot formulate ideas by which to bring order and structure into his experiences and open the way to receive and explore further experiences in depth.

The idea of God is, or should be, the most advanced of our ideas, the supreme tool of the mind, for by it we seek to synthesize all our experiences and bring them into ordered relation to each other. We have many subsystems of ideas and sentiments—of ourselves, of other people, of the world itself or things within it, an infinity of arrangements—but "God" is the interpretative idea of the whole. It is therefore important to understand not only why we ought to form the idea of God but also how in fact we do form it, to trace the steps by which we pass from crude formulations to more complete ones, and to understand the material out of which we shape the idea. This is not an exercise in logic or philosophy; it is the work of psychology.

Thinking about God is not the whole of experiencing God. There are other aspects of religious experience which must be taken into account. Language is a sophisticated achievement which only comes as the result of much experience and the effort to assimilate that experience, which we usually call "thinking." For many people ratiocination, thinking logically in concepts, remains an underdeveloped tool, often unreliable as well, and in all people there are large areas of experience which can only be verbalized with difficulty and may even be beyond verbalization, since to attempt to put them into words alters the nature of the experience. To say "I am angry" is quite different from the feeling I experience. The concept of anger and the proposition "I am angry" are different modes of experience from the anger itself. Emotions, of which anger is an instance, are the driving forces of the personality. The function of reason is to give the drives to the most satisfying forms of expression. One mark of maturity is that it displays this perfect combination of reason and emotional, instinctive drives.

The drives are present from birth but the capacity to form wide-reaching concepts, especially in religion, is not attained, as we saw earlier, before the age of ten. Up till then the drives inevitably work through their attachment to images in the search for expression in the world beyond the self. The images are the links between the world and the self. They are the outcome of previous experience.

They may be simple, that is, the result of a single experience, but usually they are constructed out of a multiplicity of experiences, which may even be conflicting with each other. It does not necessarily follow that as soon as abstract concepts are formed the emotional drives are freed from the concrete images and flow through the new concepts. In most of us the energies of the mind remain attached to the images, with the result that our abstract ideals are not very dynamic, not productive of action equivalent to their intellectual significance. We may accept the brotherhood of man, for instance, with our intellects, but this does not affect our behavior to any great extent, because the driving forces of our personality remain locked to images formed earlier. This failure of transfer of energy is a major problem in the psychodynamics of religious learning to which insufficient attention has been paid. One possible solution is to see our religious belief as mythological, so that concrete images such as calling God "Father" or thinking of him as a person can be used as symbols rather than as logical statements of truth.

The problem of how to make our religious ideas psychodramatically effective, even when they are consciously accepted as religious myths, is complicated by the existence in all of us of an extensive unconscious area of the mind, which is cut off from consciousness and which works according to infantile modes of mental activity; that is, it is non-logical, self-centered, pleasure-seeking, ruled by fantasy and not by reality. The ego, whose function it is to coordinate and control behavior, and which is the seat of consciousness, denies it recognition, yet it is able to influence our ideas, our feelings and values, and our actions by getting expression in secondary or disguised form. For instance, our ideas of God and our attitudes toward him are in large part shaped by the persistence in the unconscious of infantile images of the father.

There are two general problems here. The first is that of how to bring about healthy growth through the various stages of development toward maturity. We need to trace the development of the idea of God and its associated mental attitudes from the first simple experiences of the infant to the all-comprehending picture drawn by mature man. We have to track down the psychological sources of the material out of which that final picture is built, as well as the successive stages in integrating it. For successful religious learning we have also to ensure that the right material is acquired and that development is not arrested in any way. I have attempted elsewhere a brief outline of the main elements and the stages of development.[4] They are too complex to be even summarized here. But it can be said that the foundations of healthy religious development are inevitably laid in the prereligious stage of infancy.

The second general problem is to recognize and discover the causes of aberrations from healthy development. These are the result of fixations and repressions in the infantile stages of growth, or of the breakdown of one of the five lines of development I have listed. The failures occur mostly because something has been at fault in the relations of the infant with his mother or father, or both. Since the child's early ideas of God are formed out of his experiences with them, through the images he constructs of them, severe repressions can lead to distortion in his understanding of God and indeed may even prevent him from getting free to understand God at all. The God he professes, or rejects, may simply be the repressed fantasy image of his father projected from his unconscious upon the world. Whether such distorted religion should be called religion is another question.

Integrating Experience

The second line of growth is in the way the growing child orders his experience into connected patterns. He has an innate impulse to do so, to relate one experience to another, and to interpret each fresh experience by means of those he has already undergone that seem most closely related to it. In this way he is building up meaning. The process of integrating experience has two aspects: first, the gradual discovery of himself as a person, through the intimacy of the experience of his body; and secondly, the discovery and exploration of the world which stands over against him and with which he interacts. We shall discuss his growth as a person in the next section and for the present confine ourselves to the stages of his discovery of the world.

In the first stage of infancy, perhaps till about the age of two years, he is not conscious of himself as a knowing subject. He is immersed in the flood of perceptions, feelings, wishes, recollections of previous experiences, which, as it were, live through him. These are made up almost entirely out of contacts with his mother. Certainly all his most intense experiences have to do with her. She is his whole world. Inevitably, therefore, the first pattern which begins to emerge out of his experiences is an image of her. It must not be thought that this image is the kind of perception of her than an adult would have, like the reflection of her in a mirror. It is better thought of as a more and more closely knit pattern of familiar experiences, a central core emerging with increasing clearness from the confusion which surrounds it in his mind. When he comes to self-consciousness he becomes aware at the same time that his mother is separated from him, a different person, even though in many respects they still seem to be merged, and however strong and intimate the involvement they have with each other. The desire to recover the lost unity with the mother is one of the dominant motives in religion, but from henceforth he is locked in his own individuality and cannot escape from it. He has to discover what he is. In trying to do so he should find religion, which, according to Alfred North Whitehead, "is what a man does with his solitariness."

When the infant has sorted out the pattern of himself and his mother he can go on to clarify the general mother pattern still further and distinguish other people, his father first, and then other people and other objects. In the early stage he can only understand them by projecting himself, with his newly found self-consciousness, into them, identifying with them. That is to say, he is naturally an animist, treating everything as living. The recognition of a distinction between animate and inanimate existence is a relatively advanced achievement. It may well be that we do not easily outgrow this primal animism in some aspects of our experience, and particularly that in some people God is merely an animistic interpretation of the confused totality of things, a greatly expanded human person projected upon it, creating a tendency to see events in terms of purposes similar to the purposes they feel within themselves. They have not adjusted to reality.

In the period of childhood emphasis on objective knowledge becomes strongly developed and the understanding of causal relations more and more replaces interpretation of experience in terms of purposive intentions. In this stage the child seeks ability to distinguish fact from fantasy, truth from fiction, and to apply the test of objectivity. He is interested in getting to know the world and in learning how to manipulate it. He is outwardly directed, more concerned with knowledge and action than with feeling, even though in the process of discovering the world he is clarifying the boundaries which divide him from the world beyond him.

This stage of development raises two interesting problems for education in religion. In the first place, God and the religious sentiments may fall into the background of stories and legends, losing the vivid and pressing reality of the perceivable, tangible world of objects. Preoccupation with fact may grow to such proportions that there is little room left for interest in religion, particularly if teaching about it is not given in factual form. The belief that the scientific, empirical approach to reality is the only valid one may become so ingrained that when adolescence comes with its questioning attitude religion is easily thrown aside as a fairy tale for little children. On the other hand, because he is interested in action and getting power over things, the child may interpret God as a kind of supermagician, able to do anything and, incidentally, keeping a strict watch over human beings to punish them if they offend against him. This view too, and God with it, may be sloughed off in adolescence when other motives than the desire for power begin to emerge. If the scientific and religious approaches to reality are to be reconciled, we need to study more closely the kind of religious teaching to be given in childhood. For instance, the human aspect of Jesus, his life as an individual in his historical setting, his particularity, rather than his divinity and the divine purpose, need to be emphasized. Then again, the idea of God and creation are very interesting to a mind directed toward fact, and God ought to be discussed in relation to the world as it is rather than as over against the world. This certainly is necessary in adolescence when the pressing concern is to find the meaning of life. This links up with the third line of growth.

Becoming a Person

We are not born with ready-made unitary personality; unity has to be achieved by a long struggle. To put it more precisely, the experiences we undergo are often in seeming contradiction to each other, or our impulses drive us in opposite directions, and there is need for reconciliation of the opposites. Some experiences are pleasant and we seek for their repetition; others are unpleasant and we seek to avoid them. We desire contradictory things—for instance, to swallow our mother's breast yet not destroy it, or, later, to possess our mother and not incur danger from our father in doing so. Our interests and feelings become organized into various patterns which grow more and more complex and extensive, and over them all is the innate urge to unify them. In the prepersonal stage —that is, before consciousness of self is reached—the division is relatively simple. Some experiences are good, that is, pleasurable; some are bad, that is, unpleasurable. As we have seen, this leads to the formation of two general images of the mother, the good mother and the bad mother, which in healthy growth are later integrated. If the bad mother image is made too dominant, the work of reconciliation becomes more difficult and may not be completely achieved. In the early period of infancy the integration of experiences into a unitary personality seems to be most vulnerable.[5] The infant can develop a sound ego only under maternal care which reduces the inevitable anxiety situations of the infant to a minimum and gradually builds up in him the power to tolerate them because he comes to trust in the continuity of love and so of the overall dominance of the good. His mother's loving care of his needs and sympathy with his sufferings give him the faith to let his desires be strong, to bear an increasing measure of unpleasure, and even to experience the latter as a step toward greater pleasure and more enduring satisfactions, a lesson that he will go on learning all his life and which finds its full expression in faith in God. The root of religious faith is established in early infancy through the natural love of the mother.

The integration of impulses, emotions, thoughts, feelings into a person has to overcome many difficulties in the following stages. The most difficult of the crises to overcome is that of later infancy, the so-called Oedipus complex, in which the ego, the seat of integration, has to handle powerful wishes from within and the (apparent) threats of danger from without. If these are too strong for it, the ego sets up defensive barriers by means of repression, and the unconscious is filled with severe fixations, unresolved fears, anxieties, aggressiveness, and feelings of guilt. The images of the father and mother may become charged with intense emotions, positive or negative, which remain in the unconscious after they are detached, partially at least, from the actual parents and are then projected under God and the church and become screens to prevent a true understanding of what these are. Repression and fixation set up a division preventing the unity of the self and depriving it of the capacity to live to the full. Growth in religion is best safeguarded in the infantile period by creating relationships which promote the formation of a strong ego, and no efforts then or later to inculcate religious teaching can take its place. "Moral education is no substitute for love."[6]

Strengthening of self-identity and progress in becoming a person take place through the process known as identification. We identify with other people by imagining ourselves to be those people, living in them, as it were. The boy identifies himself with his father, the girl with her mother, but there is some degree of identification in all human relationships. Where the emotional interest is strong the identification is more extensive than where it is weak. The ego of the child takes on the admired and desired characteristics of the person with whom the identification is made, characteristics, of course, as the child sees them. They then become his own. The self adapts itself to them. The process is not confined to childhood but continues throughout life. It is the basis of all community and loyalty. It undoubtedly facilitates learning of all kinds, but it is of particular importance in religious growth. It is frequently said that religion is caught, not taught, that the teacher is more significant and fruitful in imparting religion than what he says. Good instruction elucidates what he is, but what is communicated primarily is his own religious attitudes.

The quest for personal significance and identity in relation to other people and the totality of the world becomes most urgent in adolescence as the individual is preparing to pass out of his long period of emotional, social, and economic dependence. It is no mere coincidence that this is also the period which brings most changes in religious alignments. God takes on a deeper meaning as that within which (or whom) we may truly find our identity and become ourselves. He is not something outside ourselves to whom we relate; he is that which we become, or aspire to become.

Adjustment to Reality

The fourth line of development is closely bound up with the two previous ones discussed. In the multiplicity of patterns into which we order our experience a demarcation gets drawn between self and not-self. The division is not clear at first but as we grow in experience and in awareness of self-identity the distinction gradually sharpens. We know that we have some measure of inner control over what is oneself, though there are always elements of experience which come as a surprise to the ego, almost as if they were from outside the personality. But that which does come from without has a givenness about it which puts it beyond the control of the receiver to determine its nature. It must be seen in its givenness if effective adjustment is to be made to it. The infant, however, does not recognize the quality of givenness, for he has not yet clearly drawn the line between self and not-self. He is dominated by his wishes, by the pleasure-pain principle, and by his animism. That which is pleasant appears to come to him because he wished for it. That which is unpleasant is due to aggressive forces attacking him. He is governed, that is to say, by the principle known as the omnipotence of thought, that what happens is the result of wishing. This is also the principle of magic; wish for something in the right way and it will come to pass.

We have to put the infantile behind us if we are to grow to maturity. Undoubtedly we grow out of much of our infantility, but much of it we also bury in our unconscious, and if that is strong it operates from there to influence both our behavior and our attitudes. It makes us prone to rely on the omnipotence of thought, to indulge in wishful thinking and belief in a (refined) magic. This is shown by the way we are blinded by our emotions from perceiving truth and deterred from accepting hard fact and acting on it, in the political and economic fields, for instance. Religion is a field in which infantile attitudes flourish. We create our pictures of heaven out of infantile wishful thinking; prayer is too often merely the effort to change reality by wishing; and God is the great magician whose power we call into effect by the use of the right formulas and propitiating rites. We see the harshness of reality as punishment by God, or feel ourselves assaulted by the devil. We try to avert rather than to accept the givenness of God, which we have to accept as the beginning of action.

There is no easy way to bring about reality thinking in place of wishful thinking and the omnipotence of thought. It is universal, extending beyond religion, and cannot be cured by religious instruction alone. At least it should not be encouraged in religion by presenting to children a God constructed on these modes of thinking. Infants and young children cannot help but think partially in these ways, but the challenge to them begins in childhood with the urge to distinguish fact from fairy tale, and the child should be encouraged to approach religion in the same spirit—that it is concerned with the realities of the world and is not a flight from what is unpleasant.

Becoming Moral

Man is a social being, not just because he is endowed with a "gregarious instinct" that drives him to seek the company of others, but because he develops from the beginning within a social context —the mother-baby unit—and depends upon his social environment to shape his mind, to stimulate and give direction to the wide spectrum of love impulses which form the main drives of his personality. He is a social being before he becomes aware of his individuality, and his individuality is always in relation to or contrast with other persons. To complete his development to full humanity he has also to become a moral being. He has to learn to regulate his behavior so that the satisfaction of his innate drives does not destroy satisfactory relationships with his fellowmen. Because he is a self-conscious thinking being it is not enough for him to be compelled by external pressures to conform to the code of his society and so remain acceptable; he must identify himself with the code and standards of his society, consciously accept them, make them an essential part of himself. By internalizing the standards he becomes moral, as distinct from merely social. Man has no inborn sense of right and wrong, of good and evil. He has to learn his standards as he grows. He has also to build into his personality the psychological structure which makes him feel obliged to obey the standards. This is the fifth of our lines of development. It is a long and very involved process, but it is one which must be understood for religious learning, since religion and morality have become, in Christianity at least, very closely intertwined. Here I can give only the barest outline of the development.

Morality involves control and direction, or redirection, of instinctive impulses. The incipient ego of the baby first learns some measure of control by seeking what is pleasurable and avoiding what is unpleasurable. To that, quite early, is added another source of control which may become of considerable power at a later stage. I refer to the inversion of his aggressive impulses. Frustration of his desires or deprivation of something he is enjoying stirs his aggressive instinct into action to defend himself against what seems to him hostile. He does not necessarily, particularly in the first two years, recognize what is the "enemy" that is attacking him. The anger he feels and the violence of the instinctive reactions which accompany it are not understood as belonging to himself. They are frightening and rather painful experiences, disturbing to him, and he treats them also as a danger, which he attacks. His aggression is split and part of it becomes directed inward to control his own outwardly directed aggressive impulses. This inverted aggression later attaches itself to the function of conscience; and if the individual has repressed strong aggressive impulses, as often is the case, his conscience is likely to be oversevere and true moral judgment is impaired in him. It is really a pseudoconscience he has formed.

The true conscience is formed as a result of the resolution of the Oedipus complex at the end of infancy. The child has by then learned to substitute the desire for approval and fear of disapproval of his parents, with perhaps an admixture of rewards and punishments, in place of the earlier egocentric pleasure-pain sanctions of conduct. He has learned that there are rules of conduct imposed in one way or another by the parents. He is a social being trying to conform to the rules of his social group. These rules become internalized when the crisis of the Oedipus complex is overcome by the introjection of the father image. By a complicated process of projection and identification the structure of the ego is altered. It takes into itself as a permanent modification the image the young child has built up of the father (with, of course, some elements of the mother) and this becomes a superego, part of the total self, which now commands *from within* obedience to the rules formerly seen as established from without, by the parents. Moral conduct is distinguished from merely social conduct by the inwardness of the sanctions and the sense of absolute obligation to conform.

Rules of conduct that are learned subsequently are added to this central core and gain the authority which is exercised by the superego. The early codes are enlarged, developed, modified by the influence of the many different social groupings to which each growing person is exposed, and by his reflections over his experience. One of the chief sources of moral teaching is religion. This is as it should be, but there is a danger entailed in it. God is first understood by the child by projecting the father image upon him. This is inevitable, but it is desirable that the understanding of God should not remain infantile. The superego is likewise based upon the father by the internalization of the infantile image of him. Thus God and the superego very easily become identified, with the result that our religion becomes moralistic, and negatively moralistic at that, for the superego was formed to inhibit certain strong Oedipal desires. When this happens goodness takes the form of refraining from committing the major sins, which are usually construed according to the Oedipal pattern.

The safeguard against this overemphasis on negative morality, and moralism in general, is to be found in another strand of development, the formation of the ego ideal. This is the moral aspect of becoming a person. The young child needs to feel loved to give him the sense of security to face and accept the strange world, which sometimes is harsh, and so to grow. He learns that his father and his mother prefer certain kinds of behavior over others and he forms a picture of himself winning and holding their love by doing what they want him to do and becoming what he thinks they want him to be. He forms an ideal of himself by which he will ensure being loved. At the same time, because he loves, admires, and perhaps envies them, he also wants to be like them, to become what they are, and this desire amalgamates with the other ideal. When he turns from the family to other people these processes continue to operate, and his ego ideal continually grows. He identifies himself with those whom he loves and admires and becomes in part like them, but the ideal always reaches beyond the attainment.

The ego ideal is for each person his true self, in that he cannot help struggling toward it. It calls on him to change, to become new, something better. This is positive morality. The struggle to find the ideal self and live by it reaches its greatest intensity in late adolescence, where the quests for identity and for a meaning to life become the dominating interests of the individual. It scarcely needs to be said that for the Christian Jesus is the pattern and the inspiration of the ego ideal.

Conclusion

Mature religion is attained only when all the lines of growth mentioned above are well developed and the stages of growth are gone through successfully. Unless this happens religion will retain an infantile character, which, it must be admitted, passes for good religion in many quarters. We need to establish criteria by which to distinguish mature from immature religion. The criteria cannot simply be the fervor with which we call upon God, for the God we worship may be created from our own immaturity. Nor can any particular interpretation of the Christian faith be sufficient guarantee of itself that it is right. It will always need the corroborative evidence of the study of man's development in the wholeness of his life. Religion and life are inseparable and religion cannot be learned as a special subject. Yet we have all too readily assumed that it can be in our efforts to teach it. We have aimed to impart knowledge about religion. Knowledge is necessary, but the knowledge must always be part of something far wider, just as religion must include all life. A good syllabus of instruction is useless, even harmful, unless it is an integral part and expression of a bigger purpose.

This purpose must be to help people, adults as well as children, to become mature persons. This cannot be procured by instruction alone. Teaching, whether conceived as the imparting of a given set of ideas or as concentration on methods of imparting knowledge, is too narrow a concept. We may learn a lot about God, but we only know him by living him, and religious learning is learning how to take God into ourselves, into the whole of our being. Hence nothing is specifically religious and everything is religious, religious when seen in its essential relation to God. Man cannot be made religious from outside; he can only grow into religion. To help in this we need to understand the psychology of the development of persons, for that is the psychology of religious learning. No doubt we have always desired to have full-grown Christians, but we have not known enough about the processes involved in growth.

What I have said is neither specifically Protestant nor Catholic. It applies to both. Everywhere there is a search for fresh approaches to religious education. In Great Britain the churches have been slower to move than the teachers, who in my country are responsible for religious education in the schools. But movement among responsible church leaders is rapidly gaining momentum, and the few voices hitherto crying in the wilderness are beginning to get a responsive audience. There is hope that the new perspectives opened up by psychology will reveal to all the true setting of religious learning.

THREE

Education in the Sociological Situation, U.S.A.

A. by ROSEMARY R. RUETHER

B. by MARTIN E. MARTY

A. *by* ROSEMARY R. RUETHER

WHAT KIND OF Christian education is possible in America in the third quarter of the twentieth century? What kind of Christian education is possible in a world in which old denominational identities are evaporating; where our cultural forms and institutions taken for granted as Christian have become quaint cultural artifacts and where even the name "Christian" seems a more and more parochial self-image? What kind of Christian education is possible in a world of youth and revolution, black revolution, and world challenge to American imperialism? This is the kind of context in which I shall try to pose the question of Christian education. Or rather, this is the kind of context in which I must pose the question of Christian education; because it is my own life context, and it is the situation most immediately present to the Christian community of which I am a part.

Since most of the remarks I shall make stem rather directly from this situation, a brief sketch of the autobiographical context is appropriate at this point. Reared a Roman Catholic, I experienced the not unusual sense of having outgrown this background early in college years. Nevertheless, I became interested in religion and in Christian origins in particular. I then did graduate work in preparation for the academic study and teaching of religion, in which I am presently engaged (church history and historical theology). Ten years ago I probably would have found little way to relate this work to Roman Catholicism. But the period of my graduate study corresponded to the sudden thaw of that ancient glacier, and I found myself drawn into the Vatican II reform movement. In this newly dynamic situation, the kind of thing I had been doing became very relevant. I and many other people found ourselves in a transitional process, relating ourselves back to a tradition which we had transcended in an effort to move it to transcend itself. Our position was distant from the conservative statements of this tradition; quite often distant even from the "liberal" restatements of this tradition. But convinced that the direction in which we had moved was where the tradition itself must go in order to be renewed for a future age, we related to the developments of the Second Vatican Council and tried to construct paradigms of continuity and mediation that could bridge the distance, even though these paradigms did not always correspond with our own position. We put ourselves into strange frameworks of thought, and there argued about "natural law" and "magisterial authority" in terms that did not correspond with our own presuppositions but were means of opening up the tradition and moving the dialogue to the place where our own concerns could begin to be discussed.

New Patterns Emerge

The results of this spectacular effort are now beginning to fall into some new patterns. As might be expected, a certain segment of the Catholic population, who were ready for such changes, moved quickly into escalating patterns of dissent. But the new attitudes did not, in most cases, succeed in incarnating themselves into new structures of power and institutional authority. The conservatives continued to man the hierarchical rungs. Soon after the Council ended, they began to dig in their heels. In the last year or so, a systematic pattern of resistance to change has become evident (sometimes dubbed the "counter-Council"). We see now a fairly continuous effort to purge out liberals and liberal thinking, particularly from an area which might be construed as "official." The high point of this "counter-Council" so far has been the papal encyclical *Humanae Vitae*, which put the official kibosh on a key topic where it appeared that doctrine was being reshaped by popular discussion and consensus. The Dutch Church and the Dutch Catechism have become the continual target of Roman conservativism because the Dutch Church is the prime example of a liberalized hierarchy and the place where liberal thinking has been incorporated into new governmental structures, such as a representational national council. Not only was Holland in the forefront of renewal of old structures, but some of the most avant-garde of new experimental communities, such as the ecumenical, social-action Shalom communities, where Protestants and Catholics concelebrated a free Eucharist, began in this small country. The Dutch Catechism gave the blessing of the bishops to the theological avant-garde and incorporated their ideas into the new standard for adult catechetics. The anomaly of the relation between this church, which really took the Council seriously, and the Roman tradition is illustrated by the fact that the new Catechism is the official publication of the Dutch bishops and yet had to be published under episcopal ban and without an imprimatur in the U.S.A.! In this new situation of polarization, the liberal, who once marched confidently at the head of an advancing parade, now seems more like a man clinging desperately to either side of a fissure which is opening up along an ancient earthquake fault.

In the United States in particular the forces of reform, which have a large constituency but no structural power, find themselves in a certain state of disarray. Representational organizations outside the official power structure, such as the laymen's and priests' associations, have grown up, but they have yet to find a way to make a significant impact. When the leadership of the Washington Priests' Association was summarily dismissed in their dispute with Cardinal O'Boyle recently, both the local Association and their national organization found that they had no recourse. The chief power of the reform movement lies with the press; both the secular press, which is open to extensive reporting of such disputes, and the liberal Catholic press, represented by such organs as *Commonweal* and *National Catholic Reporter*. It is not surprising that the latter particularly has come under official condemnation both from its local bishop and from Rome, because it acts not only as the central medium of communication but even as the central educational tool for the forces of reform.

The problem, however, is that, lacking any real influence on the power structure, these reformers have settled into a predominantly protest stance. The pattern goes something like this: "Priests in city X protest racism in chancery policy"; "Bishop suspends priests for protesting racism in chancery policy"; "Lay committee forms to protest suspending of priests for. . . ." The titillation of protest goes on for a few more rounds and then gradually subsides into nothing. The suspension is seldom reversed short of the priests' abandoning their original protest. The dissenters are rarely willing to go beyond dissent into constructive activity. One feels an invisible border separating protest from new autonomy, and the reformer shies away from that border with almost compulsive fear. Nevertheless, people in their daily lives cannot live in suspended animation waiting for officialdom to grant a space in which to breathe; thus a large movement of illicit communities, house churches, and *ad hoc* sacramental gatherings has grown up, but these persist in an ecclesiological limbo called "the underground." This term indicates both their unwillingness and their inability to clarify their actual relationship to the hierarchical church.

Alternatives to Present Structures

The present author has two main concerns in the present Catholic situation. The first is to articulate the ecclesiology of the "free church"; to help the "underground" to grow from adolescence to maturity where it can offer a significant alternative to present church structures. Secondly, I would like to link up the dissidents and experimentalists in the Catholic left with similar movements in Protestantism and in social reform, so that they might become an ecumenical movement vis-à-vis both institutional Christianity and contemporary American society. Only with such mature autonomy and broadened perspective can they begin to have something to say to the present historical moment. To make such a movement effective, it is necessary to think through some authentic alternatives to present denominational structures. We do not need another Methodist Church. We do need a free-forming, grass roots movement of communities, task forces, and Christian centers that could have a certain identity and media of communication among themselves, but would continue to relate to the whole structure of institutional Christianity as an ongoing catalytic agent. For antecedents to such a form we might look back to the medieval Western church, which produced numerous "parallel institutions" that came and went alongside the official structure. Movements such as the "Brethren of the Common Life"; the early Franciscans or the twelfth-century Waldensians did not conceive of themselves as starting a "new church" (neither did the sixteenth-century Reformers, for that matter). Rather they were revival movements within the whole of Catholic Christianity. Such a movement stands within the Catholic Church but outside of conventional jurisdiction, thus making a very clear distinction between the two.

In the sixteenth century such movements of "Brethren" split off into separatist churches. Such a development was difficult to avert, given the breakdown of medieval pluralism, yet such separatism really undoes the distinctive witness of this tradition. When they become "separatist," the "Brethren" tend to become ingrown and parochial, losing contact with the larger historical configuration of Catholic Christianity. Separatism also makes the "Brethren" take on an institutional structure of their own as a vehicle of historical perpetuation and this is actually foreign to their original perspective. The "Brethren" or the left-wing tradition in the church, I believe, would retain their authenticity if they remained a movement within Catholic Christianity (this would include not only Roman and Eastern churches, but historical Protestantism as well). The "Brethren" would thus both remain related to the whole tradition in their intentionality and critique and yet be quite autonomous in the forming of their own life. They should particularly avoid the efforts of the institution to domesticate them as the medieval church domesticated the parallel structures by incorporating them as "religious orders."

The "Brethren" as a prophetic voice in the community must operate outside the institution, but inside the covenant. If domesticated by the institution, they lose their prophetic voice. If they move outside the covenant, they become irrelevant to those who remain behind and must also become a new institution to perpetuate themselves. Outside the institution, but within the covenant, the "Brethren" hold up a critique of the introversion and self-idolatry of the institution and open alternative forms of life. But in order to make a contribution to the whole, they must maintain lines of communication with the whole; not simply protest and pronouncements, but valid communication which seriously discusses their critique and their soundings of new alternatives which can be assimilated by the liberals in the more conventional church structures. In this way the "Brethren" act, not as a sect, but as a leaven within the whole.

Leavening on a Double Front

This work of leavening must have a double front. It must face the traditional institution. This front must be seen in an ecumenical perspective as a renewal movement that faces the whole of institutional Christianity. Secondly, it must face the contemporary world. In this latter respect Roman Catholic reform particularly is in a traumatic historical situation, since it is simultaneously trying to catch up with all the revolutions which it has missed over the past four hundred years and also relate to a contemporary world which is itself in a state of rapid change. Democratization of social structures, liberalism in mass communication and education—these are good eighteenth-century issues, but Roman Catholicism has still not come to terms with them. It remains a social structure virtually untouched by the liberal revolutions; the last monument of the European *ancien régime.* How about biblical criticism? That is a good nineteenth-century issue. Roman Catholicism slammed that door shut in 1909 and not even the most intrepid of the liberals have really dared to open that door again. The vernacular in the liturgy? That's a good sixteenth-century issue, and I think we have that one about settled. Hans Küng seems to have taken care of the outstanding dispute between Catholics and Protestants over "justification." But even a casual perusal of Luther's *Three Treatises* will turn up a few outstanding issues from the sixteenth century—such as the papacy, priesthood of all believers, sacramentology, celibacy! None of these conflicts can be skirted. I am a convinced believer in relentless historical justice. History's demands must be satisfied. One cannot skip over or repress a historical challenge and then go on to something else without history's catching up and taking its revenge in some form.

Perhaps the historical community has a certain organic logic not unlike that of the maturation of the person. Psychiatrists today emphasize that every stage in the maturation of a person has an essential place. If the child suppresses a stage of development or does not satisfactorily solve its problems, it remains with him in a neurotic form. He cannot free himself for new possibilities until he comes to terms with these unsolved problems of the past. I am pretty sure that Roman Catholicism will not be free for a new future until it comes to terms with all these skeletons in its family closet. But we must do all this while simultaneously dealing with a whole new kind of world which has long since left behind the contexts in which these problems were formulated. As one wit has remarked, "Protestantism exercised a little birth control in having its revolutions, while Roman Catholicism insists on having all its revolutions at once." Having proved inadequate to these lesser challenges of the past, it is indeed doubtful that Roman Catholicism can prove adequate to this much more momentous challenge of the present time, short of some extraordinary upheaval of revolutionary proportions in its leadership structure. (Anyone for evicting a few bishops?) Failing any signs of political revolution in the church— except perhaps among the Dutch—the idea of carrying on a free church movement in an ecumenical context that can offer a vehicle for alternative possibilities seems at least an intermediate tactic.

The free church, however, must be historically mature itself. It must come to terms with these outstanding issues. It must clarify where it stands—theologically, historically—over against the institution, so that it can provide a depth critique and not just a disaffiliated whine. This will entail a mature theological and historical perspective on the part of its members. The free church must find means to educate its members to this depth perspective. Part of this education is provided simply by the existential life of the community itself—its ethos and its concerns. But this is still largely implicit and should be brought out in the open. When a free church community puts aside the sacramental, sacerdotal notion of celebration in favor of a free Eucharist that can be presided over by any member of the community and is celebrated by the whole community together, do they understand what they are doing? Are they still carrying over cultic assumptions from another point of view which have actually been surpassed in the practice of the community? Do they understand what that earlier point of view was, and how the assumptions on which their own practice rests differ from that? These are the kinds of questions which must be clarified in the minds of the whole community together if it is to be mature and give a mature witness.

Facing Toward the World

In addition to this critical and innovative front toward the tradition, the free church must also face outward toward the contemporary world. It should not just be an avant-garde of the church. It should be an avant-garde of contemporary society as well. This means that it should have more than a speaking relationship to the youth revolution, the black revolution, the peace movement, the struggle against Western imperialism, and the struggle against the dehumanization of technological society. It must be a part of these revolutions. This does not mean that it should be an uncritical "joiner," anxious to march under every left-wing banner in desperate hopes of becoming relevant. Such an anxiety for relevance bespeaks a very weak sense of Christian faith. The free church must relate to these movements because their cause is just, because they are the places where God's Spirit is stirring the waters of creation to renew the face of the earth. It must, therefore, stand with these movements, not as an uncritical chanter of every slogan, but as a critical witness on the side of the oppressed, alert to the ways in which good and evil intertwine in the breast of every man. Above all it must remember that its highest witness is the witness of forgiveness and reconciliation. Therefore it cannot be simply a card-carrying member of any particular revolutionary party. Nevertheless, the words "forgiveness" and "reconciliation" are not to be bandied about as "cheap grace." They are only really conferred and received when real change takes place. Marx was right when he insisted, "So far the philosophers have only interpreted the world. The important thing is to change it." The church above all tends to allow itself to be diverted from the question of real repentance and conversion to a ritualistic pronouncement and liturgical acting-out of repentance and change. All the ritual dances of the hunt are of no avail if the community is never directed to go out on the real hunt, because that is where everything that was only "interpreted" before really takes place.

A Christian community which is to be a part of this revolutionary milieu should achieve a high level of social consciousness. It must be aware of the issues. It should study the literature of the movement. It should also have the kind of theological maturity that can see the movement in the perspective of Christian faith, so that the two do not fall into separate "churchy" and "secular" boxes unrelated to each other. This means that the theology of the free church is presupposed to be a secular theology. Its theology is one which assumes that all the theological, churchly, and sacramental words are words about humanity and human life. Words like "communion," "church," "faith," "salvation" are not special nonworldly realities which point off somewhere else, but they point to the world itself; its source and destiny and the dynamic of its life. Only when "church" and "world" find a unitary perspective can the free church give the social witness in depth that we have been suggesting. Much of the education and formation for such a witness should happen simply through the praxis of the community itself, but this assumes that there is a lively dialogical life within the community, relevant reading matter is brought to everyone's attention, and the like. Emmaus House in New York is a good example of such a community, where the "education" is taken care of by the constant dialogical life that goes on in the community itself.

An Illustration

For a concrete illustration of how some of these points might be applied to a more conventional parish structure, let me turn to my own community in Washington, D.C., St. Stephen and the Incarnation Church. This is not to suggest that we have any unusual "answers," but there has been a fairly consistent effort to pose the questions. St. Stephen's is a paradigm of a church in transition between old and new possibilities. It is a parish of the Episcopal Diocese of Washington, yet it transcends the apparent limitations of that role on numerous fronts. It is ecumenical in membership, having a large number of Catholic members as well as Catholics who relate to it in a looser way. It also gathers Protestants across the whole spectrum of traditions and has an ecumenical clergy staff. More recently it has come to terms with membership for non-Christians (specifically, Jewish). It is also a peace and freedom church which is open to the social revolutions that surround it. Its physical setting is conducive to this. It is situated in the black inner city, standing on the frontier between the ghetto and the affluent society. From its front porch it can see the rows of embassies and establishment churches that run down to the White House. From its back windows it sees the blackened street gutted by riots. One of its neighbors is the "embassy" of the Black Liberation Army, which displays a Liberian flag to symbolize its claim to be the embassy of the Black People's Republic in America. The Black Liberation Army is on good terms with St. Stephen's. We worked together during the riots. They spoke during one of the stations of last year's "Way of the Cross." They have discussed their views at coffee hour, and sometimes march solemnly into back pews to hear a sermon.

The congregation at St. Stephen's crosses denominational, class, and racial lines. The greatest social tension, not insignificantly, is not due to racial or denominational plurality, but is across class lines, specifically between bourgeois "Negroes" and ghetto "blacks." Although its membership is slightly over half black, this is not so evident on Sunday morning, when the configuration is more a mixture of white liberals, young white radicals, and black bourgeoisie. Not unlike many a church in an inner-city situation, it has a constituency from outside the immediate neighborhood which supports it but which it has not succeeded in completely integrating with the neighborhood community. Thus there is a certain schism between the white liberal-black bourgeoisie Sunday congregation and the largely poor black community that occupies the church buildings the rest of the week. The schism is only partial, however, because there is some real mingling of the two.

During the last two years there have been some concerted efforts at St. Stephen's to grapple with the questions of Christian education. The basic principle enunciated by the study group was, to borrow a phrase from Marx, the "unity of theory and practice." A quotation from a study released by this group might make clear this fundamental orientation:

It is assumed that the education process of the church is not a special job or program within the life of the church, but that it *is* the life of the church. The church is a process of redemption which is constantly both forming and expressing her own newness of life. The "becoming" of the church *is* Christian education.

We must assume, also, that this process has more to do with what the church does than with what it says. No amount of "preaching" or "teaching" can impart Christian formation if this formation is not, at the same time, what we are. We do impart what we are rather than what we say, in any case. This is why Christian education programs in the past have oftentimes paid the next generation out in false coin, because we were trying to impart something we did not live. And the new generation learned from the inauthenticity of our lives and discounted our words accordingly. Consequently, we must first overcome the pretension that we have already "achieved" Christianity and are, from this vantage point, going to teach it to others. We must realize that Christian education includes us all. We are all involved in becoming Christians.

The Praxis of the Community

From this insistence on the "unity of theory and practice," it was assumed that the primary pedagogical tool of the community is the praxis of the community itself. The life of the community is our chief evidence and means of what we are trying to teach. Because the community has already, to a high extent, formed its life in terms of ecumenical and secular theology; because it has developed a life-style of social concern and openness to change, this life-style is its chief means for educating its members into the faith. Its dialogical life in sermons (our sermons are very dialogical—people have been known to clap and boo), adult forums, children's forums, and small discussion seminars can be an exposition of a faith it is really engaged in living out. For this reason the first question of new members in adult seminars is not so much a desire to know about a particular church tradition, but rather to know what it means to belong to "this community." This does not mean that the dialogue in the community is reduced to admiring self-contemplation (although we sometimes have to shake ourselves from the "we thank thee Lord that we are not as other men" line of thought). Rather it means that there is not the kind of antithetical split between theory and practice which makes real Christian preaching and teaching impossible in the typical parish short of a revolution that would burn it down. Here the community had already put its life-style and commitments into the revolution; thus the dialogical life could go forward as constructive self-criticism toward ever fuller realization of these commitments.

Community Liturgy

The chief place where the community expresses and affirms its faith is the community liturgy. The liturgy, therefore, is its chief pedagogical tool. The style of liturgy at St. Stephen's has been reshaped and almost dissolved until it has become a free-flowing expression of "life." (The little button with the slogan "Celebrate Life" was originally the creation of St. Stephen's.) The celebrants crowd around the table, some vested, others with no special garb to mark them off from everyone else. One may have on an African robe; another a sweat shirt and sandals. Many laymen (and women!), boys (and girls!) assist in the reading and the liturgical functions of the service. All this helps to break down the image of a rigid lay/clerical distinction (which is the typology of world/-church distinction). One gets the impression of the whole community as ministry. The celebrant greets the congregation at the "kiss of peace" and everyone cheerfully shouts it back. Then people turn and greet each other spontaneously without set form. Often the clergy mingle during this spontaneous greeting with the congregation. At the offertory all come up to bring their offerings, which may include baskets of food, clothing, flowering branches—just about anything. The table is a freestanding wooden plank on a spreading tree trunk that stands in a circular dais. The congregation remains around it for the blessing and Communion. The atmosphere is distinctly unpious. Almost any element of liturgical "reverence" has vanished. People are likely to be talking, reaching across to greet friends, hugging each other. In short, it is very much like a very friendly, happy family gathering for a party.

But the total configuration of the liturgy is not simply one of warm feelings. The "warm feelings" have some depth to them, and some pretty rough stuff goes on before that point of hugging and kissing. The liturgy of the word focuses on prophetic challenge. For example, in Advent there was a series of sermons by black churchmen on the relevance of the church to the black community. Their message was not one to leave anyone feeling very comfortable. During the previous Lent, a series of community leaders, such as Julius Hobson, the militant who has challenged the Washington public school system, were in command of the pulpit. They spared few feelings in "telling it like it is." After the Democratic Party's Chicago convention young radicals who had been in the streets there took over the liturgy and shaped it to express that experience. Mass media have been used several times to bring home the challenge of the peace movement. When a good militant takes over the pulpit, he often does not scruple to lash the congregation for a full hour! In other words, when St. Stephen's people stand arm in arm passing bread and wine together, they stand on the other side of some real shed blood and speak a "nevertheless" that can stand, experientially, for some real resurrection.

Adult Forum

In addition to the liturgy and as an extension if it, there is an adult forum in which the themes of the liturgy are continued. This may entail lively exchange between the speaker and the people. Sometimes there are events suitable to particular occasions; e.g., during a political campaign a three-hour panel discussion took place, with representatives from the Democratic, Republican, Peace and Freedom, and American Independent parties. Almost any current event will be likely to find its way into the adult forum. At the present writing time St. Stephen's is serving as a seminar center and housing station for the young people who are coming to town for the counterinauguration sponsored by the Mobilization to End the War in Vietnam (of which St. Stephen's has been the local headquarters). Plans for the seminars were discussed at the adult forum, members helped to plan them and will participate in them, and the regular weekly adult class will become a mobilization seminar for that occasion. After the adult forum, more informal dialogue goes on over wine, chitterlings, and greens.

During the adult forum the children of the congregation meet in their own groups by age level or in an assembly for a film or art project. The problems of structuring a children's program reflect the cultural diversity the church is engaged in trying to span. Although most of the adults are middle-class whites or blacks, the children are drawn much more heavily from the ghetto. Many come without their parents—some regularly; some drifting in, half-hopefully, half-defiantly. It thus becomes the responsibility of the congregation to adopt these children and bring them into the liturgy and the children's program. This means that the program is in a state of almost constant innovation from week to week in an effort to find forms which can hold such a diverse group together for an hour of constructive activity. In practice we find that about the only people who are capable of this kind of flexibility and imagination are young people in their late teens and early twenties. The typical older person who wants to have a structured "Sunday school class" is almost incapable of doing anything in this situation (several have fled in tears). The new breed of socially conscious youth have proved very successful here. We have been fortunate in attracting a number of such young people, both black and white, male and female, and especially some very sophisticated young black men. This is great for breaking down the stereotype of the Sunday School teacher as "old," "square," "white," and "female." Third and fourth graders have been working on biblical materials in preparation for First Communion on Holy Thursday (using the book by this author, *Communion Is Life Together*). The fifth and sixth graders have been studying black history, using it as a paradigm of human alienation and reconciliation. These classes, led by young teachers, have been particularly successful. The teen-agers discussed the New York school crisis in relation to their own school situation during the fall term (our term is broken up into fall and spring ten-week group study, interspersed with mass media projects). This spring they decided to study comparative religion, focusing on Islam, Judaism, and Christianity.

Adults, especially new members, have open to them an adult education seminar which runs one evening a week from September until Easter. Here some of the theological presuppositions of the community are perhaps more explicitly explored. The seminar serves as an educational tool for any adult, as well as a class for new

members, some of whom may wish to be confirmed, others of
whom wish to join St. Stephen's without making or altering any
denominational ties. Childhood confirmation has been almost entirely dissolved in favor of membership through baptism and early
Communion and a conception of adult commitment and ministry.
The adult seminar tries both to give a theological and historical
background and to provide an ongoing dialogue in present innovations. Every topic, then, tends to have two aspects. There is both
a review of the tradition and its historic development on a certain
point and an opening up of current views that may stand in a highly
critical relationship with that tradition. The seminar is co-ordinated
by this author and taught by a staff of theological and social experts
drawn from the Washington area. A brief summary of the curriculum will be self-explanatory. The seminar falls into three series.
The first series is on biblical theology. It covers such topics as
(1) creation and kingdom, (2) God's people—covenant and promise,
(3) prophecy, (4) Christology, (5) grace and forgiveness,
(6) community, (7) Christian hope. The second series is on problems in church history. The topics covered are (1) the church and
culture, (2) liturgy, (3) ministry, (4) church and state, (5) the Protestant Reformation, (6) the Anglican church tradition, (7) American
Christianity, (8) the ecumenical movement. The third series centers
on the church's mission. It covers such topics as (1) the nature of
mission, (2) the church and the city, (3) the church and politics,
(4) the church and the black community, (5) the church and war,
(6) the church and revolution.

Christian Initiation

St. Stephen's has too mobile a congregation to hope to carry
through a class with the same group for more than a year. This class
is an attempt to give a rapid survey of the Christian tradition and
what the church is called to be today, in a period of time that is
feasible for our people, i.e., from the fall to the climax of the Christian year at Easter. Easter time is also the time of Christian initiation for us. Adult baptism takes place on Easter Eve. This year we
will celebrate a new form of First Communion for children on
Holy Thursday. We usually try to have confirmation with baptism

on Easter Eve; this may be replaced with some service of adult "commissioning" and new membership. The relationship between Christian education and Christian initiation is one that has been extensively explored at St. Stephen's and is still being reformulated. The orientation of our education program is clearly toward "becoming Christians," and not toward joining this or that church. The context is assumed to be the whole Catholic tradition in its many forms as this comes into and confronts the present destiny of mankind. No smaller context than that is feasible to us. Baptism, sharing of the Lord's Supper, and confirmation must therefore mean a reconciliation with God in Christ and a reconciliation with one's fellowman, rather than membership in any particular denomination or even a very narrow identification with "historical Christianity" as a whole. When our members may be American black nationalists, Africans, or Jews, can we afford to be less catholic? To act in word or deed as though joining the community of the messianic banquet meant becoming a White Westerner, adopting a Graeco-Roman culture, etc., would belie the whole nature of our message. This kind of statement is often made by "Catholics" but with a superficial notion of its implications, as though such worldwide ecumenicity could still be reconciled with all kinds of cultural and institutional forms that are strictly parochial. I think we are not unaware of the fact that such commitment to Catholicity means a commitment to an ever widening challenge to all our parochialisms which we cannot expect to control or predict.

Focus for Education

. The focus of Christian initiation and education at St. Stephen's must surpass ideas of joining "the church" in an institutional sense or even becoming a "Christian" in a cultural sense. Our most concrete historical community is our own local community. The other point of reference is "the Catholic Church," which ultimately must be seen as mankind. "Joining the church," therefore, is to be understood as "joining God's revolution in the world," not just as a slogan but as what we really are doing. Adult commitment, not childhood acculturation, must be the orientation of "Christian education." A church which is oriented to the acculturation of children avoids the whole period of development that ushers in real adulthood. It tries to get the child all "wrapped up," signed, sealed, and delivered before he can ask any questions. A church for a people come of age must do just the opposite. Everything that the church has—baptism, Communion, full participation—can be extended to even the smallest child as a free gift. This is an appropriate expression of the free grace of God. But then everything which is given must be appropriated and made one's own by the adult in a voluntary commitment that really corresponds with his personal maturation. Thus the period of radical questioning that goes on in late teens and early adulthood, far from being the period avoided by the church, must be seen as the crucial period that makes possible such adult commitment. This in no way suggests a kind of underhanded way of tying young people to mother's apron strings. I am speaking about the process of rebellion and rejection itself as the means by which the young person is to pass to an adult Christianity. Unless the church is ready to accept that kind of critique and recognize it as the path of adult faith, it deserves to have only little children and old ladies in its congregation. The structure of Christian education must thus be formed to reflect the real pattern by which a person comes into personal faith.

Every individual is given a certain heritage and structure of values by his society, which is trying to form him in various ways, whether rightly or wrongly. This period of relatively passive formation goes on approximately through the sixth grade. Then there comes a period—sooner for some, later for others—when the person engages in conflict with the structure in which he has been reared. He questions its values; he doubts its faith; he rebels against its code. This period, however painful, particularly to the parental figures, is a positive and essential part of the person's coming of age. Gradually through this period of conflict, the person begins to work out his own values and develop his faith. If the values in which he has been reared were sound, he may be able to appropriate much of this "faith of his fathers," only in a new way and in a language meaningful to himself. This period of maturation may find the person coming back to the church or—if he has never physically left it—taking it up in a new way. This "rejoining" of the church

corresponds to the subjective half of baptism, one's personal appropriation of the faith. Here the Anabaptists were quite right in
demanding that baptism stand as an expression of this process. The
church still needs very much a sacrament that would express this
adult side of baptism. It is at this point that the person who previously had been given the faith, the sacraments, the life of the
church, begins to make these his own by personal decision. The
church must see this whole questioning process as an essential part
of a mature faith, putting the bulk of its task of Christian education
squarely in the middle of this questioning period; not in the sense
of "providing the answers," but precisely in the sense of being
willing itself *to be questioned.* Only in this way can we have a people
come of age, making their faith an act of personal assent in authentic autonomy.

The False Schism Between "Clergy" and "Laity"

This kind of adult "joining" of the church is also essential to
eliminating the false schism between "clergy" and "laity." Churchmen often write lamenting little books about "God's frozen people," but they persist in all the practices that make this situation
inevitable. The chief cause lies precisely in the schism between
ministerial training and the education of the people. Ministerial
training takes place in a separate ivory tower of the seminary,
where those training for the ministry hopefully get the latest word
on biblical criticism, theology, ethics, and the like. Much of this
material they would not think (would not dare) to communicate to
their people. Therefore ministerial training becomes esoteric; a
secret culture hidden from the people, passed out only to the enlightened. Much of this material is not only hidden from the people;
it is also irrelevant to their actual situation. The seminaries, hidden
in their ivory tower, do not have to confront the distance between
academia and pulpit. Thus a clerical caste is continued, even where
the notions of sacerdotal power have been relinquished. I see no
way of overcoming this kind of false distinction, which emasculates
both ministry and people, except to abolish this kind of seminary.
Christian education, including the formation of the clergy, should
take place at the level of the committed adult church member.

Perhaps there could be a training center on a diocesan level for more specialized work for all adults of the type which the typical community could not support, but this should be linked up with the dialogue and seminars going on in each community. From this level of the committed, theologically alert adult a pool of persons can be formed who can serve in a more explicit sense as ministers of the church. This itself should be seen in the context of the ministry of the whole community and simply as one function within it. With a theologically trained people, ministry could be chosen as a function to be exercised for a time rather than a "state of life." By the same token the professional ministers would not be isolated in their communities as persons with a special esoteric culture, but they could have around them a theologically trained adult leadership that can really share in the guiding of and dialogue within the community.

The Christian Doctrine of "Creation"

Finally, a Christian education which really corresponds to adult maturation must relate to contemporary culture in a very different way from that which presently prevails. It must be open to every challenge which science, historical criticism, and social change have to offer. It must see such challenges, not as the "secular threat to the church," but in just the opposite perspective as "God's challenge to his people to be open to all truth." This is not simply a cultural question. It really stands for a fundamental theological question. To be ready and open to the new is really a crucial test of whether the church has faith or is in reality "faithless." More and more today theology tends to see the future as the paradigm of transcendence. In the demands of the new, God's Spirit encounters us as a judgment upon our self-enclosed idolatries and calls us to metanoia and rebirth. A church which has kept this faith and lives in this Spirit is free and capable of being open to the new and provisional in its own life-style. Consequently the cultural task of the church today is far more radical than that postulated by the "up-daters" of doctrine. It is not a question of finding a more relevant and modern world to sacralize, but rather a rejection of all sacralizing of culture. This rejection is based on the theological critique of the relationship between man's word and God's word. The church does not appropriate God's word into its own. She remains a place where God's word can be proclaimed by placing her own reality firmly under God's word. This means that no part of the cultural expression of the gospel can be finalized as such, as the permanent and unchangeable expression of God's word. The church's images can be truthful to the extent that they are also self-iconoclastic. In this way the church's cultural incarnation of God's presence does not become a new idol, but remains in a state of constant improvisation.

This is really what is meant by the Christian doctrine of "creation," considered from the pont of view of incarnation or sacrament. Sacramentality is not a metahistorical reality, but a radically historic expression, with all the ephemerality implied by historicity. The church's culture remains sacramental—remains a disclosure of God's presence—to the extent that it does not try to hold onto what has been created but is able to let its self-expression go when its hour is done. In this way, the church's celebration of God becomes a "constant improvisation on the theme of God's presence" (to use a term dear to Gabriel Vahanian). This is the truly iconoclastic view of creation, in which creation itself is ever newly the image of God and the place of the manifestation of his glory.

Such a view of the relation of the Spirit of God to cultural expression suggests a style of life which would not only express the themes of awareness, concern, and contemporaneousness, but would also exist in its very mode of being as a constantly renewed improvisation. This means that the culture of the church should be programmatically ephemeral. It should not be made to last or be valid forever, for the longevity of man is no true image of eternity. If there is anything eternity is not, it is being out-of-date. A long history now become past history is no image of eternity because eternity is not an infinite extension of time, but the fullness of time. It is *kairos,* the decisive moment that fills the heavens with its presence and cancels the on-and-on-ness of fallen, sinful time.

Our word about God's word does not imitate God's word by seeking to last forever, but by being a constantly renewed improvisation upon the fullness of time. The forms of the church should represent in their expression and very mode of being this reformable and disposable nature of the church word about God's word. Therefore, the cultural forms of the church should not be constructed out of gold and jewels, carved from heavy, immovable blocks of marble, or displayed as "infallible doctrines" in a fixed system of thought, for such forms are misleading reflections of the value and eternity of God. The value and fidelity of God's word is quite different from this human mode of preciousness and longevity. Rather the forms of the new church must reflect a renewed awareness of the fallibility of imperfection of man's words about God's word.

The stone cathedrals, the costly vessels, the immovable thought and cultural structure of the church in the past expressed this false effort to capture God's eternity in human form. The result was a church trapped in her own history, unable to escape from her own past, her life crushed by the dead hand of her own "infallibility." The new church must be one which has stood in searching judgment upon the failure of this cultural effort and has recognized the roots of this failure in a false, idolatrous confusion of man's longevity with God's eternity. We must allow God's Spirit to wean us, little by little, from all these attachments and securities, so that we may live in the true freedom of the sons of God—not holding on to what we have made and become, but living out of that creative void of the imageless God from whose depths creation ever springs forth as the real disclosure of God's presence.

A culture which would express this existence of the church as the place of celebration of creation will not construct churches and art forms made to last forever, but it will meet in houses, on street corners, and in shops, using an art improvised from the materials of the moment. It will not be dominated in its theology and teaching by an esoteric band of professionals, but its theology will be created by the people of the community as a witness to its own ongoing life and work. The center of this Christian life is constant in the constancy of the man-God relationship established in Christ, but it is an eschatological constancy which must be ever reappropriated by being seen through concerns as timely as this week's news magazine. Such a culture reflects an understanding of a church which lives in exodus; not in temples, but in tents, which travels lightly and gathers manna from heaven afresh each day. Such a church does not erect cultural and sociological walls around the place of celebration, but celebrates in the real contexts of the dying and rising of God's world.

B. *by MARTIN E. MARTY*

EDUCATION, ACCORDING TO Martin Buber, involves a conscious and willed selection of the effective world. But educators also know that the world of effects reaches them and their students in many ways that are unconscious and involuntary. For that reason, they are and have to become increasingly more alert to that world which is perceived in many ways: aesthetically, psychologically, or sociologically.

The sociological setting has an almost overwhelming impact on education and on religious education. In a crowding and complex world, the educational establishment confronts other social forces; the religious institutions are not only social institutions, but they embody ideas about sociality which are shaped by or which counter other and competing ideas.

The Protestant who wishes to set education into some sort of context may very well know that the social setting does not exhaust the possibilities open to him, but he neglects it at his peril. In this chapter, I shall take a conscious and willed selective view of the social world from the viewpoint of Protestantism. Much of what will be seen here is perceived also by Roman Catholicism, Judaism, or secular forces, but the only responsibility here is to stress Protestant distinctives. In order to do justice to complexities and countertendencies, I shall concentrate on some paradoxes or tensions in the ways in which the social world of effects is perceived.

The Majority That Feels Like a Minority

Protestantism retains its majority status in late twentieth-century America. That status derives from its life in the thirteen colonies; by the end of the colonial period, few Jews and only about twenty thousand Roman Catholics disturbed the vision of relative homogeneity shared by many kinds of Protestants. The first half of the nineteenth century, the period of major expansion into the Southwest and the West, saw only the beginnings of the continental immigrations which were to jostle Protestantism from its secure position in the last half of that century and throughout this one.

Since the height of the immigration period, at which time significant numbers of millions of Roman Catholics and Jews appeared (along with a smaller number but significant body of Eastern Orthodox Christians), Protestantism has held to its position of numerical strength, despite many internal changes. Because of its numbers, its head start, and its effectiveness, Protestantism played a major role in shaping the culture and left its stamp on most major national institutions. This means that educators, religious or not, are preparing people to live in and interpret a more or less Protestant culture.

The impact of that culture can be felt in many ways. Those who bother to chronicle the doings of the social establishment will end up as E. Digby Baltzell did, writing of *The Protestant Establishment*[1], which still dominates the social registers and still prevails in many clubs and businesses and in corporate life. Taking on society means, for many, taking on vestigial Protestantism. Not that educators have to give lessons on social status climbing; but they do have to locate people in all types of power situations. *Who's Who* continues to have a Protestant roster at its base. While an inherited construct of beliefs may mean little to the people implied in this paragraph, it has helped them determine who and what matters and who and what are threats in their world. The outsider to their culture, through education, learns to adapt to it.

In addition to numbers and influence, one can also cite the impact on national myth, symbol, and folklore. The artist, the folk singer, the politician, and the polemicist can all imply recognition when he or she refers to religious institutions in Protestant categories. The Christmas card manufacturer who desires to portray a church building will normally reach for recall of a Congregational meetinghouse in a New England village; this is the "father's" church for the whole nation in many senses, even though a very tiny minority of living Americans derive from a population stock which ever employed such locales and forms for worship. The cartoonist who wants to get across the idea of "missionary" does not draw pictures of fraternal workers in indigenous younger churches—or whatever current missionary renewalist jargon calls them; he illustrates his concept with a Protestant missionary in a heating cannibal pot.

Similarly, the magazine cover illustrator who wants to demonstrate a concern for religious education will not show a synagogue school or a Roman Catholic parochial day school scene. He will reveal starched and bonneted little girls and implausibly neat and perky little boys in a hands-folded situation in what all readers can recognize as a Protestant Sunday school, the "normative" situation even for readers who have never been inside one.

When critics of elements of the culture, for example, kick-over-the-traces college sophomores, or the gurus who publish *Playboy* magazine want a universally recognizable symbol of repression for their attacks, they instinctively reach for the category "Puritan." The Puritan ethic, in national symbolism, produced the uptight, guilty, grim society against which liberated people must rebel. Whatever is wrong with the American business creed can be traced to the Protestant and Puritan ethic, which produced generations of work-obsessed misers. When people seek symbols of racial oppression, they attack middle-class Protestant suburban culture—forgetting quite frequently that most of the oppressed people are themselves Protestant and that many other oppressors in a backlash culture are anything but Protestant. Protestantism through many decades held the field at a time when racist attitudes were developing.

These illustrations of statistics, influence, and symbolism could be extended indefinitely; they are suggestive of the fact that educators neglect at their peril the Protestant dominance, waning though it may be, in the world of effects that surrounds them. But—and this is equally important—they will also be operating in an illusory world if they overlook the fact that to many Protestants their position does not feel like one of dominance; they belong to a majority that is coming to feel like a minority. Several reasons for this ambivalence or this paradoxical situation stand out.

First, it was Protestantism which alone had to suffer the psychic trauma that goes with giving space or yielding ground as America came to describe itself as a pluralist society. While it may have been pluralist for centuries, this pluralism was obscured (and, indeed, the word itself rarely appeared) because Protestants were able to nurture a host-culture/guest-culture complex. Catholics, Jews, nothingarians, and other outsiders may not have been driven out or actually persecuted, but it was made clear that they were here by sufferance. Not until the 1950s were sociologists and analysts of culture capable of convincing the nation that it was an authentically pluralist society.[2] In such a society, no premium is to be attached (at least legally) to those who support one creed as opposed to another, nor are there to be restrictions against those who hold to minority creeds or to none at all. "Any number can play" in the rules of the game of such a society. Other groups gained status by this definition. Protestantism yielded with so much grace that many of its advocates questioned whether the yielding was not the result of a failure of nerve. Had Protestantism lost its essentially masculine character? Was it acting overpolitely out of a new uncertainty and weakness? Such a sudden shift in the assignment of a role in society has led Protestants to begin to take on a minority complex.

Other factors less subtle than the psychological one of adjustment have been present too. The value systems associated with Protestantism have been under attack, and Protestants have done what they could to see that blame for these positions is shared as well by others. Thus in a time of racial upheaval, a new generation attacks its parents for having left a legacy of hatred, racism, or oppression—a legacy enhanced by theological support that had been developed on Protestant norms.[3] The defensive generation hastens to point out that for a century "secular man" has had just as big a role in developing attitudes of racial superiority as antebellum Southern divines ever did. True. Well into the twentieth century many of the nation's major anthropologists, sociologists, psychologists, and historians were giving sophistication to old racial theories. Or Protestantism will hurriedly point out that the most intense racial hostility occurs in "ethnic backlash" areas of Northern cities—a euphemism for Catholic territories. The act of sharing blame is also an act of yielding space and revealing minority status.

In the equally obsessive ethical issue of the past decade, the one associated with the war in Vietnam, a new questioning generation criticizes the Protestant churches' endorsement of every kind of military engagement on the part of the nation. True enough, say the Protestant leaders: We have normally been hawkish, normally we have blessed all the cannon and sanctioned all the killing. (Not really true; many whole clusters in Protestantism, for example, opposed the Mexican War from beginning to end.) But, such spokesmen continue, we have not counted for all that much. The military-industrial complex and its social and political antecedents have been really responsible. We are only "peanuts," insignificant in the overall reckoning of power. In saying something like that, the minority complex of Protestantism unfolds even more.

Today's campus generation, whether in high school or at college, often reckons that a whole tradition has been exhausted. Whether this generation takes on the passing modes of hippie or yippie, turn-on or dropout life, it centers its attack on "linear, rational, programmatic, productive," and hence "Protestant" culture as its villain. The defensive generation, in its attempt to retrieve what can be salvaged from the past and to rescue what it can of its values or reputation in the present, tries to shrug off responsibility for the old. When successful, it also succeeds in relegating to minority status the former and the present contributions of Protestantism to the old and now disintegrating construct.

So Protestantism yielded place in pluralism and wanted to minimize its past and present majority status; in both cases, it began to develop a minority consciousness. That is not all. The educator who wants to perceive the social situation from a Protestant point of view will also be conscious of the ways in which Protestantism recognizes itself to be surrounded by newly vital and attention-getting entities. In religion, for instance, much of the curiosity once extended the Protestant custodians of the culture is now directed toward the Roman Catholicism that has been so much in motion during the past decade. Protestant ecumenical endeavor elicits the public's yawn; for a few years, at least, Protestant-Catholic interaction draws attention. Protestant attempts at reform generally awaken little interest; almost everything seems already to have been tried in multiformed Protestant thought and action. Not so with Catholicism. The subtlest doctrinal readjustment there seems significant; the smallest formal change deserves chronicling.

Ernst Benz, in his book *Evolution and Christian Hope*,[4] to take one instance, ponders why it is that today's world is so taken with the evolutionary religiousness of the Jesuit father Pierre Teilhard de Chardin. Benz discovers that Anglo-American Protestant liberal and modernist thinkers, men like John Fiske, well back into the nineteenth century had worked out comparable syntheses with the thought of a post-Darwinian world. What is so special about Teilhardianism, he asks, except that this thought seems strange in Catholicism and familiar in Protestantism?

Protestantism, having long ago seen its symbols blend with those of the larger culture, seems to have little that is evocative or arcane in its resources today. When former priests marry former nuns, when nuns stage "happenings" and priests rage against the church under the glare of television cameras, when leading laymen in Latin America advocate revolution against a regime that contains Catholic admixtures—then, the public recognizes, news is being made.

Another cultural dynamism that attracts the historians', the journalists', and the public's magnetic needles is associated with racial change. This change has added to white Protestantism's minority status and has complicated the life of black Protestantism, which is also losing out to Muslim, secular, or neo-African cultism among blacks who are out to repudiate elements of their ecclesiastical past. But white Protestantism is most conscious of the change. Their churches are not engaged in holy war; no one talks about their burning down each other's parts of town; few look with fear at their threats or with hope at their promises. The American black is on the move.

Several summers ago an incident stamped this sense of momentum on my mind. I gave some lectures at a summer retreat of hundreds of (chiefly Southern) black clergymen at the Hampton

Institute in Virginia, sharing the program with Martin Luther King, Jr., who was then coming into his prime. The audience could not have been more patient, courteous, or attentive to me as I spoke on several major theological and cultural themes. I faced a sea of tape recorders, notebooks, and books to autograph. But when Dr. King would rise to speak each day, everyone in the room, myself included, could feel a difference. At my best, I would be commenting on a history, while he was making it. I was speaking of great acts of God in the past; he was inviting the audience to join in the forward march of God's people in the present. Any analyst of what we both said that week would be astonished to see how parallel the themes were. What made the difference (apart from the by no means insignificant factor of Dr. King's celebrated charisma!) was that I was speaking out of the context of settled, no longer kinetic white Protestantism. He was speaking of people who represented promise, threat, but most of all movement. Today's black (and sympathetic white) may be only seeking compensatory attention, but he is seeking academic courses on Afro-American culture and history. It would be almost inconceivable to have campus riots centering on the idea that the Protestant aspect of culture be stressed curricularly, even though it seldom is in any systematic way at present.

The white Protestant who senses the trend of curiosity to black American history, whether Protestant or not in character, is also alert to the cultural self-consciousness of the American Jewish community. As he observes the preoccupation with Jewish themes in today's novels of urban alienation; "the New York Jewish literary establishment" which, he is told, makes or breaks authors' reputations; the recognition granted Jewish humor on national television —he wonders just where his Protestant majority status is to be observed and felt.

Perhaps I have overstressed the growing sense of minority consciousness in America. Protestantism retains many kinds of political power in the South and in some suburbs. Its impact is subtly interfused with many power elements in the culture at large. But it is aware of the change. Sometimes Protestants act like a minority out of a sense of shame over their past; self-flagellation has been "in" in the past few years. Sometimes their actions grow out of a sense of defensiveness, in which case their counteractions are often extreme. Much of the American radical right is an expression of those who want Protestantism to retain a hold on the nation's power resources. Sometimes it grows out of an acquiescent and blurring vision; sometimes it involves a conscious desire for a loss of distinctiveness in the interest of what are seen to be higher and more important common values.

In sum: The educator who formerly introduced the child to a self-contained, somehow Protestant world today stands with the child (or adult, for that matter) somehow outside that world and treats it objectively, as something that may be acquired or shrugged off. And he or she looks at a once Protestant world that is now authentically pluralist, one which makes a home for millions of ambivalent Protestants.

A Most Religious, Most Secular Nation

Educators today have to deal with both the conscious and unconscious world of effects as perceived along the lines of an issue: Is our society religious or is it secular? What is it tending to become? Because of their heavy investment in the past and present and their contention over the future, Protestants are much involved in the urgent issue.

I spoke of conscious perception: Protestant theologians have become preoccupied with all the dimensions of secularity and religiousness; it is fair to speak of this perception as the obsessive theological issue of the past decade.[5] But we also note the unconscious perceptions. The American who buys the summer home and the boat away from all places of worship which he formerly frequented every summer Sunday is casting a vote on the issue. The American who rejoices in the fact that the phrase "under God" was inserted in the pledge of allegiance to the flag is making up his mind on the issue. The citizen who wants to hear a sermon on Sunday, but who wants it restricted to Sunday issues and is hostile to the preacher who comments on the world in which he lives the other six days, is doing his part to help "secularize" the world. The lady who turns her back on the churches and synagogues, but who hustles off to buy the astrology magazines at each change of the season, is involved, albeit without a high degree of formality or consciousness. America's sociological setting impinges on religion almost nowhere else with the intensity that it does on this issue; this time (in contrast to our earlier paragraphs) not only Protestants are involved, but their viewpoint is not without interest.

For the purpose of dramatizing the paradox, I shall exaggerate the two poles between which Americans live, in so far as this issue is concerned.

"We are a religious people, and our institutions presuppose a Supreme Being."[6] The United States Supreme Court coined this dictum in the 1950s and quoted it in the 1960s—a sure sign (since it seemed to be taken for granted) of a way in which Americans define themselves. While the last half of the proposition is shaky and may be demonstrably false, the first half is demonstrably true. Neither the Court nor other students have to comment on the quality or authenticity of the nation's religiousness; at this point it is necessary only to note the amount, not the character, of American religiousness and religiosity.

By almost any conventional public measure, America was and remains a religious nation. Religion (almost always of a Protestant stamp or reminiscence) was written into most of the colonial covenants, compacts, and charters on which the society was built. In the nineteenth century America became a "churched" society which took revivals of religion for granted as a rhythmic element in its history. At almost any moment in that past, an observer or a poll-taker could come away with an awe for America's preoccupation with religious themes, especially when he recalled that the nation had been born in a period when the world, by most conventional measures, already looked "secular" and seemed to destine the new nation to postreligious life.[7] Americans have shown respect for religion; anticlericalism on a wide scale had hardly been heard of until the 1960s, when clergy involved themselves in the racial struggle and in criticism of the Vietnam War. Even then, most people were cautious in their attacks against God or his church.

Sociologists would be even more satisfied with the harder-core measurable features of American religion: Through the years more and more Americans have come to affiliate with and support religious institutions—from the time of the nation's birth, when perhaps 6 percent of the population did, until the 1960s, when over 60 percent did. On any weekend over two fifths of the population will be attending religious services—an almost unheard-of-number in Western European nations. Americans spend a billion dollars a year for church and synagogue building. Their literature (from at least Hawthorne and Melville down to the present) is shot through with explicit religious images and symbols; their politicians know that it would be unwise not to invoke the deity for their causes, and impossible to be elected if they spoke out against such invocation.

The public in general nurtures the self-image of its religiousness. About four fifths of the population reacts negatively (according to the polls) when the Supreme Court decides that on constitutional grounds prayer, Bible reading, and devotion do not belong in public schools and similar institutions. As late as 1965 95 percent of the sampled population in a Gallup Poll stated that it believed in God. Conventional religion holds its own in the 1960s, despite all the talk about materialism and secularization. While dramatic reshuffling goes on inside the churches, Protestant religious vocations are relatively stable, and a Catholic decline is readily explainable on grounds other than those of disinterest in all forms of religion.

If conventional religion remains strong, unconventional religion seems almost to be on the upswing. While the switch from mood to mood may be sudden and the new devotions and attachments are anything but profound, it is in recent years that Americans have taken into their culture many aspects of Eastern religion. They have learned about Zen Buddhism and the *I Ching;* they speak about gurus and yogis and shamans and transcendental meditation. They are fascinated with peyote cults and religious visions based on the chewing of morning-glory seeds or the eating of LSD. They wear pendants with religious symbols and explore holy writings of non-violent religionists of many traditions.

Sales of astrology magazines reach all-time highs and few metropolitan newspapers could hold their readership without running some sort of column on the signs of the stars. One could make out a legitimate case that superstition is the real religion of the modern world, especially if he observes the actions and hears the words of the purportedly secular men and women on late night television. The voguish study of ESP, psi phenomena, consciousness expansion, psychokinesis, mediums, and countless other scientific and semiscientific omen worlds is further evidence.[8]

What of the future? If the future involves pure prediction, one can say what he wishes; if it follows the watching of trends, it takes no great audacity to envision some sort of continuing religious future. If it involves commitment to a philosophy of history, there are not a few people of distinction in range who make clear that they regard concern for ultimate issues to be profoundly religious and see it as part of man's essential nature.

In the middle of that world, a world which every religious educator is pressed to understand, there are countersigns; and there is a significant establishment of sociologists, artists, and theologians who warn against the illusion such signs of religiosity breed. Advocates of this position warn educators that they will miss the real meaning and the inner dynamism of our culture if they overlook its pervasive secularity.

So the world of effects contains its secular pole: Examine it.[9] The man who may have listened to the sermons of the religious revival of the 1950s and who then turned down his hearing aid for a decade, only to tune in again in the recent past, would have occasion to express surprise. With an astoundingly sudden reversal of values, the word "secular" has changed from being the dirty dog in the theological room to becoming something to be valued and sought. Once equated with materialism and baseness, it is today set forth as an aspect to reality to which the people who were once called religious ought to aspire. While the reversal has occurred chiefly in ecclesiastical circles (the conscious secular/religious battle is a very "churchy" issue), it has dealt with features of the sociological scene with which the whole society reckons. Old materials in religious education for people almost all the way across the theological spectrum are virtually worthless today; now the secular order has to be reappraised.

At least three views dominate. One implies a neutral definition of social secularity. It does not probe for theological meaning; it chronicles in matter-of-fact fashion. Thus Eric Hoffer[10] can say offhand that at some point in history God and the priests seemed to have become superfluous, but history kept going on somehow. He was not dogmatic: He did not say that God did not exist or had died, or that priests did become superfluous. These changes "seemed" to occur. Neutrally secular man does not find it necessary to make up his mind fully about these issues—even the question of secularity is in a way superfluous at such a time. Needless to say, unreflective secularity is the least welcome approach so far as theologians are concerned: It is hard to get a conversation started, hard to generate heat enough to motivate the shedding of light. At the same time, it may well be that in this form secularity is most pervasive and maddening to religious educators. People find God, church, religion to be extraneous, dismissible, neither here nor there; they find little occasion for decision. This is the secularity of the marketplace, the legislature, the academy. Almost all moderns share it in some way or other.

At the other extreme from this environmental "mere" secularity there is a dedicated form, which I call "utter" secularity. It relates to the modern phenomenon of godlessness. Now and then it may be overtly atheistic in outlook and tone. More frequently a rather studied but only slightly militant agnosticism is implied. So far as God and religion are concerned, "the returns are not all yet in." But with this assertion goes the idea that were they to be all in, God would be out of the picture, and that religion is more enslaving than liberating, more retrogressive than contributory to progress.

Utterly secular man sees the perceived universe to be made of atoms and molecules; human action is the result of mechanical and chemical forces. Only that! Such a person is cool, clear, clean. He has no experience of gods; and if he did, he could find ways to dispel it as illusory, as projection. He lives in what Buber calls an "epoch of homelessness," away from the land of the gods. But he is not waiting or expectant or dependent upon promise. He has moved beyond religion. This kind of person (and the society he fashions) seems to have much of history on his side—yet he coexists with religious man and may find contradictory elements in his own self and his own circle.

A third form of worldliness can be called "controlled" secularity —the kind of worldliness or godlessness advocated by the radical theologians of the recent past, men and women who welcome postreligious times but who reflectively attach symbols that had once been thought of as religious to the process and events. The symbol manipulators who can thus control the concept of secularity are few in number; they may be almost unheard of outside the seminaries. But they are in the business of discernment and they have indirect impact on the larger culture. They too belong to the sociological context in which religious education occurs.

To such thinkers, world-affirmation has been a neglected note in religion and especially in Protestant Christianity, with its back-of-the-mind antiworldliness or otherworldliness, its leftover asceticism and dour or grim approach to celebration. Radical theology asks for celebration and affirmation of the world as the bearer and context of meaning. While it is reluctant to engage in God-talk, since such talk cannot be verified by ordinary canons of empirical measurement, it may be very much at home with the concept of the Lordship of Christ, with aspects of recall of the historical Jesus, and with warm regard for selected elements in the Christian tradition.[11]

Out of such a complex, the affirmative secular theology has sought to be relevant to the world as it is. But it makes stronger claims than this. Drawing on teachings of Dietrich Bonhoeffer about the necessity to see the world moving into its adulthood and past adolescent religiosity, it finds in Friedrich Gogarten[12] and others exemplification of the idea that prophetic religion anticipates and gives momentum and meaning to the secular process. The prophets, Jesus, the sectarians of the Middle Ages, the Reformers, and latter-day secular theologians are in the god-killing business. They scorn solemn assemblies. They remind that at best the Sabbath was made for man, not man for the Sabbath. They ask men to wait without idols, to test the spirits, to be no longer subject to weak and beggarly (i.e., religious) elements. The church becomes part of God's vanguard, though one speaks diffidently of God and may resort to Christological terms only. The church is to set the pace for liberation and secularization, to nudge a reluctant world and church past their comfortable household deities onto the sunny plain of human freedom.

What is man? Is he essentially religious or secular? Many today claim to know. They speak of divining his essential nature; or they consciously prophesy concerning his future; or they unconsciously reveal their commitments by the ways they speak about the meaning of history. They are involved in contention over what man is, where he is tending, where he should go. Educators find they can say few words bearing on the purposes of religious education without finding themselves at the center of this debate, a debate filled with sociological sources and overtones. They live with the paradox of apparently increasing religiousness (albeit of a new kind) and increasing secularity in a single society and even in the same persons.

Devotion to Generalized and Particular Religion

For the rest of this chapter I shall bracket or shelve what I call "utter secularity" and absorb "mere" and "controlled" secularity into the general context of religion, where they seem to belong. That means that we can return to the discussion of the religious dimensions of the social scene from a Protestant point of view. And the reintrusion allows for grappling with still another paradox that confronts educators. Americans seem to be durably involved with a very generalized religion and equally concerned with celebrating distinctives and particulars. The dialectic of involvement with the common faith and the separate faiths in a single society and in single individuals remains a mystery in American life, though it has some obvious sources in national history.

The general first. For centuries citizens of what came to be and is the United States have been involved with the fabrication of or recognition of a sort of common faith, a religion held in general. Few of their forefathers came with such an intention in view; in fact, their intention may have been just the opposite. Most of them came to develop organismic but separate communities,[13] far away from the depravations and degradations of European religion. In New England, most sought a kind of Congregationalist Calvinist theocracy, which conferred full rights and full status only on those who "owned" a particular covenant. Virginia and other Southern colonies may have been more relaxed, but their intentions did not differ in substance. The middle colonies had more broadly conceived charters, but they too had to make room for exclusive communities. Even within subtle shades of Protestantism, radical distinctions were made. Heresies which would go unnoticed today served to divide whole colonies and necessitated the development of new ones like Rhode Island.

An incipient pluralism was present, however, and the colonies developed between the need for tolerance and the fear of religious anarchy. So they experimented. Some spoke of connivance toward toleration; others kept things cool by attempting to muddle through pragmatically. Yet the effect in both instances was to generate a common religious value system that was not merely Protestant or Christian, but which included a syncretistic embrace of some para-Christian and non-Christian ideas.

The most significant moment for such embrace and such fusion occurred at the time of the formation of the nation. At that time the American counterpart to the Enlightenment held sway: Many "founding fathers" were at home with British deism or the new French thought.[14] Some of them became quite critical of particular creeds; of John Calvin's God, priestcraft, and superstition. Others remained devoted listeners to divines in latitudinarian pulpits or held onto their posts as vestrymen. But men like Benjamin Franklin, George Washington, Thomas Jefferson, and James Madison united in fearing religious establishment or monopoly. They took some hope from religious multiplicity, feeling that it would have an erosive effect on the distinctives of creeds and a protective result for the larger society. At its heart, their own new creed celebrated the Enlightenment's quest for common values, a societal grounding, an embrace of universal reason, nature, and moral purpose; what the sects held individually, said Franklin, was irrelevant to common life in the nation.[15]

Coming as these concerns did at the crucial period for the formation of institutions and values, they have been bonded into the fabric of national life. Nor have the occasions which gave rise to the quest for common symbols and religious aspirations or measures disappeared. Binding up the wounds of the nation after the Civil War; calling people together to engage in common wars; inspiring common devotion—all these and other demands have evoked a consensus of values that seems to demand a quasireligious sanction and some ceremonial celebration.

The Enlightenment in America was not an ahistorical mutation. It had a Protestant reminiscence; it was non- or anti-Catholic in many of its expressions; it found little occasion to have to deal with the Jew; it was, for all that, a kind of liberal Protestant heresy.

The chief early challenge to this common faith came from reactors to the Enlightenment, from people who were themselves Protestant. In the early nineteenth century during the revivals and the awakenings, as denominationalism took form,[16] American church people became competitive and contentious, stressing their differences in religion. However dysfunctional denominationalism may seem to many in a later day, it was extremely functional at the time of its birth. It allowed people to coexist without resorting to intolerable religious warfare of the kind they had grown weary of in Europe. At the same time it permitted fanatic attachment to finely parsed definitions of doctrine. In effect, the denominational promoter was not saying that all who went different ways were going to hell, but he was able to say, in effect, "Don't be half safe. Come my way."

The separate intentions of colonists and the achievements of nineteenth-century competitors have given later-day Americans a legacy of denominationalism that is hard to interpret, transcend, or overcome. Yet they hold to it against the background of shared assumptions about ultimate values in a pluralistic society. At first these general assumptions retained their explicitly Protestant base. Ruth Miller Elson in her study of textbooks of the period, *Guardians of Tradition*,[17] makes this clear. Many citizens did not realize how profound the Protestantism of the general values was until significant numbers of non-Protestants arrived. For example, they had made the public schools into what amounted to the established churches of America and felt that having rendered them non-sectarian they had also achieved non-controversiality. When Roman Catholics arrived, they found it necessary to establish parochial schools because they could discern the pro-Protestant bias of what had looked universal earlier.

The society is no less complex today than it was in the past. Over 250 religious groups are strong enough to be reckoned with in the *Yearbook of the American Churches.* Yet the result is not mere competition or religious warfare. As many sociologists, Robin Williams most notably, have pointed out, a complex society seems to demand a consensus of quasireligious values that can be appealed to or implied ultimately.[18] Without these, people call into question the basis of their laws, their orders, their morals. When the consensus is radically questioned, society faces anarchy; when it is quietly disregarded, society manifests anomie.

When consensus religion (variously called civic, societal, political, or generalized) is evident, one would expect what the Catholics used to call indifferentism. If the society places a premium on shared religious values and finds distinctives irrelevant or even distracting, should not I, asks the individual, also find my own confessions and commitments irrelevant and distracting? Often Americans indicate that they answer the question in the affirmative; they hold to the nation's unofficial theology with more tenacity than to their private creeds; they die for one and live genially with the other. They are often denominationally mobile as they move up the status scale or laterally from suburb to suburb.

Yet—and this is a chapter of "and yet's"—they are surprisingly loyal to the particular. They are, if they are Protestant, not only so in general but also in particular. Charles Y. Glock and Rodney Stark, in dealing with this phenomenon, speak of it as a "new denominationalism."[19] It is not new at all, though they have described its contents well: It is durable denominationalism. Protestants are able to recognize some symbols or other which give them distinctiveness and identity: adult baptism, or apostolic succession, or congregationalism, or consubstantiation. They show loyalty to the men who propagate these separate views.

Evidences of this ongoing particularism in the face of generalizing religion are on every hand. Economics: It is a truism in Christian circles that the denomination is the more efficient (and the local congregation the most efficient) way to raise funds, something that is a mark of deep loyalty in America! Budgets for transdenominational or ecumenical causes are small and fragile. In organizing power, the particular symbols and structures are more efficient than are general ones. On a college campus strong denominations can outdraw interreligious programs almost any day. Churches which remain isolationistic when common Thanksgiving Day services are held will attract, ordinarily, more worshippers than will the highly publicized common goodwill services. The pace of denominational mergers in an ecumenical age remains glacial.

Education in a society where these pulls and tensions are present provides a baffling situation. Sebastian de Grazia has discussed the ways in which anomie results from confusion of directives: "Love thy neighbor, shove thy neighbor," says a co-operating-competing society.[20] These maxims from the economic realm also prevail in the religious. The young American is trained to be a good citizen in the general society, whose common religious affirmations may contradict the prophetic and distinctive elements of his own religion, even as he is trained to hold to those elements. Push the former and one has erosion and religious disaffection; push the latter, and a kind of "spiritual" anarchy results.

The Relevance and Irrelevance of Denominationalism

Within the Protestant sector we have spoken of durable denominationalism. Even within it some paradoxes or contradictions seem to be present. The denomination was designed in part for confessional integrity; in the new or durable denominationalism, a few symbols at least remain, to provide marks of recognition or agencies for eliciting loyalty. So far, so good. Yet many of these inherited symbols lack cognitive import. They belong more to the reflexive than to the reflective life of Protestants. What actually separates or unites them transcends denominational lines.

Thus it is possible to speak of a kind of two-party system in Protestantism. Each party draws on all denominations, though some denominations may be farther at one end of a spectrum or syndrome than are others.[21] Denominational leaders, knowing how important unity is, place a premium on it and tend to minimize the divisions. Only the militants on each side try hard to cause new definition, schism, or separation. Thus to hear the Methodists in denominational assembly, one would think that the act of being a Methodist would well define one's religious life. Yet one soon learns that certain kinds of Methodists have more in common with certain kinds of Episcopalians or Presbyterians than these do with some of their own denominational compatriots.

There are not even sociologically acceptable designations for these two schools of thought and action. The militants in one speak of themselves as the evangelicals, but many in the other are also evangelical. The partisans on the other side are sometimes denominated "ecumenicals," but few of them accept the designation,[22] for their ecumenical stance absorbs too little of their attention to be an exhaustive label. The former tend to be more conservative theologically and politically, in their self-definition. Yet their opponents can demonstrate that they are actually innovators, regarding some nineteenth-century values as normative for all history, whereas the "liberals" want to draw also on older norms in the Christian past. And the party of the second part is often called liberal theologically and socially, but the public finds it difficult to define liberalism today and many in this cluster would not accept the definition, considering it to be dated and applicable only to others in a different historical moment.

At the root of the two lie significant differences concerning the meaning of the gospel, the church, and its mission. Both derive from nineteenth-century evangelicalism.[23] The one has picked up the innovative individualism of that period and stresses personal revival, conversion, and salvation. The other selects the communal aspects of the past and accents plural metaphors ("the People of God," "the Body of Christ") as interpretive tools for suggesting that salvation is social in character. The former picks chiefly the areas over which individuals have control for moral reform: gambling, drinking, swearing, loose sexual conduct. The latter party stresses the immorality built into the social fabric and sets out to try to change that fabric, confronting racial deprivation when it is institutionalized, slums, poverty, ambiguous military commitments.

The Protestant observing the changing sociological scene finds it necessary to instruct the public at large concerning this division, obscured as it is by ignorance and euphemism alike. The outsider reads books on Lutheranism, Congregationalism, the Baptist churches. He learns their historic doctrines and social programs; he anticipates that the meaningful differences follow the denominational lines. But in a time of sudden change like the recent past he soon finds that all this learning is of little effect for the issues about which he must know.

The two parties need to deal with each other. They share common histories, live as common families, support common institutions. Individualistic Protestantism remains the chief missionary-conversionistic agency, constantly providing new "warm bodies for the movement." Its social and political impact is strong, if indirect. But Protestantism's public face appears more through the complex of identifications on the part of "social" Christians, who involve themselves not only in those carefully boxed-in corners (private, familial, leisure life) where a secular society tolerates and even welcomes churches, but also in the controversial sectors, where the root decisions affecting millions occur.

Today the leadership of most denominations is ecumenical and social in outlook: Their point of view prevails in the seminaries, bureaucracies, publishing centers, and the pulpits of the younger (but not only the younger) men. A public trained to expect that ministers and theologians have a vested interest in the old, of which they are the custodians, while laymen will be petitioning the churches to modernize and to become relevant to the contemporary world, is surprised to see that often the opposite is true. A coalition between intransigent clergymen and "concerned" laymen exists in almost all Protestant denominations to serve as a check or a brake against what they regard to be runaway innovators. This is not to say that the party lines follow clerical/lay distinctions—laymen were often the pioneers in each group—but only to note that much clerical leadership is today united on a side where the public ten years ago would not have expected to find such unity.

A child brought up on the educational literature of almost any of these denominations will ordinarily be introduced to a much larger world than the one he or she will greet in the local parish. However provincial that literature may seem, it will more often portray the work of a church in many disparate cultures, at work in many controversial social causes; local church leadership may often for instinctive, political, or profound theological reasons cultivate a one-class, apolitical mentality. The issues which actually separate and divide men in local and denominational settings differ from those officially propagated in the histories of most such groups.

Public Media and Private Formation

A final essential factor in discerning the sociological setting from a Protestant point of view has to do with the role public media, transportation, mobility, and exposure have in relation to private formation. The whole concept of religious education is jostled by the changes brought about specifically by the mass media. American Protestantism has been largely localistic. Even the few denominations that have interlocking (e.g., episcopal) polities have learned to express themselves in a close bond with localized power. Religious education traditionally worked to preserve that localism, to reflect inherited values of specific people in a specific place. Today no cultural outpost is not reached in advance by television, radio, mass magazines, and newspapers. It is impossible to deal with all aspects of this change, but one or two features are urgent.

On the one hand, the reader of literature on the mass media may be prepared to expect decimation of all inherited and particular values. The more extravagant prophets of the media suggest that the bombardment is so constant and pervasive that it changes not only the substance of people's hopes but the very sensibilities with which they relate to all reality. The public media being public, it is therewith also assumed that only public and general values are propagated.

Naturally, in a world where the media have an inveterate commercial tie, one would not expect propagation of particular faiths. Advertisers who must seek the broadest possible markets will do what they can not to alienate any religious groups even as they cannot confer superior status on others. What is more, the communicators themselves may hold to other competitive but embracing value systems and have a positive disinterest in privately nurtured commitments.

Why, then, has not particular formation disappeared? Or, a better question to ask: What in the particular formation has survived? What has been challenged? Here a body of empirical and theoretical study about the nature of the media provides some clues. There is no question that the media bombardment is profound and wide-ranging. The succession of images presented constitutes a problem for the traditional educator or religionist: Young people in particu-

lar are subjected to a maddening sequence of images eliciting decision about products, norms, values, and groups. Inevitably there is
a kind of trivializing or eroding of the decision process itself. When
everything is taken seriously, nothing is taken seriously. When all
the walls are battered, how does one protect against weather? What
can be retained?

On the other hand, one can put down the media and notice the
limits of their impact. The new toothpaste advertiser not only
shows toothpaste on television, he has an agent drop a sample in
people's mailboxes. The commercial writers do anything they can
to pick up secondary impact, word-of-mouth advertising. They
must know that certain realms of life are best approached personally and intimately. Joseph Klapper, William Stephenson,[24] and
others have noted that the media serve best as agents to reinforce
opinion and rarely ("all things being equal") as converting agents
for wholly new systems. It would be intolerable if men had no
protective devices built in against the tireless (or tiring) sequence
of appeals to convert. Somehow, man tunes them out.

Stephenson points out that the media have their greatest effect
in areas of opinion, attitude, and notion; they are least effective in
the realms of profoundest belief and commitment. The latter are
nurtured in areas of "social control" like home, family, nursery,
school, church, face-to-face contact. Here are the deepest ego-
involvements. The media can sway, they can affect; rarely do they
uproot and confirm. When religion is locked into the areas of "social control" in the more positive and open senses of that term, it
best serves the individual who is to be buffeted by many contradictory signals. In short: In the age of media, the greenhouse walls are
partly shattered and the door is open, but there is a greenhouse
which provides some protection for decisive stages and moments
of nurture.

Conclusion

This Protestant view of certain aspects of the sociological setting
for education has not been exhaustive. One could point to other
basic paradoxes or contradictory tendencies. In the 1950s people
were told to build up the church; in the ensuing decade they were

asked to submerge the identity of the church, to forgo attention to its good name, and to lose themselves in service of the world. It was "in" to speak critically of the sanctuary, the private rites of the withdrawn circle, the retreat, the devotional life, and to speak positively of the social-ethical involvements and identification with the world.

As time passes, we see again that here too a dialectic was operative. The church represents the cave of withdrawal and the tent for people on the march; the worship signifies withdrawal or strategic retreat for renewed open involvement; the service of God is called for both in the reserved cell and in the exposure in the streets. Ideologues may call for a simple and permanent decision between all these tendencies. The social historian need only point to them, so that the educator can deal with them. He may also commit himself enough to say that a society which makes up its mind simply and permanently on all these matters may be less confusing; it may at the same time be less humane, more dull, and less open to adventure and surprise than is the complex and contradictory one which we have inherited and in which we today move and have our being.

FOUR

Attitudes Toward an Ecumenical Orientation for Religious Education

A. by SISTER ANN PATRICK WARE, S.L.

B. by HOWARD GRIMES

A. *by SISTER ANN PATRICK WARE, S.L.*

W E C A N N O T S A Y that attempts to give an ecumenical orientation to religious education have failed; we can say that few
serious attempts have been made. This is not meant to be a para-
phrase of the saying (Chesterton's, I think) that Christianity has not
failed: it has never been tried. Innumerable efforts have at least gone
under the name of Christianity, but scarcely anyone has been
claimed to be planning and offering a fully ecumenical religious
education program.

The area is practically brand-new; history offers little precedent.
Before the time of a "divided Christendom" there was obviously no
need for it; from the time of the Reformation to the present the
accent in religious education was largely on justifying the claims
to truth and rightness of the several denominations. Vilification of
the others was not unknown. Hot tempers and defensiveness do not
make for ecumenism. Despite admirable small-scale attempts at
collaboration in educating the young in the Christian faith, there
has been nothing yet which approaches genuine ecumenical endeavor along these lines if we understand "ecumenical" as engaging the church of Christ as a whole.[1]

Because we are here concerned with attitudes, it seems appropriate to look briefly at some dominating attitudes of the past which
have had a large part in the formation of twentieth-century Christians; at essential attitudes for ecumenical orientation; at some con-

temporary explorations in the matter of attitudinal change; and finally at some of the problems inseparable from an intent to give a religious education in an ecumenical fashion. We shall make no attempt to list or to evaluate any of those ventures which their authors might like to call ecumenical religious education.

Attitudes of the Past: Hatred and Distrust

Past animosities have been deeply rooted and widespread. Professional seminary education nurtured them because the classic works of Reformation and Counter-Reformation theologians abounded in abuse. Calvin did not hesitate to refer to the pope as "the Roman antichrist"[2] or to the Mass, even when "considered in its choicest and most estimable purity, without any of its append-ages, from the beginning to the end" as "full of every species of impiety, blasphemy, idolatry, and sacrilege."[3] Clerics were those than whom "there is no class of men more rapacious, ignorant, or libidinous."[4]

Luther called Zwingli "pig, dog, or fanatic, whatever kind of unreasonable ass you are," and Zwingli returned the compliment: "fanatic, fool, bumpkin, yes a devil, murderer, and corrupter of souls."[5] Not only was it impossible for these men really to hear one another; it was not possible to look upon their followers as other than dupes. Jaroslav Pelikan claims that Roman Catholics ever since the sixteenth century have displayed "an astonishing incapacity to understand the Reformation, and an unwillingness to admit that the religious convictions of the reformers were animated by their fidelity to catholic ideals."[6]

Even after the heat of hostility cooled and the tone of reference to other Christians moved from abuse to disdain, aloofness, or polite ignoring, it was a rare Christian who thought of a Christian of another church as his brother, called by the same Father, baptized into the same Body, fed by the same Lord, in whom the same Spirit dwelt and prayed. It is true that in the early part of this century concerned Protestants and Anglicans, especially sensitive to the scandal which the divided church presented in missionary situa-tions, met together with a view toward dialogue and whatever further action the Spirit might prompt in them. They were soon joined by the Orthodox, but the Roman Catholic Church, though invited to join in the conversations about unity, steadfastly declined to participate. Consistent concern about church unity took its most noticeable shape in the formation in 1948 of the World Council of Churches.

Roman Catholics, whose ecumenical stance has been affected much more solidly by pastoral attitudes than by papal statements, might well be surprised at the intransigence of the Roman position as late as the forties and fifties in contrast with the present ecumenical activity. In 1943 Pope Pius XII's encyclical letter *The Mystical Body of Christ* was unequivocal in stating that the true church of Christ was the Holy, Catholic, Apostolic, Roman Church and pointed out that it was a dangerous error "to hold that one can adhere to Christ as Head of the Church without loyal allegiance to His Vicar on earth."[7] This was equivalent to impugning the reality of the adherence to Christ of all those Christians who stood outside the Roman communion. Although it was the specification of members *in re* of the church of Christ which received most of the theological attention, it is probable that this encyclical, which enjoyed a broad circulation and was widely studied both in Catholic colleges and in adult study groups, was one of the most significant doctrinal influences on the attitude of educated Catholics toward other Christians.

Instruction of the Holy Office on the Ecumenical Movement, which appeared in 1949, was full of warnings and caution: Bishops should keep the movement for the reunion of Christians under "vigilant observation"; they should "shield the faithful from the perils" attached to the movement. They should "exercise vigilance" in regard to the publication of literature on the subject. They should "be on their guard" against a dangerous indifferentism, scrupulously take precautions and firmly insist that in the discussion of the Reformation the faults and foibles of Catholics be not overemphasized, while the blame and defects of the Reformers are dissimulated. Non-Catholics may be told that in returning to the Catholic Church they will forfeit none of the good which the grace of God had hitherto wrought in their souls but they are not to be given the impression that by their return they are making a contribution to the church of something essential that she lacked in the past. Expressions like "exceptional watchfulness and control," "the faithful shall be prudently kept away," "such conversations are wont to be fraught with danger" are to be found on almost every page.[8]

The commentary of a noted canonist, William Conway, J.C.D., which followed close upon the document, indicates better than anything else the mentality with which it was greeted by many "prophets of doom" in clerical circles. Press reports, he said, tended to imply that the Holy Office considered round-table conferences between Catholics and non-Catholics as the principal and most effective means of achieving the *return* of those outside the church. Such a view, he says, tragically misconceives and distorts the whole tenor and purpose of the document. "The Holy Office considers these conferences not as the most effective but as the most dangerous means of furthering the work of reunion." The means suggested are prayer (by the whole Catholic world to God that non-Catholics be given light and truth to return to the true church of Christ); good example; facilities for the instruction of prospective converts; information centers; lectures on Catholic truth for non-Catholics. He concludes with the statement that all participation with non-Catholics in an act of religious worship is forbidden. "This prohibition, *of course, being a prohibition of divine law*, is absolute"[9] (italics the writer's).

It was into such a climate that Pope John's calling of the Council burst in 1959. His intention "to invite the separated communities to seek again that unity for which so many souls are longing in these days throughout the world" caused no little surprise. Quite against the better judgment of highly placed advisers, he invited observers from the Christian churches and set up the Secretariat for Promoting Christian Unity. Pope Paul continued this spirit, saying,

This is a Council of invitation, of expectation, of confidence. . . . We greet the representatives of the Christian denominations separated from the Catholic Church. We thank them for their participation. We transmit through them our message—as father and brother—to the venerable Christian communities they represent. . . . If we are in any way to blame for [our prolonged] separation, we humbly beg God's forgiveness.[10]

One fruit of this aspect of the Council was the *Decree on Ecumenism*. The whole tone and content of the document manifests a true about-face from the former admonitions and directives. The decree points out that Jesus Christ established one church. Many communions present themselves as the true heirs of Jesus Christ. All proclaim themselves disciples of the Lord but convictions clash and paths diverge. Now we are experiencing a new movement for unity motivated by the Holy Spirit. The Roman Catholic Church sets before all Catholics certain helps, pathways, methods by which they can respond to this divine summons and grace. All preconciliar directives are hereby superseded.[11]

Next the document proceeds to elucidate certain Catholic principles of ecumenism. First, every effort must be made to eliminate all untrue and unfair words, judgments, and actions toward other Christians. Second, dialogue between competent experts from different churches is to be fostered. Third, there must be co-operation in projects demanded by the Christian conscience for the common good. Fourth, common prayer under certain circumstances is not only permitted but encouraged. Finally, all must examine their own faithfulness to Christ's will for the church and vigorously undertake the task of renewal and reform where this is necessary.

Significant changes of attitude are discernible here. For one thing, with the calling of the Council there came to the surface for the first time an admission that the "guilt" for the division of Christendom was not all on one side. There is a hesitant but real tendency to allow to other Christian communions truly Christian endowments and to acknowledge their capacity to form Christ in their members. Formerly, Roman Catholics were inclined to regard anything good in non-Roman Christians as belonging to them as individuals through some gift of grace unrelated to their corporate ecclesial structure and life. The decree regards the whole movement of Christians toward unity under the image of the pilgrim church, and this represents an important departure from the image of a "return" to the one true church which has marked all official preconciliar statements. Finally, there is a hint that there may have been deficiencies in Roman Catholic dogmatic formulations of the past together with a clear acknowledgment that the hierarchy of truths which Christian faith has attempted to articulate must be respected.[12]

Such tentative admissions hardly seem worthy of notice, much less of praise, but the very fact that they were "firsts" in the official position shows to what an extent the previous attitude had been justified in its aloofness from the ecumenical movement. In fact, all steps were not forward. Some will remember the irritation which many of the Council Fathers felt when Pope Paul, on the day before the final vote, made nineteen changes in the text of the *Decree on Ecumenism,* and there was not time to discuss or vote on them singly. A reluctance to call the shining and heroic deeds of some Protestants "gifts of the Holy Spirit" reduced them to "virtuous works,"[13] and a curious hesitancy to admit that non-Roman Christians "find God in the Holy Scriptures" led Pope Paul to make the change "they seek in those sacred Scriptures God as He speaks to them in Christ."[14] Thus Samuel McCrea Cavert, while expressing a new hope for ecumenism as a result of this document, notes in his response to it the "unchangeably Rome-centered" understanding of the ecumenical movement which it expresses through its failure to reconcile an ecumenical outlook with the assumption of the primacy of Peter and of his jurisdiction over the whole church.[15]

If we have dwelt overlong on what seems to be already much explored and broadly known, it is because the problems of which we have an inkling here seem to be central to what an authentically ecumenical religious education will have to deal with in the future. It is vitally important that Roman Catholics educated before Vatican II have some clear understanding of the shift in the official attitude we have sketchily traced here. There can be no successful ecumenical religious education if this new orientation is not firmly established.[16] Whereas papal or official documents up until the time of Vatican II had their influence mainly in seminaries or clerical circles, the popular influence of the Council documents among a wide section of the Catholic laity should not be underestimated. They were in good circulation almost from the first moment of their publication and have been the subject of study in parish renewal groups. College theology departments have organized whole courses around specific documents or groups of documents issuing from the Council. At no time, it seems safe to say, have official doctrinal positions and official attitudes received such exposure among the Catholic faithful as at the present time. But also at no time has there been such a rapid shifting of both position and attitude in a matter so closely connected with the dogmatic teaching of the Roman Church as in this matter of ecumenism.

Essential Attitudes for Ecumenism

Any orientation toward a new openness in the matter of religious education must presuppose the readiness of Christians of whatever communion to accept other Christians as genuine whole Christians, not religious amputees, not deprived, not shortchanged in the area of God's grace—in short, as equals. This is much easier said than done and only the "other" can tell us the myriad ways in which we express the superiority we subconsciously feel.

Eugene Bianchi describes the attitude of the "pre-ecumenical Catholic." To such a one

. . . other Christian communities represented erroneous threats to true religion. It was, of course, admitted that sincere, individual Protestants could be saved in spite of their waywardness. Their ecclesial life, however, was considered to be of little value. The less informed but typical Catholic wondered why anyone would want to be a Protestant, unless he simply desired an easy and nominal religious affiliation. To lose one's Catholic faith was regrettable but understandable; to become a Protestant was irrational. They had no pope, no Virgin, no saints, no real sacraments and no rules. Protestantism was seen as individual interpretation of the Bible, hymn singing and doing pretty well what one pleased.[17]

Even now in the "ecumenical era" there are more subtle but just as real ways of denying to non-Roman bodies the riches of full Christian life. The *Decree on Ecumenism* says, for instance:

. . . Some, even very many, of the most significant elements or endowments which together go to build up and give life to the Church herself can exist outside the visible boundaries of the Catholic Church: the written word of God; the life of grace; faith, hope, and charity, along with other interior gifts of the Holy Spirit and visible elements. All of these, which come from Christ and lead back to Him, belong by right to the one Church of Christ.[18]

The omission of any mention of sacraments or true ministry as even capable of existence outside the Roman Church is another way of denying full stature to other ecclesial bodies in the church of Christ.[19] It is a way of repeating the stereotype described by Bianchi but all the more difficult to deal with inasmuch as it is an official statement which appears to be making concessions.

The tendency of Christians to see others not just as different but as lesser Christians is not unlike the white community's inability to recognize the black man as truly equal. The more the white man protests that he really does consider the black man his equal, the more he is condemned by the very terms and manner of his protestation. Our prejudices are subtle and very deeply ingrained. We justify them as being the logical consequences of our respective theologies and ecclesiologies, and we find ourselves unable to hear another's position without comparing it with our own. To pronounce judgments while listening is not really to hear what is being said.

. . . [In true ecumenism] a church no longer thinks solely about its own plans, programmes, interests, and concerns but takes up the otherness of the other into its own consciousness. The other is not contested. One thinks in relation to and with the interest of the other. One lives towards and with the concrete life of the other—not merely his thoughts.[20]

Our seriousness in rooting out old prejudices and treating other Christians as equals must be manifested in new attitudes, the first of which is a willingness to let the other speak for himself. For too many years the knowledge which Christians have of one another has been based on what A tells B about C's belief. Roman Catholics have been in a particularly disadvantaged position here because of strictures (now largely ignored) of canon law which forbid the reading of unapproved religious works unless the reader has episcopal permission. In many dioceses such permission was all but unattainable; in others, delays were so prolonged as to make the permission no longer useful when granted. It follows, then, that the knowledge most Catholics have of Lutheranism, for instance, has been derived from hearing or reading what other Catholics had to say about it; and the latter may well have gained their knowledge or understanding in the same way. It ought to be apparent to us that only the one who knows and loves his religious tradition can hope to manifest its riches to another. Weaknesses need no apologist.

Do we need to mention that Christians being ecumenically oriented toward religious education must give the other credit for good faith? Bianchi described the typical Catholic as wondering why anyone would want to be a Protestant unless he simply desired an easy and nominal religious affiliation. Our deep-seated convictions—they can be called only that—that the "religious other" is basically stupid, insincere, dishonest, unlike us in every way, are readily betrayed by the damning "but"—that is, "He's a Baptist, *but* he's well informed (or honest or holy or such a good man)" or "She's a Catholic, *but* she loves Christ (or is intelligent or has a mind of her own or really wants to learn)."

It will not be new for us to say, but it may be new for us to operate on the truth that no one has a monopoly on the Holy Spirit. The Spirit blows where he will, and Christians need to break out of the boxes they have decided they would operate in if *they* were the Holy Spirit. Why such hesitancy to listen to, to admire, to approve, to rejoice in the religious riches of others? Why such determination to prove that a different way of understanding or worshiping is a false way? "But there are contradictions," someone will answer. Can we be so sure? Are we not, rather, facing the variety of responses evoked in uniquely different and varied persons by the Spirit who is Lord of them all?

Once we are willing to adopt a less static view of truth, a vision of the whole Christian people growing together into the fullness of the stature of Christ, we may be willing to take that greatest risk of all: the risk of having our own most deeply cherished ideas changed.

... The most basic skill in a rapidly changing world is that of knowing how to learn continually in order to stay abreast of developments. This involves a willingness continually to question old ways and a readiness to drop them as soon as they no longer work.

The impact of such an attitude is most strongly felt in matters of *faith and ethics* [italics the writer's]. Conscience and traditions are not exempt from the willingness to question and adapt.[21]

The serious re-examination on the theological level of doctrinal statements formulated in times of heated defensiveness has shown how much common ground there can be in positions hitherto considered antithetical. On the more popular level, too, we may find a great deal of appreciation of another's positions if only we do not hinder that discovery by slogan-thinking. We attach a pejorative meaning to "compromise" and then proceed to label any change compromise, to parrot "You can never compromise in matters of truth," or to repudiate "change for change's sake" without ever seeking whether the labels fit the situations.

On the other hand, we must be willing to examine the caricatures which persist and see not only upon what they have been constructed but why, if they are untrue, they fail to die or even to be exterminated. Congar speaks interestingly in this regard about distrust of Rome:

Among the complexes that other people have about us . . . is the notorious anti-Roman complex. With varying shades in the details of its motivations and expressions, it appears to be common to the Orthodox East and the Protestant West. It is a very profound reality. We may wonder whether it is Christian, even while not excluding the idea that it may be deeply motivated by attachment to authentic Christian values (if sometimes wrongly interpreted ones). I believe it would be possible to find a formula for these values and for their disputable interpretation at the same time in Dostoievsky's "Legend of the Grand Inquisitor." I had been a priest for just a year when a Protestant pastor from Berlin and, only a few weeks later, an Orthodox friend in Paris, each named this creation of Dostoievsky's genius as the quintessential expression of their grievances. It seems likely that the attribution has some truth.

Should we not take note of it, we Catholics? Should we not give ourselves the benefit of this lucidity, and question ourselves honestly, humbly, about the reasons for this monumental fact, the persistence of which historically has been expressed in thousands of actions and records? Rome is distrusted. Men attribute to her the aims of domination and sentiments of paternalism that put them on the defensive and make them keep their distance, even though many outside the bounds of Catholicism are prepared to recognize the benefits the papacy has conferred on Christianity and on the world.[22]

In a more positive vein, the ecumenical future in all areas, but particularly in that of religious education, will have to rely heavily on a better appreciation of all truly human values. Ecumenism is not a matter of obtaining accurate information about the beliefs and religious life of those who do not share our spiritual heritage; it is to enter as openly as possible into the hopes and dreams, the mind and heart of another. It is to view other Christians as contributing to our own completeness just as all the brothers and sisters must be loved and appreciated if the family is to be whole and healthy.

Indeed, we can no longer be content with narrow Christian boundaries. We must be open to the whole family of man, all of whom are God's creation and gift, if we are to be sound, and any examination of ecumenical attitudes must somehow include these wider perspectives. For example, as the church struggles with her identity in a secular society and is determined not to repeat the mistakes of a religiously chauvinistic past, Christians will perhaps have to give up for the present the frenzied search to see how their service differs from (is better than!) that of those who have no Christian motivation. They will turn to the indisputable manifestation of concern for the brother which can be found in individuals of other religious beliefs or of no religious beliefs, admire, and rejoice in it. We are not threats to one another. We build and finish one another. There can be no orientation for ecumenical education without admiration and appreciation of and joy in all human values.

We must seriously undertake in our dialogue with others to be sensitive to the ways in which they see themselves and to root out phrases or epithets which they deem unfair or unrepresentative. For example, someone in the Christian world must begin to take seriously the charge of defamation which Jews level at the New Testament.[23] A provocative article by Jack Epstein, himself a Jew and Research Associate Professor in the Department of Neurology of the Mount Sinai School of Medicine, claims that out of the 202 explicit New Testament references to Jews, 80 are anti-Jewish. Can Christians claim not to be perpetuating anti-Semitism when they use in their religious education of children passages of Scripture still translated in such a way as to make "Jews" the enemies of Jesus, who is the embodiment of goodness, love, and charity?

There must be moderation and as much care as possible in the use of language. Since it is not always obvious what will disturb other people's sensibilities, an excellent test is to ask a representative group of people who are identified with the category under discussion and get their opinion as to whether a given generality about themselves is being validly used. . . . The issuance of an authoritative version of the scripture by a religious group is an act of more momentous social influence than is the enactment of most laws. Thus, it would not be out of place to consider the opinions of one's fellow men before deciding on those portions which will affect them. If it is to mean that more reservations and qualifications would have to be included to prevent the unjust slandering of innocent people, then it is worthwhile including them.[24]

Aware that it is a touchy matter to tamper with the scriptural word, Dr. Epstein shows that there is good precedent in already well-accepted translations and suggests synonyms for each of the eighty pejorative references. The most common synonym suggested is the term "Pharisee," and Epstein points out that there is no danger of merely transferring prejudice from one group (Jews) to another (Pharisees) since the latter term no longer designates any group in our contemporary culture.

In an essay on "The Elementary School and Ecumenism" Carl Pfeifer, S.J., spells out three basic attitudes that are radically Christian and ecumenical: objectivity, respect or reverence, and compassion. He calls objectivity the ability to see and face facts and truth as it is, independently of our previous convictions, prejudices, or fears. A love of truth, a love of life—these, he says, are ecumenical attitudes in depth. Reverence enables us to wonder at the immense goodness breaking through so much evil, the joy shining through such great sorrow, the gradual unification within so much diversity. He calls it an absolute condition for understanding and dialogue between those whose personal commitment to conflicting faiths and ideologies is deep and true. Objectivity and reverence should flower in compassion—responsiveness to the needs and troubles of all men. Here is where a child can learn the morality of Christ, whose only law is love, and whose life was but a day-to-day living out of effective compassion.[25]

A serious revamping of our attitudes calls upon us to re-examine all our educational materials both in the light of how well they set forth the positive aspects of the unity we possess, whether it be that of mankind or that of Christians, and as to the manner in which they present those common riches of the Christian faith. Do not the churches, when they speak of the church, speak too exclusively of themselves? Seldom is much attention given to the life of the churches together in the ecumenical movement and the vision of unity to which they are committed.

A study undertaken by the World Council of Churches suggests that if the present educational situation is to be improved, our curricula and educational programs should evidence the following: (1) an awareness of the fellowship of the churches together and an indication of the implications of this fellowship; (2) an awareness of how all churches (including one's own) are being changed by the ecumenical movement; (3) a taking seriously of other churches and an attempt to understand them adequately; (4) a recognition of the anomalous nature of our divided state along with an attempt to prepare people to live in it while striving to overcome it.[26]

A kind of examination of conscience follows for those charged with the responsibility of revising educational materials, and we might review our own attitudes in reponse to the questions posed. In the area of understanding the nature of ecumenical fellowship, how do we speak of the *gospel?* Is it made clear that this is not only the heart of Christian tradition, but that as such it gives us a basic unity with all Christians beyond the frontiers of the different churches? How do we speak of the *presence of Christ?* Is it made clear that Christ encounters us and works his salvation beyond the frontiers of the particular churches? Is it made clear that confession of him enables a denomination to cross these frontiers? How do we speak of *Scripture?* Is it made clear that our interpretations of Scripture are the starting points of all differences?[27]

Most churches use the *creeds* in worship and education. Are they used in such a way that the unity of faith we have with others is made clear? How do we define the relation between *church and churches?* How far is the individual church identified, expressly or implicitly, with *the* church of Christ? How far is the ecclesial reality of other churches recognized? How do we speak of *baptism?* Is it made clear that the fellowship of the baptized goes beyond the several churches and that therein unity is potentially given? How do we speak of the *Eucharist?* Is it made clear that other churches also offer real adoration and thanksgiving to God? How do we speak of the *history of the church?* Is it primarily, even exclusively, the events which constitute the individuality of our particular church that occupy our attention? Or is the activity of Christ in the history of all the churches made clear? Do we point out how much we have in common in the hymns and prayers we use—and how much they are all in question in our contemporary society?

Quite apart from doctrinal matters, we must give attention to understanding changes in our churches and our growing consensus. Does our educational material speak of *contentions* which belong to the past but which play no role today (e.g., indulgences, the monastic life, grace and works-righteousness)? Do our educational programs reflect the new consciousness of the *universality* of the church gained in the ecumenical movement? Is the new understanding of the *ministry of the laity* being adequately reflected, together with its consequences for worship and mission? Where there is consensus among the churches with regard to *contemporary problems* (e.g., war, racial division, economic justice), is discussion of such problems characterized by an awareness that here the churches speak together? Have our materials and teachings been examined to see whether, consciously or unconsciously, traces of anti-Semitism persist?[28]

Are the *pictures we give of other churches* such that they can be recognized by those churches? Do we seek, in so far as possible, to understand them as they understand themselves? Do we take into account *historical developments* and *renewal* in churches other than our own? Are doctrines and events which belong to their pasts presented in such a way that they do not distort our interpretation of the present situation?

Does our educational program help us to examine our own tradition critically as well as foster loyalty to it? Does our program provide for co-operation with others on the lines of the principle enunciated at the Lund Faith and Order Conference in 1952; viz., "that we should do together all that can be done together, and do separately only that which must be done separately"? Do we seek to provide a basis for helping our people to understand the problem of intercommunion? Finally, do we speak of the engagement of the churches in the ecumenical movement in such a way that we prepare people to be ready to take "next steps" and accept essential reforms even when the precise results cannot be known in advance?

The "Report" concludes with recommendations: (1) that a competent group of theological and historical scholars from every church be appointed to engage in a content analysis of the educational materials in use in that church in the light of the above questions; (2) that a similar group of educators be appointed to review the teaching procedures in use in the church to see whether method as well as material serves to communicate the actual present position of the church in these matters; (3) when educational materials are prepared, other churches should be requested to comment on any relevant parts: also, if possible and where reciprocity is assured, representatives of other traditions should be given the opportunity to present their own traditions in our texts.[29]

Factors in Attitudinal Change

When we speak of attitudes toward an ecumenical orientation, we are speaking mainly of changes that must be wrought rather than of an empty slate to be filled. We have looked at what precise attitudes we ought to eradicate and what positive ones we ought to adopt, but let us investigate briefly the factors which are in part responsible for our present feelings.

What is familiar to us forms an indispensable basis for our existence. It would probably come as a shock to many of us to discover exactly how much of what we take to be integral to our religious faith is merely a comfortable part of the familiarity we have with our particular church's manner of expressing itself either in creedal statements, preaching, or modes of worship. Our religious associations, like our family ties or local affiliations, constitute us an ingroup. Sociologists broadly define such a group as any cluster of people who can use the term "we" with the same essential significance. Provided that one does not rebel against his ingroup, it is here that he finds a certain security, perhaps even identity. Others outside the group become "they." It does not follow automatically that one's loyalty to the ingroup implies hostility or other forms of negativism toward outgroups, but the more defensiveness prevails within the group, the more relationships are cemented by the presence of a common enemy. Even when all defensiveness is overcome, the familiar is preferred, and what is alien is regarded as somehow inferior.

In the matter of religious affiliation it is clear that very strong ingroup pressures can be at work.[30] And the more narrowly one conceives his affiliation the more he relegates others to outgroups. Thus to conceive of oneself as an Irish American Catholic parishioner of St. X Church or a German Missouri-Synod Lutheran of the Walther League is to posit ethnic, national, parochial, and associational ingroup relations which are restricting rather than embracing. To designate "Christian" as one's primary ingroup is to enlarge enormously the "we."

One difficulty here is that ingroups grow weaker the larger their circle of inclusion. The potency of the membership becomes less as the distance from personal contact increases.

Such an image implies that a world-loyalty is the most difficult to achieve. There seems to be special difficulty in fashioning an in-group out of an entity as embracing as mankind. . . . Other languages and customs inevitably seem outlandish and, if not inferior, at least slightly absurd and unnecessary.

Such almost reflex preference for the familiar grips us all. . . . For persons neither imaginative nor well-traveled artificial props are needed. They require *symbols*—today almost lacking—in order to make the human ingroup seem real. . . .

There is no intrinsic reason why the outermost circle of membership needs to be the weakest. . . . It seems today that the clash between the idea of race and of One World is shaping into an issue that may well be the most decisive in human history.[31]

That Christians have failed to achieve such familiarity and to invent such symbols, to achieve any unanimity of will and action is painfully brought home to us by Camus's indictment that Christians by the millions, if they really wanted, could add their influence to isolated persons who, singly, are now interceding for children.

It is the mode of teaching which ordinarily stops the process of enlargement. Allport claims that most children never enlarge their sense of belonging beyond the ties of family, city, nation. How many enlarge their sense of religious belonging beyond the specific denomination of their church? The reason is that those with whom the child lives, and whose judgment he mirrors, do not do so.[32]

Linguistic factors also play a significant role in the forming of attitudes. Although ecumenical etiquette has weeded out the grosser forms of verbal abuse ("black Protestant," "perfidious Jews," "whore of Babylon," "papist plots," "monkish babblings," "treacherous heretics"), there are still labels which place undue emphasis on religious differences. Roman Catholics, for instance, do not relish being called "Romans"; likewise they must understand that they cannot expect to appropriate to their exclusive use the term "Catholic." Labels of primary potency lose some of their force when they are changed from nouns into adjectives. To speak of a Jewish artist or a Catholic teacher calls attention to the fact that some other group classifications are just as legitimate as the racial or religious. We have two attributes to know the person by, and two are more accurate than one. Allport suggests the useful rule that we designate ethnic and religious membership where possible with adjectives rather than with nouns.[33]

It is startling to discover how little real contact in the area of religion has gone on among vast sectors of the American population despite the staggering mobility of families, increased visibility by way of the communication media, and the extent of invitation proffered by church and synagogue groups to those of other religious persuasions. Roman Catholics especially have been cut off from association with their Protestant, Orthodox, and Jewish neighbors more than others in matters religious. The strict prohibition prevailing until quite recent times against active participation in, and even passive attendance (without preponderant reasons) at the worship services of others left most Catholics in abysmal ignorance of what their American neighbors were doing in Sabbath observances or Sunday morning assemblies for worship. By extension most Catholics avoided like the plague any radio sermons preached by Protestant ministers or Jewish rabbis or televised presentations in church or synagogue.

The Catholic parochial school system, which at one time made it possible for a youth to be educated by Catholic teachers and with Catholic students only from kindergarten through university, effectively cut off contact with those of other religious ideas. It is still not uncommon to find Catholics who grew up in homes where only Catholic friends and neighbors were known. Other religious educational systems have produced the same results. There are Lutheran families and Jewish families in which this same lack of contact has been the normal pattern.

We do not wish to imply that contact with various groups is a solution to prejudice, for it is a myth that the mere assembling of people without regard for race, color, religion, or national origin thereby destroys stereotypes and develops friendly attitudes. It is the nature of the contact that is important. Allport's studies led him to conclude that prejudice (unless deeply rooted in the character structure of the individual) may be reduced by equal status contact between majority and minority groups in the pursuit of common goals. The effect is greatly enhanced if this contact is sanctioned by institutional supports (i.e., by law, custom, or local atmosphere), and if it is of a sort that leads to the perception of common interests and common humanity between members of the two groups.[34]

Common ventures in religious education seem to be the ideal solution for abolishing the factors which contribute to the formation and maintenance of prejudice, for presenting "equal status contact in the pursuit of a common goal," and for achieving a strength of relationship with our fellows on a level which, if not worldwide, will at least raise us above our local, national, ethnic, or denominational ingroups. The real challenge to the churches is to see whether we wish to hear the call of the Lund principle, to do together all that we can do together, and to set seriously about seeing whether ecumenical religious education is one of these enterprises which can be done together. What would it mean if we were to do it?

Hoekendijk suggests a principle which might well guide us in our practical decisions.[35] He points out that the ordinary rules which guide the life of the church are suspended and that "exceptions" prevail when a situation is abnormal. The critical limit is passed (1) when we get into a "truly missionary situation"; (2) when we get into an "emergency situation" that was not foreseen and therefore could not be regulated beforehand; and (3) when we have passed the point of no return in our life and have arrived on the threshold of death. In these three cases, he says, the possibility usually is kept open to modify and adapt generally recognized and otherwise immutable rules of church order. Although the analysis which Hoekendijk offers was set forth in the context of dealing with the problem of intercommunion, it does not seem unrelated to the problems attendant upon ecumenical education.

In a missionary situation the presupposition holds sway that where men are for the first time faced with the gospel, theological distinctions and subtleties cannot be thought to have real priority. These fine points, the product of inner theological and ecclesiastical sophistication, can be deferred to a time when more "mature" conditions prevail. We make a mistake, however, if we suppose that a missionary situation must be located overseas. "Where the gospel comes, missionary situations originate, everywhere and always."[36] One who wants to speak authentically about a "missionary" situation has to know that he speaks about the whole world and the whole of history; in other words, about the normal setting of the church. Mission does not start at the walls of the church, but has its source at the very heart of the church. What is often admitted as an exception to the rule in a missionary situation (and then often demurely and with all kinds of ulterior thoughts) should be valid as the normal and acknowledged rule of church order.

Next Hoekendijk asks what the emergency could be which could not be foreseen and for which no regulations could be made beforehand. For a small flock of sheep sent into the midst of wolves emergencies cannot be a surprise. Refugees, church-in-diaspora, people in concentration camps, and congregations under the cross are what people have in mind when they talk about abnormal relations in which extraordinary measures may be taken. He suggests that we have all fallen into a state of emergency, where no end is in sight and in which not only individuals but whole generations live. Instead of looking upon our divisions in the church of Christ as normal, should we not view our disunity as a state of emergency in which "estrangement" has replaced suppression and persecution? And if this is the case, what dispensations may our generation expect?

The third situation in which rules break into pieces and denominational divisions are suspended is danger of death. Hoekendijk's thesis is that in the scope of our lives death has also become a normal element. On hearing the words *periculum mortis* scarcely anyone thinks of a composed deathbed for which one can prepare oneself with care and leisure. Rather the term brings to mind freak accidents, mine disasters, sudden landslides, violent explosions, unexpected heart attacks, prolonged and senseless war, and, overriding all these, the threat of the H-bomb and the forthcoming destruction of the world. The question is whether this changed attitude with regard to death and life should not have far-reaching consequences for permissible relaxations of strict rules.

What holds us back from applying emergency measures? Christians have settled into a denominational complacency and feel no compulsion to change the situation. If we could be jolted out of our complacency and ecclesiastical inertia and face up to the scandal which a divided church presents to the world, would we not dare apply these principles to areas of such obvious distress as religious education?

Taking Ecumenical Education Seriously: Challenges and Problems

Two options seem to lie open. One involves orientating the church and synagogue membership toward a stance which will affect religious education within each body by assuring an ecumenical slant to the materials used, introducing occasional speakers from other religious groups, broadening contacts, and consciously working for the improvement of attitudes. The other involves setting about religious education as a joint non-denominational enterprise. The first would mean the continuation of a religiously separated education strongly allied to an institutional commitment; the second would mean entering upon an uncharted course demanding a fresh preparation of materials, a restructuring of experiences as well as recruitment of personnel. (In such a venture one cannot speak of teachers and learners: All would be learners.) One is ecumenical orientation; the other is ecumenical education.

A working paper from the Catholic Council for Youth and Oikoumene of The Netherlands stipulates that religious education, if it is to be called ecumenical, must agree in some way with those criteria which are characteristic of the "new man." It must be actually and practically *existential* (related to men and events); *ecumenical* (related to the whole inhabited world and to each local place in which we live our own lives); *historical* (mindful of all that has happened, moving in the actuality of what is now happening, while grasping for the future which is ours); *liturgical* (useful and meaningful, ready to make sacrifices so that real signs of movement toward salvation will be established, possessing a flair for inventiveness).[37] We would wish to go a step further and insist that religious education is not truly ecumenical as long as it is given to homogeneous religious groups.

Occasional reference has been made in this chapter to the Jewish community although, in the strict sense of the word, ecumenism refers to the movement to heal the divisions of Christendom. Reference has also been made to those who have no religious affiliation as though any reaching out of the Christian community must embrace them as brothers and allies. For the moment, though, we wish to look exclusively at what ecumenical Christian education might mean. Is it possible for the churches to set aside the question of their own denominational identities and strengths and to concentrate on something larger, so large that they can tackle it only together— the presentation of the Christian gospel? Obviously there is a much more difficult problem for those churches who conceive of their ecclesiology as an essential part of the gospel, e.g., Roman Catholic, Orthodox. Is it possible for the churches to arrange a hierarchy of Christian values such that really divisive issues appear where they ought, far down on the list? This is not to call for a watering down of Christian teaching to a tasteless mass which everyone can accept. Quite the contrary. It is to act on Hoekendijk's principle that when we are in a missionary situation, an emergency situation, *in extremis*, priorities change. Those who knew they were in "abnormal" situations in prison camps or under fire are eager to tell us what has emerged as the really important Christian values in such a situation. Ecumenical faith, Visser 't Hooft says, is not the common denominator of what anyone at any time has believed, but the faith which was once delivered to the saints and which has remained the foundation of the church of Christ through the ages.[38]

More likely, the question is not how the churches are going to present an ecumenical religious education without prejudice to their own institutional strength, but how the churches together are going to educate for change, for progress, for freedom. The church is a preserver of the status quo, and in an era when the status quo presents a situation patently and grossly unjust to millions of persons, the church cannot stand without blame. If she has done nothing to create it (a dubious premise to some), it is very clear that she has done little to educate her members to change it. The shocking conclusion of sociological studies shows that there is a positive correlation between the intensity of religious training in general and prejudice. Individuals having no religious affiliation show on the average less prejudice than do church members.

This information happily does not stand without qualification. Studies show that those who have interiorized their religion have much more openness than those whose outlook can be called "institutionalized."[39] The former are those who through a personal and authentic acceptance have taken the—in this case—Christian message and integrated it so wholesomely into their modes of thinking and acting as to be truly free. They are not motivated by an unthinking conformity to commands imposed from without, by a merely habitual regularity in religious practice, nor by a mere notional assent to doctrines. "Institutionalized" Christians, as the title indicates, act in certain ways because the institutional church approves and accepts these ways. Belonging to the ingroup demands this kind of conduct or fosters these kinds of attitudes. Such persons are under pressure in their deepest yearnings, and although they are free from external duress to maintain or sever their membership in their particular church, they are not truly liberated within themselves.

If religious education hopes to form the first kind of Christian, may we not hope that an ecumenical educational experience will have much more chance of doing it than that religious education which, however much it tries not to be, has been institution-centered? Confessional loyalties are not without value and one would make a serious error in thinking that they ought to be abandoned forthwith.[40] Besides the fact that this is not possible, even if it were thought desirable, we would be forgetting our community history and family tradition if we were to renounce our confessional loyalty. But everyone agrees that loyalty to Christ takes precedence over any other loyalty, and the point we would like to make here is that it is the formation of Christ in his members that religious education ought to concern itself with. Other and choice occasions abound where commitment to the institutional church and her manner of ordering the faith and life of her members can be intensified. The family environment is one such arena and the Christian worship service is another. Formal programs of education, however, on whatever level ought to be truly non-denominationally Christian.

If the factors which have influenced this position seem non-theological, they at least have the merit of not yet having been proved wrong. Moreover, they speak to the fact that no church claims to have solved to its satisfaction the problems inextricably bound up with religious education. In fact, one can scarcely find an area of greater agreement than the gloomy admission that no one has discovered a program which is guaranteed to turn out an informed, witnessing Christian. Can we not, then, attempt to do together what we have failed to do in our religious isolation? May we not even attribute our failure in part to the fact that as divided Christians we have not been able to speak credibly about the universality of the church? Born in a rupture of continuity with the past, as Max Thurian says, we became diversified in a plurality of groups, of which no single one can consider itself "the church." Each is part, and all of them together are part of the entire church. It is normal that each ecclesiastical group, despite the division, feel the need of being open to others in order to live in certitude of the church's universality.[41]

B. *by* HOWARD GRIMES

To DEAL WITH Protestant attitudes toward an ecumenical orientation for religious education is an exceedingly complex matter. While the historic diversity of Protestantism lies at the basis of the complexity, there are other complicating factors. For example, the differences within one communion are now often greater than those existing between historically separated communions. There are, in fact, such wide diversities within the present religious scene that is both difficult and dangerous to generalize concerning almost any matter of church thought and life, and the ecumenical concern is not excluded.

Before proceeding further, we must note the ways in which the word "ecumenical" is used in this chapter. Although the original meaning of the Greek word *oikoumene,* from which "ecumenical" derives, was "the inhabited earth," the word has taken on special meaning in our time. For Protestants of recent years, it has meant the impulse and movement toward unity between the various Protestant communions, with the more recent addition of the Orthodox churches to the movement. Its institutional expression has been the conciliar movement, on a local, state, national, and world basis. Since the first years of Vatican II, the word "ecumenical" has taken on additional meaning for Protestants. It now often refers to the movement toward the efforts on behalf of the unity of all Christian groups, including the Roman Catholic Church.

The word is also used in other, and broader, ways. Occasionally it is used to include the Jewish community. Some use the word with still broader connotations to include all believers (that is, those who believe in God) in their relationships with the non-believing world.

I shall use it in this chapter primarily to denote those efforts of Protestant groups to work together, both historically and at the present time, and for the larger efforts of all Christians together, including the Orthodox and Roman Catholics. Either the context of its use or a direct statement will be necessary at times for the specific use to be understood.

A Complex Issue

The causes and the solutions to religious divisions are characterized by extreme diversity. Since these factors influence ecumenical religious education, we must at least take brief account of them.

The most obvious force at work in both division and unity is the theological factor. Persons and groups differ widely with regard to the interpretation of the biblical message even when they agree that the message of the Bible is the basis for theology. These differences range from major disagreements concerning the nature of Jesus Christ to relatively minor ones such as the method of receiving the Lord's Supper. Such differences are significant in teaching since either implicitly or explicitly all religious teaching is theological.

Interestingly, differences are often intradenominational or intraconfessional rather than interdenominational or interconfessional. There are "fundamentalists" within both Protestantism and Roman Catholicism, and although they do not agree concerning the fundamentals, their general approach is similar. There are also "liberals" within both groups—that is, those who are both willing and often anxious to discard many of the traditional beliefs of Christian faith. In most groups there are also those of a liberal spirit even among the theological conservatives. There are likewise those concerned with the manifestation and actualization of unity as there are also those opposed to the implementation of such unity. Especially among Protestant denominations, the more divisive theological factors no longer necessarily follow denominational lines.

Social factors are also both divisive and unitive. H. Richard Niebuhr showed some years ago how they worked in the formation of American denominations.[1] Both the Oxford and Edinburgh conferences of 1937, forerunners of the World Council of Churches, took the social factors into account. Recent writers have pointed to similar factors as they contribute both to division and to unity.[2] It is probable that such factors will become more intense if present trends toward a secular society continue.

Attitudes toward ecumenicity are also partly determined by economic and political views. Much of the opposition to the National Council of Churches, for example, is due to the political and economic pronouncements made by constituent elements of the National Council. Any executive of a council of churches must at times weigh the relative values of his agency's speaking or acting on an important social issue and the effect that the action will have on the support of the ecumenical enterprise as a movement toward the unity of the church.

How these differences and similarities operate within communions and across their boundaries can be illustrated in many ways. Four illustrations will suffice. In a meeting on evangelism at the Ecumenical Institute in Celigñy, Switzerland, some years ago, the real division was not between the historic Protestant groups represented; rather it was between the representatives from the newer nations and those from the older ones. Those from the newer nations found it difficult to understand the European problem of estrangement of church and people. Other misunderstandings arose. Apparently, however, the division ran even deeper and involved former colonial policies, for in one meeting a delegate from a new nation felt so strongly that he left the room.

At a convention of the Religious Education Association several years ago, a Catholic priest and a sister from the same church engaged in a rather violent argument in a discussion group concerning educational theory. One was an ardent follower of John Dewey; the other was just as anti-Dewey. Most of us found ourselves somewhat between the two, but not aligned according to denominational affiliation.

In a meeting including Jews, Catholics, and Protestants, with the purpose of discussing the possibilities for lay activity within the Armed Forces, the Catholic representatives upheld a position which would have granted fairly broad powers to laymen, under certain circumstances, to perform church rites. On the other hand, a representative of a Protestant group that traditionally has granted broad authority to the laity opposed the move.

The fourth example concerns a discussion between a Protestant clergyman and educator and a Roman Catholic diocesan worker in Christian education. The subject was interpreting Easter to children. The two found themselves in such general agreement that the discussion tended to become too one-sided. The reason, I am sure, was that both were hiers of similar educational traditions even though they belonged to quite different religious traditions.

It is not easy, therefore, to generalize concerning attitudes and practices regarding ecumenism since there is so much variety within the Christian groups. One cannot always predict who will agree with whom on what issues.

Ecumenicity and Religious Education

The factors that operate on all levels of ecumenicity are complicated by those unique to religious education. Whatever else such education is understood to be, there is always, I believe, at least some degree of induction involved in it. That is, it is concerned with the introduction of the younger members of the community to the perspective from which that community views life. Although the inducting aspects of education are usually stronger in conservative groups (because they consider it crucial that the young adhere to the faith of the fathers), I believe that they also operate in less rigid forms of faith education. It is likely, for example, that a liberal group such as the Unitarian-Universalists will want to introduce their children to the character of their tradition and its background. Induction cannot be neutral or objective even though it may seek to be fair and unprejudiced.

I do not mean to imply that religion cannot be taught as any controversial academic subject, such as political science, is taught. The teaching carried out from purely academic motives is different from that of a faith community, however. A religious community will either consciously or unconsciously want to introduce the younger members of that community to the approach that the community has found helpful. The amount of indoctrination will depend upon how essential for the welfare of the individual and/or society the group considers the religious thought and practice of the community to be.

This means, then, that when we consider the teaching that a religious faith community does, we face problems that do not necessarily operate in the ecumenical outreach of that community in other ways. Traditionally, worship has been one key stumbling block between Protestants and Catholics. Since this has begun to break down—partly because most religious groups have recognized more fully both the validity and the value of various traditions in worship—teaching may now be a more acute problem. It is in the community's teaching that we believe the formation of attitudes, ideas, and practices takes place. It may be that we expect more of formal teaching than it actually delivers, since the principal formation of the child and youth most likely takes place in less formal settings, including the family and peer groups. Whether this be the case or not, nevertheless, we still hope that part of the process of formation occurs in whatever formal teaching the community does, and we are therefore likely to guard its shape rather carefully.

It is difficult, therefore, for Protestant groups even of similar persuasions to give up their own distinctive teaching. It will be more difficult when the Orthodox-Protestant, Protestant-Catholic, or Catholic-Orthodox lines in teaching are bridged.

Religious groups, therefore, face an almost insoluble dilemma with regard to their identity as communities and their induction of the young into those communities on the one hand, and their relationship to other religious communities on the other. Religious groups are, in a sense, extended families. The more self-conscious a family is, the more likely it is to do an adequate job of introducing the children of the family to the traditions of that family. So with a religious community: The very factors which make of it an effective group can also make of it one which is concerned with its own tradition in relation to other traditions in an unhealthy way. The ingroup-outgroup phenomenon, characteristic of all societal organization, provides an individual with a sense of belonging in relation to a social grouping, and at the same time tends to put him in opposition against members of a "rival" community.

Religious prejudice may be fostered even when one group is quite willing, even anxious, to practice tolerance with regard to other religious groups. Such prejudice may creep in by innuendo, or even be implied simply in the stating of a conviction. This is to say that the first step in developing ecumenicity in religious education is for religious groups to be more self-conscious about their own faith, their attitudes toward other religious groups. This self-consciousness provides at least a beginning point for relationships with other groups.

It is also to suggest that in the growing ecumenical activities, including teaching, ways must be found for expressing both unity and diversity. I am convinced that one of the unrealistic and harmful assumptions that many religious groups make is that there is something inherently wrong with disagreement and conflict. Rather what is wrong is the unwillingness to face and deal with conflict creatively. Part of ecumenical education, then, will include help in facing up to the reality of disagreement and conflict, and means of dealing with conflict when it arises.

Emerging Structures for Religious Education

Although Chapter One deals with the history of education in America, we cannot avoid historical data as we consider the issues of this chapter. We shall therefore turn to historical information especially relevant to this chapter to show that, in the past, education has to some extent been oriented on a pan-Protestant basis. In fact, more has been done in line with this orientation that one might expect to find.

So long as Christendom remained intact, the teaching of religion was no problem. Even after the breakdown of Christendom and the growth of Protestantism in Western Europe and later in America, a problem still did not arise. Generally a nation or some portion thereof (as in the case of Germany) followed a particular kind of Christianity, and that faith was taught in whatever general education existed. The Jewish group, of course, worked out its own religious teaching with whatever freedom the nation of which it was a part allowed.

The original pattern of education and religion in the American colonies duplicated that of the mother countries. The most tightly controlled plan was that of New England, where the common school originated. Although these schools were publicly supported, they were church-controlled, in this instance by the Congregationalists. The Middle Colonies were more divided, and hence educational opportunities were usually controlled by the prevailing religious group in a section of the colony. Most education in the Southern colonies was under the auspices of the predominant Church of England.

After 1787, however, the pattern developed in quite a different way. This development was partly due to the increasing heterogeneity of the population and the consequent religious pluralism. It was due also to the principle of separation of church and state as included in the Bill of Rights and the ensuing emergence of the religious group as a voluntary institution to which people belonged not by virtue of geographical residence but because of personal preference.

In this milieu two approaches to teaching religion emerged. On the one hand there is the Christian day or parochial school, a pattern which has been developed extensively by the Roman Catholic Church and by groups such as the Missouri Synod Lutherans and the Seventh-Day Adventists. The more common pattern in Protestantism, however, is a second form, in which the *congregation* assumes responsibility for formal religious instruction. This pattern emerged in the form of the Sunday school, originally a separate institution with religious motivation. It was later adopted by the church and gradually assumed its more extensive form known as the church school, with its Sunday and weekday forms, but still controlled by the congregation.

A similar structure emerged in the Jewish community, in which the synagogue assumed responsibility for its own religious school —not to provide for the total education of the child but to supplement public school education through the teaching of religion. All of these patterns assume in one degree or another that the family is the primary agency for teaching religion to children.

The Sunday School

William B. Kennedy points to three major periods in the development of the American Sunday school, the principal Protestant structure for church education.[3] In its *first* phase, in both England and America, the Sunday school was literally a Sunday school for the teaching of the rudiments of learning to poor children who worked during the week.[4] As child labor became less common and public schools burgeoned in America, the purpose of the Sunday school began to change. It became, during its *second* period in the early nineteenth century, a non-denominational religious adjunct to the increasingly non-sectarian public school. Although the common schools continued to teach considerable Bible and were strong in their moral emphasis, such teaching became increasingly non-sectarian as society became more pluralistic in character.

For our inquiry the significant aspect of this movement is that it was a non-denominational agency.[5] I use the term "non-denominational" quite deliberately, for the Sunday school unions that sponsored the Sunday schools were usually controlled by laymen from various denominations, and they were not interdenominational efforts. The first such Sunday school society was formed in 1791, though it did not operate continuously. In 1816 the New York Society began, and a year later the Philadelphia Sunday and Adult School Union got under way. In 1824 these unions were combined to form a national society, known as the American Sunday School Union. (In England the first national society began two decades earlier.) The American Sunday School Union, a non-denominational agency, issued lesson materials that were used extensively by Sunday schools throughout the land.

One of the reasons that such a high degree of co-operation could develop was the character of the teaching carried out by the Sunday schools. As Kennedy has pointed out,[6] the American Sunday School Union served almost as a denomination itself, though its approach to Christian faith was so simple that most Protestant groups found its "common faith" acceptable. That interpretation of faith, similar to that of the revivalism which was also occurring, emphasized conversion and the living of a life of conventional morality, consisting of such virtues as honesty, truthfulness, purity, kindness, and the like. Revivalism itself tended to play down denominationalism, especially on the frontier, and since the Sunday school often preceded the establishment of an organized church, the two movements—revivalism and the Sunday school—were closely related.

Denominational reaction to the Sunday school had ranged from fairly enthusiastic support to downright opposition. By the 1820s, however, the denominations were beginning to adopt the Sunday school. By the 1840s, the Sunday school had become a regular part of most of the churches, and the denominations began to establish their own "unions." The American Sunday School Union continued, but the domination of the Sunday school shifted to the denominations by the close of the Civil War. Thus the *third* period of the Sunday school movement came to fruition from the 1860s onward, that is, the denominational phase.

Although denominational curriculum materials became increasingly common, the interchurch pattern of work also continued. For one thing, the lay movement that had led to the American Sunday School Union persisted, leading in 1875 to the First International Sunday School Convention and in 1889 to the World's First Sunday School Convention, in London. Out of the first of these movements emerged the International Sunday School Association in 1905, while out of the latter grew the World's Sunday School Association in 1907, now the World Council of Christian Education and Sunday School Association.

The International Sunday School Association remained largely lay-dominated and non-denominational. Nor did it respond to the more liberal educational and theological currents that were developing in mainline Protestantism at the turn of the century. Increasingly the denominations were also developing professional staffs for the direction of their national religious education enterprises, and these staff professionals formed the Sunday School Council of the Evangelical Denominations in 1910. This group, unlike the International Sunday School Association, was interdenominational (in that it represented various Protestant denominations), chiefly professional, and stood for change in approaches, methods, and curriculum for the Sunday school.

The two groups existed side-by-side for a time, and were then merged into the International Sunday School Council of Religious Education in 1922. Having been renamed the International Council of Religious Education two years later, it became one of the constituent groups of the National Council of Churches of the Churches of Christ in the U.S.A. on its formation. The more progressive and interdenominational agency had prevailed, and thenceforth mainline Protestantism accepted as normative the interdenominational agency that had emerged out of the Sunday school movement, now controlled by professionals rather than laymen.

Curriculum Materials

In the meantime significant changes were occurring in the field of curriculum materials. Out of a period of great variety and much uncertainty developed the International Uniform Lessons, which began in 1872. The process of their development was as thoroughly ecumenical as any Protestant enterprise of the time. Planned originally by a committee of five clergymen and five laymen under the auspices of the National Sunday School Convention, the outlines were used by churches in any way they saw fit. Later, in the first decade of the twentieth century, closely graded materials especially designed for children and youth were prepared, also on an interdenominational basis.

Two plans have been followed with respect to curriculum materials for congregational use. The less common pattern has consisted of the production and publication of the materials by the ecumenical agency. The more common pattern has been the interdenominational production of outlines and descriptions of units of study that are then used by the denominations with their own peculiar adaptations. Some materials are still published interdenominationally—for example, texts for leadership education courses and materials for use in vacation church schools are prepared by committees of the National Council of Churches and published by the Cooperative Publishing Association, which consists of denominational publishing houses. A new weekday series is a joint enterprise prepared and printed in the same manner.

The co-operative venture in curriculum building began to break down in the 1940s. Although during the two or three decades prior to this time, fewer and fewer communions used the International Lesson outlines for groups other than adults, many still continued to use the Group Graded Series (graded departmentally) and the Closely Graded Series (prepared for separate grades of children and youth). By the 1960s, however, the only curriculum outlines being developed on an interdenominational basis were the International Lesson Series. In the meantime two interdenominational projects had helped to develop foundational work for curriculum building, under the Division of Christian Education of the National Council of Churches: the Cooperative Curriculum Project and the Cooperative Curriculum Development.[7]

The reasons for this change are difficult to determine. Perhaps the foremost one was the ferment that had developed in the 1940s in the field of church education, caused especially by the movement in theology generally called "neo-orthodoxy." The ongoing process of interdenominational curriculum building did not respond to this and other changes as quickly as it might. But there is another, somewhat disturbing reason. At the time that ecumenicity was developing at a fast rate in the life of Protestant churches, there was also a tendency for separate communions to assert their distinctiveness. Since, as we have seen, the Sunday school tended toward a moralistic, non-theological approach to Christian faith, there was a general rejection in the light of these developments of what has sometimes been derisively called "Sunday school religion." While the fairly shallow kind of ecumenism that had prevailed proved inadequate, the denominations often reacted to a deeper kind of ecumenical thinking by asserting their own integrity.

Other Movements

What we have considered thus far has pertained fairly directly to the Sunday school movement. There were other movements, however, concerned with religious education on a non-denominational or transdenominational basis. For example, the Young Men's Christian Association, originally an educational agency in part, had its origin in London in 1844, with the first association being established in the United States in 1851. "One of the driving forces of the

YMCA movement from the beginning," writes Paul Limbert, one-time general secretary of the World Alliance of the YMCAs, "was a desire for greater unity among Christians."[8] The Young Women's Christian Association, with similar aims for young women, dates from a few years later.

These two groups were responsible for the first organized voluntary student work, which therefore was interdenominational (or perhaps non-denominational). Out of this original work emerged various student organizations, the first of which was the Student Volunteer Movement in 1888. Although the scope of the student movement has always been more extensive than religious education in a narrow sense, its work has always included study. Moreover, its educational impact has not been confined to its study program as such, since the contacts with members belonging to other Protestant groups has been one of its more effective means of ecumenical education.

Related to the ecumenical student movements has been another, of special importance because it has helped to provide an ecumenical orientation for the ordained leadership of the churches. The first ecumenical gathering on the seminary level was convened in 1880, at New Brunswick, New Jersey, with some 250 seminary students in attendance. Its initial concern was missionary. In 1898 the movement became the theological section of the YMCA, while later the Interseminary Movement in the United States was organized as a separate group. Still later it was incorporated into the National Council of Churches.

It is therefore clear that ecumenical efforts in education, at least on a Protestant basis, are of long duration. Although the most dramatic expression of ecumenical work has probably been in the field of the world mission of the church, the significance of the agencies devoted primarily or partly to teaching should not be underestimated. It seems clear to me that in the writing of ecumenical history, these movements have not been given their proper place in the developing of ecumenical attitudes and practices.

The movements and organizations thus far used as illustrations of past ecumenical religious education have been primarily Protestant. Two additional movements, on a broader basis, require brief comment. One of these is the Religious Education Association, organized in 1903, and involving Protestants, Catholics, and Jews. During the first sixty years of its life Protestants generally dominated, though never completely controlled, the organization. At the convention held in 1966, Roman Catholics constituted 75 percent of the more than one thousand official delegates, the largest number ever to attend an REA convention. The Jewish group was small, only 4 percent, the Eastern Orthodox 1 percent, and the Protestant 20 percent.[9]

The second of these organizations is the National Conference of Christians and Jews, founded in 1927. Although it has been only a quasireligious organization, its intention has been to break down prejudices between the three major religious groups in the United States. Its educational efforts have generally been pitched on the factual and psychological levels rather than on the theological.

During and since World War II the more conservative Protestant groups have organized interdenominationally. The National Association of Evangelicals, begun in 1942 and consisting of thirty-eight denominations, many small, is not directly related to religious education though two of its affiliates are. One of these is the National Sunday School Association, charged with the provision of curriculum outlines of a more conservative bent. The other is the National Association of Christian Schools, whose purpose is to promote Christian day schools.

Other Recent Developments

Considerable ecumenical activity, usually on a Protestant basis only, is carried out through local, state, national, and world councils of churches. Some communities still have interdenominational schools for teacher education, for example. Ecumenical youth councils, both for education, projects, and ecumenical contacts, are fairly common. Some of these now include Roman Catholic young people. Group life laboratories, for sensitivity training and a study of the working of groups, have often been sponsored ecumenically. Many, perhaps most, of these and numerous similar enterprises are for church leaders and do not involve general religious education.

Perhaps a case study of one state council of churches, both what it did and the problems it faced, may be illuminating at this point.[10]

The philosophy on which the division of christian education of this state council operated was that it should not duplicate what the denominations were already doing. One exception was the ecumenical youth council, whose main activity each year was a week-long institute in a camp setting. The purpose of this enterprise was considered primarily that of providing contacts across denominational, and later faith, lines for young people.

Financial support was a recurring problem. The council of churches was limited in what it could do, partly for lack of money to subsidize activities and partly because staff was not available to supervise them. Those who gave voluntary leadership to the various departments of the division were limited in time, since they, with few if any exceptions, were busy on denominational enterprises of one kind or another. It was also difficult to secure publicity, since the denominational educational executives were often so busy with their own church affairs that they could not see their way clear to "promoting" an additional activity, regardless of how worthy it might be. In this case, as in many others, the problem of ecumenical action was not so much opposition as preoccupation with denominational affairs.

In spite of these and other problems, several worthwhile enterprises were held during a period of seven years. These included: a conference on aging, three group life labs, a conference on children with special needs, two conferences for adults in the youth ministry, a conference for campus ministries, and regular meetings of public school teachers and administrators to consider the matter of religion and public education. The response to the latter, where promotion was through the public schools and not the churches, was unusually good and only the lack of money and staff time prevented its being a more significant enterprise.

As in the case of similar enterprises in the past, two separate purposes were fulfilled. On the one hand, training was provided for a limited number of leaders, usually, though not always, in some specialized area of religious education. The second function the enterprises served was to bring persons from different communions together and thus increase the exposure of these individuals, some quite provincial in their background, to persons of other religious groups in matters dealing specifically with religion.

Ecumenicity and the Congregation

It is difficult to assess either the importance of or the response to the kind of ecumenical education which has been described. It is often not opposition which limits the support of and participation in such enterprises; it is, rather, indifference, and this indifference exists especially in areas (such as the one described in the case study of previous paragraphs) where there are strong Protestant churches and where organized religion still seems to be prospering.

In spite of the difficulties in drawing conclusions, I shall attempt to do so with regard to ecumenical religious education of the past and present. First, there has been considerably more interdenominational activity than one might suppose. This was true in the nineteenth century; it continues into the present. But a second conclusion must follow, namely, that it has been primarily Protestant. This is increasingly being changed since Vatican II, and the situation probably will be vastly different in the decades ahead.

A third conclusion is that most of this ecumenical activity has taken place beyond the congregation or parish. Much in the nineteenth century took place on a national level, and by the time it filtered down to the congregation it had taken on a distinctly denominational slant. Increasingly, activity occurs on the state and local levels, though this too is often not directly related to congregations and parishes.

A fourth and similar conclusion is that most ecumenical education has dealt only with leadership for the church. That is, it has consisted to a great extent of training for various leadership roles and functions, and very little of it has pertained to general theological, biblical, or even humanistic education. There are exceptions, some of which have been noted, but I believe the generalization is a fair one.

Fifth—and this is the most significant conclusion of all—the denominations have generally reigned supreme on the congregational or parish level. Here also there have been exceptions: Vacation church schools have often been conducted interdenominationally. Released time is almost always pan-Protestant. Ecumenical youth councils have operated even across confessional lines. Such efforts have been sporadic in most instances, and they are, unfortunately, happy exceptions. Although the culture, with its amalgamating and secularizing tendencies, discourages religious particularity, the various communions have done but little to educate their members into an intelligent facing of religious differences and similarities.

The Need for Ecumenical Education

"The critical issue concerning ecumenical education is not whether it shall be but only what kind it shall be."[11] Thus spoke Eugene B. Borowitz, Professor of Jewish Education at Hebrew Union College in New York, at the Religious Education Association convention in 1966. He went on to point out what is an increasing fact of American society—the personal confrontation of individuals representing diverse religious and cultural orientations. These orientations are increasingly not just Jewish-Christian: They involve also religions of the East and a wide variety of cults often patterned after the Eastern religions.

Not only does the existence of cultural pluralism call us to rethink the narrow provincialism of much of our church education in the past; the decreasing influence of organized religion *forces* us to do so. We noted earlier that one form of ecumenical thinking aligns "believers" in their confrontation with "non-believers." An increasing secularism, which makes of a non-theistic approach to life a religious faith, provokes the adherents of most of the traditional religions to some degree of conversation. I am not thinking here only, or even primarily, of organized atheistic efforts such as Marxism, but rather of those movements which either deny the reality of God altogether or make into a god some temporary expression of reality, such as an economic theory, a nation, or a set of political beliefs.

This broader ecumenicity is possible because of the common and divine origin of man. The doctrine of creation makes world brotherhood and brotherliness not only possible but necessary for those of the Jewish-Christian tradition. Philip Scharper put it quite trenchantly in an address at the Religious Education Association convention in 1966: "Regardless of whether those who do not share the Judaeo-Christian view of man recognize themselves as sons of

God, we recognize them as such, and can only speak of and to them as our brother, whose dignity we have neither designed nor given, and with whose destiny we are not allowed to tamper."[12]

From many quarters there comes this urgent call to a broader ecumenicity in the years ahead. While the emerging world makes education of a different character imperative, the patterns that will follow are more confused because we are not prepared to cope with the changes. All we can do in the remainder of this chapter is to point to six proposals which give some indication of the possible character of that education in the years ahead.

Proposal One: Education Without Prejudice

On the most elemental basis, those responsible for all levels of religious education must continue to eliminate prejudicial statements from curriculum materials and teaching. We are concerned in this chapter primarily with interreligious relationships and education. An equally urgent—in many ways more urgent—matter concerns relationships with and therefore prejudicial writing concerning ethnic groups. Although many years of efforts have gone into the attempt to eliminate, or at least seriously curtail, prejudice, the case is not yet settled, nor perhaps will it ever be.

The most extensive recent study of intergroup attitudes in church school materials is that made in the 1950s by Bernhard Olson. It involved a detailed analysis of the materials of four groups —Unitarian-Universalist, United Presbyterian in the U.S.A., Missouri Synod Lutheran, and the non-denominational Scripture Press. The details of the study do not concern us here; two of Olson's findings do.

First, he found evidence in all of the materials, in differing degrees, of intergroup prejudices.[13] The second finding—and this is of special significance for our concern in this chapter—is that those whose curriculum materials were examined were more than willing to listen to his findings. "A promising omen," he writes, "is the fact that the Protestants involved in this study have been open to receiving these findings without defensiveness and with an eagerness to make needed changes in their curricula."[14]

Proposal Two: Dialogue Between Separated Groups

In spite of the pluralism that has existed in American society for over a century, many people have grown up in a restricted and provincial atmosphere. My own boyhood was not altogether untypical in many parts of the United States a few decades ago. I lived in a Protestant community where one generally avoided religious subjects outside one's own religious group except when they were sufficiently general not to be controversial. There was a Catholic church, but there were no Catholic young people in the public schools. There were a few Jews, but my own contact with them was through occasional purchases at the two stores they owned. I must confess with considerable embarrassment that my culture remained primarily Protestant but increasingly ecumenically Protestant until I served in the Armed Forces during World War II.

Fewer children grow up in such a provincial atmosphere today; yet their contacts with members of other ethnic and religious groups often remain on a superficial level. Increasingly over the last few decades, both planned and unplanned efforts have increased the level of participation. This has been due partly to the wider informal contacts across religious and ethnic lines. It is partly due to structured opportunities for discussion of ideas. Such efforts as the ecumenical youth councils, the Interseminary Movement for seminary students, and various interfaith discussion groups have contributed to the progress of this greater understanding. The most recent effort in this direction is the "Living Room Dialogues" sponsored by the Confraternity of Christian Doctrine of the Roman Catholic Church and the National Council of Churches.

Sometimes such groups remain on the ideational level. It is important to consider where we both agree and disagree, but ecumenicity cannot be built on this basis alone. What is needed is dialogue—that is, a relationship which transcends talk and draws two people together because of their willingness to listen and to be honest in what they say both in words and in non-verbal means of communication. In other words, ecumenical education takes place partly, and perhaps on its deepest level, as two persons relate meaningfully to one another.[15]

Too often we show an interest in another person's beliefs but not in him as a person. One of the refreshing dimensions of working with an ecumenical youth council (Protestant and Catholic) was the personal acceptance of these high school youths of one another. Often I was embarrassed at what seemed to me to be their insensitivity (probably lack of knowledge) concerning each other's beliefs. They needed to discuss their beliefs, but they had something that is more important than intellectual agreement: They had a will to unity which showed great impatience with their adult sponsors when they raised practical questions that, at least for the adults, seemed essential for the ongoing life of the council.

Dialogue may emerge through common work. Ecumenical work camps have led to some of the deepest levels of relationships. Albert van den Heuvel called for engagement in mission to the world in an address before the Religious Education Association in 1966. Concentration on a discussion of differences, he pointed out, usually causes hardened disagreements, while concentration on what unites us usually "creates the uncomfortable agreement of people who know the surprising measure of their unity but who do not know how to apply their agreement." "Only," he went on to say, "if we learn to theologize and worship as one body-in-service, will we understand the true scope of our disunity and the strength of our unity. Our common service and witness form the only reliable tools for establishing the real dimensions of our unity and division."[16]

Proposal Three: Common Educational Enterprises

My third proposal involves nothing new, for, as we have seen, a great deal of common educational effort by the churches has taken place in the past. Most of this effort has concerned the education of leadership for functional tasks, and there is every reason why such efforts should continue and be increased. In many such efforts, Jews and Christians can join: for example, in a group life lab (or enterprise in sensitivity training). Innovations in education affect general, synagogue, and church education in similar ways. Educational methodology is changing so rapidly that both the expense and the effort of keeping up necessitate the religious groups' working on methodology together. Much leadership education can and should be done in common.

Protestant congregational education may be done in a better manner in many situations if denominations pool their resources. This is obvious in a small community, with two, three, or even four struggling Sunday schools; it might be equally true in an urban community. For example, several downtown churches might carry on a youth ministry co-operatively. Churches in the inner city may need to join in common educational endeavors even when they are not joined together in organic unity. Churches might plan youth ministries around high school affiliation rather than congregational identity, since the lives of young people so clearly revolve around their school experience.

Such joint educational enterprises imply that we are willing to risk institutional success in order to achieve more in dealing with persons. Unfortunately, many congregations are not yet willing to take such risks. We are often too concerned with institutional self-maintenance to place persons above institutions. If present trends in religious disaffiliation continue, however, we may be driven by circumstances to such ecumenical efforts.

As churches move nearer to some form of unity, the areas of co-operative effort will naturally increase. "Flexibility in co-operation" is the principle that has been adopted by the Christian Education Committee of the Consultation on Church Union.[17] It is accepted that all ten participating denominations will work together in the immediate future on certain problems; for example, they will consider educational strategies and important decision points where it is urgent that there be no overlapping of efforts. Other activities will be carried on by fewer groups; for example, some clusters are already sharing curriculum materials, and it is expected that this activity will increase in the future. It may be that separate congregations will maintain their identity even after some form of union is achieved; for example, there may be a First Presbyterian and a First Methodist congregation on opposite corners; what they do in common will increase; duplication of efforts will diminish; and thus the quality of their work will be improved.

Proposal Four: Religion and Public Education

The proposals to make possible some relationship between religion and public education cannot be discussed here. Probably the most common is that suggested by Mr. Justice Clark in connection with his opinion declaring unconstitutional the mandatory reading of the Bible in the public schools of Pennsylvania. He not only made clear that the decision did *not* include a negative response to the inclusion of religion in appropriate ways in the general curriculum; he also declared that adequate education *must* include due recognition of the place of religion in American culture.

For our purposes, it is not appropriate to support any one proposal concerning the relationship of religion and public education. The significant thing is that the problem can never be solved except on an ecumenical basis. There has been a surprisingly small amount of free discussion by religious groups of the issues and possibilities involved. The point has been established, rightly, I believe, that the public schools cannot favor any one religion nor develop their own (as the New York Regents' prayer was in danger of doing). We have been told what can *not* be done; we have hardly begun to explore on an ecumenical basis what *can* and *ought* to be done in the face of recent Supreme Court decisions. Such discussion must occur on the broadest possible ecumenical basis, and the religious education that results should be also broadly ecumenical.

Proposal Five: Curriculum Development

We have already noted that much common curriculum development was carried out during the nineteenth and early twentieth centuries. Although there has been less of this common effort within recent years than formerly, it has not ceased to be. Curriculum design received the attention of the Cooperative Curriculum Project in the 1960s. Vacation church school materials, weekday materials, and materials for special groups such as the inner city are either being done or are projected on an inter-Protestant basis.

There is the possibility that a common curriculum will be developed in the future for those communions entering unions such as that proposed by the Consultation on Church Union. Instead of a common curriculum, however, I believe that we are more likely to see co-operative development of curriculum resources. Rather than having one curriculum, or even a common outline, to be followed by every congregation, I think we are more likely to provide several designs, and a variety of resources from which congregations can construct their own curriculum.

One such design, for example, might be related to the content of general education. I have come increasingly to believe that a useful kind of teaching, especially for youth but also to some extent for children, would be to use in the systematic study of the congregation some of the same basic materials used in the public schools in such areas as history, literature, and related subjects. The church would then supply interpretive material, resources, and resource units to accompany the public school material. I am aware of the many problems connected with such an enterprise, one of which is the variety of materials used in the public schools. I do not believe we have explored the possibilities of this kind of curriculum nearly as extensively as we should. Any exploration would almost of necessity have to be done on some level of ecumenical activity.

The use of common materials on all age levels and from a variety of perspectives will certainly increase in the future. Books are already used by adult study groups without reference to the denomination of the writer. Why can this not be extended to all adult materials? Because of their expense, audio-visual materials have only rarely been made for the exclusive use of one communion. As the cost of innovations in teaching rises—for example, programmed instruction—we will be forced to draw upon our common resources rather than go on our own. Perhaps most of these resources will be developed first on a pan-Protestant basis; increasingly we will find areas where Catholic and Protestants can co-operate, and, at least on a limited basis, where the Jewish-Christian division can be overcome.

Proposal Six: Education for Ecumenicity

Thus far we have considered ecumenical efforts aimed toward various forms of religious education; we turn finally to education

for ecumenicity. To be sure, dialogue between members of different religious groups is both education in an ecumenical setting and
education for deeper ecumenicity. Indeed, the concomitant learning in many of the proposals made thus far will be in the direction
of increased ecumenical concern, and will therefore be education
in ecumenicity.

There is need for specific education for ecumenicity, however.
This will occur through units of study prepared by denominations
or prepared co-operatively. It will occur as common worship, with
its accompanying preparation and follow-up, takes place. A wider
variety of such efforts is needed if we are to move in the directions
which have been noted in this chapter. We cannot assume that
either general goodwill or the hard facts of a secular world and its
accompanying pressures on the institutional church will convince
churchmen of the necessity for increased ecumenicity. We must
continue to plan for many years, therefore, ways to encourage
persons toward increased ecumenical activity.

Conclusion

The prospects for the developing of an ecumenical orientation in
religious education naturally vary from communion to communion. Perhaps in every denomination, however, there are three
classes of persons. There are the ecumenical enthusiasts who provide leadership for ecumenical efforts outside the separate groups.
Their number is increasing, as is also the will to unity. This is
undoubtedly the ecumenical age, and the future surely belongs to
this group.

There are also in most, if not all, groups those who oppose any
form of interdenominational or ecumenical effort. Some do so because they feel that their own interpretation of life is ultimate.
Others do so because they oppose certain actions of councils of
churches, especially their social pronouncements. Others oppose
organic union because they fear increased bureaucracy. Some oppose ecumenical efforts on other grounds.

By far the largest group of Protestants, however, are indifferent.
Neither actively opposed to nor actively in favor of ecumenicity,
they are willing to be led in either direction. Education for

ecumenicity must be aimed especially toward this group. If, as many believe, God is today drawing the church to some form of unity, no human effort can be spared to clear the way for his work of healing. Whatever else ecumenical religious education is—and it is much more—it involves at least this: to prepare God's people for understanding what God is doing in our midst as he seeks to reconcile those who are separated.

FIVE

Some Bases of Common Concern in Education

A. by JAMES J. MEGIVERN, C.M.

B. by GERALD E. KNOFF

A. *by* JAMES J. MEGIVERN, C.M.

THE SECOND VATICAN Council "exhorts all the Catholic faithful to recognize the signs of the times and to take an active and intelligent part in the work of ecumenism."[1]

The fact that this remarkable statement has not met with either sympathy or compliance among certain segments of the church should cause no surprise. Change is more difficult in the religious sphere than in any other area of life. In particular, the peculiar circumstances that prevailed in the post-Reformation era led Catholics to an outlook that virtually made immutability a mark of the true church. This outlook finds the entire phenomenon of *aggiornamento* bewildering. For if one's chief orientation in theology has been apologetical and polemical, the realization that renewal and reform imply imperfections in the status quo can be uncomfortable. This is why opposition to ecumenism is usually only one aspect of a syndrome opposing liturgical renewal, modern biblical advances, catechetical changes, and the whole enterprise of renewed theology.

To grow out of such opposition is the basic challenge facing the generation of Catholics whose academic training took place before Vatican II arrived on the scene. The fundamental requirement is an openness of spirit that is willing to accept that something *new* has happened, that a former mentality is no longer adequate or justifiable. Unless this is accepted, all else is in vain. In his opening speech on the first day of the Council, October 11, 1962, Pope John XXIII left no doubt as to where he stood: "The Council now beginning rises in the Church like daybreak, a forerunner of most splendid light; it is now only dawn. And already at this first announcement of the rising day, how much sweetness fills our heart." He knew that there were those who saw things differently, some of them his closest collaborators, who saw nothing but reason for fear in modern developments, and would therefore counsel against any kind of change. But he also knew that such an outlook had little to do with the Gospel. "We feel we must disagree with those prophets of gloom, who are always forecasting disaster, as though the end of the world were at hand. In the present order of things, Divine Providence is leading us to a *new order* of human relations which, by men's own efforts and even beyond their very expectations, are directed toward the fulfillment of God's superior and inscrutable designs. And everything, even human differences, leads to the greater good of the Church."

By setting this tone on the very first day, Pope John opened a new period in Christian history. We who were raised in the former era will undoubtedly find it difficult to make some of the adjustments called for by the new era, "to recognize the signs of the times," to live in the overlap bridging two epochs. But this is no excuse for inertia or indifference, let alone opposition.

What has been said above applies to the entire order of renewal and is very evident in the progress of the ecumenical movement. Before the Council, the word *ecumenism* did not exist in our common vocabulary. This alone could make one wonder how it suddenly became a concern of such great importance. But this is misleading; the word itself is derived from the Greek and signifies "the inhabited world." In adjectival form it has been a common Christian term especially designating those gatherings of the bishops from all parts of Christendom that were known as "ecumenical councils."

Pope Paul VI has used two different forms of the noun on several occasions: *ecumenism* and *ecumenicity.* The latter is used in very much the same sense as the word "catholicity"; it is a perennial mark of the church, her orientation toward the whole of mankind. It expresses the hidden correspondence that exists between the church and the world. The church is meant for the world; it has no other goal than to become coextensive with mankind. This is the heart of the church's mission and mandate: She is as "world-embracing" as the cross of Christ. To be otherwise would be to renounce her very being.

What then is Catholic ecumenism? It is a program, an activity, a concrete effort and plan of action to bring this essential trait of the church, her ecumenicity, to full realization, to bring it out of the field of theory into that of practice. It is a *movement* to close the gap between what we *say* we are and what we *see* we are. The *Decree on Ecumenism* from Vatican II gave this movement its Magna Charta, its official endorsement, so that participation in it is not a matter of indifference for a Catholic.

Why is this so? Are we merely following the whimsy of a pope or council? The basic theological principle answering this question is stated in the first paragraph of the Decree: "Christ the Lord founded one Church and one Church only" . . . yet we find a multiplicity of Christian churches, professing to be His followers. . . . As a result, "such division openly *contradicts the will of Christ*, scandalizes the world, and damages that most holy cause, the preaching of the Gospel." Simply to accept this scandalous division and do nothing about it is to share in its sinfulness by ignoring the fervent prayer of Christ that all his followers might be *one*.

The starting point of ecumenism is the painful admission that the present divisions among the Christian churches are a supreme scandal illustrating the sad fact declared in another conciliar document, that "believers can have more than a little to do with the birth of atheism."[2] For divided Christianity is a spectacle of contradiction that prevents the world from seriously considering our claims. A great step forward has been made in the Decree when we have at last officially made the frank and humble admission that we Catholics share the responsibility for this scandal. It marks a major breakthrough in that whole Counter-Reformation mentality which Bishop de Smedt characterized so concisely as "triumphalism." But the staggering task that still remains is to bring this change of mentality down to the parish level.

One thing that should be obvious at this point is that the *Decree on Ecumenism* was, so to speak, a "natural" product of Vatican II.

The central concern of the entire Council was the understanding of the church itself. Consequently, the chief result of the Council was a new theological vision of the church. Oversimplified notions of the past were made more complete. The excessively Platonic approach that spoke of a church existing off in some world of ideas, unreal, untainted, and unvanquished, gave way to a more biblical and realistic appreciation. To recognize that the Church is people, God's people *(The People of God)*, is to bring back into view the fact that there is a fragile, human element subject to human limitations. It is to recognize that, due to controversy, the divine element had been emphasized in the past, with the result that such things as the church's unity, truth, and holiness were seen simply as existing gifts, present ever and always, forgetting that they are just as truly *tasks*, challenges facing every generation that would call itself Christian.

From this vision of renewal the *Decree on Ecumenism* was born. It simply spelled out the implication of this new self-awareness for relations with the other Christian churches by asserting a fresh realization of the manifold richness of the *mystery* of the church. In its magnificent *Constitution on the Church*, the greatest product of Vatican II, the Council Fathers have given us the necessary context for understanding most of the other documents, and this is especially true of ecumenism. In trying to bring back our attention to the full span of biblical images describing the church, Vatican II[3] effectively shows the shortcomings of considering the church as something static and unchangeable that can be expressed in permanent legal terms. It is just as truly an *event-in-process* as an institution. This is the reason why it is not only desirable but necessary that there will always be movements (such as ecumenism), concerted efforts within the church to close the gap between theory and practice, to answer the challenges arising from the very gifts with which Christ has endowed her.

A point that has received all too little attention is the solid basis on which the Council rests the need for participation in the Ecumenical Movement by *all* Catholics. In the concluding words of the first paragraph, reference is made to the purpose of the Decree: ". . . to set before all Catholics guidelines, helps and methods by which they too can respond to the grace of this divine *call.* "

The call to unity in Christ is part of the Christian call itself, the vocation received in baptism. It is not something optional. "The concern for restoring unity involves the whole Church, faithful and clergy alike. It extends to everyone, according to the talent of each, whether it be exercised in daily Christian living or in theological and historical studies."[4] What makes one shy away from such truths, however, is the uncomfortable consequences. To turn a phrase, we might say "the name of the game is *change*" and, as mentioned earlier, this hurts.

What kind of changes does the practice of ecumenism entail? The first one, and by far the most difficult one, is basic to the Christian life itself, the primary response to the gospel, the first demand made by Christ himself: *self-change.* "There can be no ecumenism worthy of the name without interior conversion. For it is from *newness of attitudes* of mind, from self-denial and unstinted love, that desires for unity take their rise and develop in a mature way."[5] This then is what we are called to by Christ in ecumenism: to change our minds, our attitudes, our hearts, our conduct, our way of speaking. To recognize that we are burdened with prejudices toward other Christians is a difficult thing to do, God knows. It is always much easier and more comfortable to take refuge in the caricatures of the past, to continue to think of Martin Luther as a disobedient, runaway monk who did nothing but damage and divide the church. But the perpetuation of such historical distortions is one of the grave sins for which no one any longer has any excuse. The new *Dutch Catechism* that informs the Catholic child of the religious genius of Luther is simply an early example of the kind of change demanded by ecumenical honesty.

Because of the immobilism of the past, the change of posture now called for is all the more difficult. But this is no excuse for refusing to answer the call. To do nothing to foster unity now is to share in the sin of disunity. As we have seen, the first change called for is self-change; "this change of heart and holiness of life, along with public and private prayer for the unity of Christians, should be regarded as the *soul* of the ecumenical movement, and merits the name *spiritual ecumenism.* "[6] But this is not all. Ecumenism, like charity, to which it is so closely related, begins at home but dares not end there. It is a movement *toward,* an *approach* to other Christians. It is a rejection of the idea of the church as a "closed shop." It is an opening of the arms to embrace all whom Christ has embraced in baptism.

But this requires more than merely good will. "We must get to know the outlook of our separated brethren. Study is absolutely required for this and it should be pursued in fidelity to truth and with a spirit of good will."[7] The immediate objection raised by an anti-Protestant prejudice is that when it comes to faith we have nothing to learn from non-Catholics. Such naïveté would have us ignore the monumental works of men like Karl Barth, Dietrich Bonhoeffer, Emil Brunner, Paul Tillich, and Rudolph Bultmann, to mention only a quintet of modern luminaries. To ignore such men is to limit oneself ironically to being less Catholic rather than more Catholic. The Council Fathers are unequivocal on this point: "From such dialogue will emerge still more clearly what the situation of the Catholic Church really is."[8]

One change implied here is dictated by common honesty. We can no longer, as a matter of course in apologetics, point to what is worst in others and compare it with what is best in ourselves. Offensive general statements will have to disappear from our conversations. Facile judgments of other people, based on our ignorance of them, will henceforth be recognized for what they are—sins against the eighth commandment: "Thou shalt not bear false witness against thy neighbor."

All of this is the simple consequence of taking our own theology seriously. By baptism we believe ourselves to be made brothers of Christ with all the baptized. All subsequent separation is a result of sin, sin which we make our own when we in any way continue the separation by our attitudes or deeds.

It is necessary to underline that the Decree speaks of other Christians as "brothers separated *from us*": the term in no way passes judgment on their relations with Christ or with the rest of Christians. All that is stated is that there is a barrier that has arisen between themselves and ourselves, and that we have a mutual responsibility to try to remove it. In the vast majority of cases, the barriers fall into the category of the "non-theological factors" of division. This is especially true of our relations with Eastern Orthodoxy; this rift has its deepest roots in the psychological, sociological, cultural differences between East and West.

It is precisely at this point that the absolute necessity of *dialogue* appears. As long as we talk *about* one another rather than *to* one another, it will be possible to continue writing scandalously superficial textbooks that reveal nothing but how greatly we have misunderstood the chief difficulty in coming to know each other. Augustin Cardinal Bea, who played such a key role in promoting ecumenism during the Council, expressed the problem succinctly in a talk at the University of Fribourg, Switzerland, in late 1961, a year before the Council opened: "While persevering in love of truth and fidelity to faith, what we Catholics have to learn today in our teaching, our writing, our conversation, is to understand *from within* the preoccupations, difficulties, and modes of thought of Christians separated from us. . . . Many prejudices and misconceptions of Christians are founded on an historically inaccurate understanding of the events of the Reformation and of the persons who were involved in them. They will only be dissipated by a re-evaluation of history based on a study of sources."

In the light of this necessity, the decision of Pope John to invite Orthodox and Protestant observers to be present at every discussion of Vatican II can only be described as a stroke of genius. The very fact that those spoken about were actually present, listening to every word, immensely affected the whole atmosphere. Many Latin bishops who had never had any contact with Protestants thought twice before publicly displaying untenable conceptions of people whom they had never met, nor listened to, nor seriously studied. Pope John had thus set up a built-in condition of dialogue, inviting, or rather insisting, that the observers inform him personally, and in writing, of their reactions, objections, and suggestions. Just a few years before the Council, a prominent American Protestant theologian had remarked that "Rome has never really listened to the witness of the Reformation."[9] Thanks to Pope John, he could not make that statement today. In listening to the Protestant observers during the four sessions of the Council, the bishops of the church at least made an honest attempt to do justice to what was valid in the "protest" of Protestantism. The work is by no means finished, but a good beginning certainly has been made. And, be it noted, the benefit has been mutual. Through the Council, we have seen a fascinating double process restoring lost riches to all involved. There has been a Catholic "return" to Scripture and a Protestant "return" to tradition.

Most Catholic laymen, however, are undoubtedly as yet unaware of the extent and consequences of the transition that is taking place. The excitement of our age is often caused by scientists making successive breakthroughs that leave one breathless. But anyone who views Vatican II seriously will see that the Catholic theologian of today has at least an analogous opportunity. The Council has drawn the curtain on the age of theological imperialism; there were historical reasons for fostering a single theology in the past, but this is obviously a very unhealthy enterprise. "The principle of catholicity implies that other theologies too have a right to exist within the Church."[10]

In what may well be the most revolutionary paragraph to come out of Vatican II, the eleventh paragraph of the *Decree on Ecumenism* is nothing less than a call for a *new* Catholic theology. What are its characteristics to be? First, its mode of expression is to be such that it "in no way becomes an obstacle to dialogue with our brethren." It is an explicit demand for a truly "ecumenical" theology, or might we better say, for a truly "catholic" theology? Far from setting out to demolish "opponents," its explicit intent and conscious concern will be to attain intelligibility by plunging past surface differences to grapple at a deeper level with the significance of Christian revelation for all: "Catholic belief must be explained *more profoundly* and precisely, in such a way and in such terms as our separated brethren can also really understand it."[11] It would obviously be just one more form of triumphalist conceit to think that we can accomplish such a project on our own. It will require "Catholic theologians . . . searching together with separated brethren into the divine mysteries." Here the Council gives reason for the desirability of inviting good Protestant theologians to join Catholic theology faculties.

A second future characteristic of Catholic theology is also expressed in this same paragraph: that is, a systematic awareness that "in Catholic doctrine there exists an order or "hierarchy" of truths, since they vary in their relations to the foundation of the Christian faith." This practically puts an end to the approach of presenting tract after tract of theology as if all were on the same level and of equal importance. This neglect of the interrelation of the various truths of faith goes a long way in explaining why peripheral matters (such as indulgences, purgatory, etc.) could grow all out of proportion and become the "tail that wags the dog." It was Archbishop Pangrazio of Gorizia, Italy, who was responsible for the addition of this important statement to the Decree in its final stage in the fourth session of the Council. He explained at greater length the distinction between truths that are on the level of our *final goal,* and truths that are on the level of *means* toward salvation. He pointed out that: "Doctrinal differences among Christians have less to do with these primary truths . . . and deal mostly with truths on the level of means, which are certainly subordinate to those other primary truths. But we can say that the unity of Christians consists in a common faith and belief in those truths which concern our final goal. If we explicitly make these distinctions in conformity with the hierarchy of truths . . . I think the existing unity among all Christians will be seen more clearly and it will become evident that all Christians are already a family united in the primary truths of the Christian religion."[12]

That such a remarkable statement could be made by an Italian bishop before the assembled hierarchy in Rome is itself sufficient proof of the revolutionary, even miraculous, nature of Vatican II. In the words of the prominent Dominican theologian Fr. Schillebeeckx: "For the first time in her history the Church has officially relinquished her religious monopoly."[13] It is forthrightly acknowledged that Protestant churches "can engender truly a life of grace, and one must say, can aptly give access to the communion of salvation. . . . Although we believe they suffer from defects . . . they have been by no means deprived of significance and importance in the mystery of salvation. For the Spirit of Christ has not refrained from using them as means of salvation."[14]

Such is the change of attitude brought about by the Council. It is unquestionably challenging to Catholics raised in a different spirit and atmosphere. But the Council Fathers felt that today's Catholics are sufficiently adult to make the adjustment. They assert in their final paragraph: "We confidently look to the future. . . . This Council declares that it realizes that this holy objective—the reconciliation of all Christians in the unity of the one and only Church of Christ—transcends human powers and gifts. It therefore places its hope entirely in the *prayer* of *Christ* for the Church, in the *love of the Father* for us, and in the *power of the Holy Spirit.*"[15]

B. *by* GERALD E. KNOFF

N O D O U B T E V E R Y contributor to this volume has thought as he began his chapter, "How impossible it would have been ten short years ago to imagine the preparation of such a book!" The sociological situations surrounding education seemed not to share common features; there was little or no ecumenical dialogue; it was the differences, not the similarities, much less the common roots, of worship which impressed us.

If such reflections that have come to the minds of the writers of the other chapters, they have similarly come to the writer of this section. An early slogan in the history of Protestant co-operative church work was "Theology divides; action unites." That aphorism was never much more than a half-truth. For if there is not enough commonalty in thought and reflections, action never really takes place, much less does it unite. Just as true it is, moreover, that action divides as well as unites.

The revolution which has occurred, therefore, has happened just as much in the practical spheres of the churches' action and mission as it has come about in theology and ecclesiology. It has been a revolution which has begun from just as minimal beginnings as in the more speculative and theoretical arenas of the life and thought of the churches. The history of each is brief. Prehistory is not far removed from any one of the disciplines.

There is no need here to review the factors which have converged to bring about a more hopeful day. The story of the emergence of the ecumenical movement is well known. The formation of the World Council of Churches in 1948, growing out of two principal taproots, Faith and Order on the one hand and Life and Work on the other, happened barely two decades ago. The formation of the National Council of the Churches of Christ in the U.S.A., bringing together twelve independent interchurch agencies, came in 1950. The issuance of the call to an ecumenical council by Pope John XXIII is even more recent, and the decision by Pope Paul VI to continue the Council convened by his predecessor is as if it were done yesterday.

How swiftly events have moved since then! How widespread and how various have been the overt moves toward co-operation in common Christian concerns of Catholics, Orthodox, and Protestants. One does not need to compare the frequency, variety, or importance of each advance toward the common center of thought and action; there is enough in the record of all confessions these past few years to make splendid the account of any one.

It is for us now to explore the terrain for common educational activities. It is not, however, the intent of this chapter to propose a shopping list of eighty-seven items which could profitably be undertaken. There will be some practical and definite suggestions, to be sure. In general, however, the purpose will be to survey the educational landscape and take into account some of its more salient features, point to some clear advances which seem to be generally possible, and then leave the filling in of the details of the panorama to those who carry out their discipleship in particular localities. We shall do well, first of all, to ascertain what is operative in the educational work of the churches and how these agencies assist our local efforts.

Operating Structures for Exploration

On the Protestant side there operates the Division of Christian Education of the National Council of Churches. It is not true, of course, that every venture in common programs of education will be even indirectly related to this agency of the national denominations, but it is true that as Catholics and Jews join hands with Protestants and Orthodox in common endeavors, they will probably discover that most of the churches with which they are becoming acquainted are associated with this co-operative agency through their national bodies.

There are boards and agencies of forty-one denominations, in the larger churches sometimes as many as five or six boards from each, who join in this working fraternal association, in common programming, in the experience of continuing learning, and in the planning for the future in this Division. Though the Division as a part of the National Council of Churches is young, the inherited experience represented in it goes back for nearly a century and a half, for in 1832 there was established the first interchurch enterprise in the experience of the American churches.

Specialized departments, the Department of Educational Development, the Department of Higher Education, the Department of Education for Mission, and the Department of Ministry, serve the interests of the churches, and are officially committed by them to represent them in specifically defined responsibilities. The program and interests of the Division reach out through a double stream; the member denominations and the associated state and city councils of churches, to the local communities and to the local churches of the nation.

At the beginning of this section of the chapter, the phrase "on the Protestant side" was used. As I wrote those words I started to correct them by adding the words "and Orthodox," for it is true that the Division of the National Council of Churches has churches of both persuasions belonging to it.

On second thought I decided to let the less than accurate words stand, in order that they may be a symbol of one of the weaknesses of the National Council of Churches, a weakness which is to be found in literally every department of its variegated work. The Council has a long way to go to be, in fact, what it is in theory, genuinely representative of the thought and life of the ancient Eastern Orthodox churches in America. Each of the agencies which came together in 1950 to form the Council was an exclusively Protestant body. Vigorous attempts have been made, and are now being made, to make it sensitive to the Orthodox communions which are constituent members of it. No great success has resulted from these endeavors, it must be admitted, and for the most part the National Council of Churches remains as it was born, a Protestant body.

The practical result of this failure is to be seen in the local educational situation. There are cities and communities, to be sure, where the Protestant churches have a lively interest in the well-being of their Orthodox neighbor churches, and in which the Orthodox congregations have effective educational exchanges with their Protestant cousins. On the whole, however, this is not the typical situation. Orthodox and Protestants are usually as much strangers to each other as Catholics are to either, in education as well as in the other aspects of the churches' life.

For the Catholic congregation, therefore, which wants to explore the possibilities of common educational effort with Orthodox people, the local council of churches may be an effective point of contact. Again, it may not be. In such an instance it will be sound for ecumenically minded Catholics to make direct overtures to their Orthodox brothers, meanwhile keeping whatever inter-church structure there exists informed.

In any case it is important that Catholic participants in the growing ecumenical dialogue understand just what a local council of churches is, and just what the National Council of Churches is. A local council is not a congregation and the National Council is not a denomination. These agencies are just what their name implies, "councils." They possess no more authority and no more power than the member churches (local or national, as the case may be) give to them.

Perhaps it is helpful here to quote a most influential statement about the nature of a council of churches. This document, "The Church, the Churches, and the World Council of Churches," was received and commended by the Central Committee of that body at its meeting in Toronto, Ontario, in 1950.

As the conversation between the Churches develops and as the Churches enter into closer contact with each other, they will no doubt have to face new decisions and problems. For the Council exists to break the deadlock between the Churches. But in no case can or will any Church be pressed to take a conviction against its own conviction or desire. The Churches remain wholly free in the action, which, on the basis of their convictions and in the light of their ecumenical contacts, they will or will not take.[1]

Catholics may discover as they enter into co-operative arrangements through a council with Protestant and Orthodox leaders in a state, city, or town that sometimes the council cannot "deliver all its members." It will contribute to sympathetic understanding if it is remembered that nowhere is the principle of voluntarism so regnant, sometimes paralyzingly regnant, as in a council of churches. We shall achieve more if we recognize this built-in limitation.

On the Catholic side the two educational agencies with which Protestant educators have had most frequent contacts are the Confraternity of Christian Doctrine and the National Catholic Education Association.

The Confraternity of Christian Doctrine is a unit of the United States Catholic Conference, the official national administrative body of the American Catholic bishops. It was established in 1918, as a result of the 1905 encyclical of St. Pius X. It assists parents in the Christian nurture of their children. It works with the education of elementary and high school pupils. It carries on programs for college students and for parish adults. Relationships between the Confraternity and the Department of Educational Development, one of the units of the Division of Christian Education, are growing and a considerable amount of mutual sharing and interchange is already taking place.[2]

The National Catholic Education Association brings together individual educators from a wide variety of professional educational work. Its annual meetings are vast assemblies, attracting thousands of educators; priests, lay brothers, nuns, and lay teachers of both sexes. It was organized in 1904 to "unite Catholic educators, create mutual understanding and encourage mutual assistance for safeguarding and promoting Catholic educational interests in the U.S." Membership in 1965 was more than fourteen thousand.[3]

It is well to know, moreover, that there are *ad hoc* structures created from time to time by the bishops of the Catholic Church for the accomplishment of specific tasks. Sometimes their influence is felt in local communities; sometimes direct influence is not apparent.

If Catholics need to be warned against the tacit assumption that a council of churches ought somehow to behave as a church, Protestants need to have corrected their common misunderstanding that the Catholic Church in education, as in other activities, is a monolithic establishment. Protestants have assumed that when the pope, the apostolic delegate, or some faceless functionary cracks the ecclesiastical whip, all the faithful fall in line. They do not. As a matter of fact, the Catholic Church in the United States, as elsewhere, exhibits variety, which becomes more and more amazing to a Protestant inquirer the deeper he explores it. Administratively speaking, the Catholic Church in this nation is a loose association of independent dioceses, and within the diocese the bishop is the actual head. To be sure, bishops seem now to seek more and more advice from their priests and others about appointments, policies, and programs, and there is a concern that the national hierarchy find structures and methods of operation which allow for a more unified and united witness and mission.

In this exceedingly fluid situation, however, Protestants must not assume that because certain ventures in common educational efforts have been well spoken of by somebody at the top, they will be automatically approved either in the diocese or in the local Catholic church down the street. A particular bishop and a particular priest in his diocese may have altogether differing evaluations about the worth of weekday released time, for example, and unless the program commends itself to the local authority it simply will not come to pass. Protestants will do well to remember this diversity-in-unity.

Catholic and Protestant Co-operation in Higher Education

The campus world is a universe all its own. Those who work in the campus establishments, however, find that there is a considerable network of related structures that has been built up across the years. As a result of working in the regional accrediting associations, by their mixing in such organizations as the Association of American Colleges, the American Council on Education, and through advisory committees, general and specific, of the United States Office of Education, Department of Health, Education and Welfare, Protestant and Catholic leaders in higher education have shared in an impressive and continuing experience.

It is likely that in the experiences provided over the years by the

Association of American Colleges and in its Commission on Christian Higher Education, presidents and deans of Catholic- and Protestant-related colleges have had their most fruitful contacts.

The Association of American Colleges was founded in 1915. It promotes and interprets the concerns of colleges of liberal arts and sciences, including those which are integral parts of universities. It conducts research and studies in fields of interest to its member institutions and holds an annual meeting in mid-January attended by presidents, deans, and other officials of these liberal arts institutions. Its Commission on Christian Higher Education has grown in effectiveness during the past few years and provides a common meeting ground for Catholic and Protestant educators within the liberal arts tradition.[4]

To be sure, all possible fruitful contacts in the college and university world are not exhausted by the annual trips of the administrators to the January meetings of the AAC. Student and campus work contacts have been perhaps slower to develop, though there are scores of campuses on which mutually enriching associations have been normal and accepted as a matter of course over many years.

These local, mutual involvements with the task of understanding the role of the university in the light of the Christian faith now find their task materially assisted by the growing common involvement at the national level of those church leaders concerned for the same exciting, but demanding, intellectual task.

In 1960 a significant breakthrough occurred on the national scene when at its annual assembly the National Student Christian Federation completely reorganized itself. It admitted into its membership two Catholic agencies, the National Newman Student Federation and the National Federation of Catholic College Students. As it did so it changed its name and became the University Christian Movement. Since that step was taken, Catholic students, priests, and lay advisers have moved easily among Protestant colleagues in guiding the destinies of this interchurch movement.

Of course, it is on the local campuses that the most exciting action takes place. The exploration of the ecumenical imperative and of the ecumenical manifestations called forth in response to that imperative, the involvement in common social action and social protest movements (notably peace and race), the appointment of

Protestant scholars to faculties of Catholic colleges and the reverse, the new restructuring of prominent institutions to allow for greater freedom from ecclesiastical control and for the inclusion of lay members on their boards of trustees—these and other developments have led to new and deepened contacts, undreamed of a decade ago.

Many of the college and university campus workers of the 1950s yearned for such an atmosphere of openness, but it was denied them. Those who work on the campuses of today, though their major problems seem to multiply fourfold every year, have this inestimable advantage of being in a freer world, and of rejoicing in the support of those who are in policy-making positions in national bodies.

Joint Effort in Scripture Translation

One of the most heartening instances of Protestant-Catholic co-operation in educational matters is the growing association in the work of Scripture translation. At first glance this may seem a long way removed from the practical tasks of educational co-operation on the Main Streets of America, and in a sense it is.

As long as Protestants and Catholics in this country utilize, however, for reasons which seem good to themselves, different versions of the Scriptures, just so long will there be occasion for reluctant Christians of either persuasion to assume that "they" somehow read and follow an inferior version of the Holy Bible. It is *unfamiliarity* which often breeds contempt. The opportunity for hostility for the bigot is even more serious.

A second impulse has caused an upsurge of interest in a closer approximation of Catholic and Protestant versions of the Scriptures: the imperious needs of the mission fields. In an interview with the writer in the spring of 1966, Monsignor Jan Willebrands declared the absurdity of the efforts of Catholic translators working on a portion of the Old or New Testaments when down the road a few miles in Africa, for example, a group of Protestants were doing the same thing, or, worse yet, had completed a satisfactory translation. A Protestant might well have made the same comment about unnecessary Protestant labors.

Both the sense of this absurdity and the possibility of rectifying it were made possible by the new stance of the Roman Catholic Church with respect to Bible translation. In 1943 Pope Pius XII issued his famous encyclical *Divino Afflante Spiritu*, a pronouncement which allowed Catholic scholars to work for the first time from the original Hebrew and Greek texts instead of basing their translation upon the Latin Vulgate of Jerome, itself a translation of the original languages.

One of the most remarkable drawings together has been that of the United Bible Societies with the activities of the Catholic Church in Bible translation and distribution. Shortly after the conclusion of Vatican II, Walter M. Abbott, S. J., an editor of *America*, was called from that position to the Vatican with responsibilities, among other duties, of seeking out and cultivating relationships with the United Bible Societies and their member national units, and of encouraging, wherever possible, joint endeavors in Scripture translation and distribution.

The Catholic Edition of the Revised Standard Version

The account of the efforts on behalf of a common English version of the Scriptures is too long to be recounted here in detail. It deserves a separate chapter of its own in another volume. But because Catholics and Protestants can now use for educational purposes almost identical texts of the Bible, the basis of our common Christian faith, a short account may be helpful.

The story began in Great Britain, where the Catholic Biblical Association in the early 1950s began attempts to bring forth a modern version of the Scriptures in a style usable in the Catholic day schools in Great Britain, based on the original languages, and produced according to the most rigorous standards of scholarship. After much work and labor, the translators came to the conclusion that the task they had set for themselves had already been accomplished, for the most part, in the Revised Standard Version of 1946 and 1952.

Accordingly an inquiry came to the Standard Bible Committee to ascertain if the Revised Standard Version, with some as yet undetermined changes, might be so used. The response of the committee was generous and immediate. The matter, they said, was surely worth investigating. No significant obstacles were seen from their point of view.

In this spirit of tentative permissiveness a conference was scheduled for London in the summer of 1954 with representatives of the Division of Christian Education, the Catholic Biblical Association, and of a British publishing house attending. Discussion centered upon the preparation of a series of New Testament readers for the day schools of the church with the possibility of an Old Testament sequence to come. Certain ground rules were established and agreements were reached for further scholarly endeavor and ecclesiastical clearances.

The work went ahead on both sides of the Atlantic and by the time the next conference of the three parties was held in 1956 the desires of the CBA had changed. Now it was desired, instead, that there be a complete Bible, Old and New Testaments including the deuterocanonical books. The approval of the Archbishop of Westminster, Bernard, Cardinal Griffin, had been secured and he had prepared a written foreword for the edition. Clearances were made by the Protestant representatives in a conference at Lambeth Palace with the Archbishop of Canterbury in order that the officials of the Church of England might be fully informed.

Cardinal Griffin died ten days after he wrote the foreword. It was then decided that the enterprise could not wisely be pushed ahead, while a successor had not yet been chosen and installed. When that choice was made, and when the new Archbishop of Westminster, William Godfrey, was elevated to the cardinalate, it developed that he had grave misgivings about the project. Taking counsel over a long period of time both with British and with American bishops, he decided in late June, 1958 that the project could not be supported on the basis that it would give offense to the faithful.

For five years the venture languished until the autumn of 1963, when a new archbishop in turn occupied the see of Westminster, John Heenan, formerly of Liverpool. Soon Archbishop Gordon Gray of St. Andrews and Edinburgh announced his willingness to give his imprimatur to the project, he having become well acquainted with the text of the RSV, with the changes in the text of the New Testament desired by the Catholic Biblical Association and assented to by the Standard Bible Committee, and with the "Explanatory Notes" attached.

In 1965 the New Testament, Revised Standard Version, Catholic Edition, appeared with a foreword by the apostolic delegate to Great Britain commending it to Catholic readers. On May 22 of that year a specially bound copy was presented to Pope Paul VI in his private library at the Vatican. He bestowed upon those who had collaborated in the work the apostolic blessing.

Events moved without interruption from that point on. An American printing appeared, upon approvals from American ecclesiastics.

In the meantime a decision was made by the Catholic principals, unexpected among the Protestant colleagues. In the New Testament it had been deemed necessary that a number of changes be made in the text. Ninety-two verses were affected, involving thirty-three distinct departures from the original RSV text. For the Old Testament, however, its inspection being done in later years and in a changed ecclesiastical climate, it was decided that no changes should be made in the basic RSV text. The "Explanatory Notes," then being prepared, were deemed sufficient to make clear Catholic doctrine and interpretation. Again, as had been the case with the New Testament, American ecclesiastical endorsement was secured in addition to the approvals of British prelates. In 1966 the complete text of the Catholic Edition of the Revised Standard Version of the Bible was published. John, Cardinal Heenan supplied the foreword for the British printing; Richard, Cardinal Cushing, that for the American printing.

Cardinal Cushing's action was taken on behalf of a Bible whose Old Testament contained the deuterocanonical books in the accepted Catholic form and placement. Within a few months, however, there came an action by Cardinal Cushing which was even more of a break with precedent.

The publishers of another volume, the *Oxford Annotated Bible*, had incorporated into it the RSV Apocrypha in the separated Protestant form and placement. Later its scholarly notes were carefully inspected by a chosen group of Catholic scholars and a few revisions and expansions included. With this work done, ecclesiastical

approval was sought by the publisher, and Cardinal Cushing's imprimatur was promptly granted.

Thus it is that English-speaking readers, Catholic and Protestant
alike, for the first time since the English Reformation may use
almost, but not wholly, identical versions of the Holy Scriptures
with ecclesiastical approbation. The edition mentioned first above
incorporates changes in the New Testament, but has the
deuterocanonical books in their familiar order and place for Catholic readers. The other edition has no verbal changes in the text, but
contains the apocryphal books according to the Protestant placement, and with their Protestant headings.

As we come together in common educational ventures it will be
helpful and encouraging to remember that Protestants and Catholics alike have in the Revised Standard Version of the Bible and
its Catholic variant, if not a completely identical accepted version
of the Scriptures, texts which are very nearly the same. No longer
do we need to refer back to different English versions, and for that
all Christian educators in both households of faith should be profoundly thankful. No doubt the future will see us separated Christians even closer together in biblical matters, but it has been given
to the present generation to see the greatest drawing together in
the use of the Bible in the four hundred years of ecclesiastical
separation.[5]

Meeting Emergency Educational Needs

Catholics and Protestants are just beginning to learn the techniques of meeting the emergency educational needs of the nation
in which they live. Sometimes crisis situations teach with an intensity that more placid times fail to drive home. We are accustomed
to think, of course, that crises are abnormal and unusual, and that
times of slow, thoughtful planning and construction are the normal
and usual patterns of educational progress.

It may just be that we shall be living more and more in times of
crisis in this nation, and that along with the more leisurely pattern
of work we have long known, we shall have to devise new models
of common action; or indeed, of individual action, where that seems
to be needed.

In the spring of 1968 leaders in all segments of our society were looking forward with foreboding to the "long, hot summer" ahead. Time was, only a few years before, when those adjectives referred only to climate, temperature, and the calendar. From 1968 on they became words of ominous prediction, or, at best, expressive of gnawing uncertainty.

All kinds of psychological and sociological overtones were carried along in those words. Some thought only of how to avoid civil disorder, and how to stop it by police and military action. Others were aware of the underlying causes below the possible social tumult. There were some, no doubt, who looked forward to the outbreak of hostilities, some of these persons hoping to redress encrusted wrongs, others to show the blacks once and for all who was in command of the regulatory, not to mention the punitive, forces of society.

In that kind of uncertain social situation the president of the National Council of Churches, Arthur S. Flemming, called an emergency meeting of leaders of the churches affiliated with the Council. They met in late February at San Diego, adjacent to the meeting of the General Board of the Council.

Impressed with the urgency of the problem confronting the churches and the nation, an unprecedented "special order" was adopted, marshaling the resources of the Council and, in so far as it was possible, of its member churches as well, in a united effort with legislative, educational, and social action aspects. The "special order" declared:

This crisis demands unprecedented action by the churches working together. We, therefore, direct that a special action program be undertaken at once to reorder, strengthen, accelerate and fully coordinate the resources of the churches and the National Council of Churches in the crucial struggle for justice in the nation. . . .[6]

Because of the alertness and ingenuity of the staff of the National Council's Department of Educational Development, it was possible to convene only a fortnight later a representative group of editors, age-group specialists, and general executives to consider what educational materials might be prepared to meet this unprecedented need.

The meeting was not authorized by any of the regular established processes of the Council, and only those who are well acquainted with that body's elaborate protections against unauthorized staff actions can appreciate the careless abandon of the group to a desired outcome and the untypical neglect of denominational clearances.

The proposed action was all the more remarkable in that it envisaged the replacement of previously prepared denominational curricula for Sunday church school groups with a new piece prepared under emergency conditions. A local group was to use a new Council-prepared guide as a temporary summer replacement.

To the casual reader that innovation may appear inconsequential indeed. Those who are familiar with the modes of operation in American Protestant churches, however, are aware that one of the most jealously guarded denominational prerogatives is the preparation and distribution of basic Christian education curricula for local congregational use.

In this instance, however, the urgency of the situation and the clear need for common community action indicated the wisdom of preparing materials which could be used, not by one denominational group, but by as many as possible. Thus it was that swift and unanimous action was given.

Adult classes, older youth groups, women's societies, community gatherings, and other discussion groups soon began using these materials, the denominational boards and publishing houses acting as distributors for the study-action guide, *Crisis in America—Hope Through Action.* By the end of May more than two hundred thousand copies of the guide had been sold, and hopefully a large percentage of that number were actually in use in the cities and towns of America.

The educational usefulness of the guide commended it to educational leaders of the Catholic Church, some of whom were in the initial planning meeting in early March. Soon it was decided by them that the booklet, with some changes in the bibliography and minor editing in the text, could be helpfully used in Catholic parishes. Arrangements were soon worked out to make possible a third and revised printing, with a joint foreword signed by the Council's president, Mr. Flemming, Archbishop Iakavos of the Standing Conference of Orthodox Bishops, and Archbishop John F. Deardon.

Accompanying this interest of Catholics was a simultaneous interest of some organized Jewish bodies and a desire to join in the joint commendation of the booklet. It proved impossible, on further study, for all Jewish bodies to join in this common effort, but the Union of American Hebrew Congregations was able to become one of the cosponsors. This decision meant, of course, careful scrutiny of the text of the third printing in order to make it useful to Jewish participants in study groups, but with minimum alterations this was accomplished. So it was that *Crisis in America—Hope Through Action* (Interreligious Edition) was born.

For the first time in American religious history, the four large faith groups in the United States officially collaborated in preparing for local church and synagogue use adult education materials dealing with a contemporary social situation with theological and spiritual dimensions. Whether this first step will be followed in the near future by other common efforts remains to be seen. Prompt duplication of this unprecedented collaboration may not be of the greatest importance.

It may be, however, that mature reflection after the act may reveal that there were factors in this situation which, in part, are repeatable, and if the prepared materials are well received in local situations, encouragement may be given to make similar efforts in other directions.

Significant advances in interchurch or interreligious co-operation come about both by progressive advances on the part of national leaders and by joint action agreed upon in local communities. Influence spreads from the national centers outward, but just as effectively it comes from the periphery of the circle to the center.

In this instance the response of Protestant congregations, Catholic parishes, and Jewish synagogues will be crucial. If there are successful experiences in local communities, if each faith group feels that its deepest religious convictions have been adequately dealt with, yet yoked creatively to the deepest spiritual inheritance of others, and if the whole endeavor points to recognizable advances in religious and ethical understanding—in this case the responsible understanding of the problem of "white power"—then there will have been generated power and determination for further experimentation in common adult educational efforts.

Dual School Enrollment Plans

One of the achievements of the decade of the 1960s has been the breaking of the Protestant-Catholic impasse on Federal aid for public education. Perhaps historians of American education will see this development as one of the most significant advances of the quarter century.

The temptation to speculate about what would have happened if Cleopatra's nose had been an inch longer must, of course, be resisted. History is full of unpredictable twists and turns. Perhaps Federal aid would have come to our desperately needy state and community school systems even if Catholics and Protestants had continued their deadlock and had persisted in presenting before the committees of the Congress and in the arenas of public debate diametrically opposing points of view. But if this had happened, it is safe to say that the legislation would have been much delayed and the climate of acceptance would have been one of asperity and acrimonious controversy.

It seems only yesterday that the principle of Federal aid to the state and local school systems of America was sharply contested in church assemblies, government circles, and the public news media. Today there is discussed only the wisdom of differing administrative provisions or the specific amounts which ought to be made available. The basic propriety of Federal assistance seems generally acceptable. Its administration, in spite of some differences of judgment in particular instances, seems competent, and the effects of the assistance appear beneficial to the schools, the authorities, their patrons, and the children.

How has this change come about? By wise and careful legislation in the first place, and by sensitive and judicious administration in the second instance. Most influential of all, perhaps, was the pervasive sense of felt need in the towns and cities of the nation. We can all be thankful that the Federal Government has found the way to make possible across-the-board support and other specialized support for our public school system.

How did the Federal Government find the way? More particularly, how did the Congress find the way? In part, by the determination of Catholic and Protestant educational leaders to find a creative solution to a vexing question of public policy.

That dispute, of course, was the contentious matter of public aid for private schools. "Private schools" was almost a euphemism for "Catholic schools," since few other institutions were involved in the controversy. To be sure, Seventh-Day Adventists, Missouri-Synod Lutherans, and Christian Reformed congregations maintained systems of religious day schools, as did the Orthodox wing of Judaism. For the most part, these churches and synagogues were content to meet the total expenses of their own educational establishments without making demands upon public funds.[7]

Just because the dispute was based upon dearly held convictions, it was unyielding and often contentious. Catholics deeply believed that the denial of this assistance was an act of discrimination against those American children in private schools who were entitled—morally, legally, and constitutionally—to all the benefits the state conferred upon their playmates in publicly controlled schools.

Protestants believed for reasons just as deeply grounded that such support was a clear violation of the First Amendment to the Constitution, that the adoption of the practice in the face of American religious diversity would mean a practical impoverishment and perhaps the termination of American public education, and that to force a portion of a taxpayer's wealth to the support of a religion he did not believe in was a violation of his inalienable religious freedom.

In the spring of 1961 this issue received national attention in the daily press and in the weekly newsmagazines. The late Frederick G. Hochwalt of the National Catholic Welfare Conference and a representative of the National Council of Churches presented vigorous and sharply opposing statements before the House Education and Labor Commiteee and a crowded committee room audience while the House unit was in process of considering an aid-to-education bill.

Later similar and opposing testimony was presented to a corresponding Senate committee. Again, legislators, sincerely trying to find a way to aid the beleaguered and needy public school systems, were confronted with the unnerving spectacle of contending churchmen, unhappy for a Christian to behold, ominous for a politician to contemplate. Thus nothing was done; Federal assistance, so greatly needed, languished. The children of America were the losers.

Reflecting upon this unhappy outcome, two educational leaders began to ask themselves, "Can we find a way ahead? Is there a new creative solution?" The late O'Neil C. d'Amour of the National Catholic Education Association and Rolfe Lanier Hunt of the National Council of Churches staff began talking to one another. Soon out of their conversations and soul-searchings there was convened a conference of educational leaders from the Catholic and Protestant churches to see if a new way ahead might be discerned.

The meeting was held in Washington, D.C., in an atmosphere of common concern. At this meeting Harry Stearns, a Presbyterian layman, then superintendent of the public school system of Englewood, New Jersey, presented a paper advancing the idea of "shared time" as a possible new pattern.

According to this concept, Catholics could give up their attempts to provide full-time instruction of their students in parochial schools and settle for something else and less. That something less was instruction in the church school of pupils in those subjects for which religious faith had the most relevance—i.e., history, literature, social studies, religion and ethics—while those subjects with the least immediate connection with religious or theological concepts—mathematics, the physical sciences, shop, domestic arts, etc. —could be taught in the public school and for the benefit of all the children of the community. Schoolmen were quick to see that the Catholic transfer to the public school of these particular subjects, the most expensive in the curriculum, would prove to be a most substantial monetary saving.

Full-time non-Catholic students would belong to only one school as heretofore, but Catholic students would enroll in two schools, spending part of the day (or part of the week) in each institution.

As the later discussion developed in subsequent sessions and in later meetings held in Washington and in New York City, it was seen that there were no legal or constitutional barriers to such a plan. It was acknowledged that while there were undoubted administrative difficulties, these complications were not incapable of solution, and that the proposal might go a long way toward alleviating the very real financial difficulties of Catholic educators.

It was recognized that Jewish leaders would have to be involved. Accordingly, one of the later conferences was composed of representatives of the three faiths. For the most part, however, Jewish leaders remained either skeptical or opposed to the proposal, believing that the plan presented impossible operating difficulties, and that it would be in time a stepping-stone to the advancing of other claims upon public monies for religious schools.

The interchurch consensus, however, was impressive, and it was therefore possible at the next session of the Congress to sidestep the old debate. Representatives of both faiths assured the Congress that this idea of "shared time" (later called "dual school enrollment") deserved local experimentation and might prove to be a partial answer to the problem.

The continuing needs of the nation, combined with this assurance from religious leaders, seemed to be conclusive to the members of the Congress. Thus it was that the first Federal aid to education legislation on a broad and inclusive basis was passed.

Such co-operation by national bodies enormously increased local community ventures. There were in the national discussions representatives of community and city school systems, both Catholic and public. Several commitments for local experimentation were made in the meetings, and before long conversations were inaugurated between heads of systems in the same locality and between them and the general public.

Soon ventures were established in several states, and remarkable acceptance has been noted on the part of Catholic educators and parents, of public school administrators, and of the general citizenry.

These arrangements do not, it must be admitted, solve the basic problem, that of the skyrocketing costs of education. Several of the Protestant denominations mentioned above are now considering, in the light of rapidly rising costs, whether they can continue to support parochial education as they have done in the past. For Catholics the problem is especially acute, made so by the strength of their convictions that this type of education is both educationally defensible and spiritually desirable.

If the conviction continues among Catholics, if the dual school enrollment plan fails to win support for any reason, if the state or

Federal treasury is seen as a legitimate source of fiscal relief, and if no new and as yet unforeseen answer is worked out, then Catholic and Protestant educational leaders may be headed for more controversy. Protestants are probably not going to come around in the observable future to approve the use of Federal, state, or local monies for the support, even in part, of the teaching of religion, or of a particular expression thereof. It is to be hoped that either by the demonstrated success of this compromise plan or by some other device cherished convictions on both sides of the Christian household may be protected, and that the needs of all American children for a better education may be generously met.

Education and Some Contemporary Needs

In an address given at a Religious Education Association convention in 1966, John C. Bennett, president of Union Theological Seminary, New York, spoke on "What We Should Do Together." To his question he replied by saying that there were five suggestions he would like to see explored: a common witness on the theological front; co-operation in the struggle for civil rights; advances toward the solution of the problem of poverty; common commitment to international economic and social justice; and joint efforts for peace.

If these are the *shoulds* of common endeavor for Catholics and Protestants, how shall we appraise where we are and the prospects for significant advances? I am not ommicompetent to review the prospects for Catholics and to avoid highly subjective judgments about the Protestant outlook. My views may, however, have some correspondence to the state of things as they are, and readers may make their own corrections and modifications.

On the theological front of which Dr. Bennett speaks, I believe the prospects are decidedly encouraging. The Protestant churches have a revived interest in matters of Faith and Order as symbolized by the establishment in the National Council of Churches in 1959 of a Department of Faith and Order, a radical break with its own tradition and with the traditions of the agencies which preceded it. Taking their lead from the example of the national agency, numerous state and city councils of churches, perhaps eighty of them, have established similar units which are working persistently with the constituent congregations or judicatories and utilizing the considerable resources of talent resident within their territories as well as leadership from more distant places.

In Protestantism the forces of Christian education have not been notably interested in the questions which have long preoccupied Faith and Order experts. For the past quarter century most of the denominations have experienced a revived interest in the place of theology in programs of Christian education, but this concern has often been expressed in denominational terms. Not often has it found face and form to explore the issues of the unity and the divisions which are alike characteristic of our present ecumenical situation.

Nor have the Faith and Order specialists been concerned to enlist the competencies of the educational leaders of the churches. Too often religious educators were regarded as mere technicians or Sunday school enthusiasts. In the summer of 1968 the picture changed for the better. There is a widespread interest on the part of the educational leaders and there is a desire to effect a working relationship with them on the part of Faith and Order persons.

The Faith and Order Colloquium held at the University of Notre Dame in the summers of 1967 and 1968 found Christian educators and theologians meeting in a common quest for the answer to the problem "How may we make clear the unity and the divisions which are ours, and communicate them to the people of our churches; adults, young people, and, yes, even to children in language and in spirit appropriate to them?" There is a growing partnership which promises to be more and more effective as acquaintanceship grows and mutual trust and respect deepen.

President Bennett spoke also of civil rights. Here again the picture has some encouraging details. Some new developments have come about within the past few years.

Those of us who are zealously concerned about these issues in the 1960s ought not to assume that the concern began with us, nor that interchurch co-operation in such matters began in our day. It is clear, as one looks at the record of the Department of Racial and Cultural Relations of the National Council of Churches and the work of the department of the same name which preceded it in the former Federal Council of Churches, that Protestant and Catholic collaboration in these issues and in ways appropriate to their times was carried on effectively and persistently by J. Oscar Lee and his predecessor, the late George Haines.

These efforts were limited, however, partly because of mistrust and inhibitions within Protestant circles and partly by the same hindrances in Catholic arenas.

Today, however, there is free and generous interchange on the part of religious leaders in general and of Christian education persons in particular. They are united in their common concerns to educate the whites in our churches for the responsibilities of power which realistically has been theirs; power which so often has been used as a means of perpetuating class privilege and racial bias, and which now must be shared with the black community.

Dr. Bennett declares,

Certainly in the sphere of religious education imaginative understanding can be encouraged and careful distinctions made and we can help to prepare our constituencies for the courage and the commitment and the wisdom that will be needed in the midst of innumerable local and regional situations in which we shall have to act and take sides on political choices when we would prefer to wait until there is a clearer choice.[8]

It would be interesting to do a research study on the manner in which church school curricula have dealt with the matter of civil rights. It is my impression that, particularly in elective courses for youth and adults, where there is considerably more opportunity for timeliness, a rather gratifying record would be revealed.

Such an evaluation, even at best, would naturally be only relative. Not gratifying in the eyes of God, surely, not yet gratifying as measured against what ought to have been done in the light of moral imperatives and obvious social needs. A more modest standard of measurement would have to be utilized: gratifying in the light of the common thinking and practice of the church at that time.

The involvement will increase in the next few years. The temper of the times, and the general determination of denominational Christian education leaders to shape up a relevant program and curriculum will see to that.

So far as Dr. Bennett's third point is concerned, poverty, I am less sanguine than with the first two issues. It is true that studies of the economic backgrounds of Protestant church people show a remarkable and unsuspected congruence to the economic backgrounds of the American people at large. But such studies embrace the whole spectrum of American Protestantism, not only the people of the churches affiliated with manifestations of the ecumenical movement.

While there are exceptions to the generalization, on the whole the churches which have elected to remain outside the ecumenical movement are not the churches which display a lively interest in the moral problems raised by the scandal of the persistent pockets of poverty still to be found in every section of the nation and among all racial and ethnic groups.

Within the ecumenical movement the churches have their own impediments to effective education and action. To be sure, these church bodies have been prolific with their pronouncements. Educational forces have assumed their special roles. James Myers and Cameron Hall, along with other distinguished and able church leaders, have rendered effective service.

Yet the insensitivity and lethargy of most Protestant congregations has rather effectively insulated them against a disturbing awareness of the problems of American and world poverty. Our unprecedented affluent society has built up something akin to an illusion that these issues are either relatively minor or, worse still, non-existent. One has only to observe the still continuing boom in the erection of new church buildings to be aware both that the churches have money and that a distressingly large amount of it is being spent on themselves.

Against this trend the boards of education, the boards of national missions, and the boards of world missions have lifted their voices (and their pens), through their own direct channels, to the congregations. In one recent year they have also collaborated in their regularly established instrumentality, the Department of Education for Mission in the National Council of Churches, in their stated annual theme for mission study, "Affluence and Poverty", for which emphasis twenty-two separate pieces of material were prepared and distributed to the churches.

If there are notable and widespread examples of Catholic successes in bringing these urgent problems home to the attention of prosperous congregations and eliciting from them relevant and effective action, Protestant church leaders would be grateful for any shared insights. On the whole, Protestants have not been conspicuously successful.

Professor Bennett mentioned as his fourth and fifth points international economic and social justice and the cause of peace. For our purposes we may take them together.

How effective are our educational efforts on behalf of this cause? Not very effective, if one is aware of the realities of the world in which we live, observing as we do almost omnipresent international economic and social injustice and war, both civil and international, in almost every quarter of our bleeding globe.

Yet the churches, and in particular their educational boards, have been responsibly at work in the attempt to create a better state of things: if not a warless world, as the romantic efforts of the 1930s sometimes put it, at least a world in which war would be contained and the machinery for the settlement of international disputes would be increasingly trusted and utilized.

In Protestant structures there are often found within a single denominational body three agencies with a special responsibility for international economic and social justice and the furtherance of peace. The boards of world missions have been intimately involved in world affairs for more than a hundred years. They have an accumulated competence in terms of present personnel and inherited experience. The church units on world peace and international justice are of more recent origin. They are composed of specialists in the work of international relations, most of them working in close co-operation with the Churches' Commission on International Affairs of the World Council of Churches. Sometimes these bodies are independently constituted by the churches, sometimes structured within more inclusive boards of social issues. Perhaps most effective in reaching the constituency of the local church are the departments of women's work and their National Council agency, Church Women United, which with its predecessor agencies has had a remarkable skill for getting things done with a minimum of red tape, a maximum of local involvement, and an altogether admirable verve and *élan* in the process.

Youth and student groups within the Protestant churches have made an impressive record for themselves in their advocacy of international order, often to the embarrassment of their seniors. The pacifist movement of the 1920s and the 1930s and the student demonstrations against the present war in Vietnam have found church youth and student groups deeply involved. Not all the involvement has been on the demonstrative and strident side, moreover, for serious study and reflection shot through with solid theological understanding has characterized youth and student responses.

If the Roman Catholic observer comments that this is a remarkably diffuse structuring in Protestantism for the prosecution of so important an issue, the answer has to be "it is." Church structures usually come to be the way they are as results of historical growth. They are not often created according to a predetermined plan or organizational chart. Those in the Catholic Church who wish to find possible connections will find the attempt not difficult. For all the apparent diversity there is a significant amount of collaboration within the churches brought about in some instances by denominational program-co-ordinating bodies.

In spite of the sense of growing unity which is so happily a characteristic of our times, there remain real differences between the divided members of Christ's church. It will do no good to minimize them in public or private discussion, nor to act as if they were inconsequential. Time and the goodness of God will resolve them, we hope.

Meanwhile church identity must not be put in jeopardy, for (who knows?) cherished insights lightly put aside may turn out to be the truths that others in time will recognize. Meanwhile, taking full cognizance of the still effective barriers which hinder our complete collaboration, there are more roads opening these days to useful common educational efforts than any of us will have the time to explore.

In the happy exploration of these new paths God is opening up for us, both congregational and parish efforts and national strategies and policies have their roles to play, each supplementing the other. Each man and woman, each disciple of the Lord of the church, can be faithful to the task apportioned to him in his own place.

SIX

The Church's Worship as Formative of the Christian Community

A. by GEOFFREY I. KEATING, S.S.E.

B. by IRIS V. CULLY

A. *by* GEOFFREY I. KEATING, *S.S.E.*

As I HAVE examined this area of thought, I have thought of several possible ways of developing the chapter. The concept in the title which has struck me as most important is contained in the expression "Christian community." And as a post-Conciliar Catholic dwells on these words he immediately makes a distinction, for they can be thought of in two different ways at a very fundamental level. First, "Christian community" refers to that unity which exists (or should exist) among all those who profess Christ to be Lord and Master. Second, it refers to the unity of those who are members of the Roman Catholic Church. We have become very aware of the first meaning in recent years through the ecumenical dialogue. The second we have always had with us, often in very exaggerated forms. Sometimes we refer to the first-described community as the catholic (small "c") church, and to the latter as the Catholic Church. Accordingly this essay will be divided into two major parts:

1. The church's worship as formative of the catholic (small "c") community. Here we will stress the need of a much greater integration of the liturgical and ecumenical movements.

2. The church's worship (liturgy) as formative of the Roman Catholic community. Here we will speak of the great liturgical crisis in the Catholic Church.

I would like to point out that the title of this essay was given to me. For that reason I have limited myself to the consideration of *Christian* problems, even though my own interests are gradually going (and growing, I hope) beyond this very limited and limiting perspective. I have also taken certain liberties in my interpretation of the title. I have taken the expression "church's worship" to mean liturgy. And I have interpreted the word "formative" very loosely, for liturgy not only *forms* Christian community, but also *expresses* and *celebrates* it; and I cannot get myself to speak about the liturgy without bringing in these words and the ideas that they impart.

I have accepted the challenge to write this chapter with great reluctance because I am very aware that a realistic treatment of it would be impossible without touching upon some of the great theological, pastoral, and catechetical issues of the day. To state an increasingly obvious truth, any study of the liturgy's relationship to Christian community is a very complex undertaking, from both a theoretical and practical point of view. Furthermore, I share the Catholic post-Conciliar introspection and, let us be frank, confusion, to which many of my friends will gladly testify! Also, anytime I speak or write on this or related topics I run the risk of involving others in this confusion, and this frightens me. So whenever I say *anything* these days I do so as one engaged in a search, not as one offering clear, definitive answers to very profound problems. This last fact is probably the main reason for my reluctance to write this essay in an ecumenical publication, as I am supposed to represent the "Catholic point of view" (whatever that is), and I am sure that many who read this will wonder just how "Catholic" the author is. In any case, to satisfy this requirement I have limited myself in choosing sources almost exclusively to contemporary Catholic authors, realizing that the "Catholicity" of many of these has already been questioned.

Recently I have been reading for the second (third?) time Gregory Baum's *Credibility of the Church Today* and came across this passage:

There are in the Catholic Church progressive Catholics who wish to renew Catholic life according to Vatican II, then there are conservative Catholics who prefer the preconciliar Church, and finally there is the "third man."

Who is the third man? The third man believes that God has acted in Jesus Christ on behalf of all men and that this divine salvation is available in the spirit in the celebration of the Catholic Church. The third man is a Catholic. He regards the Church as his spiritual home. He is deeply attached to the Catholic tradition. At the same time, he takes the institutional Church with a grain of salt. He loves Catholic teaching when it makes sense to him, when it gives him access to new life and enables him to respond to the demands the world makes on him; but if the teaching does not make sense to him, he does not bother with it. He does not wish to argue with other Catholics about it. It would not occur to him to argue with Bishops or the Pope. If these teachings make sense to other Catholics, the third man thinks that they should accept them wholeheartedly. Similarly, the third man loves the sacramental life of the Church. He participates in the Sacraments when they make sense to him, when they deepen his awareness of God's presence and strengthen him in his involvement with other people. But when they do not make sense to him, when they become barriers to worship and community, then he does not bother with them. Again, he does not feel like arguing about it. He makes his own choice; he does not feel guilty about it. He wants to leave other people free to make up their own minds. The third man, moreover, acknowledges the law of the Church. He is no rebel. He believes in law and order. And at the same time he realizes that human life is complex and that there are situations in which ecclesiastical law does not promote the spiritual well-being of persons. In those cases he feels free to act apart from canon law and, if necessary, move to the margin of the ecclesiastical institution.[1]

I promise that this will be the longest quotation of this essay, but some people have told me that it is a rather graphic description of myself. With certain qualifications I am forced to agree. I mention all this not to talk about myself, but to warn unsuspecting readers of what is to follow.

The Catholic (small "c") Community

Before we can come to any sort of conclusions about the relationship of liturgy to Christian community it is imperative to discuss somewhat the meaning of "Christian community." As I understand it, Christian community is found wherever any group of people is united by love of Christ and each other, sustained by faith in his reality and hope in his promises, and dedicated to sharing that faith, hope, and love with all men. As easy as it is to say these words, the history of Christianity makes it clear that thinking Christians have had great difficulties in agreeing as to whom these words actually apply. The Catholic of today has his difficulties because he is trying to break the long-standing habit of thinking within very narrow limits and at the same time assimilate the special insights which contemporary knowledge (especially history, sociology, and psychology) brings to the problem. And he is finding out that this habit is not easily overcome, no matter how "liberal" or "progressive" he may think himself to be. For he is hard put to reconcile that habitual view (i.e., the *true* and *full* Christian community is identified with the Roman Catholic Church) with the more ecumenical (and less definable) view which includes all believers in Christ within its limits. From what I observe there is a similar phenomenon happening in many branches of Protestantism, but others will have to speak of that. Actually, and I hope that this is not an exaggeration, the arrival of the third man (described above) on the Catholic scene is very directly related to the psychological upset involved in passing from a very exclusivist view of Christian community to a much broader one. I am sure that everyone who is trying seriously to make this transition has experienced those awful moments when he was sure that the bottom had fallen out of everything and that he was about to experience one of those "crises of faith" which we hear about so much these days. And the depth of this experience should not surprise anyone, because this person who has been brought up with the "infallibility syndrome" finds himself, to his own amazement, admitting that one Martin Luther had some very good ideas indeed, and that the official church has a history remarkable for its consistently bad judgment.

Of course, the documents of the Second Vatican Council not only help us make this transition, but also give us the mandate to do so—at least in several passages. But even here there are not a few problems of consistency, for we keep moving from one theological world to another in these documents.[2] I suppose that this was inevitable given the makeup of the hierarchy present at the Council and that it is a healthy sign of recognition by the bishops that there is room for, and need of, theological diversity even at the "top." Indeed, this theological diversity permeates contemporary Catholic literature even, and, I dare say, especially when fundamental issues are under consideration. This is especially true today when the topic is the "church," "Christian community," or the like. For as one surveys this literature he finds that such expressions mean different things to different people.

If one reads, for example, much of the present Catholic literature on the liturgy and sacraments, the very clear impression is given that what is envisaged when the word "church" is used is the Roman Catholic community made one by participation in the liturgical and sacramental life of the church.[3] This is, of course, the exclusivist or particularist view already mentioned. In this view liturgical celebration is seen as formative of community as well as expressive of it. And the community in question is Roman Catholic. The classic statement of this view is *The Constitution on Sacred Liturgy* of the Second Vatican Council, in which the word "church" is consistently used in a very exclusivist sense.[4] In the last analysis, even though all can learn much from this document, it is written for Catholics and about Catholics.

An altogether different impression is given when one examines some contemporary ecclesiology or, for that matter, some of the other documents of the Council. Here we find a much broader concept of church and Christian community.[5] Not that there is a denial of the uniqueness of the Catholic Church and tradition, but there is recognition of the validity of other churches and "ecclesial communities."[6] This recognition is so strong and so explicit that the post-Conciliar Catholic finds himself becoming very cautious when he uses these words. All of which makes it clear that there is evolving in the Catholic mentality a way of thinking about the church of Christ which is quite different from that of the past few hundred years. In contemporary Catholic writing the most profound and responsible statement of this mentality is to be found, I think, in the book by Hans Küng entitled simply *The Church*, from which I quote here one brief passage which summarizes so well this attitude:

The Church exists in the world. But it can lay no exclusive claim to certainty of salvation vis-à-vis to the world nor to spiritual authority. What it wants is quite different: to give selfless and unpretentious service to the salvation of the world. To be truly catholic the Church must think of itself not as synonymous with the world, nor yet on the other hand as an exclusive society of those already saved, but as an open community of people dedicated to serve and work for the salvation of all, of the whole of mankind.[7]

It is my contention that we Catholics cannot make much headway in solving the profound problems implied in the title of this chapter unless we learn to handle and to live with both of these outlooks with equal ease and emphasis. An exclusivist view, when overemphasized, not only leads to a distorted liturgy and theology, but also makes a farce out of all ecumenical endeavors. In other words, the ecumenical dialogue will have to enter more and more into our liturgy, which is supposed to be the celebration and formation and expression of the whole Christian community. Of course, there is no guarantee that all other ecclesial communities will be co-operative in this, and it will be very difficult to come to terms on many points; but if we mean everything we say about the ecumenical movement, if we really thirst for unity, we should take the initiative; we should be extending the invitation.

On the other hand, because of our belief in the "uniqueness" of the Roman Catholic Church we have the obligation to celebrate and express that belief. Granted that this may have been overdone in the past and needs to be corrected, it is still true that the achievement of balance is most difficult and will continue to be so because so many Catholics see that uniqueness and nothing else as worthy of celebration.

So how are we to achieve that balance whereby we celebrate in our liturgy the uniqueness of the Catholic community as well as the unity of all men who, in the name of Christ and out of love for him, are a "people dedicated to serve and work for the salvation of all, of the whole of mankind"?

It seems to me that this will come about only if the following conditions are met:

1. The recognition that a plurality of liturgical forms is required to meet the demands of the ecumenical dialogues.

2. The search for the liturgical celebration of Christian unity must be engaged in by all interested parties—and this with a sense of urgency.

3. A massive program of grass roots education in ecclesiology.

I can already hear someone saying that the first two conditions, at least, are being met. My answer to this is that what we have up to this point is not much more than tokenism. One cannot deny, of course, that in some circles there is a lot of talk about plurality of forms in liturgy, as in other aspects of Christian life and thought. But it all seems to be accompanied by so much fear and hesitation that one has to wonder how much conviction there is behind it. Also, co-operative ventures among Christians in liturgical celebrations, though rather widespread in some areas, are still very limited, at least in this country. This may be so because the whole "program" is just getting off the ground , and nobody seems quite sure of the direction in which we are going or of what must be retained and what can be sacrificed for the common good. But speaking as a Catholic (and others will have to speak for other ecclesial communities) I feel that we are not really trying hard enough to implement these two conditions.

The reason, I think, why the first two conditions are being met in such a limited way is that the third condition is hardly being met at all. At the grass roots level, though there is much friendship and interaction among Christians in our very pluralistic society, there seems to be very little conscious ecumenism and even less interest in it as such. I do not think it an exaggeration to say that the formal ecumenical movement and dialogue is limited to a very small elite of fairly well-educated people who know some history and theology, or who are interested in learning some. Outside this group there is no "movement" and very little dialogue. This should not be surprising, because those who have little or no appreciation of the sources of division or of the bitter hostilities of the past cannot be expected to thirst for lost unity. Moreover, speaking of the Catholic community (and, from what I see, this is very true of many Protestant groups), there is very widespread suspicion that the ecumenical dialogue and its search for unity is nothing more than a sellout, bound to end in unhealthy compromises.[8] From my point of view this is all very sad and can be corrected only by education at all levels regarding the true nature of the church. As in everything else, ignorance and suspicion can be overcome only by education, and what we are dealing with here can be reduced to suspicion and ignorance.

What all this adds up to is that within the Catholic Church there has not been a significant integration of the liturgical and ecumenical movements.

This being the case, are there some signs of hope that there will be in the future a greater integration of these two movements? I think that there are. And the greatest sign of hope is found in the recent developments of ecclesiology among many Catholic theologians. I have already spoken somewhat of the exclusivist view of the church, very widespread among Catholics, and based on a long and strong tradition. But there is emerging another view which is non-exclusivist, which admits the validity of more than one authentic tradition, and which advocates unity amid great diversity. I have also mentioned this view previously, and I personally opt for it. And when I said before that we need grass roots education in ecclesiology it is a less exclusivist concept of the church which must be taught. Only when this is understood by Catholics will the ecumenical movment have a chance or realizing its goals and will Christian community be celebrated, formed, and expressed through an adequate liturgy.

Since I believe that these two views of the church are somewhat incompatible (in theory, at least), and because I think that the great theological debates of the future will center around these views, and because I am convinced that one's thinking about liturgy and ecumenics is totally dependent on one's thinking about the church, I will now attempt to compare these two views in some detail.

The thinking of one who has this exclusivist view of the church goes as follows: Jesus founded a church and that church has been and continues to be realized in its fullness in the Church of Rome. Whoever enters that church enters the Christian community in its fullest and most authentic form and remains a member of that community through loyal obedience to the legitimate successors of Peter and his fellow apostles. Every Christian community not affiliated with this true church is, for that very reason, incomplete. According to this view, the community pre-exists any choice to join it by an individual, for that "community" from the beginning was brought into existence by Christ. That all sorts of changes have taken place throughout history is gladly admitted, but the essential elements have been there from the beginning: The fullness of the Christian community is found wherever Peter and the apostles are.[9]

Personally, I do not see how a Catholic could deny this version of apostolic succession and still remain, or want to remain, in the Catholic Church. But I do think it is legitimate to question the exclusivity of this claim, i.e., that it is the one, true church. The following statement of Gregory Baum's seems to capture the spirit behind such questioning:

There are many good reasons for being Protestant. I do not see how a Catholic of the post-conciliar Church can still desire the conversion of Protestants to Roman Catholicism. What we desire for our fellow Christians is what we desire for ourselves: that they live more deeply from the Gospel and participate in the renewal of their Church so that all Churches come closer together in common obedience to Christ.[10]

If anyone agrees with these words, as I do, the implications for the ecumenical-liturgical movement are inescapable. For implicit in these words is the admission that the claims of other churches are also authentic, or, at least, that these communities have the adequate means of salvation within their grasp. They do not *need* the Roman Church. The Catholic version of Christian life is defensible, but so are the versions of other ecclesial communities. And what each Christian community should be in search of is not primarily uniformity of doctrine and/or theology, but rather a renewal, a search for greater fidelity to the gospel in the light of their own basic principles, insights, and traditions, and a total renouncement of any kind of competition for souls.

This is not to deny, of course, that we can learn a lot from each other. In fact, this is what the "dialogue" is all about. And as we look to the future, if we are sincere in this dialogue, we can expect to find how much faith, hope, and charity we have in common; how much we are already forming a united, but pluralistic, community.

If there is any truth in all this, and for the sake of the gospel there had better be, we agree with those authors who have proclaimed the death of the "Counter-Reformation."[11] We also agree, as a consequence, in the truth of these words:

Controversial theology can be distracting. By controversial theology I mean discussion on those doctrines which divided Christianity at the time of the Reformation. The theological discussions should revolve around the question that is of primary importance to all believing Christians today, namely, how modern man can live and present authentic Christianity to the non-Christians in their own country so that it does not appear to them as a spiritual and ceremonial museum piece. This is the urgent task of all confessions. Common effort on this problem will contribute more to Christian unity than a concentration on the old questions of controversial theology.[12]

I do not deny that some doctrinal discussions will always have to take place and that at this point in history agreement on many issues is impossible. Again it is a question of emphasis and balance; and if we are to avoid the mistakes of the polemical past we should de-emphasize controversy.

If all this be true, we can say that, at this point in history, the most significant Christian communities being formed are those which involve the co-operative efforts of believers from a variety of backgrounds searching together to learn and live genuine faith, hope, and love. And as we engage in this pursuit, while retaining much variety, we shall also be looking to develop ways to express and celebrate this newfound unity of faith, hope, and love. The most significant liturgical breakthroughs will be those which do this. Conversely, the least significant liturgical renewals in any church will be those which, consciously or not, perpetuate the divisions of the past without adequate attention paid to the ecumenical present and future.

All of this indicates, of course, that the Christian community of the future will be marked by great diversity in unity, and this will be celebrated, expressed, and formed by liturgies not yet invented. The best description of this church which I have found is by Hans Küng, speaking on the New Testament teaching on the church:

In the New Testament Christ's Church is not seen as a centralized egalitarian or totalitarian monolith. The joyless constricting uniformity of a standardized institution or a standard type is foreign to it. It is not part of the nature of the Church to have a uniform form of worship, nor uniform hierarchies, nor even a uniform theology. In light of Ephesians 4:4–6, the opposite would seem to be true. Diversity in worship: one God, one baptism and one Lord's supper—but different peoples, different communities, different languages, different rites and forms of devotion, different prayers, hymns and vestments, different styles of art and in this sense different Churches. Diversity in theology too: one God, one Lord, one hope and one faith—but different theologies, different systems, different styles of thought, different conceptual apparatus and terminology, different schools, traditions and areas of research, different universities and theologians, and in this sense again different Churches. Diversity finally in Church order: one God, one Lord, one Spirit and one body—but a different order of life, different laws, different nations and traditions, different customs, usages and administrative systems, and so in this sense too different Churches.[13]

I consider such words to be prophetic and I would be deluding myself if I thought that most Catholics agreed with them. Above all, it is certain that most representatives of the official *magisterium* do not agree, which creates problems for the Catholic! In any case, such words do pinpoint a great problem which has been stated much more bluntly by another theologian: "The struggle in the Church today is largely one of uniformity against pluralism."[14]

In concluding this part I would like to say that I am very much aware that I will be called a dreamer, a romantic, totally lacking a realistic view of the past, present, and future. To this I can only say that, though I do not dare *predict* the future, I know quite a bit about the past and live in the hope that most of it will not be repeated. What I have described is a vision, not a plan. If I had a plan, or could find one, I would certainly shout it from the rooftops. Moreover, I remain quite realistic, at times almost cynical, because I know that the real question right now is whether or not we Christians have enough tolerance among us to make this dream of unity a reality; whether we are willing to convert past and present controversy and conflict into a healthy tension creative of a pluralistic Christian community.

The Roman Catholic Community

As I said at the beginning we shall take up in this part an analysis of the Catholic liturgy in so far as this is the expression, celebration, and formation of the Roman Catholic community, which, according to our faith, is an authentic historical embodiment and channel of Christ and his redemptive work.

In a recent work Gabriel Moran and Maria Harris have written as follows:

. . . it is necessary to keep in mind the liturgical crisis affecting the whole Catholic Church. The long years of liturgical reform came to a glorious conclusion, it was thought, with the official approval of the new liturgy early in the Council. But as we have several times pointed out, if one is going to leave a carefully defined system, one had better be ready for a quantum leap. To this day it does not seem to have come through to church leaders that translated prayers, inserted hymns and changed rituals leave everyone malcontent. A few years ago there was a clear-cut battle between liturgists who wanted change and the conservatives who wanted no change. More recently, the lines have become blurred; the roles often seem to have reversed. People who had steadfastly resisted any of the liturgy business now often sing the loudest, offer their petitions and hit all the proper responses. In contrast, the progressive who once diligently worked for all these things can now often be found outside the chapel or, if inside, standing mute with a pained look on his face.[15]

This passage, written in the context of the renewal of religious life in the Catholic Church, pinpoints one of the great paradoxes of recent Catholic experience. At this point in history, after several decades of hard work (and widespread unpopularity) by so many activists of the liturgical movement, one would have expected a golden age to have emerged. Had not the official church enthusiastically endorsed the outlook and approach and programs of this movement? But what we have is anything but a golden age. William Buckley registers his reaction to the present-day mass and efforts at participation in it: "I think that the whole thing is an absolute mess."[16] It is as if the liturgical movement had had the effect of opening a can of worms. And this is probably the great contribution of that movement. Having brought up so many questions for discussion about the liturgy, it paved the way in the Catholic Church for much deeper questioning about prayer, spirituality, catechetics, history, and theology. In other words, the liturgical movement, to its eternal credit, has been responsible for much of the critical questioning in the Catholic Church, but the questions themselves have led the askers into areas where the study and practice of liturgy have proven to verge on almost total irrelevancy. In terms of questions being asked previous to Vatican II, the ideas and proposals of the liturgists were radical and daring. In terms, however, of post-Conciliar experience, the liturgist finds the burning questions to be outside his "field." Even as Vatican II was in its initial stages, most informed Catholics were wondering how the fathers would handle the liturgy. And by the end of the Council, and during the past few years, fewer and fewer Catholics really seem to care very much. Or, if they do care, they have become resigned to the fact that the liturgical dimension of life is in a state of crisis and that not too much should be expected from it at the present time.

I have, of course, been dealing in some sweeping generalities. All that I have wanted to point out is that the liturgy in the Catholic Church, for better or for worse, has rapidly moved away from center stage in Catholic life—which it had apparently begun to hold in the decades preceding Vatican II; that the experience of the past few years necessarily leads one to re-examine this statement of that Council: "Nevertheless, the liturgy is the summit toward which the activity of the Church is directed; at the same time it is the fountain from which all her powers flow."[17]

Without a doubt this statement has to be a challenge to all thinking Christians, for, though it is the concise statement of a principle, it seems to contradict the experience of the past few years.

Some will say in response that if you really understand what is meant by liturgy you could not have any serious trouble with this statement. Maybe this is so; but just what do we mean by liturgy? It is important, before going any further in our examination of the Catholic liturgical crisis, to summarize, according to Vatican II, the Catholic theology of liturgy. In doing this we will follow the *Constitution on Sacred Liturgy* where it speaks of the nature and purpose of liturgy.[18] In this document the following points are made:

1. (No. 2) "The liturgy is the outstanding means by which the faithful can express in their lives, and manifest to others, the mystery of Christ and the real nature of the true Church." Here, basically, the liturgy is seen as the means of expression of faith in the mystery of Christ, and as sign to others of that faith.

2. The liturgy is not merely an outlet for personal piety, but it is the whole church's proclamation of the mystery of Christ.

3. It is also the "exercise of the work of salvation," through which one is "plunged into the paschal mystery of Christ" (No. 6) and by which the whole church celebrates that mystery.

4. Especially through liturgical celebrations Christ is always present in his church (No. 7), carries out his work of salvation, and continues his worship of the eternal Father.

5. The liturgy is the "action of Christ the priest and of his Body the Church," and in which the "sanctification of man is manifested by signs perceptible to the senses."

This brief summary of Vatican II on the theology of liturgy is sufficient for our purposes. This whole document of the Council is without a doubt an excellent presentation of Catholic thought on the subject as developed especially since the 1930s. And to admit the validity of this thinking demands a very profound act of faith in Christ and his continuing real presence in history through a church and its liturgy. The liturgy is certainly the expression and celebration of the church's faith in the mystery of Christ, but, in the Catholic view, it is also the infallible guarantee of the presence of the living and saving Christ. If one makes this act of faith, the liturgy is indeed the summit of all Christian life and the source of all the church's power, influence, and witness.

But let us face it. We Catholics have a huge pastoral problem, because so many Catholics are not making this act of faith. I do not know how many hundreds of times I have heard in recent months from Catholics about their doubts concerning the importance of the liturgy and its centrality in their lives. This is especially true of young adults, but by no means exclusively.

Many reasons are given for this lack of interest and/or participation in liturgy by many Catholics of the post-Conciliar church. Of all the reasons proposed to explain this phenomenon the following seem to be among the most relevant:

1. As Catholics become more and more educated there is bound to be a profound questioning of the whole sacramental approach to the practice of faith, which is such a strong characteristic of the

Catholic Church. One author refers to this as the danger of spiritual snobbery, and there may be some truth to this.[19] However, it may well be that this growing suspicion of the sacramental "system" may be the predictable outcome of some very bad teaching about what the sacraments and liturgy really are and have been in the Christian tradition. It may also be a symptom of a maturing process among Catholics which will have to be met by much better teaching.

2. Some have noted that the rise of "personalism" in the twentieth century has had the effect on many Catholics (and others) of searching for the real presence of Christ in persons, not in sacred things and symbols. The thinking behind this is based on the judgment that excessive preoccupation with sacraments has tended to distract Catholics from carrying out their responsibilities in and for this world. The following passage reflects this very clearly:

> By staking so much on the liturgical reform, and by making it the key to all other reforms, the liturgical movement has provided people with a means of evading their full responsibilities in the world.[20]

3. Very closely connected with the previous point is the idea that a development of Christian spirituality which concentrates on this world and Christian responsibility for it has led many to an extensive re-evaluation of the whole validity of the sacraments and liturgy, which focus so much on the "other world" and the "world to come." It is almost as if the whole secularization process of Western civilization has finally caught up with Catholicism, that many Catholics are experiencing, consciously or not, the "absence of God"; and the liturgy which emphasizes so much God's (Christ's) presence in our midst is more and more difficult to accept. I certainly am not saying that all of this is good. But there is an awful lot of evidence that it is true. Maybe the development in recent years of a "theology of hope" and the great renewal of interest among theologians in eschatology are symptoms that what we have been saying is very true.

4. As I mentioned earlier, there has been some very bad teaching in Catholic circles about liturgy and sacraments. Just speak to young Catholics about this dimension of the spiritual life and you will find that many have rejected the "sacramental life" (confession

and mass) because they have concluded that there is too much superstition and hypocrisy (their favorite word) connected with it; or that it too mechanical to suit their needs. Again, I do not say that this is good, or that I agree with their evaluation, but this is the situation. Or speak with older-generation Catholics and you will find that many have such an individualistic piety that they are at a complete loss if you try to explain the communal dimension of liturgy and sacraments. I recently asked a group of about forty middle-generation Catholics what they thought of making weekly mass completely optional by removing the obligation (binding under sin) of attending. There was general agreement that the churches would have an awful lot of empty pews on Sundays. Which suggests to me that part of the poor teaching in the past has been precisely an overreliance on legal and external threats.

5. The whole life-style and values of contemporary civilization do not lend themselves to religious faith and its celebration. It is not just that the life of man has become secularized; it is also hedonistic and materialistic. Hence, though we live in a world flowing with secular "myths" and symbols, religious values and their corresponding symbols seem to fall on deaf ears. There are many who lose interest in, or never get interested in, liturgy because they are typical representatives of our times, of our world which has no interest in God because simply "it is excessively engrossed in earthly affairs."[21]

The preceding points have been made to present a partial explanation of the present crisis in liturgy in the Catholic Church. Each could be elaborated upon and others made to complete the explanation, but we have at least touched upon some of the more obvious aspects of the problem.

The question now arises as to what, if anything, can be done to bring the liturgy through its present crisis. I shall attempt to indicate in the following paragraphs some fundamental needs which, it seems to me, will have to be met if we are to come through the present crisis.

As I mentioned at the outset, I seem to be a "third man" Catholic. It should not be surprising, then, that my initial remark is a quotation from Daniel Callahan, who says, in explaining the failure of the liturgical movement: "The liturgy should never have been considered the source and center of the Christian life. It is important, indeed vital, but it shares its importance with many other aspects of the Christian life."[22] I agree wholeheartedly with this statement. The failure of the liturgical movement is due, in great part, to the fact of an exaggerated sense of the importance of the liturgy. If we are to come through the present "mess" (William Buckley's word) we will do so only if liturgy takes its proper place within the hierarchy of Christian values, and this is not at the top, or center, or source.

Another point has been made recently by Frank Sheed and it is an important one. In speaking of the liturgical changes of the future, he says: "They will be good or less good, according as they express the mind and heart of the worshippers. The danger is, of course, that liturgical experts may take over: and they are more likely than not to be out of touch with the mind and heart of the rest of us."[23]

Mr. Sheed has put his finger on one of the crucial points in any liturgical renewal. A liturgy created by experts in many ways will be sound because it will preserve historical continuity and protect the dignity of worship. On the other hand, it will almost certainly be beyond the reach and understanding of the faithful. But if liturgical celebration is an expression of the mind, will, and emotions of the faithful, and is not in some way guided by experts, we are in for an endless period of "fads," because liturgy will be cut off from the experience of the past. Certainly we are already witnessing some rather strange phenomena in the name of experimentation and relevance. So what is needed is a balance: communication between the minds and wills of the worshipers and the erudition of the experts, as the details are worked out.

If any of this is to happen, however, what is needed more than anything else is effective and permissive leadership. At the present time there is developing a plurality of forms within the Roman liturgy itself: folk masses, young people's masses, and the like. But there are also some striking variations occurring all over the place in the so-called "underground church." The underground church and its liturgies do not appeal to me in the least. But I certainly can and do understand why priests and laity are attracted to it.[24] There are many reasons why there is such a phenomenon today. Certainly one of the major reasons is frustration with church leadership; for among church leaders (the hierarchy) there is, in this country at least, an almost universal unwillingness to sponsor any innovations which could be called daring, as well as widespread lack of permissiveness. In saying this I in no way wish to imply a denial of episcopal authority, but I certainly do question the way it is often exercised. What I suggest to church leaders is that they read, or reread, the last statement of Bishop Hallinan on the liturgy, especially this passage:

This brings us to the problem of the experimenter or adapter. You already know that I feel a grassroots approach to experimentation is absolutely essential if our liturgy is to be truly expressive and creative of a people dedicated to God. . . . we cannot call a halt to our efforts to seek experimentation from the bottom up, to complement those experiments which we have received from the scholars and theorists. Each community, each diocese represented here, must engender a creative spirit in its community which can produce and encourage the formation of experimental rites.[25]

I suppose what I am saying is that a plurality or diversity of rites and liturgies is essential for future developments; and if this is not accomplished within developing ecclesiastical structures and policies, it will happen outside—or, at best, on the fringes of the organized church. I am also saying that there is a need for much greater spontaneity in liturgy. In saying this, however, I do not subscribe to the "cult of spontaneity," which would lead to total chaos.

I have already mentioned more than once that there has been some pretty bad teaching in the Catholic Church on liturgy and sacramental theology (as well as in many other areas). I do not wish to give the impression of total condemnation of the past, for I am sure that each age has its share of good teachers and thinkers. Nevertheless, in the light of the theological developments of the past few years (including and beyond Vatican II) we are faced with a massive educational task in the church, as many have been saying. This task includes all age groups and all phases of theology and spirituality. This is not the place to go into this problem in detail, but the most important challenge for the church in the present and future is the educational one, the full and enlightened implementation of the teaching office of the church. Evidently many Protestants feel the same urgency, as is seen in these words:

Within Protestantism we face a massive educational task that members may be acquainted not only with their own Reformation heritage, but with a heritage that pre-dates the Reformation both in east and west. But the educational task may be easier than we suspect. Never before has there been such a stirring of interest among the laity of our Churches. It is possible that there will be widespread reception of a liturgy that permits the people to participate not passively, but actively in the dialogue of Christian worship.[26]

I agree enthusiastically with the above observation about the great stirring among the laity. But speaking from my own experience in the Catholic Church, I have seen only minimal signs of an adequate response to these stirrings on the part of teachers, official or otherwise, in the church. Also, given the present state of the liturgy, I have very serious doubts about any significant fulfillment of this massive task through liturgy. The liturgy will always serve *an* educational function, for it will be of its very nature, a vehicle for teaching, reminding us of the great Christian truths and realities; namely, Christ and his redemption. But the many implications of our faith in Christ, i.e., of our response to Christ at a given moment of history, will be achieved, for the most part, outside the liturgy in the strict sense, through educational programs of all sorts and through the wise employment of professionally qualified teachers of religion.

Conclusion

I hope that one concludes from what I have said that, from my vantage point, at this point in history, the church is not a very good teacher at all. I have talked about the bad teaching in the church about sacraments and liturgy, and I have said that however the church faces its massive educational task, it should not plan on too much help from liturgy in carrying it out except in a very rudimentary way. I deliberately did not dwell on the "communication gap" that exists in the church between its official teachers and the faithful. (I have just read in a newspaper–March 1969–that in the Roman

Catholic diocese of Worcester a survey shows that 43 percent of the faithful have never heard of the Second Vatican Council! I am sure that this *must* be an exaggeration; but it is indicative of some kind of gap.)

Now all of this is very depressing and negative. And I would like to finish with some optimism. My optimism is rooted in two judgments which I have made about the church. The first has to do with the Second Vatican Council (the people of Worcester notwithstanding), which, if nothing else, has certainly pulled us from a rut. It was the beginning of something big; the present restlessness indicates this. This Council did open up a new vision of the Christian life for Catholics, even though at present we are not exactly sure of what that vision is, or where it is taking us. For Catholics who tended to be triumphalistic (and there were, and are, a lot of us) this should be interpreted as a healthy sign. We had to be shaken up. But ultimately my confidence about the future of the church lies in hoping against hope that the lack of understanding, foresight, and tolerance, which is such a part of the fallen human grain, will not prevent the Holy Spirit from carrying out his mission "to instruct the hearts of the faithful." I do not intend this appeal to the Holy Spirit to be an escape from responsibility; but, good Catholic that I am, my ultimate hope is not in plans and structures devised by men for the church, but in the promise of Jesus to send his Spirit.

B. *by* IRIS V. CULLY

WORSHIP IS THE church's expression of adoration to God, and any effect or value it has for individuals or the community is derivative from this purpose. Without deliberate intention, it has been the basic way by which people have learned what it means to be a Christian.

Worship as a Way of Teaching

The Sunday assembly for worship involves everyone. American Protestant churches used the phrase "the family pew" to denote the tradition that the whole family attended the service together. The box-shaped pew in old New England meetinghouses emphasized by its structure the gathering together of families, who faced one another rather than facing toward the pulpit. Only since the early twentieth century, with a concern to help the young child understand worship, has this unity been broken and the emphasis placed upon group worship services in connection with the Sunday church school. Current trends encourage the inclusion of children for all or part of Sunday congregational worship. This means, theoretically, that since all have shared in the same event, adults will explain to one another and especially to children what has been happening. Clarification and deepening of understanding can come through such discussion. Randolph Crump Miller writes:

Here is an opportunity for some of the most significant education that a congregation can develop. Here, at the center of the Church's life, we can be educated to be the Church. The only way to learn to worship is through worshipping, and not just by talking about it. Everything must be done to provide meaningful-participation.[1]

While it is hoped that seasoned Christians find continual learning through participation in the service, this is a new learning experience for children and for adults who are just entering the Christian community. The adult forms his first understanding of the meaning of the Christian faith through this experience. His previous introductions through relationships to individuals and groups doubtless encouraged him, but the encounter through worship is an understanding of how the community sees its relationship to God. This appears notably in the hymns, the use made of Scripture in preaching, the nature of the prayers, and the total congregational involvement. With the variant modes of worship service available among Protestants, these considerations become factors in the decision to become part of one tradition rather than another: a formal or an informal service, a classical tradition in hymnody or subjective hymns expressive of feeling, Scripture readings chosen for present need or a lectionary, formal prayer or informal petitions, a previously prepared or a spontaneous sermon. Whatever the form of the service, the child (or the newcomer) absorbs a particular interpretation of the Christian faith as he listens and participates each week.

Today there are more variations within specific denominations along cultural-educational lines than there are among different denominations. Thus in a large city or suburb, the service would be similar among half a dozen "First" churches of six denominations, but members of any of these congregations might feel uncomfortable in a small congregation of their own denomination in another part of the country—and vice versa.

Such weekly participation gives the new member the basic understandings from which to ask questions and to pursue further a knowledge of the meanings of the Christian faith.

This happens because any service of worship expresses in some way the message of the gospel. There is usually a unity in the way in which this expression is developed. The writer has been in congregations where the whole emphasis was on the substitutionary theory of the atonement: expressed in hymns, interpreted in Scripture and preaching, voiced thankfully in prayers, and indicated by the form of the Lord's Supper. "Christ died for me" was the theme, and the congregation derived strength from that assertion. Another congregation may find its theme each week in the affirmation "Jesus loves me." Gospel hymns express this; Scripture, preaching, and prayer emphasize the theme. Lutherans and Episcopalians have followed the liturgical year, affirming the Gospel events from Advent to Pentecost, a pattern being increasingly followed by other denominations. Some congregations give religious meaning to national holidays.

The service of worship also indicates an understanding of the relationship to God as the emphasis is placed on praise or petition, joy or penitence, receiving or giving, learning what God has done or what man is expected to do. All of these are themes in worship, but the stress denotes a congregation's (or denomination's) awareness of how God meets man and how man responds. It indicates the extent to which the gospel is understood basically in personal terms (I am saved, forgiven, loved, must be good, will go to heaven) and to what extent it links the Christian community around the world in a sense of historical continuity that feels obligated to spend itself for the life of the whole community. When members of any tradition put into words their understanding of what it means to be Christian they will be reflecting the service of worship to which they have been exposed week after week and year after year. Worship is deeply formative, not only of the individual, but of a whole culture when that culture is deeply infiltrated by members of a particular religious tradition.

Congregational worship involves the whole Christian community, of all ages and conditions, and thereby silently asserts the fact that there is no such thing as a solitary Christian—except under extraordinary circumstances. To the churchgoer who says, "I can listen to a service on radio or television," the reply comes, "Can you participate in the Lord's Supper this way?" Millions could be listening to the studio preacher and choir but they remain solitary. Minister, deacon, and parishioner surrounding the Lord's Table in a home or hospital room become a Christian congregation.

The regularity of the gathering of the community every Sunday is an important expression of this cohesiveness. It is not a matter of attending special festivals, although admittedly some confine their attention to such Sundays. Christianity, like Judaism and Islam, has set aside one day weekly for the gathering of God's people. The Sabbath is the weekly reminder that God created man and delivered his people Israel from bondage. Christian worship on the first day of the week is the reminder of the risen Lord's coming among his people, and most of the resurrection narratives in the Gospels record his appearance among a group of disciples. Whatever psychological and sociological factors bring people into particular worshiping congregations, once there, a specific understanding of Christianity is formed by inclusion and participation in the weekly service of worship. The strength of any congregation can be measured by the size of the worshiping group in relation to the size of auxiliary weekday activities. While it is possible that the small congregation represents the earnest beginnings of a new Christian community, it might instead be representing a group which feels "set apart" from the rest of the world or a group that has so abdicated its responsibility to the whole community that only a remnant remains. This has happened in cities where a few people gather from the suburbs to their "home" church, while the neighborhood is ignored. The weekly gathering reinforces the assertion that Christians are a community, while at the same time it helps to form that community.

There is also a deeply personal and individual reference in the gathered community. Each person brings himself, voluntarily, even when he does so with a sense of obligation. He is personally asserting his faith in God's presence among the community. He comes as a way of expressing his relationship to God. He expects to receive help in this encounter whether he be in doubt, perplexity, sorrow, guilt, joy, or any other of the manifold needs to be found within a congregation. Some Protestants would say that there is no need to be part of a congregation in order to fulfill spiritual needs, yet this voluntary participation acknowledges the fact that part of the new strength comes from the realization that others share these needs and give mutual support. Even the person who comes alone can perceive this. He is formed by the community, even as his presence in worship helps to form the community.

Actions of all sorts are involved; "methods" for learning. The worshiper sees the chancel area and his understanding is formed by the relative positions of table and pulpit (either of which may be centered in a Protestant church), by the use of symbols, by the position of Bible or liturgical book. He experiences the seating arrangement. The long nave with center or side aisles suggests attention toward the front. The semicircular arrangement brings people closer to one another. The existence and position of the communion rail suggests the kind of participation: sometimes close to the altar, sometimes at the foot of the chancel area. In some traditions the congregation will come to the communion table or altar; in others the elements will be distributed by lay deacons, thus preserving the sense of the total gathering. Action is specifically involved in the giving of the offering. Congregations have been taught about stewardship and are encouraged to think of this action as symbolic of self-giving. There is a trend toward bringing the elements for the communion service into the offering procession, thereby signifying the commonalty of bread and wine. Stained-glass windows, chancel hangings, the use of liturgical colors are all visual methods for the formation of understandings.

Hearing has been predominantly the mode of communication in Protestant usage. Emphasis has been placed on hearing the Scriptures and listening to the sermon, which has had the key place and around which the rest of the service has frequently been structured. Hearing is not entirely an intellectual exercise, although a highly educated congregation might prefer it to be. Hearing may be emotionally stimulating, and this fact has been the strength of the preaching in evangelistic Protestant groups. An appeal to emotion has been the emphasis in revival preaching, as the etymology of the word suggests.

The congregation, hearing, has its own opportunity to respond. They sing the hymns, speak responsively in the Psalms, sometimes affirm their faith in creedal formularies, and unite in prayer, most frequently through the use of the Lord's Prayer. Perusal of a standard Protestant hymnal would indicate that most of the historic elements of Christian worship can be used if set to music. Congregations which avoid "set" forms of prayer will repeat familiar prayer hymns. Affirmations of faith, resolutions to Christian living, paraphrases of the Psalms are all to be found within the pages of the hymnal. The specifically Protestant character of such hymns is indicated by the fact that newly compiled Catholic hymnals draw heavily from the sections containing hymns of praise and thanksgiving but have little need for the kind of hymns represented in other sections. Those thoughts are voiced in words through the congregational response within the liturgy.

Worship, further, has been a basic form of teaching because the sense of history is involved. No Christian congregation exists alone, even when it has been newly formed in a developing community. Its people are the "gift" of the parishes they leave, sometimes deliberately in order to "colonize." Financing will doubtless come from some church agency or another parish. The roots are in a continuing past. Every Sunday morning worship service is a reminder that Christians have continued this action for many centuries. Even staunchly evangelical traditions reflect their own historical beginnings, whether in the sixteenth century or the nineteenth. Within a Protestant denomination, the historical range of the hymnal is a perceptive index of where it sees its roots. The words in the worship service celebrate God's actions, affirm his love shown in the past, and look with hope toward the fulfillment of his rule in the world. So far as is known, only man among all creatures can have some awareness of the past, however fragmented. If he seeks to live only in the past, his experience will be stultified. If he ignores the past, life becomes shallow. If the past is held in remembrance to give roots for the present, life can become enriched. Liturgy does this when it tries to use sensitively whatever in the past speaks to the present and tries to interpret the heritage in ways which give perspective.

Instructional Elements in Worship

However broadly worship is interpreted in terms of action, there is an instructional core. Immediately one remembers the warning given by H. Massey Shepherd that the liturgy may be considered a resource for instruction in the faith but never a source. He writes:

For it is not one object in our referent attention and use, however important and significant. The liturgy is the subject of God's own invisible action and working. . . .

If we set out, however, with the notion that the liturgy is a "significant factor" in an educational program and the "liveliest access to the resources of the Church," we risk making it subject to a standard or norm outside of itself, whether this be the Bible, or the faith considered as a set of doctrines, or perhaps some particularly idealized way of life.[2]

This instructional core has been called the mass of the catechumens, or the service of the Word. Basically it consists of hearing the Scriptures read and interpreted. A carefully chosen lectionary will include for each Sunday two or three lessons (Old Testament, Epistle, Gospel) which illumine each other, accent the day in the Christian year, and speak to some understanding of God's work and the Christian's response. The preacher's task is to indicate for his people in his sermon what the original writer was trying to say for his time, how this is illumined by biblical studies, and what guidance is given for the immediate congregation seeking to live the gospel through the work of the coming week. Faithfully stated and attentively received, this should bring to both pastor and people a continued knowledge and understanding of key biblical passages and could possibly make this ancient word become a vital word for them: encouraging, illumining, assisting. No matter how weak preaching may sometimes become, or how irrelevant some lectionaries may seem, there is no need to lose sight of what this part of the worship is meant to be. Most people will only become acquainted with the contents of the Bible through what they hear on Sunday morning, despite centuries of emphasis, among Protestants, on personal Bible reading.

This gives point to the new Lutheran lectionary with its three lessons and the new United Church of Christ and Presbyterian lectionaries, based on a two- or three-year cycle. A common practice among ministers in many traditions has been to choose their own Scripture readings. In addition to the duplication of effort involved, it can lead to a use of favorite passages, an emphasis on a personal point of view, and a choice of lesson principally to illustrate a sermon idea. The practice could bring a sense of immediacy in the material chosen, but it also avoids the task of struggling with a given biblical passage to see what it can say for the preacher and his people. The sermon instructs even while it "proclaims." Themes may come from current events, personal problems, or any form of Christian teaching. E. Nicholls, writing in one of the brief volumes of the Studies in Ecumenical Worship series, says:

The preacher is the Servant of the Word. His sermon puts at Christ's disposal the living language of the present day, with its associations with the everyday life of the congregation. It permits Christ to preach his Word through the contemporary Church, as He has already through the apostolic church.[3]

Instructional material is also imbedded in the canon, where the account of the institution of the Lord's Supper from I Corinthians II is recited wherever the Holy Communion is celebrated. Thus the worshiping congregation is reminded of the origin of the rite. In the simplest of Protestant forms, the words of institution become the substance of the service, introduced by the invitation and concluded with a prayer of thanksgiving.

The actual participation in the rite is a form of learning. In some Protestant traditions, the communion service has been distinct from the form of service used on other Sundays. Hence, one "learned" as often or as seldom as the rite was observed. This might be as infrequently as four times a year, a tradition which the Methodist Church inherited from frontier days, when that was as often as an ordained minister could get around his far-flung parishes. It might be bimonthly, a long-held Presbyterian and Congregational practice; or monthly, as in Lutheran custom. The early Sunday weekly celebration has long been a part of Episcopal practice. Protestants have sometimes had the feeling that an action repeated often would become routine and meaningless. The idea that a frequent celebration might, on the contrary, become deepened and enriched in meaning for the worshipers is new among Protestants. The solemn respect which surrounded the infrequent observance of the memorial rite is giving way to an interpretation of joyous thanksgiving for the risen Lord. The quarterly Communion frequently becomes a bimonthly one and the latter becomes a monthly observance. The early service moves up to a late morning family Eucharist and once more the Lord's Supper becomes central for the worshiping community. Participating in it, they learn about it, and they learn to become what they are meant to be: a worshiping and witnessing community for their Lord, Jesus Christ.

How Worship Forms the Community

Now learning theory enters the picture. Conditioned learning (operant behavior) in many forms is a focus for educational theory today. The oft repeated pattern where rewarding approval follows correct response brings persistent learning. Repetition and satisfaction are key words. Cumulative learning builds, enriches, and deepens learning. Christian worship is an experience repeated at regular intervals. The favorable (approving) circumstances which lend reinforcement to learning can be provided by those responsible for the service and all who participate in it. If the worshiping group welcomes the young and the newcomers, these will feel at ease and will learn as they take part. This welcome is shown by the helpfulness of someone nearby who finds the place in prayer book or service sheet, shares the hymnal, and gives no hint of negative reaction to the restless child or the adult who makes incorrect responses. Assurance can also be given the learner through clear written or oral directions. Those who are familiar with a service never realize how uncomfortable the learner feels, and rarely discover from the latter how to write or give directions at the time most needed and in a way which makes these easy to follow. Protestant services, when they do not follow the form in a service book, are frequently outlined in a mimeographed or printed bulletin listing the order of service, the numbers in the hymnal, the Scripture reading, unison response, and indications as to when to sit or stand. The regular congregation knows exactly at what introductory phrase to rise for the singing of a hymn and senses exactly at what point to rise for the reading of the Gospel. While these movements are easily and quickly followed, they point to an internal sensitivity to the rhythm of a service acquired by regular participation. As one becomes familiar with the action and at ease in responding to the situation, he feels comfortable, "at home."

Learning takes place more easily when there is an internal logic to the structure of the service so that it moves in an easy sequence with a correlation of word and action. The stranger to an Episcopal service, for example, would be puzzled to understand why one rises for the Gospel when read at the Eucharist but not when it is read at Morning Prayer. If response belongs to the people, it seems unfair to frustrate this expectation by using an elaborate sung setting designed for a choir—but this happens. The reading from the Scriptures is more impressively the foundation for preaching when the sermon follows immediately upon the reading than when it is placed at some later point in the service, as frequently is the case in a Protestant service. The meaning of the sermon becomes reinforced when the closing hymn echoes the theme rather than negates it.

The vocabulary of the service is another aid to comprehension and ease of learning. When a person does not have to struggle to attach new meanings to archaic words and phrases, learning can come more quickly. This is part of the urgency for bringing liturgies and biblical translations into contemporary language. It may be easier to translate from an ancient language than from a classical form of the vernacular: easier because the translators are not enmeshed in familiarity and a sense of the poetic.

Negative reinforcement, which inhibits learning and repels the newcomer or the young child brought to the service of worship, is the other side of the coin. Anyone who sits week after week feeling awkward and uncomfortable, wondering if he seems strange or out of place, wishing to be spoken to (or, conversely, wishing to be left alone by an effusive greeter) will be too busy nursing his feelings to learn and to become integrated into the worshiping community. This may be the initial reaction to a service different from the one normative to his experience. If he has been used to following a written order of service or a service book, he will feel lost in having to sense each element of the service from the actions of his fellow worshipers. If he has been used to an easy informality, he will be bewildered trying to find the place in a service book. Lack of comprehension can lead to boredom: "I don't know what this is all about" or "This doesn't mean anything to me" as the inner response, and the listener "turns off" the whole procedure.

Too much pressure in the service can also cause a negative reaction. Emotional hymns with deeply personal words, erotic imagery, or death symbols—where there has been no positive correlation in the past (as for those familiar with the allusions)—can cause discomfort and avoidance. Intense moral pressure has a similar effect: hymns in which the participant affirms a climb toward moral perfection or, conversely, avows a complete unworthiness; or sermons whose emotional intensity causes recoil rather than stimulus.

The child has his own areas of negative conditioning, such as sitting with legs dangling above the floor, trying not to wriggle (even though his capacity in this regard is limited by the physical possibilities of his muscular development), trying to seem polite when he cannot understand what is being said, or trying to pay attention when he is seated far from the center of interest (children prefer to be on top of the action; unsure parents would rather avoid being conspicuous). This does not exhaust the list of inhibiting factors but merely points out that these cause learning difficulties and even rejection of participation in the group. Another factor comes into focus during adolescence. Young people may avoid the community of faith in which they have been brought up. The church may seem out of touch with the world. Furthermore, it represents the security of the family pattern at a time when adolescents are trying to develop an individual life-style. They feel some inner necessity to leave in order later to return "on their own."

One other point is suggested by reinforcement learning. Words and actions regularly performed in company with others eventually become a part of the self. The response is internalized, in one sense automatically, but also more personally. Because the forms are used without thinking, the mind is free to understand the meaning. Personal knowledge is a real form of knowing. Understanding makes knowing more complete. It can become so much a part of a person that even if he should leave the community for a number of years and return later, the forms would quickly return to his memory and the meanings become clear again. Active participation strengthens this kind of learning. It does not happen in the same way to the person who watches on radio or television or who reads the service when alone. Only from a background of congregational participation can these solitary forms have participatory meaning.

Learning to Become Aware

People can also learn through a restructuring of a situation so that new meanings emerge and become clarified. The sudden "flash" of insight can bring a new solution or a different understanding. This could happen at any point in which the participant is actively engaged in the service. A phrase of a hymn might suddenly speak to him in italics; a new translation from the Scriptures may help him see a passage in a different light; a phrase in the liturgy may take on new meaning in response to some experience of the past week. Since each person comes to church on Sunday from a differing structuring of life events, it is possible for this to happen.

The sermon is the place where clarification and new awareness is usually one of the built-in purposes. In preparing the sermon, the preacher has been letting a particular passage of Scripture work within his own consciousness, asking what God is saying to his people in these words. He will share his insights and hope either that this will be new and helpful to them, or that something in his words will illumine the Scriptures for them. Here Christians recognize the work of the Holy Spirit, for when words have changing power for a person or a congregation, even if scientifically explainable, they still seem wonderful to the person who has experienced change. People speak of "living the liturgy" as a way of cultivating new insights for living. The intercessions of the pastoral prayer can be an opening to new dimensions of Christian living. The offertory could do this if the worshiper would think of how one makes money and on what basis contributes it.

Insight alone is not enough. Any restructuring of understanding must be followed by a shift in attitudes and must result in changed ways of acting, new habit patterns. This is a matter of practice, of failing sometimes and succeeding other times, until persistence and encouragement strengthen the bonds of the new learning. The force of a sustaining community is essential. When social awareness leads to a change of action, this new way can become permanent if the community approves and encourages; it will quickly fall into disuse (however religiously motivated) if the community disapproves, unless the person feels enough security from the assurance that God gave the insight, approves the change, and will sustain when fellowmen rebuff. The liturgy is the beginning of the common work. The work continues in the days that follow.

Some Protestant services lay heavy emphasis on the conceptual: Religion is rationally presented in order to be intellectually understood. Others make use of visual symbols—objects and color. Some express worship through action, from the informality of Pentecostal groups to the formal liturgy of Episcopal rites. The educative process through the service is further suggested by realizing that it expresses the total "structure" of the Christian faith. This is accomplished when the key themes of the gospel are enunciated: praise to God and joy in his saving work, in his continuing presence, and in his power expressed through the community. Not all services are so inclusive. Whole denominations have been established by the emphasis on one phase of the gospel thought at that time to be neglected by the "established" churches. With the freedom in most Protestant traditions for the minister to develop a service (although a general pattern is always discernible), his own preferences may be expressed continually in choice of hymns and Scripture and in the themes of preaching. The wholeness of the structure could be lost.

The Persons Who Learn

The community is formed as persons develop through their individual involvement in worship. Each person brings to the Sunday gathering his whole self and some find it easier to be open to the influence of the service than do others. One must be free in order to learn. Anyone who has tried to make changes in a service soon discovers how few people have such freedom. They say, "The old form is superior in beauty of style and theological understanding," but an important unrecognized factor is that the long-established form has special meaning for their life. It has expressed their longings, comforted their needs, and assured them that something is stable in an uncertain world. Until new forms have existed long enough to do this for a whole generation, they cannot gain whole-hearted acceptance.

Some people tolerate change more easily than do others. Individual resistances are a bar to change in structure or in language (some Protestants are uncomfortable with the Revised Standard Version of the Bible), and these appear also when new hymns are introduced or a new hymnal bought. Feelings are brought sharply into the open when changes are made in the chancel, for that place is the focus of attention. Yet in the past twenty years innumerable Protestant churches have removed the center pulpit in favor of a divided chancel, symbolizing (but not entirely carrying out in practice) a change from a sermon-oriented service to an emphasis on the totality of the service. There has not been, as one might have expected, a centrality to the service of the Lord's Supper, although there has been a trend to more frequent observances. Today this same challenge of change is faced by Episcopal and Lutheran churches, whose marble altars often are firmly fixed to wall or retable and whose chancel-based choirs are the closest witnesses of the people's Communion. Money is not the real barrier to change; the security of the customary is.

Symbols are a form of visual learning which can either attract or repel according to the reminders (sometimes unconscious) they suggest to the worshipers. Initials or emblems *(XR, IHS)*, engraved on table or pulpit or in stained-glass windows seem to have little meaning for contemporary Protestants beyond being decoration, despite some efforts at revival. Much deeper power is embodied in the meanings derived from the basic elements used in liturgy: water, bread, wine, fire (flame), and breath, air (spirit). Protestant usage has most frequently taken symbols descriptively, using them in hymn and sermon to explain the basic Christian experiences. For example, the symbol of blood may mean life or death, love or suffering. In some forms of evangelical Protestantism, the "blood of the lamb" is offered either as invitation to those who need thus to be cleansed, or as assurance for those who know themselves to have been saved.

Giving the self is a difficult and sometimes impossible procedure for some people, yet participation in congregational worship requires it. Protestants have resisted the idea that one goes to church to fulfill a divine requirement (reacting against the Catholic tradition of "obligation"). Frequently it has been assumed that if one "had" to go, one could not "enjoy" going; thus the act would not be voluntary. One could only fulfill a responsibility voluntarily. This reflects a high degree of individualism. Since he did not feel that he would sin by staying home, neither did he feel it an act of personal devotion to attend.

The essentially lonely person could find no comfort in such a situation. If he had a need to withdraw from other people, he would stay away from a service, but the person who had any desire and slight ability to reach out toward others could find strength in the gathering. An usher meets and shows him to a place. This is a face-to-face meeting, intended as a welcome, but not necessarily seen as such by the visitor. Standing to sing together is an opportunity to voice ideas and feelings, to hear sound—the sound of oneself and of others nearby. Perhaps people are seated on either side (although some churches provide plenty of quiet corners). At the time of the offertory, the collection plate is passed from one person to the next. Both in making his offering and in receiving and passing the plate there is human contact. A similar form of intercommunication is found in those denominations where lay deacons pass the trays of bread and trays of small juice-filled cups for Communion. These are passed by the congregation too from one to another, literally serving one another. It is impossible here to feel that Communion is so intensely a personal act as when one receives directly from the celebrant. Greeting neighbors has been a custom among Protestant congregations, and frequently they are encouraged to be especially mindful of visitors. Such customs make attendance at worship a highly sociable act which could disconcert the withdrawn person but offers encouragement to the lonely, incapable of human interaction. J. J. van Allmen writes:

Let us begin with the pedagogic usefulness of the cult. Worship . . . is the very background for the teaching of the church. In worship we learn to be Christian, to encounter God, the world and our neighbor. We learn faith, hope, and love. . . .. The presence of the brethren, respect for the role in worship which each of them exercises, the bread broken with them—

all this makes the corporal nature of the Church alive, delivers us from the pride of aloofness, and teaches us to see mysteriously in our neighbor a member of the body of Christ, a Christ-bearer.[4]

Since Christian theology has emphasized service to the neighbor as an expression of love for God, it might be suggested that a service which encourages outgoingness assists in a deepening of the person's relationship to God by making possible a kind of openness in many directions. Recently there has been an introduction into the communion service of the "Pax," a custom wherein each greets his nearest neighbor with a handclasp and the words "The peace of the Lord be always with you." Comments one churchgoer in a letter to the editor (aftermath of an article on the proposed new Episcopal liturgy): "I am glad to greet my neighbor, but I'll be darned if I shall hold hands with him."[5] Forms of emphasis on Christian community bring varied responses!

Symbolic Learning Through Liturgy

Some say that symbols have little meaning for modern man, or that since the historic symbols of the Christian faith cannot be filled with meaning anymore, new symbols must be developed. Protestant tradition has frequently followed this theory. One can go into many churches, staunchly biblically oriented in a nineteenth-century tradition, where the few symbols used in colored glass or on pulpit are derived from biblical stories (thereby becoming shorthand evocations of the story itself): a sheaf of wheat, the lily, the vine. The theological symbols for Christ or for the Trinity are lacking. The cross is the most widely used symbol, although some groups do not use it among the congregation but display a lighted cross outside the church as a witnessing symbol of the atonement.

The arrangement of the meeting place for worship holds its own symbolism: the placing of pulpit, table, baptismal font; the use of the cross; the kind of music used (a few groups still allow no organ); the placing and use of the Bible.

If the language ceases to be communicated to the next generation and falls into disuse, there is always a question as to how well it can be revived. Is it worth the time needed to teach a language anew? Shall the symbols survive simply as decoration? Should new sym-

bols be developed? Protestant churches today seem to be finding
the symbols for Christ meaningful: the monograms IHS, XR, and
the sign of the fish have become popular in new churches. Such
symbols become reminders of who we are as a congregation. In a
functionally oriented society, those symbols are most likely to survive or to be revived which enhance the purposes of worship. The
encouragement given artists and craftsmen in fashioning varied
forms of the cross bespeaks a desire to see the meaning of that event
for today's world.

The placing of the communion table in relation to pulpit and
congregation indicates thought about the relationship of all three.
(In continental Reformed churches table and pulpit are being
placed side by side.) New Christian (Disciples of Christ) churches
are placing the baptismal font at the front and side of the chancel
so that baptizands literally descend into it in the sight of the congregation and then emerge. This replaces an earlier custom of having
it built to the back of the chancel area, half hidden by curtains,
where the rite was only partly revealed to the attendant congregation and the place of baptism concealed during all services except
this one. The symbolism of the chalice as the common cup is being
re-explored by Protestants, trained since the 1917 influenza epi-
demic not to drink from another's cup. Meaning is attached to the
question of leavened or unleavened bread, the use of wafers, small
squares, or a broken loaf. The forms become symbolic.

Protestants are more responsive to word symbols than to picture
symbols because the latter have been excluded for centuries as
"graven images." A glance at any hymnal indicates a wealth of
verbal imagery to describe the doctrine of redemption, to describe
the being and work of God, to suggest eternal life. At the same
time, Protestants are sparing in their use of traditional word symbols expressed in creed and historic liturgical forms. While the use
of the Apostles' Creed is part of the service in Presbyterian, Lutheran, Methodist, and Episcopal (who also use the Nicene Creed)
traditions, it has been avoided by those in the free-church tradition,
partly because it was a "set" form and partly to avoid repetitive
elements in the service. (Some tend to question continual use of the
Lord's Prayer.) Moreover, through a century of intensive biblical
and theological inquiry known as the "liberal" movement, many

questioned giving lip service to words whose literal meaning they questioned. The proposed Episcopal liturgy tries to be both traditional and liberal by translating the creed in the "we" form, thus affirming this as a corporate act rather than as merely a personal confession. The creed is increasingly regarded as a symbol and summary expressive of the gospel, thereby avoiding the implications of a doctrinal pósition to which assent is being given.

The form of the service has symbolic implications. There is no room here to consider the baptismal liturgy, which should be a congregational expression of worship, but its form and language are under serious review among those in both the Anabaptist traditions and other Protestant groups. The symbolic implications in the Lord's Supper have been such that as the denominations developed in expanding nineteenth-century America they sought to avoid theological entanglements by opting for what seemed to be a simple biblical re-enactment. Assuming that I Corinthians 11 was a literal description of a communion service in the primitive church, they used this basic framework, prefacing the biblical words with a brief prayer of preparation and concluding with the distribution of the elements. This was added to the end of the regular preaching service (or, for Disciples of Christ, at the beginning of the service): the service of hymns, Scripture, preaching, and prayer which has been normative for Sunday morning worship. It is only within the past few years that the validity of the development of the service in the early centuries has been accepted and the framework of the Eucharistic prayer recovered. This is evident in the new United Church of Christ and United Presbyterian liturgies. It became evident that the service for the Lord's Supper has always had theological content—even, indeed, at its institution. Traditions which have had a more catholic service have been concerned, in their liturgical revisions, to make the language clearer, to avoid archaisms, and to let the structure of praise stand out in simplicity so that the congregation is involved in joy and praise, climaxed by participation in Communion, and ending quickly with the call to serve. The symbolic action becomes clear. The present problem is to find a writing style which is directly lucid. Protestants, used to a poetic style, have difficulty in listening to colloquial writing.

Interpreting Liturgy

The service of worship itself teaches those who participate, but there is a further need to interpret and strengthen this learning. It is no longer assumed that whole families attend church together and afterward explain the service to the children. The first attempt to make congregational worship meaningful to children was through the age-group worship service which came into extensive use a generation ago with the emphasis on graded curriculum arranged either into a three-year (group-graded) or a one-year (closely graded) format. Children's church school classes were divided into departments for preschool, primary (grades 1–3), junior (grades 4–6), junior high, and seniors. Classes within each age-group gathered, usually at the beginning of the Sunday church school session, for a service led by their teachers or the department superintendent, consisting of hymns, prayers, Scripture, and sometimes a biblical story. By helping children become accustomed to a service that increased in length and formality but was always within their intellectual understanding, it was expected that they would develop habits of interest, attention, and participation. This would prepare them for eventual attendance at the main service of worship, usually when they became confirmed or joined the church by some other rite. While this plan has merit and is still widely used, several denominations have begun to encourage gradual inclusion of the children in the congregational service of worship, sitting with their families and perhaps leaving at some point to attend classes.

A main source for interpreting the service lies in units of study as part of the church school curriculum in which the meaning of worship is explored and the elements in a worship service are studied. Such a unit may be accompanied by a children's reading book carrying a description, with pictures, of a morning service. There may be a similar unit at a later age but frequently the subject is approached then through the confirmation material, usually at the junior high level. Teaching about baptism and the Lord's Supper will be referred to as a part of units on the life of Christ, but are more likely to be studied in depth under the themes of worship or Christian belief.

Several methods have been used to induct older children into participation in the service of the Lord's Supper, for since it is not usually the main service of worship, it is unfamiliar to most children even if they attend the service regularly. Sometimes a course of study will suggest that a demonstation service be acted out, with minister and elders celebrating for the class at a table in an informal setting. Discussion follows. Sometimes this becomes an "explained Eucharist," when pauses are made in the celebration for a reader to explain the action. Confirmed adults present receive the elements at the appropriate time. The house celebration is another way of familiarizing people, especially adults or whole families, with the meaning of this sacrament. It is useful because a small group in a familiar setting helps the newcomer feel at home before joining in the larger parish group which is already familiar with the liturgy. People who have belonged to a particular tradition for many years do not realize its strangeness to someone familiar with another form.

Some clergymen make a place at announcement time for explaining, week by week, a brief portion of the service to increase awareness and to bring new insight to the familiar. Others do this through notes in the Sunday bulletin, so much a part of Protestant church life, or in the less frequently published parish newsmagazine. Denominations publish booklets which find their way to the narthex pamphlet table.

Well-chosen hymns can be a way of explaining the service. The opening hymn sets the mood of praise and the closing hymn should (but does not always) dismiss the congregation into everyday life. There is a wealth of great hymnody meditating upon the meaning of the Lord's Supper. Sung by choir or by people, or simply suggested for meditative reading, these hymns deepen understanding through the insights of other Christians. Popular types of hymnody have not found their way into the hymnals of the larger denominations with the exception of Christmas carols and a few spirituals. Evangelical groups have continued the use of nineteenth-century revival songs, characterized by easily singable tunes and repeatable choruses, but the theology expressed has tended to oversimplify the Christian message.

Hymn practice is another way of explaining the service. This is especially useful to help children become familiar with the content of the service. All too frequently, Protestants ignore the words and remember only familiar tunes. Careful teaching helps the participant to understand what he is singing. Children also need practice in learning responses, and young children need practice simply in saying lines responsively, whether these be versicles or a Psalm. The Lord's Prayer is often the subject of a curriculum study unit in first grade so that as the child is beginning to read he can correct some of the mistaken words he may have picked up in earlier oral memorization. Now he can begin also to think about the meaning of this prayer of the church, a meaning that can deepen every year. Denominations which use the Creed regularly try to introduce its phrases informally as illustrative material in curriculum units. The first affirmation has meaning as soon as children are studying about God's creative work; the second affirmation encapsulates the life of Christ. Study in depth of the Creed usually awaits the confirmation course.

Some ministers have a custom of introducing the Scripture lessons with a few explanatory sentences giving the setting and even the main thrust of the passage. The church year is another form of interpretation for the liturgy, for what happens in each service, the proclamation of the gospel, is lived week by week through the seasons from Advent to Pentecost. The readings and collect are held together by a theme. The colors in the chancel set the mood. In some traditions the vestments add to the emphasis.

The liturgy forms the community as the worshiping congregation participates, listens in order to understand, and takes opportunities and finds further opportunities to learn its meaning. This requires both participation for worship and reflection upon it afterward. Religious education contributes toward this purpose through Sunday and weekday classes, confirmation instruction, and many forms of adult groups.

Worship and Action

Liturgical renewal today has as one emphasis sending the worshipers out with renewed strength to live the Christian faith. Comfort there may be, promise and assurance, but also strength, new courage, and incentive to bear witness to the love of God at any cost. The attitude is summed up by C. F. D. Moule:

> Worship is work. But, conversely, all work done and all life lived for God's sake is, in essence, worship. That there is any distinction at all between worship and work, or for that matter, any other aspect of life, is due only to the fact that we are creatures of successiveness, moving in time and space, and unable to concentrate on more than a little at a time.[6]

People have known this. They have been grateful for the final blessing, "The grace of the Lord Jesus Christ" or "The peace of God which passes all understanding." This has helped them to face the problems awaiting them once outside the church door.

What they are less enthusiastic about is a new note which says "go forth into the world" and then gives them a list of things to be done. They had not bargained for such muscular Christianity in the parish church. This is the cutting edge of liturgy today. People are beginning to make a connection between the words "service" and "work" and to realize that the term "liturgy" implies something similar. They prefer to make individual definitions of what is meant by work. A few experimental parishes may see the Christian community as a consecrated group at work. Observant ministers would agree with the finding of a survey in which more than half of those persons asked said that they expected the church to provide comfort. How does one help them to see that the only real comfort is in strengthening and that reassurance, unless tied to reality, is a false hope? This is not a new problem in the life of the church but it becomes acute in those generations when the social implications of the Christian faith are stressed. This has been a facet of Protestant thought since the late nineteenth century in the United States (earlier in England) and never fails to arouse anxiety and concomitant hostility. In a recent book on worship and mission, J. G. Davies writes that worship is a necessary part of mission, not a preparation for it:

> ... we must now repeat our emphasis ... upon the necessity as contrasted with the utility of worship. If we think in terms of utility, then ... worship becomes the occasion of gathering preparatory to sending. ... Worship, it may be said, strengthens us for mission. ... Against this it has to be affirmed that worship is not a means to mission; it is one facet of the divine

activity which also includes mission. We do not therefore prepare for mission by worshipping, although we should be missionary in our worship. The cultus is not an isolated activity, but part of the totality of the divine movement through Christ and by the Spirit in which worship and mission are united.[7]

The task of religious education in the formation of the community through worship is to help interpret the gospel message enacted there so that Christians may accept their responsibility to live as they worship.

SEVEN

The Discipline of Theology—
Seminary and University

A. by BENEDICT M. ASHLEY, O.P.

B. by RANDOLPH CRUMP MILLER

A. by BENEDICT M. ASHLEY, O.P.

A. The Concept of "Priestly Formation"

FORMATION VS. EDUCATION

The *Decree on Priestly Formation (Optatus Totius)* has made the term "formatio" standard for the preparation of candidates for the priesthood or other ministries in the Roman Catholic Church.[1] In English, this is not pleasing, since it seems to confirm the impression that Catholics prefer a clergy passively conformed to a traditional pattern. Yet we have been forced to use this term because "education" has come to mean merely academic, intellectual preparation (or, even worse, vocational training given in an academic setting). The frequent complaints of Protestant churchmen that theological schools are turning out academicians and not "men of God" or "good shepherds" explain why Catholics too believe that the preparation of a priest must somehow help him develop his entire Christian personality, and not only his scholarly capacities, if he has any.

IMITATIO CHRISTI

In the Gospels we see Jesus of Nazareth preparing his apostles by calling them to share his own ministry, its problems, successes, disappointments, puzzlements, and sufferings. Through daily experience, he forms them in his own spirit. Although the evangelists do not report in any detail the debates among the apostles, now and again we get a revealing glimpse that shows this dialogue was often lively, and that Jesus did not intervene until needed. This formation was intellectual, since it involved both a gradual growth in theological understanding and not a little training in the techniques of rabbinical argument; but it was far more a remolding of the apostles' personalities, a growth into a new mode of feeling, striving, willing, thinking, seeing, and being.

Now this formation was not completed on a graduation day, not even at Pentecost. The Spirit came to teach the apostles "all things," but as Acts shows us clearly, he taught them in the very experiences and trials of their continuing ministry. The term "formation" seems suitable to express the totality of his work required to "form" a man called by the Father to serve in the pattern of Christ.[2] The human educators who co-operate in this formative work do so only as instruments of the Spirit.

St. Paul does not hesitate frequently to advise his followers to imitate himself, as he imitates Christ. "That is why I beg you to copy me, and why I have sent you Timothy. . . . He will remind of the way that I live in Christ, as I teach it everywhere in all the churches." (I Cor. 4:16; cf. Gal. 4:12, Phil. 3:17, I Thess. 1:6, etc.)[3] This formation by the Spirit in the likeness of Christ through an apprenticeship to an authentic follower of Christ, that is, by personal identification and life participation, appears in the New Testament as a logical consequence of the idea of ministry as a "witness through service."

The Son of God teaches us by entering our lives, living with us, forming a community among us, serving us in that community. Through this experience with him we become like him, losing ourselves in order to gain ourselves. The imitation of Christ by imitating his apostles is not, therefore, a mechanical conformity, but a living identification through which the individual discovers his true self. Certainly, the Apostle of the Gentiles imitated Christ, but in doing so he was all the more that vivid individualist, Paul of Tarsus.

This Christian mode of discipleship receives an analogous confirmation from comparative religion (see the relation of guru and pupil in Hinduism) and from modern psychology. The human personality is formed and developed not so much by precepts of behavior, or by external discipline, as by a process of imaginative and affective imitation and identification of a living model. The Christian note comes from the fact that this identification comes through the work of the Holy Spirit, who incorporates and vivifies the disciple in Jesus Christ, Lord and Redeemer.

In the Roman Catholic tradition, this New Testament conception of the formation of a priest through the *imitatio Christi* has always been the fundamental principle which has inspired the great diversity of institutional structures, whatever their defects. These structures have been principally the following: (1) the pastoral apprenticeship; (2) the monastery; (3) the canonical community; (4) the university theological school; (5) the pious fellowship; (6) the seminary. Without attempting to give a history of these, even in outline, it is useful to indicate the characteristics of each type.[4]

B. The Traditional Structures of Priestly Formation

THE PASTORAL APPRENTICESHIP

Up to the Council of Trent in the sixteenth century the underlying and predominant method of priestly formation in both East and West was the pastoral apprenticeship, a direct application of the New Testament norm just described. The bishop commonly lived surrounded by a presbytery of priests and lesser ministers. A young man who believed himself called to the ministry was taken into this household and instructed in the Scriptures, the rites and canons of the church, and its modes of pastoral care by a progressive participation in these functions. The bishop and the priests furnished the pattern of Christ for his imitation.

Our information on the actual effectiveness of this type of formation is very sketchy, but from the writings of the Cappadocian Fathers in the East, or of St. Augustine or Jerome in the West, we gather one important fact. For a long time, the young man who entered this apprenticeship brought with him a liberal arts education received in classical schools that were still pagan.[5] This meant that he had a struggle to achieve a creative synthesis, or to endure a schizophrenic compromise between two conceptions of life and truth: the Greek ideal of scientific, objective truth and of a life dedicated to the harmonious actualization of human potentialities; and the scriptural ideal of a truth of faith and a life of service. The bishop, as the pastor of a community of service, as the interpreter of the Scriptures, as the witness of Christ, and at the same time as a Roman philosopher and rhetor, had to present himself somehow as the reconciliation of these two ideals, like the catacomb paintings of Christ in the guise of Apollo. Amazingly, a St. Basil or a St. Augustine played this complex role with success.

THE MONASTERY

This tension, however, was so great that it is not surprising that it received a radical solution in the form of monasticism. The monk might very well be a man of classical learning, but he withdrew to the monastery to meditate on the Word of God alone.[6]

The monastery was never intended to prepare ministers for the church. The typical monk was not a cleric. Indeed not a few men fled to the monasteries to escape the dangerous burden of the priesthood. Yet in time the needs of the church required that men formed in prayer, discipline, and sacrifice should be called from the monasteries to be bishops and priests. In the East, where the priests commonly were married, the bishops were drawn from the monks, because celibacy seemed more suitable for the office of the good shepherd ready to lay down his life for his sheep. In the West celibacy was eventually required even of priests and deacons, and along with it the whole monastic ideal tended to mark the preparation of all ordained ministers, who were formed to think of themselves as men reluctantly drawn into the active ministry out of charity to men and respect for the needs of the church, but at heart contemplatives who would have preferred their quiet cells.

After 800 this pattern was reinforced by the growth of monastic schools in which future clergy could receive not only theological training, but the liberal arts training presupposed to it in the Christianized synthesis of Augustine and Boethius.[7]

THE CANONICAL COMMUNITY

St. Augustine himself, however, instituted a type of formation more consciously directed toward the formation of the ministry. He conceived and realized the idea of a *canonical community*, that is, of a *presbyterium* of men called to be priests and ministers, not monks, who nevertheless lived with their bishop a life somewhat like that of the monks, devoted to common prayer, study of the Scriptures, fasting, and communism of property. These canons were not monks reluctantly called to pastoral duties, but priests by vocation who adopted a disciplined community life in order to be spiritually better formed for apostolic service.[8]

St. Augustine and those who later adopted this ideal explicitly had in mind a return to the "apostolic life"; i.e., the kind of life lived by the Twelve and the primitive Christians, described in Acts 2:42–47:

These remained faithful to the teaching of the apostles, to the brotherhood, to the breaking of the bread and to prayers. The many miracles and signs worked through the apostles made a deep impression on everyone. The faithful all lived together and owned everything in common; they sold their goods and possessions and shared out the proceeds among themselves according to what each one needed. They went as a body to the Temple every day but met in their houses for the breaking of bread; they shared their goods gladly and generously; they praised God and were looked up to by everyone. Day by day, the Lord added to their community those destined to be saved.[9]

In St. Augustine's community and in others, there were to be found some learned priests, and these became the theologians and teachers of the novices, first in the liberal arts, then in the Scriptures. In the Middle Ages this resulted in the cathedral school.

THE UNIVERSITY THEOLOGICAL SCHOOL

At the beginning of the thirteenth century the cathedral school gave rise to the university with its several faculties, one of which was that of theology or divinity. In many ways, this new structure was a synthesis of the previous types. In its pursuit of the liberal arts and philosophy, it was a revival of the pagan schools. It usually received its charter from the bishop or the pope and its students and faculty were legally clerics, so that it was linked to its pastoral origins. In places such as Oxford, it was made up of residential colleges, each of which was designed like a separate monastery. Finally, with the entrance of the canonical community of the Dominicans[10] and other similar mendicant orders, it tended to become a collection of such communities of priests, each with its own particular theological tradition.

Thus the university was characterized by pluralism: a pluralism of disciplines reacting on each other, and a pluralism of scholarly communities debating their diverse theological systems—Augustinianism, Thomism, Scotism, etc. The candidate for the priesthood formed in its atmosphere was exposed to this interaction, although unfortunately his loyalty to his own order or profession often made him a partisan rather than a thinker.

Along with its advantages university formation had serious faults. First of all, for social reasons, the university was accessible only to a small part of the clergy. But even if it had been open to all, how useful would its abstruse scholastic theology have been to the average parish priest? One has only to glance at the marvelous and original analyses of the virtues and vices in the Secunda Secundae of Aquinas' *Summa Theologiae* to see that it stops short a big step from the concrete problems of the confessional. In the post-Tridentine period when the *Summa* was used in some places as a seminary textbook, it was necessary to add manuals of casuistic "practical moral theology" to fill this gap.

Second, this formation tended to isolate the students from the bishop and the ongoing life of the church. The bishop chartered the university and occasionally censored the original flights of its theologians, but faculty and students jealously guarded the autonomy of their schools. They came from far and wide to international centers, remote from any parish in which they might later serve. They were formed to be canon lawyers, teachers of theology, perhaps scholar bishops, but not pastors. Certainly, a learned episcopacy is a blessing, but we can only observe that scholastic learning did not seem to furnish a practical guide for church reform, so much needed in the fourteenth and fifteenth centuries.

Finally, the scholastic theology which these students learned was stimulated more by the recovery of Greek science and philosophy than it was by concern for the problems of medieval people. It was a creative theology, but not a pastoral one. The Renaissance with its effort to develop a Christian humanism inspired by a study of the Scriptures in their original languages might have corrected this one-sidedness, but it too was a bookish learning which did not bring about a fundamental reform of the universities. The chief Reformers insisted on a scriptural theology, and on a clergy which was university-educated so that it might preach the Scriptures. While only a small part of the Catholic clergy had been formed in the universities, the typical minister of the Reformation received his preparation there. But while the Reformers had some success in reforming the church, they had little in reforming the universities, with the result that their scriptural theology was soon hardened into the scholastic mold, indeed that of ossified scholasticism, lacking the creative vitality of the thirteenth-century thinkers.[11] Calvin's *Institutes* is quite as formidable a scholastic textbook of theology as Peter Lombard's *Sentences*, and less dialogic in its method.

However, there was one important modification of ministerial formation in the university due to the Reformation. Although the Reformers stressed and expected piety in the clergy, they provided no new structures to foster it, and the introduction of a married clergy broke up the surviving monastic and canonical institutions within the university.

THE PIOUS FELLOWSHIP

This concept is not easy to define and is typical of the Reformed rather than the Catholic tradition, yet it had its Catholic parallels, and is typologically important as a reaction to the defects of university formation. Its clearest examples are to be found among the free churches, and especially in German pietism and American Methodism. It is marked out by two characteristics: (1) the conviction that the evangelistic minister should not be distracted from his urgent task by an excessive concern for theological learning, but rather should be piously devoted to the personal meditation of the Scriptures; (2) the emphasis on the individualistic sense of vocation, which is supported by the fellowship of believers but is independent of it. The fellowship is thus the appropriate context in which the minister receives his call and formation from the Holy Spirit, but it is not itself formative.[12] It would be a mistake to pass over this tradition lightly, since St. Paul himself could be cited as in some respects its prototype with his defense of his highly individual experience and calling, and his emphasis on the "foolishness" of his gospel. Certainly in American experience, a ministry of this type continues to play a very considerable part, and has even received an institutional embodiment in our many Bible schools.[13] The recent emphasis in some Roman Catholic circles on the gift of prophecy, as a special calling distinct from hierarchical structures, suggests that in the future it may play some role in the development of the Catholic Church in America.[14]

THE SEMINARY

The Council of Trent in its twenty-third session in 1563 attempted a radical reformation of the Catholic clergy by the institution of the seminary system. As O'Donahoe has pointed out,[15] the Council Fathers really thought that they were reviving the old system of cathedral schools for poor youths who wished to become priests. The schools were under the immediate supervision of the bishop, assisted by two of his senior canons, and with a faculty drawn from priests in the diocese who had degrees. The students were to be tonsured clerics, living under clerical discipline, and already sharing in some of the liturgical functions of the church. Their studies were to be closely related to their pastoral duties:

They shall study grammar, singing, ecclesiastical computation, and other useful arts; shall be instructed in Sacred Scripture, ecclesiastical books, the homilies of the saints, the manner of administering the sacraments, especially those things that seem adapted to the hearing of confessions, and the rites and ceremonies.[16]

Only a few reforming bishops, like St. Charles Borromeo, were in any hurry to implement the decree, and it was really the Society of Jesus which initiated the system as we actually know it, on a somewhat different basis than Trent foresaw.[17] The Jesuit pattern, devised principally for the formation of members of their own society,[18] was a synthesis of elements drawn from Renaissance humanism and the older university scholasticism.

The significant features of these colleges were: (1) they maintained the university pattern of liberal arts and humanistic studies for basic education, followed by a systematic scholastic philosophy and theology; (2) they did this outside the university with its pluralism of disciplines and schools of thought; (3) they aimed at an extensive program of character formation and "spiritual direction." It must be noted, however, that the Jesuits, at least for their own members, also insisted on a considerable degree of practical training during the course of studies through hospital visitation and other charitable work, and by practice in public speaking and teaching.

The aim was an intensive formation of the individual in a regular pattern of life, containing elements of prayer, meditation, study, and moderate asceticism. Above all, stress was put on the virtue of obedience and of responsibility to duty. The college was not so much a community as it was a place for individual discipline and personal spiritual direction by a counselor. The hope was to develop in the individual a sense of dedication and a disciplined manner of life which would sustain him throughout his entire ministry.

When in the middle of the seventeenth century this basic Jesuit pattern was adopted in France by the Vincentians,[19] Sulpicians, and other religious congregations dedicated to educating future clergy, it spread throughout the church, where it remained fundamentally unchanged until Vatican II. The secularization of the principal universities of Europe in the eighteenth and nineteenth centuries had excluded the religious orders from these centers and had forced the development of a parallel system of Catholic schools. These included (1) Catholic graduate faculties of theology in Rome and elsewhere, to which more talented seminarians might be sent to complete their studies; (2) a vast number of seminaries giving only basic priestly formation, usually without any degrees; and (3) "houses of study" for the religious orders, whom university secularization had expelled from the schools where formerly they were the theological masters.

This atomization of centers of priestly formation was controlled by the fact that a uniform seminary pattern was more and more enforced everywhere by ecclesiastical legislation, tending to obliterate the variety of older traditions. The last stage of this was reached when the philosophical and theological system of St. Thomas Aquinas was made authoritative for all seminaries.[20] Supporting this was a system of personal and spiritual formation, having little relation to Thomism (if not in contradiction to it), based on the spiritual tradition of the Jesuits and of the French school of Bérulle and Olier. The latter school was very traditional in its emphasis on the *imitatio Christi*, but it laid an extraordinary stress on the theologically strange view that not only did the Word of God *empty* himself in becoming man, but that in the hypostatic union the humanity of Christ was emptied of its human personality when assumed by the divine person. This meant that the priest in imitating Christ also needed to imitate this abnegation of human personality.[21]

Is it any wonder that the slogan "self-fulfillment" has become central in the recent reaction against this system? It is not unfair, I believe, to note that this antihumanistic strain in the seminary tradition was related to the Augustinian pessimism which was all too evident in Reformation theology. The Council of Trent had repudiated this tendency, yet paradoxically it had its influence on the seminaries set up by Trent to safeguard the orthodoxy of the clergy. It seems a law of theological development that polemics (since they never seem to lead to substantive resolutions of issues) always end by a mutual contamination of both parties with the errors they most feared.

Vatican II in its *Decree on Priestly Formation* says:

Major seminaries are necessary for priestly formation. Here the entire training of the students should be oriented to the formation of true shepherds of souls after the model of the Lord Jesus Christ, teacher, priest, and shepherd. . . .

This asserts the continuation of the seminary system, but there is evidence in the *Decree* that it is generally felt that the system as it has been no longer in fact meets the pastoral ideal given as the very reason for its existence. We can only conclude that the "seminary" must undergo a radical change, and this in fact is what is happening throughout the world.

C. *The Relation of the Seminary to the University*

SHOULD SEMINARIES MOVE TO UNIVERSITIES?

In the minds of many Catholics in the United States, the obvious answer to the problem of formation is the abolition of the seminary, at least as the sole path to the priesthood, and an emphasis on training future clergy in the universities.[22] There are three main arguments put forward for this position:

1. No isolated seminary can maintain a theological faculty of sufficiently high quality to meet the needs of today's priest. Today the priest must lead a community of which a large part is university-educated. Moreover, theology itself has branched out into many rapidly developing fields, each of which requires specialized training to teach.

2. Modern theology is no longer self-contained, but develops in close relation to other disciplines, especially the behavioral sciences and the communication arts. Many students expect to develop their special personal talents in these secular fields. Only a university can provide the theological faculty and its students with the opportunities for this interdisciplinary work.

3. The church in the United States has moved out of its ghetto. Hence in its ministry the priest will be constantly at work with the ministers and members of other churches and with secular agencies. From the beginning of his formation, therefore, he must acquire a broad, ecumenical point of view.

Against these, there are certain counterarguments:

1. As the student rebellion proves, the university today is an unhealthy institution. Professing an exaggerated notion of "objective truth," it ignores the problem of "values," and has abdicated its task of criticizing the culture and structure of the society to which it is enslaved. It has ceased to be really creative, and forces its students into the conventional mold of which its degrees are the symbols. How then can a priest, who is to be a *prophet*, be adequately prepared in such an establishment?

2. The university today is, as it was in the Middle Ages, isolated from daily life, and especially from that of the underprivileged.

Although it has largely abandoned its philosophic, contemplative atmosphere in order to service our vast utilitarian, technological society with information, it has not really faced the problem of the relation of theory and practice. How then can it prepare a priest to serve all men, especially the neglected, with genuine insight into their life problems?

3. The university does build a certain kind of character and personal integrity, but it is the integrity of the research worker devoted to objective truth. Its language is that of science and scholarship, technical, cerebral. How can it help form a priest who must speak to people in religious symbols which reach the depths of human life and express a truth which is creative, evocative, and mysterious?

4. The university is often a place of intense and jealous competition, through which the student passes as a lone individual, and where the faculty are isolated in laboratory or library. Today it is hardly a place of intellectual dialogue, let alone of human community. How can it prepare a priest to express the gospel of reconciliation, of interpersonal communication? It may have its own asceticism of devotion to research, of exposure to the criticism of colleagues, but it has little room for prayer or liturgical communion.

Hovering over both sides of the argument is the problem of finance, which serves to force theological faculties and bishops to face the question. It is not clear, however, that a move to universities will really reduce costs although it certainly can be argued that it will mean "more for the money."[23]

THEOLOGY IN THE CATHOLIC UNIVERSITY

When Catholics debate this problem of moving the seminary to a university, some are envisaging that the university will have a Catholic faculty of theology, others suppose that it will have a non-denominational faculty, others that the seminary will have to continue as a theological school, but that the university will supply the secular disciplines.

If we consider the first alternative, there are at present in the

United States only six full-fledged Catholic university departments of theology (i.e., offering the doctorate); at the Catholic University of America (which is the only long-established department); Fordham, Loyola in Chicago, Marquette, and St. Louis universities (which have been developed mainly by incorporating Jesuit houses of study within a Jesuit university); and Notre Dame. There are also the newly developing ecumenical clusters of seminaries with some university relationship: the Graduate Theological Union in Berkeley, the Iowa Association of Theological Schools in Dubuque, the Catholic Theological Union in Chicago, and the Boston Theological Union. There are also some twenty-two M.A. programs in various colleges and universities (some of them in religion or religious education) which conceivably might develop into doctoral programs.[24]

The second possibility, namely, attendance of candidates for the Catholic priesthood at non-denominational schools of theology, does not seem very practical for the present at least at the level of the "first professional degree." Such schools are still predominantly Protestant in tradition, and it is difficult to see how they could give the Catholic beginner an adequate contact with his own tradition and pastoral practice. The ecumenical clusters mentioned above are more promising. As for locating a Catholic seminary near a secular university, this would have advantages, but would not guarantee the quality of the theological program itself.

THEOLOGY OF THE LAITY

The education of the clergy in a few university centers cannot be evaluated without taking into consideration the broader questions of the religious education of the laity. As Franklin Littell has pointed out,[25] the concept of the "universal priesthood of the laity" entails a refusal to distinguish sharply between clerical and lay education. Vatican II, by emphasizing that the role of the priest is to help the laity exercise their own share in Christ's priesthood, raises this issue for Catholics.[26]

In the United States by 1930 there was an extensive system of Catholic universities and colleges, most of them operated by religious orders. They all required that students as a part of their general education take some courses in "religion," but these were not very important in either quantity or quality. This was a reflection of the fact that in Europe religious education for the laïty ordinarily terminated in the secondary school. Students going on to the university were entering some specialized field, and only the cleric or the rare lay theologian would be going on to theological study. The undergraduate college is essentially an American peculiarity. Consequently the Catholic colleges did not have a precedent for a program of religious studies for the general student. Nor did Protestant colleges furnish a model, since they seldom required anything more than a course or two in "Bible." Consequently, the average Catholic college contented itself with what was largely a *remedial* program intended to correct inadequate study of the catechism in high school.

In the 1930s a movement, largely centered at the Catholic University of America, undertook to intensify and improve the quality of such "religion courses." The impetus back of this was the consciousness, produced by the depression and the strength of the labor movement among Catholics in the New Deal period, that the average Catholic did not see the social implications of religion. The emphasis of the new programs was on religion as a dynamic force for Catholic action, and the application of the "church's social doctrine" as found in the social encyclicals of the popes.

This in turn led to an awareness that the Catholic college ought to supply lay leaders who understood their religion. At that time Jacques Maritain was the theoretician of the Christian Democratic Movement in Europe and South America, and his presentation of Thomism was very influential in the United States. As a consequence, priests of the Dominican Order, especially Walter Farrell, in the name of Thomism began an attack on the current religion programs in Catholic colleges as anti-intellectual, rhetorical, and shallow. Father Farrell urged that the laity needed to study not "religion" (which he pointed out was a moral virtue, rather than an academic discipline), but theology. By "theology" Farrell meant the systematic scholastic theology of Aquinas, which he believed would furnish a solid natural law doctrine as the basis of the Catholic social movement. This movement of "theology for the laity" spread throughout the Catholic college and university system in the form of a program of twelve to eighteen hours of theological study required of every student. Not all bought Farrell's strongly systematic approach. Jesuit schools in particular inclined rather to a "humanistic" presentation of theology which stressed its positive basis in Scripture and tradition.[27]

Since Vatican II, and the general movement away from Thomism to personalistic and existentialistic approaches, these programs have greatly changed. Today Catholic colleges are not attempting to present a systematic coverage of theology, but commonly require the student to take a certain number of courses as a part of his program of general education, which he may choose from a considerable variety of theological offerings. It still remains true, however, that every Catholic college is attempting to give its students an adult education in the field of theology, usually with emphasis on the themes of Vatican II and the changing situation within the church.

However, more and more Catholic students are going to non-Catholic schools, especially to the state universities, both for financial reasons and because they wish to escape the Catholic ghetto. In these schools the majority of students receive no further religious formation than they may have had in high school. The church is attempting to meet this situation through the growing number of Newman centers, a form of campus ministry.[28] During the 1940s and 1950s, these centers attempted to develop supplementary theological programs in which university students might engage along with their regular studies at the secular school. It was hoped that the universities would recognize these courses for credit, and some have done so. However, the trend now seems to be against this. Rather Catholic Newman priests are hoping that the state universities will establish departments of religious studies which will include Catholic professors capable of presenting the Catholic theological tradition in an ecumenical context. If this develops, then the campus ministry will occupy itself not with the presentation of formal academic courses, but rather with enabling the student to integrate all his studies with his personal life as a Christian and a member of the university community.

THE FUTURE

In view of the two developments just described, (1) the trend of Catholic seminaries to move to the university or to a university-related ecumenical cluster, and (2) the trend toward a fairly high level of theological sophistication among college-educated Catholic laity, what picture is likely to emerge?

I believe we can predict that the coming generation of Catholic clergy will receive their *academic* theological training (1) in a department of theology in a Catholic university; (2) in a Catholic school of theology clustered ecumenically with Protestant schools of theology, and with access to interdisciplinary relations with a university.

We can also predict that the growing number of Catholics at secular universities will be an important factor in the development of departments of religious studies in such universities, in which the Catholic tradition will be adequately represented, and from which Catholic students will be able to acquire an adult religious education as part of their general education.

Finally, we can predict that the major Catholic universities will develop graduate departments of theology open to both clerical and lay students, and that these will attempt to achieve the ecumenical breadth of the programs of religious studies in the secular schools. The Catholic colleges will develop undergraduate programs of a similar character.

PROBLEMS AHEAD

In view of the typology given at the beginning of this paper, which indicated some of the factors that must enter a satisfactory program of priestly formation and the negative factors that must be avoided, we can already perceive two major problems that will have to be met very soon.

The first of these is the problem of *pastoral formation*, the interrelation of theory and practice. We have seen that the fundamental Catholic tradition, stemming from the New Testament itself, is that a priest should be formed not merely through academic study, but by a kind of apprenticeship undertaken in the actual context of ecclesial life, under the guidance of the bishop, in whom the pattern of Christ is seen as a contemporary reality.[29]

The lack of such formation was a grave defect of the seminary, and it will not be corrected but perhaps even exaggerated by the move to the universities. Granted that only in the university, or in schools closely related to a university, is an adequate academic program in theology possible, it remains true that the academic program is only one part of priestly formation. In Protestant schools the realization of this problem led to the development of the clinical pastoral programs and field education that commonly occupy one year of the three required for the first professional degree for the minister. It is generally admitted that this solution is not wholly satisfactory. In particular, it is difficult to integrate the clinical and academic programs, so that there is a *reciprocal* effect of theory on practice and practice on theory.

The second of these problems is that of *personal spiritual formation.* The Catholic tradition has always regarded this as basic, and even in the medieval university attempted to provide it. Protestants today admit frankly that its lack is a serious defect of their university-located theological schools.[30] How can this be met?

In my opinion, these two problems are closely related, and in the remainder of this paper I shall discuss them together.

D. *Pastoral and Spiritual Formation*

THE PASTORAL ORIENTATION

From the typology presented above we can list some mistakes that must be avoided:

1. The pastoral apprenticeship and the pious fellowship did not provide adequate academic learning. Today it seems that this can only be provided by a university.

2. The university has not provided adequate pastoral or spiritual formation.

3. The monastery provided intense spiritual formation, but of a kind directed toward the contemplative rather than the pastoral life.

4. The seminary attempted to combine the academic program of the university with the spiritual formation of the monastery. But the isolation from the pluralism of the university and the practical life of the people to whom the priest ministers prevented it from giving either adequate academic or pastoral formation.

5. The pastoral apprenticeship and the pious fellowship had the advantage of forming the priest in the actual life of the church, but the latter suffered from an individualistic conception of spiritual life and of the ministry. It had the strength, however, of emphasizing the universal priesthood of the believer.

The theology of Vatican II presents a concept of the pastoral orientation of the ministry which is helpful here. It first stresses the priesthood of Christ. He came as suffering servant to redeem us in love. He performed for us the service of a shepherd in gathering us together in community. He performed the service of prophet or teacher in enlightening us with the vivifying Word of God. He performed the service of priest in uniting us in worship of the Father and of reconciliation with him and one another.[31]

Through baptism every Christian shares in this priesthood of Christ. The Reformers were correct in emphasizing this truth. Hence every Christian is called to share in community life, to witness to the Word of God, and to unite in worship of the Father. This threefold ministry of Christ therefore belongs to every Christian, and every Christian requires to be formed for ministry. When we speak of "priestly formation," therefore, *we ought first of all to think of the formation of the laity in their priesthood.* The formation of the clergy, consequently, is not something separable from the problem of Christian education, but ought to be seen in its context. This should be expressed practically by opening theological schools to the laity, and by developing constant and close relations between clerical and lay students at every level of formation.

The Reformation theology, however, was inadequate in the negative conclusions it drew from this stress on the universal priesthood. The fact that Christians are a "priestly people" does not negate the fact that within the church as an organic community there is a diversity of gifts of the Spirit. These gifts are given not to make one member superior or dominant over another but to enable each member to serve the others. These gifts constitute *particular* ministries within the universal priesthood. Central to these is that of the bishop, or shepherd, who as successor to Christ and the apostles stands in the community as a source of unity.[32] He is not there to dominate, however, but precisely by his unifying leadership to assist in the formation and fruition of the ministries of all the members of the community. He has the plenitude of the priesthood, but only that he may serve the members so that their priesthood may be fully realized.[33] As Christ came not that he might be a priest but that we might be priests, so the bishop is priest not for his own priesthood, but for ours. Hence the hierarchical priesthood in the church is not contradictory to the universal priesthood of believers, as the Reformers tended to think, but is in its service and for its sake.

The priests and other hierarchical ministers share in this plenitude of the bishop's priesthood in various modes, forming with him a college of brethren who assist him in his work of service. They are not merely functionaries, but with him they have a special mode of existence, namely, they exist *for* the members of the church. As Christ by the incarnation existed as a servant *for* men, so ordination constitutes a man a servant (indeed a slave) for the free men, who are the redeemed members of the church. Thus the priesthood is not merely a function, it is a *state* of dedicated responsibility, as is parenthood.[34]

Every Christian by baptism is also in a state of responsibility, namely, a responsibility *for* the world. It is in this service to the world that he becomes fully aware of God's presence in the world. The Word of God which he witnesses in faith becomes relevant and meaningful to him, not merely in contemplation, but in the experience of secular reality, since God speaks to us not simply in Scripture and tradition considered as a static *depositum fidei,* but as Scripture and tradition become the living Word in the actual circumstances of our life of faith, hope, and love.[35]

Thus the *spiritual* formation of the Christian is a *pastoral* formation. He grows in the Spirit by serving the world in the Spirit.

From these considerations some Catholics today are drawing the conclusion that the monastic, contemplative tradition, and the form of spirituality which it fostered, and which in the past so influenced the formation of the clergy, was essentially mistaken. This assertion is reinforced by stressing the undeniable fact that dualistic ideas stemming from Neoplatonism, and perhaps even from the Essenes of Qumran, played a large part in the monastic tradition.

In my opinion, however, this is a mistaken conclusion, and a repetition of the failure to distinguish between the universal priest-hood and the diversity of special ministries. The universal priest-hood of every Christian, including the monk, is pastoral, apostolic, directed to the service of the world. But within the church the monk has a special gift, and a special ministry, that of prayer and penance. He is called to witness to the church the indispensable need of prayer, reflection, silence, discipline. By devoting himself exclusively to this, he reminds every Christian that Christ and every one of his followers must from time to time go into the desert to fast and pray.[36]

Christian tradition, therefore, was not mistaken in learning from the monks something of the importance and the discipline of the contemplative life. The mistake, however, was to apply the monas-tic model too univocally to other states of life. Those elements of monastic spirituality which *separate* the monk from the world can-not be carried over into those ministries which are directed pre-cisely to *encounter* the world. In learning from monastic experience we must constantly rethink it analogically in view of the pastoral orientation of the whole church, and of the specifically pastoral ministries.

THE COMMUNITY AS FORMATIVE

We have seen above that in the history of the church the structure which most explicitly aimed at making use of monastic experience in developing a truly pastoral center of formation was the canonical community as conceived by St. Augustine and as exemplified in the canonical religious orders of the Middle Ages.

Could we again today imagine a bishop of a diocese living sur-rounded by a college of his clergy, including some men of special theological learning and others of special pastoral experience and practical creativity, in a community in which the candidates for the clergy would be spiritually and pastorally formed?

The first objection would be that this could not give an adequate academic formation. I believe that is true, certainly in the United States. But this could easily be met by allowing the student members of such a community to take their academic work in a university school of theology. They would then bring back into the pastoral community what they had learned, for reflection, discussion, criticism, and testing in pastoral practice. In this way, the student would not be victimized by the university's academic mentality, but would be able to achieve a certain distance from it and to criticize it. Also the learned members of the community, by seminars or tutorials, could provide for the deficiencies of the university's academic program. The student in turn would bring to his university classes the stimulus and experience, the questions and doubts gained from his pastoral experience and community discussions. This would be a service to the university department of theology itself.

The student might also receive training in some special pastoral skills, not at the university but in other centers or agencies of the secular community. Thus he might have practice in pastoral counseling at a hospital, or in the communication arts at a communications center. His life and apprenticeship to the church, however, would take place in his community.[37]

A second objection is that such a conception is totally unreal, considering the fact that the average bishop today is the administrator of a large and complex diocese, who must turn the formation of his future priests over to the faculty of a seminary. Undoubtedly, at present, communities of the type I am proposing would have to be under the supervision, not of the bishop, but of his delegate. Nevertheless, this simply illuminates the fact that the bishop's role in the church at present does not look very much like that of the Good Shepherd in the Gospel. In the church of the future, bishop and people must be brought more closely together, and this is impossible if the bishop does not first come very close to his clergy and to future clergy in formation. The exodus of priests from the church at the present time is dramatic proof that this gap must be closed.

A third objection is that this formation through a community is proper to religious orders and unrealistic for the diocesan priest, who will have to live alone or with two or three others. This objection arises from the false conception of a rigorous line dividing the clergy from the laity. The parish priest does not live alone; he lives with his parishioners. As the bishop should live with his clergy to form them to priestly service, so the priest in the parish must live with the parishioners to form them to *their* priestly service. Of course, the parish is not a single residence, but it must become a community in which dialogue, reflection, common prayer go on. Hence the clerical formation community must be conceived as an *open* community, one which is in continual contact with the laity and can serve as a model for the parish itself. This will be all the more true if, as many think, the territorial parish will be replaced or at least supplemented by congregations based on occupation, common interests, etc.

A fourth objection will be raised by Protestants and those Catholics who expect that soon there will be a married clergy in the Catholic Church. How can this formative community idea be reconciled with a married clergy? Has not Protestant experience proved that the married clerical student cannot be fitted into a real community, since his family displaces it?[38] I think it must be granted that celibacy does give to a cleric a freedom for community life both with fellow clerics and as a member of a congregation which does not exist for the married minister. Nevertheless, it seems to be quite false to think that a Christian community must be monastic. Is it not conceivable that a community can be made up of both celibates, and families? The celibates will help to give cohesion to the community, but the married couples will help to give it an openness and a continuity with the common life of the church and the world which, as we have just seen, will have to be a feature of the formative community.[39]

A final objection is that communities of the sort we have been discussing would be too large to be real communities. If a diocese had one hundred men in its seminary, how could these be gathered in a community with the bishop at its head? The obvious answer to this is that the reality of the church in its catholicity demands that we do not conceive of Christian communities as tiny, sectarian groups. The pious fellowship, as has been noted, tended to end in antiecclesial individualism. Each community, to be Christian, must reflect the church in its totality and be open to the other communities and the whole church. In a large diocese there will have to be a number of formative communities, each with its head delegated by the bishop, but these communities then must devise methods of interchange which express the unified mission of the diocese as a whole.

THE MONASTIC IDEAL

The pastoral or apostolic formation just outlined is above all a formation *through experience of intense Christian community life.* The Christian apostolate is a witness to the gospel, but the gospel is the announcement that men are reconciled to each other and to God in Christ. Reconciliation, *agape* are the restoration of human community in God, so that man enters into a fellowship with Father, Son, and Holy Spirit.

What we have seen and heard we are telling you so that you too may be in union with us, as we are in union with the Father and with his Son Jesus Christ. We are writing this to you to make our own joy complete. (I John 1:3-4)

How then can we form an apostle or a pastor unless we help him to experience in actual life this mystery of Christian community? The descent of the Holy Spirit at Pentecost was such an experience, in which by the gift of tongues the barriers to communication produced by human pride at the Tower of Babel were broken down. At that moment the meaning of the gospel, until then obscure to the apostles, was made plain. To teach the future minister about this is not enough. He must experience it in daily life. It is this experience which is the basic formative process.

The monastic community remains historically as one of the most explicit and perennial realizations of this ideal of a formative community.[40] What were its elements? First of all, it involved a withdrawal, a separation from "the world," patterned after Jesus' custom of withdrawal to the desert, the mountain, or the garden for prayer. This aspect of separation colored every phase of its style of life. The cloister, the habit, silence, abstention from physical pleasure, withdrawal from married life by celibacy, poverty, restriction of study to the Scriptures—all this negative aspect was not intended to be life-denying, but rather was intended to "sweep clean the house" (Matt. 12:43–45) since "The love of the Father cannot be in any man who loves the world, because nothing the world has to offer—the sensual body, the lustful eye, pride in possessions—could ever be from the Father but only from the world; and the world, with all it craves for, is coming to an end; but anyone who does the will of God remains for ever." (I John 2:15–17)

The hermits, however, learned from experience that the house swept bare can be an invitation to "seven other devils." The answer to this was the cenobitic community. By dedication (expressed both in the vow of obedience and the vow of "stability"), the monks gave themselves to the community and undertook to live in charity and mutual service, so that they might learn to love God not only by direct communication with him and by an anticipation of the kingdom by an "angelic life" on earth, but also by loving their mortal brothers. A community of sinners, they were to suffer and labor together. This community, however, was not merely a human community; it was a community in Christ. Christ was present in it and gave it unity. As sinners, the monks shared in his suffering and lived the life of this age, but as redeemed they contemplated him resurrected and transformed in glory. This presence of Christ was both an object of contemplative faith and an experience given through the sacraments. The Eucharist and its extension in the sacrament of penance and liturgical prayer were the climax of this, but community life was itself a sacrament, a perpetual experience of mutual forgiveness and charity. This sacrament of community centered in the abbot, who was not merely an official, but rather the sacramental sign of Christ's presence, Christ as shepherd leading the community and binding it together by his example of humble service. He assisted the Spirit of Christ to form the monks through their daily life.

The first element of this daily life was *prayer.* This prayer was the essential life of the monk, because it was direct communication with God, an entering into God's triune life. But prayer was not merely the monk's own activity, it was rather his response to the Word of God. God calls to us, or we would not know he is there. This Word of God comes through the Scriptures, so that the *lectio divina,* the reading and meditation of the Scriptures, is the basis of prayer. Furthermore, this Word of God comes not merely through a book, but through the witness of the community, by ecclesial tradition; and it is not merely words, but an event, an enactment. Hence, this meditation of God's Word extended not only to private prayer, but to communal prayer, to the liturgy, especially the Eucharist, and to the Divine Office with its public Scripture readings and its psalmody.[41] In later monasticism and the canonical communities, this prayer was also supported by *study,* that is, by a more formal study of the Scriptures and of auxiliary subjects. This spirit of prayer and study was supported by preaching and spiritual colloquia or discussions, on the positive side, and by silence, on the negative side. It was said of St. Dominic that he "spoke only to God or of God," and this was the spiritual ideal of communication which took place always in God.

Prayer, however, although it is to be continuous, cannot be the only human activity. Prayer must express itself also in the bodily work of this life. By poverty, manual labor, and a disciplined routine, the monk hoped to turn this work into a support of prayer, a kind of physical, sacramental prayer in the service of the community and of the poor or the stranger who came to the community for help. This unselfish devotion to service was supported by the physical austerities intended to detach the monk from personal dependence on material needs as far as possible, so that he might be physically free for service, and mentally free for prayer.

As we look at this tradition today, a multitude of psychological and sociological questions arise in our mind, and without a doubt we need to apply this new knowledge to the reform and renewal of the monastic ideal. Yet when we look over its history, and observe that its great leaders were constantly striking the note of *moderation* and that the institution has in fact again and again balanced its own excesses, we cannot help but conclude that fundamentally it respects the requirements of the human condition. That it is deeply Christian in inspiration is proved by the saints it has produced and the creative periods of Christian culture which it has influenced.[42]

THE APOSTOLIC AND PASTORAL IDEAL

If we now ask ourselves how by analogy this model of Christian community life can be realized for the formation of apostolic and pastoral ministers without falling into the too univocal mistakes of the past, a number of issues appear.

The basic one is how to remove the conception of *separation* from the world and still achieve a depth and intensity of Christian experience. It should be obvious that in some measure, the formation of a Christian minister does not require *withdrawal* from immersion in the secular culture. The "world" requires redemption. It is a confusion of exaggerated values, of "idols." Its reality is shallow, unanalyzed, dispersed, uncriticized. Man loses himself in it, and God is hidden in it behind false gods. To serve this world in a redemptive way, the minister must first have the opportunity to withdraw from it, to see it as it is, to discern the spirits within it, to discover himself, and to hear God speaking "out of the whirl-wind." Furthermore, since formation in a new life also entails a kind of psychological regression (as takes place in psychoanalysis), there must be a kind of "novitiate," a return to the womb and to the primitive, a breaking up of the fixated personality, so that it may be freed to reform itself, to be re-created. All the evidence of comparative religion and religious psychology seems to make clear that this moment of distancing, of return to the sources, of reflection and criticism, of strategic withdrawal is necessary for the apostle and pastor.

To look at it in communal rather than individual terms, a community cannot become really intimate and open within itself unless it distinguishes and isolates itself from the surrounding community. The study of group dynamics indicates how necessary this process of group withdrawal is.

How can this paradox be overcome? I would suggest that in a formative community the key here is the bishop (or his delegate) or, better, the bishop and his college. The unity and cohesion of the community must depend on persons who have in their own personality and their relations to one another overcome the paradox of being "in the world and not of it"; for the world, but not enslaved by it. When the formative community centers in a group of men who have achieved a deep personal life, supported and fed by close community with each other, such a group can be flexibly open to the world. They can, therefore, guide those in the community who have not yet achieved this integration in a life which is both open to the world and yet detached from it.

Thus the formative community must have at its nucleus a permanent community. This is why in its way the university has proved a viable institution. The senior faculty with its tenure and dedication to research has made it possible for the university to endure through the flux and flow of classes of students and yet remain relatively open to the changing world. This openness, however, is based on the dedication to objective, scientific truth, which is the shared value that was the standard of admission to the faculty and its point of contact and cohesion. At the present moment, we see the universities in great danger of breaking up because this conception of truth ("the value of being value-free") has proved inadequate to the needs of today's world. Similarly the strength of monasticism and of the seminary also rests in the dedicated groups that form the nucleus of the community; and the cohesion of these groups depends on a conception of faith in God reinforced by structures of vows and hierarchy of offices. These too are proving insufficient to meet the needs of a rapidly changing world.

What is needed, therefore, is a community of formation whose nucleus is made up of Christian ministers bound together by a deep experience of Christian community based on a theological understanding that is thoroughly apostolic and pastoral. They must be able to see that the God who is met in silent prayer is the same God present and speaking through secular realities.

Conclusion

It appears to me that Catholics if they are to retain the values to be found in their tradition in the formation of priests must begin experimentation with *formation communities.* The main body of these communities would be small enough (say not more than thirty, preferably half that many) to make close interaction possible. These communities might include, however, families and other single persons less closely knit to the group, yet sharing many of its activities.

The nucleus of a community would be three or four priests who possessed both theological knowledge and pastoral skill and experience, headed if possible by the bishop or in close contact with him, meeting frequently with him. These men would first be trained together and would have developed a mutual dedication and understanding at a deep personal level.

This community would be located near a university center, and would also have close contacts with other agencies that could furnish training in pastoral skills. It would follow a daily program in which liturgical worship, time for study, reflection, and meditation would be safeguarded. It would also give itself time for regular recreation together and for times of discussion with respect to both the interior community life and the needs of the world around it. It would carry on some apostolate or service to this community as a team, and its individual members would be progressively engaged in the actual ministries of the church. The members would bring back from the university the problems raised at a theoretical level, and with the assistance of the permanent members would attempt to criticize and supplement this learning.

The detachment of the community from the pressures of the society would have to be assured by simplicity and poverty of life to the degree that this could be attained. Furthermore, it would have to be tolerant of the freedom of both students and permanent members to separate from it if conscience or personal development demanded.

The basic problem of such a group would be precisely its stability, since its openness and relative freedom from supportive and restrictive structures would make it very open to disruption. But the solution to this must be found in a Christian way, not by laws and regulations but by the development of a deep inner realization of the reconciling presence of Christ in the community, in the church, and in the world about them both.

B. *by* RANDOLPH CRUMP MILLER

RELIGION as a topic of study has become accepted in most of the state universities of this country. The situation has been changing so rapidly in terms of the establishment of departments of religion and the expansion of course offerings that even a current survey is out of date by the time it is published.[1] Because this is where the action is, some careful thinking about the significance of religion in the humanities should precede a consideration of theology in the university, and both of these developments may provide new insights for "doing theology" in a divinity school or seminary.

The significance of the study of religion in state universities is at least twofold. First, within a few years it is estimated that 90 percent of students at the college and university level will be in state universities. Therefore one might welcome this development because it is the only way in which a majority of students will receive any knowledge of religion at an academically respectable level. Second, the study of religion apart from denominational allegiance or professional training within a pluralistic society now becomes possible in a new way.[2]

The Place of Religion in the University

Within the scope of a secular university, religion is a discipline that includes the study of both the quality of human experience designated as religious and the beliefs that constitute the structure of religions.[3] It is a recognition that "the sacred is possible."[4] The phenomena are considered to be "in the public domain."[5] Claims that religious beliefs are based on revelation may be examined, but there can be no insistence on the acceptance of such claims. As a humanistic field of study, it has no distinctive methodology, but it makes use of methodologies from many disciplines and fields. However, it is a subject of study in its own right, although it may also be studied within the scope of other disciplines and fields, such as sociology, psychology, history, anthropology, and philosophy.

Clyde A. Holbrook writes, "Stated in comprehensive terms, religion embraces the study of those forms of conviction, belief, and behavior and those systems of thought in which men express their concerned responses to whatever they hold to be worthy of lasting and universal commitment."[6]

Such study is to be "objective." That is, although the need for imaginative projection and perhaps empathy for the experiences being analyzed is recognized, such teaching is not confessional. Whatever is taught needs to be intelligible to both the believer and the non-believer. Such teaching needs to be free from charges of indoctrination or of antireligious bias, so that both the believer and the non-believer take a risk by being exposed to such teaching, although the content is not loaded in either direction. Objectivity is not sterility or indifference.[7]

The objective teaching of religion operates on three levels. The first is a descriptive and analytical approach to the many phenomena that are called "religious." There is little involvement at this level, but it may be the best approach to the foundations of religious study. The scope may be wide or narrow; the approach may be through a variety of methodologies; the emphasis may be on anthropology, sociology, or psychology; the cultural roots may be explored; the impact on daily living may be examined; the belief-structures may be compared.

The second approach takes current religious traditions and in the light of their histories seeks to discover the sources of their energies. Here one may turn to myth and cult, to the power of community, to the place of law, to the Scriptures and sacraments.[8] This information is to be sought in historical data, for religious meanings arise in history and can be understood in their cultural contexts. In such a study one discovers the similarities in the various traditions; if this element is overemphasized, one may miss the distinctiveness of each major tradition; however, if this element is underemphasized, the uniqueness of each tradition may be considered as different in kind (so that one may say that Christianity, for example, is not a religion and therefore cannot be compared with other faith-systems).

Religion is marked off from other disciplines and religions are distinguished from each other in terms of religious language. Today, when even the possibility of religious language has been questioned, the historical evidence is that the category of religion has its own language or languages. Within the scope of religious thinking, one finds a logic that is internal to the language, and this makes it difficult for the outsider to understand the meanings. One element of involvement that the non-religious person must risk in attempting to understand religious behavior and thought is to acquire some capacity to grasp the self-involving and performative nature of religious language.[9]

The third approach is a comparison of and analysis of belief-systems. Here one comes close to "doing theology," which will be discussed later; but there is a place for looking at theologies and meanings of life as a purely academic procedure. The self-understanding of man in relation to God comes to the fore at this level of study. In some situations this cannot properly be called theology and should be considered as philosophy of religion; but in other cases philosophy and theology overlap in both methods and conclusions; yet, in contrast, in the thinking of some theologians theology has no clear relationship with philosophy. These distinctions are important and will be considered in any broadly based comparative study of belief-systems. It would be proper, also, in this regard, to make a careful study of a single system of thought, such as Protestant thought after the Reformation, or Catholic thought since Vatican II, or Moslem theologies of the Middle Ages.

Religion, then, offers a complex field of study with a variety of methodologies and approaches. Most of the elements making up the total field can be categorized in different ways: the religions of the world; the textual study of the Scriptures of all the religions;

historical, psychological, sociological, and anthropological approaches to all the religions; comparative theologies; and specialized approaches.[10] No university can hope to cover the whole field, and some subjects will be omitted because of the lack of trained personnel. Possibly, because of the pluralism of American religions, an attempt should be made to cover most of the live options for American students, and this may be done in terms of competent scholars on the faculty without concern for representation of committed members of all the churches and synagogues and other institutions. Some degree of specialization must be expected, or else all teaching will be watered down.[11]

What marks off teaching in a state university from that in a divinity school or even from that in some church-related or Jewish colleges is that the state university seeks specifically to avoid evangelization, conversion, and indoctrination. Holbrook has an excellent chapter on "Purposes of Religious Instruction." He stresses both the materials and methods of the field and the needs of the student. The first objective is stated as follows: "To acquaint the student with the perennial questions which men have raised and attempted to answer concerning their meaning and destiny as these are reflected in systems of thought, cultic acts, and characteristic attitudes and beliefs."[12] This approach is to be both descriptive and evaluative, and the criticism should be on the basis of internal logical and moral consistency.

The second objective, according to Holbrook, is to dispel ignorance and to assist the student in formulating his own view of the meaning of life. This involves some degree of appreciation and understanding of human experience in the field of religion, combined with freedom to make one's own decision.[13] In other words, guidance of the student's self-development is at the center of the university's concern, and the teaching of religion may contribute to this guidance. Many students hope to develop a philosophy of life during their educational experience, and they also want to become competent in their fields of knowledge. To achieve this a student "needs practice in criticism and the self-esteem and confidence that will enable him to stand in opposition to pressures of authority and of the immediate social group. He also needs models of independent thinking, a general climate of freedom in his college, and a rule structure that is appropriate to his stage of development."[14]

There is a risk here that the result will be commitment to the religious goals of the teacher. But where the teacher is fulfilling his role with enthusiasm for his subject, change in the student is to be expected as a by-product. The important element is that the student be challenged to face the issues and to make decisions, and therefore to develop as a person. That he may decide to accept the position of his teacher is therefore a risk that has to be taken; and this is true in courses in political science, philosophy, ethics, and most other subjects.

In order for such a possibility to exist, not only must religion exist as an academic pursuit on the campus, but the field must be representative of the live options of the day. The danger does not come from the opportunity for commitment (for any living subject includes this possibility), but in the limitation by those in authority as to the acceptable form of commitment. At this point the university has a freedom and integrity that is not often possible for a denominational college or a theological seminary: and perhaps the freedom of the university might serve as a model for other institutions of learning.

There is another set of purposes that needs recognition. So far, we have talked about the non-professional concerns of students of religion. However, there are students within the university who are planning on graduate work in religion, teaching in elementary and secondary schools, or entering training for the Christian ministry. These students normally have some degree of commitment and some kind of vocational plans. Decisions about course offerings need to be made with these students in mind, just as courses are planned for premedical, prelegal, and other preprofessional students. This will not change the focus of university teaching of religion, but it may broaden the base of course offerings, especially in the area of theology, which is often neglected in current university faculties.

Who Should Teach?

There is a great deal of discussion concerning departments of religious studies as the proper organization for teaching religion at the university level. Some would prefer to have religious subject matter included in other academic disciplines. There is much to be said for both approaches, but perhaps the warning of E. Thomas Lawson should be noted: "When religion is taught as an aspect of other academic disciplines it is not adequately done. Even if a person is a trained historian, it requires specialized training in theology, which few historians have, to teach a course in the history of Christian thought."[15] There should be a faculty of religion, whether in a department or not, and at the same time it needs to be recognized that religion has always been involved in any understanding of the economic, political, literary, artistic, and philosophical approaches to human activity, and therefore should appear in any course where it is relevant.

But what of this faculty of religion? In the American scene, with its pluralism carelessly classified as Catholic, Protestant, and Jewish, some faculties have followed what is called the "zoo" approach.[16] Representatives of each of the three faiths serve as exhibits A, B, and C and are exponents of their own positions, and students can take an "eeny, meeny, miney, mo" approach. This is a distortion of what actually happens, and in the best example of this approach, at the School of Religion at the University of Iowa, one finds highly qualified representatives of a fully academic approach to religious studies.[17]

What the issue comes down to is qualified personnel, without too much concern for denominational or faith commitments. When a policy has been developed concerning offerings in religious studies, with recognition of the richness of the field and the limitations of the university, each institution must decide where to specialize. This decision in turn is qualified by the availability of trained instructors. The requirement for faculty is based on academic expertness and involvement rather than commitment. As Holbrook writes, "a distinction not always noted is that between the professor's enthusiasm for the study of his field and the religious commitments which may or may not underlie his interest in the field."[18] The experts in religious scholarship and teaching have not always been exponents of the faith they have studied.[19]

Many competent scholars have received their graduate degrees from church-related institutions and theological seminaries. They are likely to have commitments, but this does not disqualify them. In the future, as graduate departments of religious studies in the universities develop, not only will there be a supply of trained scholars and teachers for university faculties, but it is to be expected that they will also teach in divinity schools. This interchange back and forth will be a good thing.

On "Doing Theology"

So far we have dealt with the scope of religious studies in the public university, which is where most of the action is today. But a casual study of the offerings at these universities exhibits a lack in theology (even when one discovers some courses in the history of Christian thought), contemporary Christian thought, and occasionally in the theology of Aquinas, Barth, or the Niebuhrs. There is even less evidence of such teaching concerning Jewish theologians.

Part of this, I think, is due to misapprehension concerning the nature of theology, which is often thought to be a closed system of indoctrination based on a revelation not in the public domain and not open to analysis in terms of the human experience of religious phenomena. That some theology fits such a description is obvious. Theology is simply "the-truth-about-God-in-relation-to-man." For the Christian it has its roots in the Bible and the history of the church, but it operates in terms of verification based on history, reason, and spiritual experience. Although theology has a narrower boundary than the field of religious studies, it is a specific discipline within that field.

William Temple suggests that *"the primary assurances of Religion are the ultimate questions of philosophy."* He goes on to say that religion has three central convictions: (1) "the conviction that Spirit is a true source of initiation of processes," (2) "the conviction that all existence finds its course in a Supreme Reality of which the nature is Spirit," and (3) "the conviction that between that Spirit there can be, and to some extent already is, true fellowship, at least such as is involved in our conscious dependence on that Spirit."[20] "Theology starts from the Supreme Spirit and explains the world by reference to Him. Philosophy starts from the detailed experi-

ence of men, and seeks to build up its understanding of that experience by reference to that experience alone."[21] This leads to an
uneasy but necessary alliance between theology and philosophy,
which is theological philosophy or natural theology. Temple goes
on to establish this on the basis of revelation, which he defines as
"the coincidence of event and appreciation,"[22] something possible
in every aspect of knowledge and therefore not limited to theological issues.

In this view no propositions are revealed. They are the result of
the thinking of men about events which have aroused appreciation,
sometimes of a unique sort. This approach eliminates any dogma-
tism in theological statements, although it allows for them as significant propositions interpreting events. Ian T. Ramsey speaks of
moments of discernment or disclosure, where the "light dawns" or
the "ice breaks." Ideas "come alive" in specific situations and then
are tested in daily living. For Ramsey these experiences occur in
"characteristically personal situations,"[23] while for Temple "all oc-
curences are to some degree revelation of God."[24] For both the
certainty lies in the discernment and not in the propositions. Ramsey says that "being sure in religion does not entail being certain
in theology."[25]

Bernard Meland, in a chapter on "The Appreciative Consciousness," develops the first part of the claims of Temple and Ramsey,
utilizing William James's claim for the depth in immediate awareness that underlies conscious experience but which an attentive act
as such can never achieve.[26] As a regulative principle in thought,
says Meland, "the appreciative consciousness . . . can best be understood as an orientation of the mind which makes for a maximum
degree of receptivity to the datum under consideration on the
principle that what is given may be more than what is immediately
perceived, or more than one can think. . . . Call it what one will:
intellectual humility, wonder, reverence, or simply open awareness, some such mood is essential to the orientation of the mind we
are describing."[27] Tillich, who claims to be no empiricist, makes
the same point at the beginning of his *Systematic Theology:* "The
theological concepts of both idealists and naturalists are rooted in
a 'mystical a priori,' an awareness of something that transcends the
cleavage between subject and object."[28]

There is, then, a dual nature to theology. First, there is a concern with the appreciative consciousness as such; second, there is concern with the object of that consciousness. When put in the language of faith, there is faith as trust or commitment and there is faith as loyalty to the one who claims such faith, which involves a critical analysis of faith both as an activity and in relation to the object or objects.[29]

The critical function of theology is the crucial one in the current scene. Verification in terms of scientific checks or the appeal to sense experience seems to many to be impossible, and yet the empirical anchor, as Ramsey calls it, cannot be ignored without reducing theology to some kind of impossible speculation that is not open to adequate analysis. It is no accident that Van Buren's approach in *The Secular Meaning of the Gospel,* using a strict theory of verification derived from logical analysis, seems to turn Barth's theology on its head. As against both Van Buren and Barth, there are those who claim that theology provides a complex presentation of evidence demanding some kind of decision that takes account of many subtleties and includes the attitude of the one making the decision. A theology calls attention to a way in which facts may be seen and understood.[30]

Theology has been a way of analyzing and evaluating faith-systems. This has been its most important function. In doing this it has often operated in terms of seeming authority that in due time has been undercut by new insights and new formulations. Partly this has been due to increased information and new techniques of investigation, which may supplement or improve some theological systems and threaten others. Today most of the pressure is in terms of serious questioning of all theological formulations. As one commentator has put it, we no longer have viable systems, we do not even have foundations, and all we can do is to take soundings once again.[31] The "death of God" movement was evidence of this vital re-examination of theological method and systems, which has now moved on to new ways of formulating theological questions which may produce new propositions or resurrect theological positions that were in temporary eclipse.

Theology is also concerned with communication. It is at this point that it has often failed miserably, especially with the lay person and the undergraduate student. Although many people are eager to consider what their life means and to ask questions about the nature of God, they do not find intelligible answers among the professional theologians. When someone writes a book like *Honest to God*, its popularity surprises the professionals not only in theology but in other disciplines. The popularity of Paul Tillich, Hans Küng, and James A. Pike on university campuses is another significant factor, for these men have not been popularizers or interpreters of religion in general but have spoken on theological issues. The recent developments in linguistic philosophy, especially the writings of Ian T. Ramsey, Donald Evans, and Dallas High, may lead to new ways of communicating what theologians wish to say.

Approaches to Teaching Theology

Obviously there are many ways to teach theology in a secular university. The simplest way of introduction for many is to do a study of existing theological systems, in terms of the history of Christian thought or of comparative current systems. Such courses are being taught successfully, often as survey courses. They may deal only with the results of such thinking, so that one compares Barth, Buber, and Rahner in a manner similar to a comparison of a Corvette, a Ferrari, and a Mustang, not in terms of how they were made, how they perform, or what they cost, but only in terms of how they look. But if one gets inside the system, discovers the principles of construction, the methods of handling the evidence, and the criteria for judging the final model, he is on the way to "doing theology" himself. It is this involvement that the student needs in order to achieve his own abilities in the field and to make a decision. Many students make this kind of effort in deciding what car to buy, although some are satisfied with advertising claims or the amount of chrome on the car.

This approach may be used with any theology derived from any religious tradition. Those universities which can provide adequate personnel may offer courses in the theologies of various Moslem schools of thought—or of others. There also are the many varieties of Christian theology. In all cases the purpose is the study of any theology and theology as a whole as an academic discipline in its own right.

In the case of Christian theology, this means adequate critical acquaintance with the Scriptures as the basis for theology. This is the point at which almost all curricula seem to be adequate, although not necessarily in the focus of being a foundation for theologizing. The check on such teaching should be only in terms of professional competence, not in terms of some institution's orthodoxy. It might be hoped that both believers and non-believers would find such courses helpful. At Oxford University, it is said that "for believers the present performance of the faculty of Theology is not constructive enough, while for unbelievers it is not open and relevant enough."[32]

Bernard Meland describes an approach in philosophy of religion that applies also to "doing theology." He writes, "I am trying to point a way between a purely objective procedure and an overburdened subjective concern with knowledge, realizing that a serious loss of perspective follows when the personal equation intrudes too zealously."[33] This means taking seriously the "appreciative response," seeing it in action in the human experiences which may be recounted. This is the note of elemental religion, as seen at a high level in some of the Psalms. This principle of selection could be applied to primitive religion, to medieval Christianity, to great personalities, and to the current scene. With this beginning Meland takes his students through relevant literature and on to the existential issues of today's world, using art, poetry, and music as well as theological works. Such an approach, Meland believes, gives philosophy of religion a sense of function, moves it out of a negative atmosphere, accepts the modern secular mentality at the start, and makes such study restorative. Chiefly, though, the students "are there to develop reflective powers, to inform the mind, to widen the imagination; but all this so that they may sharpen their capacity for insight, that they may be both critically and appreciatively aware of data which bear significantly upon those crucial inquiries which come to men, either in moments of solitary reflection or in situations of extremity, or in society when one finds other human beings confronting one."[34]

When philosophy of religion or theology is taught in the way that

Meland describes, the student is on the way to "doing theology." Meland is quite clear that he is talking of theology that operates within "the human level of meaning,"[35] and this may be a severe limitation for some. It is one thing to insist that theological meanings carry one beyond man's limitations (as do most of the sciences) and another to insist that theology relies on other than human propositions or tools in order to accomplish its goals. Some theologies, if seen in this latter way, could very well appear in a course in the history of Christian thought or even in a course in contemporary theology, to be looked at with the tools and attitudes proper to humanistic learning. One can learn that the doctrines promulgated are not considered open to human inquiry, that authority may not be questioned, or that this is a command from on high. Such claims are frequently found among some of the sects and occasionally among the major theologians of some traditions— Christian and otherwise. But normally this understanding is not "doing theology" as far as one learns to use the tools proper to a university setting.

In the United States today most of the research and creative thinking in the field of religion has occurred in the theological seminaries and private universities and colleges. This has been so primarily because there was no home for the professionally trained religious scholar in the universities. But a new day is dawning. The resources for research and creative scholarship will gravitate toward the graduate departments of religious studies in the great state universities. Already some of the best research is occurring in such institutions. This will not eliminate research in the seminaries but will provide healthy competition. It also means that competent undergraduates and graduate students will be participating in such research and scholarly activities. The geographical movement of the seminaries into university communities is partly a recognition of this development. Furthermore, the free university may have fewer restrictions on its research than a denominational seminary.[36]

Of course, this movement toward the university community is also a recognition that the church cannot live apart from the world. "Academic theology," says Howard E. Root, "has lived on its own fat."[37] There is a whole new world to be explored by theologians in a worldly setting, and out of it may come a bolder natural theology that has a proper place for the Christian revelation. This may be the kind of thinking one finds in books by John Cobb, Schubert Ogden, and Charles Hartshorne,[38] in which metaphysics regains its place in theological reconstruction.

Theology is taught out of situations for dialogue. Such dialogue can be between those representing various viable theological positions or between those in theology and those in other disciplines. But for such dialogue to be effective, certain conditions must obtain. First, dialogue is not achieved when there is an interchange of ignorance. Herman Wornom suggests that participants must be advocates of the position they defend, but others would claim that good teachers can represent various positions with empathy and understanding.[39] Second, the curriculum must provide enough religious knowledge to make dialogue fruitful. The basic courses in today's universities usually provide this. Third, there needs to be some common basis of agreement about epistemology, so that what counts for knowledge can be discussed. Sometimes this is a question of what "language game" is to be used, for even among theologies one finds language used in different ways.[40] Fourth, there must be freedom to explore ideas. Since this is basic to the university, one would hardly think that this requirement needs mentioning; but it is a fact that many state universities have not permitted free discussion of religious issues.

Such dialogue should continue between theology and other disciplines. This could be done strictly on a comparison of disciplines dealing with theological questions, or it might involve the ways in which various disciplines approach crucial issues in politics, social ethics, race relations, community living, medicine, technology, or church life. This is not a question of making theological pronouncements about the other disciplines, although this also is within the province of theology, but of assisting the theologian in making his theology more relevant and communicable in the modern world.[41]

The objections to the approaches suggested are not likely to come from the academic community, except among those who are avowed secularists, or from the religious community, except for extreme conservatives among Catholics, Protestants, and Jews. Because "religious studies must be liberal and open, seeking to understand as a part of the community of learning rather than the community of faith,"[42] the universities will not be doing the jobs of churches and synagogues and will offend those who are not open to the humanistic study of religion and theology. Most approaches to religious studies will satisfy neither the religious conservative nor the non-theist. This is the risk that must be taken, because religion is properly an academic subject within the community of learning.

The Protestant Divinity School

Traditionally the Protestant divinity school has conceived its purpose as training of men for the parish ministry, with little concern for other possible ministries or for the work of men in Christian service. Within this framework theology was a major subject of academic study, but this study was oriented to a denominational tradition and to an acceptable point of view. Some competent theologians were on seminary faculties, but many men taught theology as something received from the tradition.

Today all this has changed. The seminaries are not sure of their purpose; the vocations for which men and women are being trained are not clear-cut; curricula are under radical revision; clusters of theological schools, both Protestant and Roman Catholic, are being located near major universities.

The students entering these seminaries are not sure of why they are there. Many of them disavow the parish ministry but have romantic ideas about other forms of ministry; they are uncertain about the nature and function of the church; they are doubtful about the truth of many theological statements; and yet they are attending seminaries in increasing numbers in order to find out what it is all about. Not all of these students are carefully selected, however, and often they are incapable of work at the graduate level which seminaries claim for their post-B.A. degree (B.D. or M.Div.).[43]

In such an avowedly confused situation, seminaries are attempting to rethink their purpose and to restructure their curricula and organizations, even moving into new geographical areas or considering mergers. Although we cannot deal in any detail with such complex situations that vary from one institution to another, we need to keep them in mind as we look at the emerging sense of purpose and the place of theology in the life of a Protestant divinity school.

At the academic level the purpose of a divinity school has been described as "educating men in theological thinking," which includes "development of the student's awareness of the relationships between theological conceptions and the historic experience of the community, its present life, and its hopes and thrusts into the future." Essential to "education in theological thinking" is "practical contact with the changing world."[44] The theological school is the "intellectual center of the Church's life. . . . a community of students in communication with one another, with the common subjects or objects studied, and with companions of the past and present in like communication with the objects."[45]

It also has as its purpose education for service in and to the church and to mankind, including the professional and ordained ministry but also the lay ministry. It is vocational and professional, as well as academic and graduate, training in religion. It lacks the secular neutrality of a state university, although it seeks the same degree of objectivity and scholarly competence.

Because it is in the service of the church, a divinity school, even if part of a university, has as part of its function concern with commitment of its students. It aims at what is called *formation* of its students for their work of ministry. This is a point at which Protestants can learn much from Roman Catholic practice.[46] Already there is a community of committed faculty, a life in some kind of Christian community including worship and fellowship, and a sense that this is the church in action, but often this has led to withdrawal from the secular world and therefore from concern for the needs of mankind.[47]

This points to the seminary's need of the university at two levels. First, the recent development of religious studies at the university level leads to the expectation that students will come to the divinity school with better preparation in religion at the undergraduate level, some with background in comparative religions and the relation of religion to culture, some with a degree of expertise in "doing theology," some with a broad outlook on the secular scene, some with a great intellectual interest in religion but with no commitment except for academic excellence, and some already capable of dialogue between theology and secular disciplines.[48] Second, when a theological school is related to a university, the university is a resource for theological education. Students may take many of the courses needed to make up deficiencies in any subject (including religion), they may take secular subjects that are needed for a broad training for their particular ministries, and they may use the resources of university life and library for greater breadth and depth of learning. Furthermore, the university faculty may become agents of dialogue with the divinity faculty. When there is a cluster of seminaries in the vicinity, such dialogue may cross various denominational and faith lines.

In our discussion of "doing theology" at the university level, we dealt with the appreciative consciousness. It is expected in a theological school that personal involvement will exist to an unusual degree, even when there is confusion about beliefs and vocational goals. H. Richard Neibuhr suggests that such study is "hazardous; the involvement may become so personal and emotional that intellectual activity ceases and the work of abstraction, comparison and criticism stops."[49]

If in the university there is the risk of commitment in an academically neutral community, in the divinity school such commitment is expected or hoped for as part of the process. Not only what goes on in the classroom but the support of the community impels the student in this direction, often to the accompaniment of indoctrination rather than "doing theology."

Granted the differences in environment and commitment, I cannot see that the purpose in teaching one to "do theology" in the seminary is different from what it is in the university. One learns to reflect theologically on the meaning of experience, dealing with the ultimate issues of life in all of its forms. Theology includes the study of "God and man-before-God in their interrelation," including reflection on the life of the church and the world.[50]

Seminaries have not done a good job of helping students to think theologically, even when they have filled them with theological systems and ideas. Charles Feilding writes, "I have persisted . . . in asking how theology is learned, how the faith of the communities of Christians in past history is learned today, how it is apprehended as something with which present Christian faith and life is continuous and by which it may be illuminated and criticized, and how that faith may illuminate our own time and become the ground for living the Christian faith now. I have found it difficult and often impossible to find articulate replies to questions of this kind."[51]

Students today, we are told, want to start with basic questions. They are moved by the "God is dead" movement, by the radical and secular theologies and moralities that are popularized, by the relevance of some of the ideas they have accumulated in university life, and they are not satisfied with the traditional methods and approaches of most theological systems.[52] If we are going to reflect theologically upon the current scene, we may need historical knowledge for perspective but we need new methodologies in order to relate the Christian interpretation of reality to daily life. Feilding suggests that the theology which comes alive for many students is that taught through clinical training or field education, but that this is often a theology different from what is taught in a theology class.[53] A theology that is the private property of theologians and clergy is not likely to become a functioning part of ministry among lay people.[54] This suggests that theology needs a pastoral orientation, says Karl Rahner, with communication to lay people both verbally and through ministry as basic. This may involve a new kind of scholarship and research every bit as demanding as the mastery of abstruse and abstract ideas.[55] Theology must be functional without losing its academic respectability. This is what "doing theology" or "thinking theologically" really means.

To some extent this marks off seminary theological teaching from both the undergraduate and the graduate programs in the university. Except for the students who are continuing beyond seminary into a graduate program, most of the students need to learn how to "do theology" within the Christian community, with an emphasis on the functional aspect, as the minister becomes a teacher of teachers.

"Doing Theology" in a Protestant Divinity School

If theology is no longer the queen of the sciences, it is still the chief element in a theological education. No matter what the subject taught, its chief value in a theological school is that it contributes to "doing theology." This focus is primary, for all that the student learns is for the purpose of assisting him to reflect on the

theological meanings in all aspects of life and to act on these reflections in terms of ethical decisions and obedience to his Christian
conscience, which may be stated best under the model of "the will
of God."

To do this adequately, then, requires some degree of unity of
purpose on the part of the faculty, so that they are agreed on what
they are trying to do. Theologizing underlies every subject and
every subject contributes to the process of theologizing. The school
is dealing with "the-truth-about-God-in-relation-to-man" at every
level of learning activity.

Such agreement as to purpose does not entail agreement on the
results of theologizing or even on the methods. The chaos in the
field of theology today, which many consider to be a healthy situation, means that there is an openness as to both methodology and
subject matter that promises new insights and degrees of commitment.

Our concern in this chapter, however, is with theology as a
discipline. We may recognize that other elements in the curriculum
are intimately concerned with theologizing, but we are concerned
primarily with "doing theology." Much of this endeavor will be
identical with what goes on in the university at both the undergraduate and graduate level, but in the theological seminary other
approaches and other claims may be recognized and emphasized.
In the secular approach of the university most theology will be
examined in terms of natural theology or philosophical theology.
In the seminary it is possible to start with the claim of revelation
as something distinctly other than natural theology, as in the
thought of Karl Barth. In the university Barth's position may be
presented and examined, but in the seminary his theology may be
presented as conviction or at least shared as such by the students.
The freedom of the university may permit acceptance of Barth's
position, but in the seminary it may be presented by an advocate
without considering the philosophical or metaphysical conditions.
But in the seminary, also, where there is genuine academic freedom, the student and teacher are free to reject any specific theological system. The primary goal is not indoctrination, even in a
seminary closely controlled by a confessional denomination. For
the seminary as for the university, we cannot escape the fact that

theology must operate in the public domain. On the other hand, both institutions need to recognize the validity of the use of language of belief even when there may be no evidence of verification on humanistic grounds. It may be that involvement is essential to getting at the meaning of a theology, although, as we have said, there can be involvement without commitment. In a survey course one may become involved in a number of theologies without being committed in terms of any one of them, just as one may become involved in the meanings of other religions without sacrificing one's Christian commitment. But in the seminary it is expected that the result of "doing theology" will be that one not only thinks straight but also illuminates his commitment.

For many in the seminaries the beginning point of such theological involvement that may lead to commitment will be in terms of Christology. The focus of much theology today is Christology; the response to questions about belief in God has been that we must start with Jesus Christ. Pusey and Taylor state this clearly: "Christ is the message, contemporary, basic, urgent, underlying all theological endeavor."[56] But others will ask if this can be so unless one already believes in God. Does Christology precede or follow belief in God? Does the special revelation of God in Christ have priority over the revelation of God himself in the experience of mankind? As one deals with such questions, he begins to develop his own methodology in terms of a perspective that comes from his prior way of examining reality.

For others the beginning point for theological reflection may be the current doubts of what has been called "radical theology." This requires what has been called "apologetics," a consideration of the evidence for Christian belief. But such an approach will be entirely different from traditional apologetics. One approach is through language study, as described by Dallas High: "When *looking at and seeing* language at work (not idling), it is the case clearly that we do not give 'reasons' in quite ordinary ways for the beliefs we 'own' and 'own up to' including religious (credal and doctrinal) beliefs. Moreover, performing an act of believing or holding a belief implies that we will not entertain such utterances, at least seriously, unless we are also willing to 'back them up,' 'give reasons,' 'justification,' or 'grounds' if asked or pressed, or if we think about it."[57]

When one says, "I believe," there are involvement and commitment and a willingness to stand back of the statement or proposition. One anchors his beliefs in experience, history, authority, or Scripture, and this is open to the examination of others.[58] What one is working for is not agreement about what is true or false but agreement in the language one uses which points to a form of life. This style of life is illustrated by the theology one holds, and often one's theology is commended more by a style of living than by a logical system.

Competence in "doing theology" relies on two kinds of internal discipline, the historical and the comparative. Both deal with the sources of faith, but from different perspectives. The history of Christian thought needs a broad base in the development of the culture and the church. Within this framework, the student can learn both how theology was done in those days and what the results were. There is as much to learn, for example, from Augustine's or Anselm's methodology as from their conclusions, and in some cases the methodology may be borrowed and different conclusions reached. Historical continuity and discontinuity in the development of method and doctrine need to be understood. Theologians from the same or different periods can be compared. The dynamics of theological conflicts, as exhibited in the early councils, the Reformation, the modernist-fundamentalist controversy, and other conflicts will be helpful.

The comparative study of theology can be looked at historically but will be more fruitful when concerned with the live options in today's world. Theological opinions are changing rapidly, and in some cases there have been revivals of positions prematurely pronounced dead. The negative criticisms of the more radical theologians, for example, have turned some thinkers back to the empirical theological methods of the 1920s and 1930s. The new hermeneutics may be a revival of some earlier kinds of biblical study with new twists. The developments in linguistic philosophy, at first detrimental to theological study, have become an invaluable tool in the hands of such men as Ian T. Ramsey and Dallas High. As background for the current scene, one could take the theologians from Schleiermacher onwards mentioned in *A Handbook of Christian Theologians*[59] or *Twentieth-Century Religious Thought*,[60] and then turn to the thinkers in the *New Theology* series.[61] With some selection from such lists and use of the original writings of these men, a comparative approach to methodology and belief could lead to exercises in "doing theology."

Besides the use of historical and comparative approaches to theological thinking, there are also the dogmatic and the systematic. In some vocabularies these two approaches either overlap or are identical, but if dogmatics is the presentation in a systematic way of a given theology of the church, we can consider systematic theology as the building of a system of theological thinking. When one is a member of a denomination with a distinctive theological heritage, this can be learned through a study of dogmatic theology. Granting that there are variations in dogmatic emphasis, Catholic, Eastern Orthodox, and Lutheran theologies are more suitable for dogmatic presentation than those of the Free Churches or Anglicanism.

Most theologians today would not claim to be explicating the official doctrine of the church. They have their own systems of theology. The study of any of these theologians, especially when one gets inside the point of view and grasps the methodology, is an invaluable discipline as background for "doing" one's own theology. But there is the danger that such theologizing will be of the "hothouse" brand if it is purely an intellectual exercise. Charles Feilding has warned us that theology comes alive for students within some kind of practical situation, and that this theology may have no relation with what is taught in the more traditional classroom approach. This suggests that in the systematic theology classroom there be concern with a methodology that takes account constantly of the world of daily living, that theologizing be a continuing process in relation to all that happens to the student in the seminary and outside, and that this kind of theologizing be recognized as the chief purpose of the divinity school. For unless theology provides an interpretation of the meaning of the world, can operate in the public domain, and can do this for lay people as well as for technically trained leaders, it will be sterile and deserve the opprobrium from which it often suffers.

Theology, then, is neither an intellectual nor a practical exercise but a combination of the two. The distinction between "theology as content" and "practical theology" as found in many seminaries is a false one and guarantees sterility, irrelevance, or shallowness. With all the varieties of ministry now open to seminary graduates, the theological school must assist them to reflect theologically on what is involved in a broad field of activity. In religious education, for example, theology provides perspective and guidance, but in turn the findings of educators *as educators* may modify the theological approach. There is here a kind of dialogue between disciplines and even between interdisciplinary fields that provides the possibility of some kind of unity in one's approach to ministry.

This leads to a final point: the need for dialogue. First, there needs to be opportunity for dialogue between representatives of various theological traditions. In the larger seminaries this is possible; and in the move toward clusters of seminaries even greater varieties of dialogue may develop. In the isolated small seminary, however, the one professor of theology may be found talking to himself unless he is enough of a scholar to bring many possible positions into the classroom through books and his own ability to make objective and yet impassioned presentations of positions not his own—obviously a mark of a great teacher not often found in a small seminary. Those seminaries near colleges and universities have access to theologians on other faculties. All seminaries can provide the setting for dialogue among students, either in classes or in non-classroom activities.

Second, there needs to be dialogue between representatives of all the disciplines on the faculty. Every teacher in a theological school is dealing with theology in his own way, and his subject contributes to the process of theologizing. Multiple teaching teams, conceived in terms of genuine interchange of ideas, especially with small classes where students can participate in this discussion, may be especially illuminating. Students may be encouraged to meet informally with faculty and outside guests to discuss their own choices of issues. The problem is both to overcome the pigeonhole effect of the average curriculum and to achieve an overall view of what it means to "do theology" against the background of the complex riches of the curriculum.

Third, there needs to be dialogue between theology and the world. This involves dialogue between the theological school and the university, between theology and secular disciplines. The Niebuhr, Williams, Gustafson study puts it this way: "If the Christian faith must enter a dialogue with contemporary thought and culture, a student has not been introduced to the core of theological education until he has entered into this conversation between Christian thought and the many disciplines which are concerned with man and his world."[62] One cannot assume that this has happened in the student's previous training. One cannot simply hope that it might happen. It needs to be built into the curriculum. Here again the cluster of divinity schools around a university suggests a way out. When students are encouraged to take courses with a purely secular orientation, the seminary can provide periods of theological reflection on what has been learned. The student needs many secular subjects, including psychology, sociology, and philosophy, as a basis for ministry, but these are not adequate resources until they are part of his person as a theological man.

Some of the most interesting experiments of the seminaries are in terms of knowing the world. Intern years are more likely than before to be in secular situations. Students are encouraged to participate in summer-in-industry programs. It is suggested by some groups that students should spend a year between college or university and seminary in some kind of secular occupation. Students are being offered housing in inner-city situations, where their field education and classroom work are centered. It has been suggested that such centers of training for ministry be mandatory, with focus on a life-cycle ministry, institutions, business and industry, political process, crisis (civil rights, poverty, war), and the arts.[63]

We have talked about clusters of seminaries. One purpose of such clusters is the establishment of ecumenical dialogue, which may be between various brands of Protestants, between Catholics and Protestants, or between Christians and Jews. Already there are clusters of these kinds, providing rich resources for dialogue and for co-operative education. The interdenominational seminaries, especially when university-related, already have these resources, but they need much greater exploitation. The isolated divinity school could consider adding a faculty member of another faith (although this reflects the "zoo" approach) to teach within the existing framework, or seek an expert on the other faith as one does in presenting the comparative study of religions.

Conclusion

Theology, when properly conceived as "doing theology," has its proper place within both the university curriculum and that of the theological school. The focus of the institutions differs, however: for the university is a secular institution in which religion and theology have proper academic standings, and the seminary has an overriding theological purpose for education in theological thinking. The university accepts commitment among students and professors but does not expect increasing or new commitments from the academic approach, although the involvement necessary for any appreciation of religious reality and "doing theology" involves always the risk of commitment. The theological school is supposedly a community of the committed, although increasingly this is not so, and works for fuller, stronger, and sometimes different commitments. The university is concerned with the welfare of its students and hopes for the development of an overall view of the meaning of life, but does not think of this in terms of Christian faith. The divinity school is concerned with the formation of its students for Christian ministry, lay or ordained, in its many varieties and new developments. Everything that happens in the theological school is for the development of theological reflection about the world in which we live in all of its dimensions. Theology is the dominant interest, and all other subjects have value primarily as they feed the process of "doing theology."

There is continuity between theology as taught in the university and seminary. "Doing theology" involves methodology and reflection, no matter what the environment may be. Furthermore, the sources are the same in both instances. In many cases, the syllabus for a course in the university at either the undergraduate or graduate level could conceivably be the same as in the seminary. The difference could come at the level of attitudes toward revelation in a secular university, or in the possibility of teaching dogmatic theology as a single option, or in the expectation or requirement of commitment to the object of study.

The development of religious studies in the university frees the seminary to do more advanced work with its incoming students, although the university courses are conceived in humanistic and not in professional or preprofessional terms. The university is concerned primarily with religion, including theology, as a proper academic discipline for all who elect such subjects for any reason whatever. Such endeavors may or may not provide intelligent lay people for the churches or seminarians. What will result is a sector of the public that is not religiously illiterate, and this in itself justifies the efforts of the university. Through its graduate programs, some teachers for seminaries and universities will be developed, but again this is for the enrichment of the teaching profession as such, not for the good of the church or the seminary as a primary objective. But the side effects, in terms of commitment and professional competence, may prove in the long run to be as valuable as the achievement of the primary goal.

EIGHT

Implications of Catholic-Protestant Educational Dialogue

A. THE DECLARATION ON CHRISTIAN EDUCATION

B. DIALOGUE WITH NON-BELIEVERS

C. by KENDIG BRUBAKER CULLY

EDITOR'S NOTE

In this section we offer two important documents from the Roman Catholic Church: *The Declaration on Christian Education* (the footnotes being omitted), promulgated by Pope Paul VI on October 28, 1965, and containing the statement on Christian education emerging from Vatican Council II; and *Dialogue with Non-believers* (the Introduction being omitted), issued by the Vatican Secretariat for Non-believers in October 1968. These are the officially issued texts, presented here as an integral part of the total discussions from a Catholic standpoint. The concluding portion of this section is the editor's summation of some implications for the Catholic-Protestant educational dialogue as it proceeds in the years immediately ahead.

A. *THE DECLARATION ON CHRISTIAN EDUCATION*

Prologue

THE SACRED ECUMENICAL COUNCIL has considered with care how extremely important education is in the life of man and how its influence ever grows in the social progress of this age.

Indeed, the circumstances of our time have made it easier and at the same time more urgent to educate young people and, what is more, to continue the education of adults. Men are more aware of their own dignity and position; more and more they want to take an active part in social and especially in economic and political life. Enjoying more leisure, as they sometimes do, men find that the remarkable development of technology and scientific investigation and the new means of communication offer them an opportunity of attaining more easily their cultural and spiritual inheritance and of fulfilling one another in the closer ties between groups and even between peoples.

Consequently, attempts are being made everywhere to promote more education. The rights of men to an education, particularly the primary rights of children and parents, are being proclaimed and recognized in public documents. As the number of pupils rapidly increases, schools are multiplied and expanded far and wide and other educational institutions are established. New experiments are conducted in methods of education and teaching. Great attempts are being made to obtain education for all, even though vast numbers of children and young people are still deprived of even rudimentary training and so many others lack a suitable education in which truth and love are developed together.

To fulfill the mandate she has received from her divine founder of proclaiming the mystery of salvation to all men and of restoring all things in Christ, Holy Mother the Church must be concerned with the whole of man's life, even the secular part of it insofar as it has a bearing on his heavenly calling. Therefore, she has a role in the progress and development of education. Hence this sacred Synod declares certain fundamental principles of Christian education, especially in schools. These principles will have to be developed at greater length by a special post-conciliar Commission and applied by episcopal conferences to varying local situations.

I

All men of every race, condition and age, since they enjoy the dignity of a human being, have an inalienable right to an education that is in keeping with their ultimate goal, their ability, their sex and the culture and tradition of their country, and also in harmony with their fraternal association with other peoples in the fostering of true unity and peace on earth. For a true education aims at the formation of the human person in the pursuit of his ultimate end and of the good of the societies of which, as man, he is a member, and in whose obligations, as an adult, he will share.

Therefore, children and young people must be helped, with the aid of the latest advances in psychology and the arts and science of teaching, to develop harmoniously their physical, moral and intellectual endowments so that they may gradually acquire a mature sense of responsibility in striving endlessly to form their own lives properly and in pursuing true freedom as they surmount the vicissitudes of life with courage and constancy. Let them be given also, as they advance in years, a positive and prudent sexual education. Moreover, they should be trained to take their part in social life so that, properly instructed in the necessary and opportune skills, they can become actively involved in various community organizations, open to discourse with others and willing to do their best to promote the common good.

This sacred Synod likewise declares that children and young people have a right to be motivated to appraise moral values with a right conscience and to embrace them with a personal adherence, together with a deeper knowledge and love of God. Consequently, it earnestly entreats all those who hold a position of public authority or who are in charge of education to see to it that youth is never deprived of this sacred right. It further exhorts the sons of the Church to give their attention with generosity to the entire field of education, having especially in mind the need of extending very soon the benefits of a suitable education and training to everyone in all parts of the world.

II

Since all Christians have become by rebirth of water and the Holy Spirit a new creature so that they should be called and should be children of God, they have a right to a Christian education. A Christian education does not merely strive for the maturing of a human person as just now described, but has as its principal purpose this goal: that the baptized, while they are gradually introduced to the knowledge of the mystery of salvation, become ever more aware of the gift of faith they have received, and that they learn in addition how to worship God the Father in spirit and truth (cf. John 4, 23), especially in liturgical action, and be conformed in their personal lives according to the new man created in justice and holiness of truth (Eph. 4, 22–24); also, that they develop into perfect manhood, to the mature measure of the fullness of Christ (cf. Eph. 4, 13) and strive for the growth of the mystical body; moreover that, aware of their calling, they learn not only how to bear witness to the hope that is in them (cf. I Pet. 3, 15) but also how to help in the Christian formation of the world that takes place when natural powers, viewed in the full consideration of man redeemed by Christ, contribute to the good of the whole of society. Therefore, this sacred Synod recalls to pastors of souls their most serious obligation to see to it that all the faithful, but especially the youth who are the hope of the Church, enjoy this Christian education.

III

Since parents have brought children to life, they are bound by the most serious obligation to educate their offspring and therefore must be recognized as the primary and principal educators. This role in education is so important that only with difficulty can it be supplied where it is lacking. Parents are the ones who must create a family atmosphere animated by love and respect for God and man, in which the well-rounded personal and social education of children is fostered. Hence, the family is the first school of the social virtues that every society needs. It is particularly in the Christian family, enriched by the grace and office of the sacrament of matrimony, that children should be taught from their early years to have a knowledge of God according to the faith received in baptism, to worship him and to love their neighbor. Here too they find their first experience of a wholesome human society and of the Church. Finally, it is through the family that they are gradually led to a companionship with their fellowmen and with the People of God. Let parents, then, recognize the inestimable importance a truly Christian family has for the life and progress of God's own people.

The family which has the primary duty of imparting education needs the help of society as a whole. In addition, therefore, to the rights of parents and others to whom the parents entrust a share in the work of education, certain rights and duties belong indeed to *civil society* whose role is to direct what is required for the common temporal good. Its function is to promote the education of youth in many ways, namely: to protect the duties and rights of parents and others who share in education, and to give them aid; according to the principle of subsidiarity, when the endeavors of parents and other societies are lacking, to carry out the work of education in accordance with the wishes of the parents; and, moreover, as the common good demands, to build schools and institutions.

Finally, in a special way, the duty of educating belongs to the Church, not merely because she must be recognized as a human society capable of educating, but especially because she has the responsibility of announcing the way of salvation to all men, of communicating the life of Christ to those who believe, and, in her unfailing solicitude, of assisting men to be able to come to the fullness of this life. The Church is bound as a mother to give to these children of hers an education by which their whole life can be imbued with the spirit of Christ and, at the same time, to do all she can to promote for all peoples the complete perfection of the human person, the good of earthly society and the building of a world that is more human.

IV

In fulfilling her educational role, the Church, eager to employ all suitable aids, is concerned especially about those which are her very own. Foremost among these is catechetical instruction which enlightens and strengthens the faith, nourishes life according to the spirit of Christ, leads to intelligent and active participation in the liturgical mystery and gives motivation for apostolic activity. The Church esteems highly and seeks to penetrate and ennoble with her own spirit other aids also which belong to the general heritage of man and which are of great influence in forming souls and molding men, such as the media of communication, various groups for mental and physical development, youth associations and, in particular, schools.

V

Among all educational instruments the school has a special importance. It is designed not only to develop with special care the intellectual faculties but also to form the ability to judge rightly, to hand on the cultural legacy of previous generations, to foster a sense of values and to prepare for professional life. Among pupils of different talents and backgrounds it promotes friendly relations and fosters a spirit of mutual understanding, and it establishes, as it were, a center whose work and progress must be shared together by families, teachers, and associations of various types that foster cultural, civic and religious life, as well as by civil society and the entire human community.

Beautiful, indeed, and of great importance is the vocation of all those who aid parents in fulfilling their duties and who, as representatives of the human community, undertake the task of education in schools. This vocation demands special qualities of mind and heart, very careful preparation and continuing readiness to renew and to adapt.

VI

Parents who have the primary and inalienable right and duty to educate their children must enjoy true liberty in their choice of schools. Consequently, the government which has the obligation to protect and defend the rights of citizens must see to it, in its concern for distributive justice, that public assistance is given in such a way that parents are truly free to choose according to their conscience the schools they want for their children.

In addition, it is the task of the State to see to it that all citizens are able to come to a suitable share in culture and are properly prepared to exercise their civic duties and rights. Therefore, the State must protect the right of children to an adequate school education, check on the ability of teachers and the excellence of their training, look after the health of the pupils and, in general, promote the entire work of the schools. But it must always keep in mind the principle of subsidiarity so that there is no kind of school monopoly, for this is opposed to the native rights of the human person, to the development and spread of culture, to the peaceful association of citizens and to the pluralism that exists today in ever so many societies.

Therefore, this sacred Synod exhorts the faithful to assist to their utmost in finding suitable methods of education and programs of study and in forming teachers who can give youth a true education. Through the associations of parents in particular, they should further with their assistance all the work of the school, but especially the moral education it must impart.

VII

Feeling very keenly the weighty responsibility of diligently caring for the moral and religious education of all her children, the Church must be present with her own special affection and help for the great number who are being trained in schools that are other than Catholic. This is possible by the witness of the lives of those who teach and direct them, by the apostolic action of their fellow-students, but especially by the ministry of priests and laymen who give them the doctrine of salvation in a way suited to their age and circumstances and provide spiritual aid in every way the times and conditions allow.

The Church reminds parents of the duty that is theirs to arrange and even demand that their children be able to enjoy these aids and advance in their Christian formation to a degree that is abreast of their development in secular subjects. Therefore, the Church esteems highly those civil authorities and societies which, bearing in mind the pluralism of contemporary society and respecting religious freedom, assist families so that the education of their children can be imparted in all schools according to the individual moral and religious principles of the families.

VIII

The influence of the Church in the field of education is shown in a special manner by the Catholic school. No less than other schools does the Catholic school pursue cultural goals and the human formation of youth. But its proper function is to create for the school community a special atmosphere animated by the Gospel spirit of freedom and charity, to help youth grow according to the new creatures they were made through baptism as they develop their own personalities, and finally to order the whole of human culture to the news of salvation so that the knowledge the students gradually acquire of the world, life and man is illumined by faith. So, indeed, the Catholic school, while it is open, as it must be, to the conditions of the contemporary world, leads its students to promote efficaciously the good of the earthly city and also prepares them for service in the spread of the kingdom of God, so that by leading an exemplary apostolic life they become, as it were, a saving leaven in the human community.

Since, therefore, the Catholic school can be such an aid to the fulfillment of the mission of the People of God and to the fostering of the dialogue between the Church and mankind to the benefit of both, it retains, even in our present circumstances, the utmost importance. Consequently, this sacred Synod proclaims anew what has already been taught in several documents of the magisterium, namely, the right of the Church freely to establish and to conduct schools of every type and level. And the Council calls to mind that the exercise of a right of this kind contributes in the highest degree to the protection of freedom of conscience and the rights of parents, as well as to the betterment of culture itself.

But let teachers recognize that the Catholic school depends upon them almost entirely for the accomplishment of its goals and programs. They should therefore be very carefully prepared so that both in secular and religious knowledge they are equipped with suitable qualifications and also with a pedagogical skill that is in keeping with the findings of the contemporary world. Intimately linked in charity to one another and to their students and endowed with an apostolic spirit, may teachers by their life as much as by their instruction bear witness to Christ, the unique teacher. Let them work as partners with parents and, together with them in every phase of education, give due consideration to the difference of sex and the proper ends divine providence assigns to each sex in the family and in society. Let them do all they can to stimulate their students to act for themselves and even after graduation continue to assist them with advice, friendship and by establishing special associations imbued with the true spirit of the Church. The work of these teachers, this sacred Synod declares is, in the real sense of the word, an apostolate most suited to and necessary for our times and at the same time a true service offered to society. The Council also reminds Catholic parents of the duty of entrusting their children to Catholic schools wherever and whenever it is possible, of supporting these schools to the best of their ability and of cooperating with them in the education of their children.

IX

To this concept of a Catholic school all schools that are in any way dependent on the Church must conform as far as possible, although the Catholic school is to take on different forms in keeping with local circumstances. Thus the Church considers very dear to her heart those Catholic schools, found especially in the areas of the new churches, which are also attended by students who are not Catholics.

Attention should be paid to the needs of today in establishing and directing Catholic schools. Therefore, though primary and secondary schools, the foundation of education, must still be fostered, great importance is to be attached to those which are required in a particular way by contemporary conditions such as professional and technical schools, centers for educating adults and promoting social welfare or for the retarded in need of special care, and also schools for preparing teachers for religious instruction and other types of education.

This sacred Council of the Church earnestly entreats pastors and all the faithful to spare no sacrifice in helping Catholic schools fulfill their function in a continually more perfect way, and especially in caring for the needs of those who are poor in the goods of this world or who are deprived of the assistance and affection of a family or who are strangers to the gift of faith.

X

The Church is also concerned with schools of a higher level, especially universities and colleges. In those schools dependent on her, she intends that by their very constitution individual subjects be pursued according to their own principles, method and liberty of scientific inquiry in such a way that an even deeper understanding in these fields will be obtained and that, as questions that are new and current are raised and investigations carefully made according to the example of the Doctors of the Church and especially of St. Thomas Aquinas, there may be a deeper realization of the harmony of faith and science. Thus there is accomplished a public, enduring and pervasive influence of the Christian mind in the furtherance of culture, and the students of these institutions are molded into men truly outstanding in their training, ready to undertake weighty responsibilities in society and to witness to the faith in the world.

In Catholic universities where there is no faculty of sacred theology, there should be established an institute or chair of sacred theology in which there should be lectures suited to lay students.

Since science advances by means of the investigations peculiar to higher scientific studies, special attention should be given in Catholic universities and colleges to institutes that serve primarily the development of scientific research.

The sacred Synod heartily recommends that Catholic universities and colleges be conveniently located in different parts of the world, but in such a way that they are outstanding not for their numbers but for their pursuit of knowledge. Matriculation should be readily available to students of real promise, even though they be of slender means, and especially to students from the newly emerging nations.

Since the destiny of society and of the Church herself is intimately linked with the progress of young people pursuing higher studies, the pastors of the Church are not only to expend their energies on the spiritual life of students who attend Catholic universities, but, solicitous for the spiritual formation of all their children, they must see to it, after consultations among bishops, that even at universities that are not Catholic there should be associations and university centers under Catholic auspices in which priests, religious and laity, carefully selected and prepared, should give abiding spiritual and intellectual assistance to the youth of the university. Whether in Catholic universities or others, young people of greater ability who seem suited for teaching or research should be especially helped and encouraged to undertake a teaching career.

XI

The Church expects much from the zealous endeavors of the faculties of the sacred sciences, for to them she entrusts the very serious responsibility of preparing her own students not only for the priestly ministry, but especially for teaching in the seats of higher ecclesiastical studies or for promoting learning on their own or for undertaking the work of a more rigorous intellectual apostolate. Likewise, it is the role of these very faculties to make more penetrating inquiry into the various aspects of the sacred sciences so that an ever deepening understanding of sacred revelation is obtained, the legacy of Christian wisdom handed down by our forefathers is more fully developed, the dialogue with our separated brethren and with non-Christians is fostered, and answers are given to questions arising from the development of doctrine.

Therefore, ecclesiastical faculties should reappraise their own laws so that they can better promote the sacred sciences and those linked with them and, by employing up-to-date methods and aids, lead their students to more penetrating inquiry.

XII

Cooperation is the order of the day. It increases more and more to supply the demand on a diocesan, national and international level. Since it is altogether necessary in scholastic matters, every means should be employed to foster suitable cooperation among Catholic schools, and between these and other schools that collaboration should be developed which the good of all mankind requires.

From greater coordination and cooperative endeavor greater fruits will be derived, particularly in the area of academic institutions. Therefore, in every university let the various faculties work mutually to this end, insofar as their goal will permit. In addition, let the universities also endeavor to work together by promoting international gatherings, by sharing scientific inquiries with one another, by communicating their discoveries to one another, by having exchange of professors for a time and by promoting all else that is conducive to greater assistance.

Conclusion

The sacred Synod earnestly entreats young people themselves to become aware of the importance of the work of education and to prepare themselves to take it up, especially where, because of a shortage of teachers, the education of youth is in jeopardy.

This same sacred Synod, while professing its gratitude to the priests, the religious men and women, and the laity who by their evangelical self-dedication are devoted to the noble work of education and of schools of every type and level, exhorts them to persevere generously in the work they have undertaken and, imbuing their students with the spirit of Christ, to strive to excel in pedagogy and the pursuit of knowledge in such a way that they not merely advance the internal renewal of the Church but preserve and enhance her beneficent influence upon today's world, especially the intellectual world.

Each and every point stated in this Declaration has satisfied the fathers of the sacred Council. And we, by the authority bestowed on us by Christ, together with the venerable fathers, approve it in the Holy Spirit, we decree it and we enact it; and we order the promulgation, to God's glory, of what has been enacted synodically.

Rome, in St. Peter's Basilica, October 28, 1965

Paul, Bishop of the Catholic Church
(The Fathers' signatures follow)

B. *DIALOGUE WITH NON-BELIEVERS*

NATURE AND CONDITIONS
OF DIALOGUE

1. Dialogue in General
Documentation

By the word dialogue, used in a general sense, we here understand every form of meeting and communication between individuals, groups, and communities to bring about a greater grasp of the
truth and to achieve better human relations in a spirit of sincerity,
respect for persons, and mutual trust.

Dialogue is particularly important and complex when it is established between people of different and even sometimes opposed
positions, who are attempting to overcome their mutual prejudices
and broaden, as far as possible, their areas of mutual agreement,
whether this take place on the plane of simple human relations or
that of a quest for the truth or of collaboration to attain ends of a
practical nature.

All these dimensions are to be found in each of the different
forms of dialogue, but according as one or the other of them plays
a central role, one can distinguish three fundamental types of dia-

logue, which can be classed as follows:

—Encounter on the plane of simple human relations, with a view to drawing the interlocutors out of their isolation and mutual mistrust, and creating an atmosphere of deeper understanding, mutual esteem, and respect;

—Encounter on the plane of search for the truth regarding questions of the greatest importance to the persons involved, by striving in common to attain to a deeper grasp of the truth and to a fuller knowledge of reality;

—Encounter on the plane of action, which aims at establishing the conditions for collaboration towards fixed practical objectives, despite doctrinal differences.

Although it is to be desired that dialogue be achieved at all three of these levels simultaneously, each of them, in so far as it is an interpersonal encounter, has its own peculiar value.

All dialogue, inasmuch as the parties involved both give and receive, implies a certain reciprocity. Wherefore it differs from teaching, which is ordered towards the doctrinal enrichment of the pupil. Since dialogue can, however, aim at the benefit of the public at large through the diffusion of information, it can in this sense be considered a form of instruction and even an implicit announcement of the truth of the Gospel message.

Dialogue, as it is here understood, also differs from polemics and controversy in so far as these are ordered principally to the defense of a position and to the demonstration of the falsity of its opposite.

Furthermore, dialogue is not simply a confrontation of views, because it implies on both sides a movement of rapprochement and a deeper understanding. Finally, even if each of the interlocutors may legitimately aim at persuading the other of the value of his own position, dialogue is not of its nature directed towards this end, but rather towards a mutual enrichment.

2. *Doctrinal Dialogue*

I. POSSIBILITY AND LEGITIMACY OF THIS TYPE OF DIALOGUE

The very possibility of doctrinal dialogue is often brought into doubt. The question is raised as to whether it is not necessary to set aside all absolute truth if dialogue is to be sincere—whether it is required that the participants remain indefinitely in an attitude of enquiry if dialogue is to be open. Further, if absolute truth is admitted, the very possibility of engaging in dialogue is questioned; where one believes that he possesses the truth real dialogue seems impossible, for it seems that a disposition to engage in dialogue demands that doubt about absolute truth be entertained.

Furthermore, it is possible to enter into dialogue if one starts from two different systems of thought? If it is true that each affirmation acquires its precise meaning only in relation to the whole of its system, is there any place for genuine dialogue when the points of departure are diverse systems?

Further yet, an analysis of the notion of truth held by men of our times shows that, for them, truth is immanent in man himself and depends on man and his freedom, to such an extent that there can be no truth, which does not derive from man himself. Thus all basis for dialogue would be lacking, as Christians, who reject this principle of immanence, have a completely different notion of the truth.

Concerning public dialogue, one wonders whether the faith of an assembly not sufficiently prepared for controversy can be legitimately exposed to the risk of challenge.

For these reasons we should like to point out, in the remarks that follow, some directions in which the solution of these difficulties should be sought.

Doctrinal dialogue is a discussion conducted with courageous sincerity in an atmosphere of complete freedom and respect on doctrinal matters in which the participants are in some way personally involved. Though holding different positions, those taking part wish to reach a deeper mutual understanding, to discover their points of agreement and, as far as this is possible, to enlarge them. It can thus come about that the parties can mutually enrich one another.

On the one hand, therefore, dialogue requires that one pay attention to the personal character of the acquisition of truth. The uniqueness of each individual in his particular situation, as well as the limitations under which everyone labors in this search for the truth must be taken into account. Awareness of the limitations of individuals and of historical communities creates a readiness to consider the opinions and the efforts of the other, and to embrace the elements of truth contained in both positions. By this process the minds are enriched and the greater truth is furthered.

On the other hand, in so far as it is also a quest for the truth, dialogue has no meaning unless one believes that the intellect can attain objective truth, at least to some extent; that it can always grasp some aspects of the truth, even if these may be mixed with error; and, finally, that each individual has a contribution to offer in the search for truth which others should take into account because of the very fact that he attains a view of reality which is proper and unique to himself.

In these conditions the affirmation that it is possible to attain the truth is not only compatible with dialogue; it is a necessary condition for it. There can be no question, then, of bringing the truth in doubt, as it were subordinating the demands of truth to those of dialogue, as certain forms of irenism seem to do. On the contrary, dialogue must come about as a result of the common moral obligation of seeking the truth in all matters, especially in religious questions.

Furthermore, the fact that each of the participants considers his own position to be true does not render the dialogue futile, for this persuasion is not contrary to the nature of the dialogue. In fact, dialogue arises from the confrontation of two different positions and it aims, not at destroying them, but rather at clarifying them and, as far as possible, bringing them closer together. Thus it suffices that each of the participants believe that his grasp of the truth can increase through dialogue with another.

Now, such an attitude would be adopted and fostered in all sincerity by believers. Although the truths of the faith, since they are revealed by God, are in themselves absolute and perfect, they are always inadequately penetrated by the believer. Consequently he can always grow in his understanding of them. Besides, not everything that is believed by Christians is derived from Revelation. Thus dialogue with non-believers can help Christians to distinguish what is derived from Revelation from what is not, as well as to read the signs of the times in the light of the Gospel.

Further, Christian faith does not dispense the believer from a rational enquiry into the rational presuppositions of his faith.

Rather, it urges him to embrace whatever is rightly postulated by human reason, for the Christian is convinced by his faith that reason can never be contrary to faith. In fine, the believer knows that his faith does not provide all the answers to every question under discussion; for from his faith he only learns in what spirit and according to what norms he should guide his judgment, especially in the temporal order, in which vast areas are still open to investigation.

Regarding the difficulty arising from the internal unity of a system of ideas, let us recall that dialogue exists even when the participants can agree only on certain points. If every system of thought contains certain truths and values which do not necessarily receive their sense and importance from the system itself and can thus be separated from it, it will suffice to place these truths and values in their proper light to reach a certain degree of agreement.

Even amongst men separated by radical differences of opinion, some points on which agreement and communication are possible can always be found. While keeping in mind the internal unity of the systems under discussion, one will have to distinguish, in any particular discussion, the different levels at which dialogue can take place, because it can happen that dialogue be possible at one level and not at another. Particularly, let it be recalled that the secular sphere retains a certain autonomy; consequently divergences in religious matters do not exclude, in principle, a certain amount of agreement in temporal affairs.

Nor is it to be denied that dialogue may become more difficult because the participants hold different notions of what constitutes the truth and do not agree on the very principles of reasoning. If this occurs, the purpose of dialogue will be to try to come to a notion of the truth and of principles of reasoning that all participants can agree upon. If this is not possible, dialogue has nevertheless not necessarily been fruitless; it is no small matter to have found the limits beyond which the dialogue cannot proceed. After all, dialogue is not to be pursued at all costs.

The risk of diversity of opinions is in some way inevitable in a pluralistic society like ours. Hence it is necessary to prepare believers to face this risk, especially in public dialogue, which, if properly conducted, can contribute much to a maturation of the faith. Besides, public dialogue affords the interlocutors the possibility of proposing their positions to an audience which they would not otherwise be able to reach.

Dialogue between believers and non-believers, while involving certain risks, is not only possible but desirable. It can be brought to bear on all subjects accessible to human reason, such as for example philosophy, religion, politics, ethics, sociology, economics, the arts, and culture in general. Fidelity to all spiritual and material values obliges the Christian to recognize these values wherever he finds them. Dialogue with non-believers can also deal with the benefits to human life and culture that can be derived from truths of the supernatural order.

2. THE CONDITIONS FOR DOCTRINAL DIALOGUE

To attain its objectives dialogue must respect the demands of truth and liberty. It must sincerely seek the truth . . . Thus doctrinal dialogue must be excluded when it is apparent that it is being "manipulated" as a means to attain particular political ends. Greater difficulties arise in dialogue with those Marxists who adhere to communism because of the intimate connection which they establish between theory and practice; a factor which makes it extremely difficult to keep the different levels of dialogue distinct, and which sometimes even reduces dialogue that pertains to doctrine to the level of practical dialogue.

Fidelity to the truth demands, furthermore, an effort to be clear in presenting and comparing the respective positions, lest the use of words that sound the same but have different meanings for the participants conceal differences instead of resolving them. This requires that attention be paid to the sense in which the same words are used by both parties, so that, avoiding all ambiguity, the discussion may proceed properly.

Doctrinal dialogue also demands the courage, both to expound one's own position with complete sincerity and to recognize the truth wherever it is found, even when this obliges the participants to revise, at least in part, their doctrinal and practical standpoints.

Dialogue will be really profitable only if those who prepare it and those who engage in it are truly competent. Otherwise the benefits obtainable would not outweigh the dangers involved. Finally in dialogue truth should only prevail by its own innate force; thus the freedom of the interlocutors must be juridically recognized and effectively safeguarded.

3. DIALOGUE ON THE PLANE OF ACTION

Dialogue can also be initiated with a view towards establishing collaboration between individuals, or between groups or communities, with different or even opposed doctrinal positions.

In the first place, we must note that movements which have their origin in doctrines which a Christian may not accept are sometimes capable of evolving towards positions which are no longer essentially those from which they were derived. In the second place, as we have already stated, divergencies which render systems, taken in their totality, mutually incompatible do not prevent these same systems from agreeing with one another on certain points. In particular, divergencies on the religious plane do not themselves exclude agreement in the secular sphere, which according to the Constitution Gaudium et Spes, retains autonomy in its own sphere.

Finally, even when doctrinal agreement is not attained, it is possible to reach mutual agreement concerning particular practical objectives. That this agreement and collaboration be legitimate, certain conditions must be fulfilled: The objective sought must be good in itself or reducible to good, and what the parties to the dialogue agree upon must not compromise values which are more fundamental, such as integrity of doctrine and the rights of the human person (such as civil, cultural and religious liberty). To judge whether these conditions obtain when a particular dialogue is contemplated, the programmes proposed by the participants and past experiences must be taken into account.

Whether such cooperation is opportune will thus be determined by different circumstances of fact, time, and place. Although it is primarily the prerogative of laymen to evaluate these circumstances, it is the duty of the hierarchy to be watchful and to intervene when religious and moral values need to be safeguarded—always, however, respecting the legitimate freedom and competence of the laity.

PRACTICAL DIRECTIVES

The following directives are to be understood as corollaries to the foregoing considerations on the nature and conditions of dialogue. They are necessarily of a general nature because situations vary considerably from country to country and because it is left to the prudence of pastors and the faithful to apply particular directives to different specific situations. For example, there are differences between countries which are traditionally Christian, countries in which the Gospel has so far not been preached, and countries in which atheistic rules govern over populations composed to a great extent of Christians. Besides, it is expected that further experiences may recommend the amplification of these directives in the future. It is the function of the episcopal conferences to lay down the general norms for each country, adapting them to the local conditions.

1. Directives to Promote Dialogue

In the light of Vatican II it is desirable that public opinion in the Church be awakened to the urgent need for dialogue.

1. In the education and formation of the clergy it is necessary that their philosophical and theological instruction be imparted in such a manner that, "equipped with a correct understanding of the mentality of their age, seminarians be thus properly prepared for dialogue with the men of our times," including also the non-believers. Thus future priests should be led to a profound knowledge of the principal forms of unbelief, especially those prevalent in their respective countries, and to a knowledge of the philosophical and theological foundations of dialogue. These ends must be further pursued, at a more serious academic level, in ecclesiastical universities and faculties.

2. In promoting pastoral renewal of the clergy (through courses, seminars, congresses, etc.) special attention is to be given to the problems of dialogue with non-believers, above all in the concrete situations in which the clergy exercise their apostolate.

3. Likewise, courses of higher religious education on dialogue with non-believers, specialized courses for experts as well as workshops and congresses should be organized for the laity; this applies

especially to young people and those who are engaged in the apostolate.

4. Preaching and catechetical instruction must also take this new dimension into account, for today the Church is open to it and ready for it in a special way.

5. Dialogue and the study of atheism will be carried out by diocesan and national organizations, attached in some way to the Roman Secretariat for Non-believers and established under the authority of the local hierarchy. These bodies will seek the collaboration of ecclesiastical and lay experts of both sexes to promote research, studies, courses, and meetings.

6. It is desirable that ecumenical collaboration between Catholics and other Christians be established in this field on an international, national, and on a local level.

7. This collaboration in establishing dialogue with non-believers must also be extended to those who belong to the non-Christian religions, especially Jews and Moslems.

2. *Particular Directives*

The first distinction to be made is that between public and private dialogue.

For *private* dialogue, that is for spontaneous discussions or organized meetings open exclusively to certain individuals or restricted groups, one cannot give particular directives beyond urging the exercise of prudence and understanding, virtues which must regulate all responsible human and Christian activity.

In particular we suggest the following:

1. To achieve more fruitful dialogue it is necessary to have sufficient knowledge about the subject under discussion, not only being familiar with the viewpoint of the other party, but above all with the Christian teaching on the subject.

2. Whenever a Christian realizes the inadequacy of his preparation, he must himself have recourse to the advice of a competent person or direct his interlocutor to such a person.

3. Also to be taken into account is the important moral responsibility of not betraying the authentic content of one's faith by ceding to irenism or convenient syncretism, and of not imprudently endangering one's personal adhesion to the faith.

4.   Nor should the extent to which the testimony of an upright life led in conformity with one's faith can contribute to the efficacy of human encounter be underestimated.

Public dialogue, on the other hand, is dialogue between men who are qualified representatives of their communities, even if they do not participate in their official capacity. Planning such encounters between believers and those who hold different doctrines and belong to movements which differ from and may even be opposed to Christianity requires greater prudence in view of the repercussions on public opinion. Here too we limit ourselves to a few general recommendations:

1.   Christians, whether they be priests or laymen, who take an active part in this type of dialogue, while possessing the moral qualities enumerated above for private dialogue, must excel both in doctrinal preparation, in which they must be truly qualified, and in the other qualities which public dialogue calls for, such as moral authority, efficacy of speech and presentation.

2.   If, as is supposed here, it is a question of public dialogue at an unofficial level (without the formal authorization of the respective authorities), to guarantee the freedom necessary for true dialogue it seems opportune that persons who occupy positions of such importance that they could compromise the public authorities, their own office, or the institution which they represent should not take part in the dialogue. On the other hand, the participants must remain faithful to the general standpoint of the community in whose name they are speaking.

3.   Official dialogue (formally authorized) cannot be excluded "a priori," but the conditions favoring such dialogue between Christians and non-believers are found only rarely, either because most non-believers represent only their individual positions and not that of some community or group, or because of the great differences that obtain between the Church or religious community on the one hand, and a political party or a cultural organization on the other. In such cases it is important to avoid all ambiguity regarding the meaning of dialogue itself, the objectives to be obtained, and the willingness of all parties to work together.

4.   Dialogue may only be undertaken in circumstances of time

and place which guarantee its authenticity. Thus, for example one should avoid excessive publicity and the presence of an audience not sufficiently well informed for this could disturb the serenity of the debate and cause it to degenerate into an unseemly argument. As a rule, then, discussions among a few experts on both sides will prove more profitable. At times the rules for the conduct of the debate will have to be established beforehand. Finally, when it is evident that public dialogue is intended purely as an instrument in the hands of one of the parties, it ought to be declined.

5. Sometimes, to avoid misunderstandings or scandal, it will be necessary to make a declaration beforehand, clearly stating the meaning, the aim, and the content of the dialogue in question.

6. Priests should obtain the consent of their own Ordinary and that of the Ordinary of the place in which the dialogue is to be held. All the faithful will respect the directives of the ecclesiastical authorities. These authorities, for their part, will carefully respect the legitimate freedom of the laity in temporal matters as well as the general conditions in which they live their daily lives.

Besides the spoken form of dialogue there also exists a written dialogue. This can be achieved through the collaboration between believers and non-believers in newspapers, in editing and publishing periodicals, magazines, and journals, etc.

This form of public dialogue is more exacting because of the greater repercussions and wider diffusion of the written word. It is also more demanding because of the greater responsibility and obligation in conscience that falls upon the believers who participate in it. On the other hand, it offers greater guarantees in so far as it is easier to avoid improvisation and superficiality. For dialogue of this nature believers are advised to submit their writings before publication to the judgment of competent persons. All the faithful are further urged to faithfully observe the canonical norms already in force, as well as any new ones that may be passed in this connection.

C. *by* KENDIG BRUBAKER CULLY

W HEN WE SPEAK of "educational dialogue," what, somewhat
more precisely, do we mean?

In the Buberian sense, dialogue has come to mean an
interpersonal relationship based on intuitional capacity to have empathy with the other on the deepest levels of awareness.[1] It is
common knowledge that much of Christian pastoral theology in
recent decades has been profoundly influenced by Martin Buber's
"I-Thou" perspective; formal educational theorists, especially of the
existentialist variety, have dealt with this level also, as have students
within the theological, biblical, and historical disciplines.[2] "Relationship theology" has been defined by Randolph Crump Miller as
"a term used to describe both the sources of theological truth and
the means of communicating it."[3]

Some highly activistically motivated theorists (who usually
repudiate theorizing as too intellectualistic and "abstract") have
been arguing in recent years that the very concept of "dialogue"
tends to connote a quiet, contemplative mutuality of sharing, especially in the realm of ideas and feelings, and is inadequate for a more
violent age, in which confrontation through power struggles constitutes the chief, most viable theater of operations, sociologically and
educationally. Such a point of view still has not been adequately
formulated on a theoretical basis (and perhaps will not be, since the
"confrontation" or "involvement" approach finds ideological for-

mulation either repugnant or as the negation of the sphere of action).

"Dialogue," in the sense in which it has been used ecumenically, certainly does not imply mere conversation. There has been ample conversation *in* ecumenical dialogue, to be sure, but that has been historically necessary due to the long separations which the various Christian traditions represent; and, perhaps, psychologically necessary, for—as every analyst knows—it is important for "patients" to talk out their feelings—aggressions, hostilities, fears, etc. However, it can also be pointed out that action has been as much a part of ecumenical dialogue as mere verbal exchange. There has been the pragmatic desire to bridge old gaps, to implement a felt oneness in Christ, and to do something about the scandalous divisions. Sometimes, even, outright efforts have been made to explore the grounds of reunion and actually to reunite, as has happened in notable instances of church mergers, such as the Church of South India, the United Church of Canada, the United Church of Christ, the United Presbyterian Church, and the United Methodist Church. It has become apparent that the educational dialogue of Catholics and Protestants—still in its infancy—has been characterized by an openness to change, accompanied by a willingness to learn from one another in actual change-producing situations.

Inhibiting Factors

As many of the chapters in this book have indicated, the dialogue is impeded, however, by certain given ingredients in the church situation that tend to inhibit dialogue, both conversationally and actionally. These factors are often deeply rooted in history and are not resolved quickly. People who have lived in isolation from one another for long centuries have many mental and emotional readjustments to make when they are suddenly thrown into the close proximity of face-to-face meeting.

It must be admitted, also, that many vested interests are involved in the various "establishments" out of which churchmen speak. Denominational concerns often center in statistical matters, publishing houses (as has been pointed out by Professor Grimes), buildings, departments of operation, and other matters of a primarily institutional sort. The bureaucratic mind often finds a most comfortable abiding place in ecclesiastical headquarters, and this is often reflected in lay attitudes as well. After all, did not one's family bend every effort, when one was an infant, to assure that one would grow up to be a devout member of the church where roots were planted? That could be a matter of basic personality security, but it is more often a camouflage for an unwillingness to seek ultimate religious security, which finds its roots not in the local or parochial but in the catholic wholeness of baptized faithfulness.

The dialogue is impeded, likewise, by the type of education to which many are exposed in the church—a religious education that takes on so indelibly the coloration of a particular time-bound tradition that openness is hard to come by even when persons desire it. The advent of the ecumenical age calls for an educational approach that will condition church people to react ecumenically, just as in earlier days they were conditioned to react confessionally. This surely can be accomplished without impairing the loyalty to one's own church tradition. However, only teachers and pastors who are themselves so committed will be able to communicate such a feeling-tone to the younger generation.

Directions for the Dialogue

If the ecumenical dialogue vis-à-vis education is to emerge into profitable new directions, there would appear to be certain inevitable accompaniments. We are assuming that the process of education, if ecumenically conceived, will be the result of such directions as well as the maker of the directions.

In this book the various writers have suggested some of these directions. For one thing, there will certainly be a fuller appropriation among all concerned of the history held in common by the total church.[4]

There will be a willingness to discover areas in which there can be relatively unanimous agreement with regard to common subject matter for study. This could often include scriptural, historical, and other substantive material as well as the more distinctively methodological considerations, which seem to flourish universally despite theological divergencies.

In this connection it is interesting to note ideas included in the "designs for an educational system" as set forth in an official pronouncement of one of the Protestant denominations, the United Presbyterian Church, as the basis for a new church school curriculum. Whatever the eventual critical reaction to that emerging curriculum may prove to be, it is doubtful if any church—Catholic or Protestant—would find anything in the statement with which to disagree violently. For example, under the heading "Why the Church Must Teach," several propositions are enunciated.

The church teaches:

"because its worship of God is a response to the message of reconciliation . . .

"because God's reconciling act in Jesus Christ is a mystery its members must explore . . .

"because the new life in Christ requires discipline and nurture . . .

"because the scriptures, which through the Holy Spirit bear unique and authoritative witness to Jesus Christ, require interpretation . . .

"because it has a mission of reconciliation in the world. For the sake of that mission 'the church, guided by the Spirit, humbled by its own complicity and instructed by all attainable knowledge, seeks to discern the will of God and learn how to obey' in all the concrete situations and crises of its day. . . ."[5]

The reader may compare the above statements with the propositions stated in *The Declaration on Christian Education* that emerged from Vatican Council II (the text is included earlier in this section). There too we read of the same phenomena—mystery, new life, the way of salvation, worship, discipline. The phraseology may vary and the context, ecclesially speaking, may be different in each case, but the Spirit is the same Spirit; so much so, that one might say the spirit with a small "s" is the same in both instances also.

Emerging directions also point toward a full and complete sharing of pedagogical techniques, even of facilities and institutions. Common publication of basic textbook material is not impossible within the near future, since already, as has been pointed out by Dr. Knoff, the Revised Standard Version of the Bible is available in both

Protestant and Catholic editions with only the most minor variations of text; and in an area such as race relations in the U.S.A., not
only Catholics and Protestants were able to rely on an identical
resource for teaching, but Jews as well.

There doubtless will be a fuller sharing of institutional facilities.
Already it is not uncommon for seminarians from both Catholic
and Protestant schools to cross-register, or even to participate in
jointly planned courses of study. In Berkeley, Dubuque, Boston,
and elsewhere theological unions have been formed which unite for
many aspects of theological education the faculties and facilities of
schools which a few years ago scarcely realized that one another
existed, or had had only polite academic nods for one another.

On the grass roots level similar exciting developments have tran-
spired. "Living room dialogues" have captured the imagination of
Catholics and Protestants in many parts of the country, enabling
neighbors to meet for frank, informal discussion of their common
existence in the world as well as of their similarities and differences.

These matters are not mentioned so much for the purpose of
painting an optimistic picture of emerging directions as for the
accenting of the existent *fact* of educational dialogue-action. All
who are sensitive to the magnitude of the tasks lying ahead will
realize that formidable barriers will continue to exist. But Christians *have* been discovering one another, on various levels.

Some Viewpoints

While preparing for this chapter, I asked some religious educators to share viewpoints held concerning the possibilities and difficulties of ecumenical educational dialogue. Several perceptive
comments and analyses are recorded below, with the gracious permission of my correspondents.

Will "Dialogue" Become Antiquated?

"The development of joint programs, structures, and activities in
theological education is stimulating; and eventually from this may
come new constellations of religious commitment and action not
tied to present denominational rigidities. The movement up from

the bottom—not waiting for change from the top down—which characterizes the present decade is offering the opportunity for new styles of 'piety,' of religious life, which may antiquate 'dialogue' between Protestants and Roman Catholics." —*J. Gordon Chamberlin*, Professor of Christian Education, Pittsburgh Theological Seminary.

Person-to-Person Communication

"Speaking as a Roman Catholic high school teacher of religion, I feel the need for some built-in way to communicate with high school teachers of other confessions on a person-to-person level. True, theoretical problems and insights are aired, are shared, in journals. The need I feel, however, is at a practical, personal level. . . . Things come out in a person-to-person exchange that never surface in journals—tones, enthusiasm, practical insights and ideas; yes, even a mutual growth in faith.

"I wish, too, that my own students could meet with students of other confessions—not to share information and to air differences, but rather to share attitudes, concerns, and insights into the person of Christ. I would like them to share with one another their own faith and prayer experiences. I feel that they could greatly assist one another by voicing the common problems they have with regard to the faith and faith-witness in the world today. I think such a mutual, personal faith-encounter would be infinitely more valuable than having them read shelves of books or view miles of film. Personal faith is the key issue today. We must meet each other at a personal faith level." —*Mark J. Link, S.J.*, St. Ignatius High School, Chicago.

Divergent Approaches

"Roman Catholic-Protestant dialogue in Christian education has been sparse. American Catholic religious educators have conversed far more with their European counterparts at *Lumen Vitae*, Brussels; the Institut catholique, Paris; the Canisianum, Innsbruck; and the Higher School of Catechetics, Nijmegen, the Netherlands. Protestant Christian educators have conversed mostly with Teachers College, Columbia University. The persons with whom they choose to dialogue betray the divergent approaches which Catholic and Protestant Christian educators take to religious education. Catholics come at the task theologically. Protestants come at it educationally. Both desire a religious education that is theologically integral and educationally sound, but their initial approaches largely determine their final emphases. Catholic curricula end up heavily theological. Protestant curricula end up conventionally educational.

"If any issue presents an invitation to cross-fertilization between the two traditions, it may be Gabriel Moran's alerting Catholic educators to the inner relationship of method and content.[6] Protestants may be surprised that the suggestion is welcomed as a veritable proof of continuing revelation by Catholics. They will have remembered it as the central argument of John Dewey's *Democracy and Education* in 1916.[7] They will recall Betts's[8] and Bower's[9] wrestling with the relationship in their call for a child-centered curriculum in the 1920s. They will recognize having struggled with it at a thousand National Council of Churches curriculum meetings over the last three decades in the quest for an 'organizing principle.'

"American Catholic religious education has only recently forsaken memorization of the Baltimore Catechism as its method and content. Now that it is producing posthaste curricula for various age-groups of the life-span, it may be sensitive to the lessons Protestant planning boards have learned through a century of experience. The first may be that the problem of interrelating content and method remains largely unsolved at the level of curriculum planning and rarely operative at the level of live curriculum. A second may be the impossible dream of developing the perfect centrally planned lifelong curriculum which Protestant planning boards are finding an increasingly futile exercise. Conversely, Catholics may learn to see the 'creative mess' of their present religious education as not necessarily the worse of two worlds. There is an advantage in the absence of a church school tradition. Catholics may discover far more effective learning environments than the classroom in meeting what is for them the new challenge of free-time religious education. Wearying of an arid Sunday school, Protestants may profit from the experimentation.

"Protestant Christian education may also learn much from some Catholic theological emphases. It is axiomatic in Protestant circles that the Holy Spirit exercises a 'transforming influence' upon the learner's learning. They are silent about the same Spirit's acting through the teacher's teaching—a subject which Catholic catechists like Hofinger and Grasso warm to. Is there here a residual prejudice of the Reformation that the Spirit can work upon a person but not through one person upon another? Candid dialogue may enlarge the horizons of all.

"Another Catholic emphasis from which Protestant Christian education can learn is the liturgical and sacramental accentuation. Even the most staid of Catholic settings are enlivened by para-liturgies and celebrations. By contrast, Protestant education is bookish. The divergence is much deeper than appearances and methods. It is profoundly theological. One wonders whether the most serious and open dialogue can bring a meeting of minds. The difference deals with the meaning of the sacraments. Are they extensions of the incarnation? Are they effective signs which involve persons in the paschal mystery of Christ? Are they acts of the risen Lord? What would be the reaction of educators in the Reformed tradition to the affirmations of Schillebeeckx's *Christ, the Sacrament of the Encounter with God*[10] and Vatican II's *Constitution on the Sacred Liturgy?*[11] Catholic religious education has welcomed Protestant emphasis on Scripture. Can Protestant education welcome Catholic emphasis on the liturgy?" *—James R. Schaefer,* The Aquinas Institute, Princeton.

Liberals and Conservatives

"Those whom I have observed are clergy—Protestants, Catholics, and Jews; all graduate students. . . . Some of the Roman Catholic clergy are the most vocal liberals in regard to theology and educational theory. Any conflict that occurs is between liberals and conservatives and not between Catholics and Protestants as distinct groups. The worldly concern, rather than the theological emphasis, makes it possible for Jews to be brought into complete dialogue with the others. In summary, I have observed no difficulties between Catholics and Protestants as such in regard to educational philosophy, and much valuable sharing of ideas." —*Lee A. Belford,* Chairman, Department of Religious Education, School of Education, New York University.

An Involvement in Mission

"Since the fall of 1967 the Roman Catholic seminary at Maryknoll and two Protestant seminaries, Union Theological Seminary and New York Theological Seminary, have been engaged in a joint venture in education.[12] Students from the three institutions meet for a weekly session that involves the study of one urban issue for the semester, including opportunities for firsthand knowledge of the problem, a seminar on mission and ministry, and periods of worship and biblical study. The students remain together in the city overnight, and thus have unusual opportunity for informal dialogue.

"In the course of the program it became quickly apparent that the students were not entering into dialogue across some kind of traditional barricades. Their focus was on the task of urban analysis and its implications for mission. While they brought different experiences and traditions to bear on their task, the unifying concern for faithfulness in Christ's mission quickly provided a sense of unity that simply bypassed any sense of Catholic-Protestant 'dialogue.' In the years ahead, I am convinced that these men will work with a vital sense of one mission with Christians of whatever traditions they find engaged in Christ's mission in their particular *locus* of service." —*George W. Webber,* President, New York Theological Seminary.

The Dialogue Partners

"In my opinion about 'possibilities and difficulties' which may arise in Catholic-Protestant discussion of educational philosophy, I would say that a great deal will depend on how one defines the dialogue partners. Many conservative Catholics would find the difficulties substantial, as doubtless would conservative Protestants. But on the ecumenical level things have certainly changed a great deal."[13] —*George N. Shuster,* Assistant to the President, University of Notre Dame.

Needed: Greater Openness

"In some ways there is more creativity among Catholics than among Protestants, due to Vatican II and the stimulus which that Council gave. We Protestants have not really had some major event in recent years to shake us up. On the whole Catholics are open to Protestants. Their new freedom has almost left them compulsive in exploring our positions. It is too bad that we Protestants have not been as open to what we could learn from Catholics. I frankly believe that the present dialogue has real possibilities for Protestants to look again at catechetical approaches to learning. I do not mean by this the parrotlike fashion of asking questions and giving answers; rather, what I have in mind is the present emphasis in Catholic education upon a systematic and comprehensive approach to Christian faith. Furthermore, we need to be much more open to formational learning, or the emphasis upon the formation of the person as a man in Christ. . . . Probably the most significant thing that the Catholics are providing Protestants is an opportunity to explore the meaning of celebration. . . ." —*Allen J. Moore*, Professor of Religious Education, Southern California School of Theology, Claremont.

In Conclusion

Doubtless the viewpoints quoted above would be echoed by many others who exercise leadership roles in religious education.

What the non-professional thinks of the educational work of the church in the light of ecumenical developments will be even more important as time goes on. To date only a relatively small proportion of the memberships of Catholic and Protestant churches have been involved in authentic encounters with their counterparts. As ecumenical dialogue-action spreads more widely among the people, the church will have to face even more earnestly than it has done to date: Do we know how to teach?

NOTES

ONE, A: JAMES MICHAEL LEE

1. Jerome Edward Diffley, "Catholic Reaction to American Public Education, 1792–1852," unpublished doctoral dissertation, University of Notre Dame, 1959, p. 303.
2. J. A. Burns and Bernard J. Kohlbrenner, *A History of Catholic Education in the United States*, Benziger, 1937, p. 206.
3. Ibid.
4. Quoted in Vincent P. Lannie and Bernard C. Diethorn, "For the Honor and Glory of God: The Philadelphia Bible Riots of 1844," *History of Education Quarterly*, VIII, Spring 1968, p. 55.
5. Daniel Dorchester, *Romanism Versus the Public School System*, Phillips and Hunt, 1888.
6. Lawrence H. Fuchs, *John F. Kennedy and American Catholicism*, Meredith, 1967, pp. 164–88.
7. Quoted in Burns and Kohlbrenner, op. cit., p. 137.
8. Pius XI, "The Christian Education of Youth," in *Papal Teachings: Education*, trans. by Aldo Rebeschini, Daughters of St. Paul Editions, 1960, p. 236.
9. Ibid.
10. Second Vatican Council, "Declaration on Christian Education," in Walter M. Abbott, ed., *The Documents of Vatican II*, trans. under the direction of Joseph Gallagher, Herder and Herder, and Association, 1966, p. 647.
11. Cleo C. Berry, "Public Schools and Religion: The Opinions of Nine Eminent Educators," unpublished doctoral dissertation, University of Southern California, 1961, p. 410. (These nine educators were Henry Barnard, Horace Mann, William Torrey Harris, Francis Wayland Parker, G. Stanley Hall,

John Dewey, Herman Harrell Horne, William C. Bagley, and William Heard Kilpatrick. Kilpatrick was the lone dissenter.)

12. Neil G. McCluskey, *Catholic Viewpoint in Education*, Doubleday, 1962, p. 8.
13. Educational Policies Commission, National Education Association, *Moral and Spiritual Values in the Public Schools*, The Commission, 1951.
14. Alcuin C. Walker, "Moral and Spiritual Values in Certain Basal Readers," unpublished doctoral dissertation, New York University, 1963.
15. Neil G. McCluskey, *Public Schools and Moral Education*, Columbia, 1958, p. 7.
16. See Richard Bruce Dierenfield, "An Examination of the Current Relationship between Religion and the American Public Schools," unpublished doctoral dissertation, University of Colorado, 1958.
17. American Association of Colleges of Teacher Education, *Teacher Education and Religion*, National Education Association, 1959.
18. Commission on Religion in the Public Schools, American Association of School Administrators, *Religion in the Public Schools*, Harper & Row, 1964.
19. Jack Joseph Cohen, "The Dilemma of Religion in Public Education," unpublished doctoral dissertation, Columbia University, 1959, pp. 259–62.
20. James Michael Lee, *The Purpose of Catholic Schooling*, NCEA and Pflaum, 1968, pp. 10–11.
21. See D. Pumpinase and I. Zwetschken, *Unterfluss und Herzkontakt*, DaBalaia, 1968.
22. Jeffrey Keefe, "The Learning of Attitudes, Values, and Beliefs," in James Michael Lee and Patrick Rooney, eds., *New Dimensions in Teaching Religion*, in press.
23. Andrew M. Greeley and Peter H. Rossi, *The Education of Catholic Americans*, Aldine, 1966. Michael Schiltz, senior study director of NORC (which sponsored the investigation) discussed this finding at length in conversation with me.
24. Ibid., p. 221.
25. "Minutes of the Meeting of the NCEA Board of Directors," *The National Catholic Educational Association Bulletin*, LXV, August 1968, p. 222.
26. Their position was against federal aid. See M. Gabrieline Wagener, "A Study of Catholic Opinion on Federal Aid to Education, 1870–1945," unpublished doctoral dissertation, University of Notre Dame, 1963.
27. Of interest here is that in 1840 the "typical" teacher in many Catholic schools was a lay person. See Burns and Kohlbrenner, op. cit., p. 127.
28. This information was supplied by Winifred Long, research specialist in the NCEA, in a telephone conversation with me in December 1968.
29. See James Michael Lee, "Catholic Education in the United States," in James Michael Lee, ed. *Catholic Education in the Western World*, University of Notre Dame Press, 1967, p. 304.
30. John Tracy Ellis, "Lay Trusteeism in New York, January 25, 1786," in John Tracy Ellis, ed., *Documents of American Catholic History*, Bruce, 1956, p. 155.
31. See Benjamin S. Bloom, ed., *Taxonomy of Educational Objectives: Handbook I, Cognitive Domain*, McKay, 1956; also David R. Krathwohl, Benjamin S.

Bloom, and Bertram B. Masia, *Taxonomy of Educational Objectives: Handbook II, Affective Domain*, McKay, 1964.

32. See James Michael Lee, *The Purpose of Catholic Schooling*, op. cit.
33. Xavier Harris, *A Study of Per Pupil Expenditure in a Midwestern Diocesan Catholic High School*, Department of Education, Notre Dame University, 1963.
34. Ibid., p. 99.
35. Mary Janet Miller, *Catholic Secondary Education: A National Survey*, National Catholic Welfare Conference, 1949, p. 103.
36. Harris, op. cit., p. 4.
37. Ibid., pp. 5 and 339–42.
38. For a further explanation of this social science approach to religious instruction, see James Michael Lee, "The *Teaching* of Religion," in Lee and Rooney, op. cit.; also James Michael Lee, "Religious Instruction: What is it?" *Discovery: A Forum for High School Religion Teachers*, I, March 1968, pp. 1–3.
39. Patrick C. Rooney, "Religious Instruction in the Context of Catholic Schooling," in *Discovery*, ibid., pp. 1–3.
40. Gerard S. Sloyan, Address to students in the graduate department of education, University of Notre Dame, July 1967.

ONE, B: D. CAMPBELL WYCKOFF

1. Edward D. Myers, *Education in the Perspective of History*, Harper & Row, 1960, Ch. 2.
2. Bernard Bailyn, *Education in the Forming of American Society*, Vintage, 1960.
3. Malcolm S. Knowles, *The Adult Education Movement in the United States*, Holt, Rinehart & Winston, 1962.
4. Bailyn, op. cit.
5. Jerome B. DeJong, *The Parent-controlled Christian School*, unpublished doctoral dissertation, New York University, 1954.
6. August C. Stellhorn, *Schools of the Lutheran Church—Missouri Synod*, Concordia, 1963.
7. S. A. Wittmer, *The Bible College Story: Education with Dimension*, Channel, 1962.
8. Horace Bushnell, *Christian Nurture*, Scribner's, 1888.
9. George Albert Coe, *A Social Theory of Religious Education*, Scribner's, 1917.
10. Louis Filler, ed., *Horace Mann on the Crisis in Education*, Antioch, 1965.
11. James E. Loder, *Religion and the Public Schools*, Association, 1965.
12. John Dewey, *A Common Faith*, Yale, 1934.
13. Ward Madden, *Religious Values in Education*, Harper & Bros., 1951.
14. Cf. the pronouncement of the 189th General Assembly of the Presbyterian Church in the U.S.A., published in *Social Progress*, July 1957.
15. W. W. Charters, *The Teaching of Ideals*, Macmillan, 1927.
16. Alexander Miller, *Faith and Learning*, Association, 1960, and Charles A. M. Hall, *The Common Quest*, Westminster, 1965.

Additional Bibliography:

Walter B. Beck, *Lutheran Elementary Schools in the United States*, Concordia, 1965.

Cawthon Bowen, *Child and Church: A History of Methodist Church-School Curriculum*, Abingdon, 1960.

Kendig Brubaker Cully, ed., *The Episcopal Church and Education*, Morehouse-Barlow, 1966.

Robert W. Henderson, *The Teaching Office in the Reformed Tradition: A History of the Doctoral Ministry*, Westminster, 1962.

Clyde A. Holbrook, *Religion, a Humanistic Field*, Prentice-Hall, 1963.

William Bean Kennedy, *The Shaping of Protestant Education*, Association, 1966.

Robert W. Lynn, *Protestant Strategies in Education*, Association, 1964.

Edwin Wilber Rice, *The Sunday School Movement and the American Sunday School Union, 1780–1927*, Union, 1927.

TWO, A: ROBERT P. O'NEIL

1. James Michael Lee and Louis J. Putz, eds., *Seminary Education in a Time of Change*, Fides, 1965; C. M. Cuyler, ed., *Programs and Procedures of the Minor Seminary*, Catholic University Press, 1965.
2. Neil G. McCluskey, ed., *Catholic Education in America*, Columbia, 1964; E. J. Power, *Main Currents in the History of Education*, McGraw-Hill, 1962, Chs. 14, 15.
3. Andrew M. Greeley and P. H. Rossi, *The Education of Catholic Americans*, Aldine, 1966.
4. Ibid., p. 87.
5. J. Kirvan, *The Restless Believers*, Paulist, 1966.
6. See the series, e.g., produced by Allyn and Bacon, Sadlier, The Paulist Press.
7. J. H. Flavell, *The Developmental Psychology of Jean Piaget*, Van Nostrand, 1963, p. 165.
8. Ibid., p. 203.
9. I. S. Sigel, "The Attainment of Concepts," in M. L. Hoffman and L. W. Hoffman, eds., *Review of Child Development Research*, Russell Sage Foundation, 1964, Vol. 1, p. 241.
10. Robert P. O'Neil and M. A. Donovan, *Sexuality and Moral Responsibility*, Corpus, 1968, p. 12.
11. I. S. Sigel, "Developmental Trends in the Abstraction Ability of Children," in *Child Development*, 1953, 24, pp. 131–44; R. J. Harper, C. C. Anderson, et al., eds., *The Cognitive Process: Readings*, Prentice-Hall, 1964; R. C. Anderson and D. P. Ausubel, eds., *Readings in the Psychology of Cognition*, Holt, 1965; M. A. Wallach, "Research on Children's Thinking," in Sixty-second Yearbook of the National Society for the Study of Education, University of Chicago Press, 1963, pp. 236–76.

12. Statements in this section are representative of the mainstream of thinking in developmental psychology; see, e.g., E. B. Hurlock, *Developmental Psychology*, McGraw-Hill (3d ed.), 1968.

13. L. Kohlberg, "Development of Moral Character and Moral Ideology," in *Review of Child Development Research*, op. cit., pp. 383–431; O'Neil and Donovan, op. cit., p. 9.

14. For a review of the research and its application in this area see O'Neil and Donovan, op. cit., pp. 8–12, 25–31.

15. L. Kohlberg, op. cit., p. 426.

16. Greeley and Rossi, op. cit., p. 72.

17. J. Adelson and Robert P. O'Neil, "Growth of Political Ideas During Adolescence: The Sense of Community," in *Journal of Personality and Social Psychology*, 1966, 4, pp. 295–306.

TWO, B: ROY S. LEE

1. Cf. Ronald Goldman, *Religious Thinking from Childhood to Adolescence*, February, 1968.

2. Cf. Ian Ramsey, *Religious Language*, SCM, 1957, and Macmillan, 1963.

3. See, e.g., Anna Freud, *Normality and Pathology in Childhood*, International Universities, 1966. Ch. 3.

4. Roy S. Lee, *Your Growing Child and Religion*, Macmillan, 1963.

5. Cf. D. W. Winnicott, *The Maturational Processes and the Facilitating Environment*, International Universities, 1965. Chs. 3, 4.

6. Ibid., p. 97.

THREE, B: MARTIN E. MARTY

1. Random House, 1964.

2. Best known of the books which achieved this result were John Cogley, ed., *Religion in America*, Meridian, 1958, and Will Herberg, *Protestant, Catholic, Jew*, Doubleday, 1955.

3. For examples, see Winthrop D. Jordan, *White Over Black*, University of North Carolina Press, 1968; I. A. Newby, *Jim Crow's Defense*, Louisiana State, 1965; David M. Reimers, *White Protestantism and the Negro*, Oxford, 1965.

4. Doubleday, 1966.

5. For the religious point of view, see Herbert W. Richardson, *Toward an American Theology*, Harper & Row, 1967; the most comprehensive of the secular-oriented books, though not written in America, is Arend Th. van Leeuwen, *Christianity in World History*, Scribner's, 1965.

6. The texts of the main recent Supreme Court statements on religion and the public realm are in Arthur Frommer, ed., *The Bible and the Public Schools*, Liberal Press, 1963.

7. See Seymour Martin Lipset, *The First New Nation*, Basic Books, 1963, especially pp. 140ff.

8. William Braden surveys the field in *The Private Sea*, Quadrangle, 1967.

9. The best sellers on this subject were Harvey Cox, *The Secular City*, Macmillan, 1965, and Daniel Callahan, ed., *The Secular City Debate*, Macmillan, 1966.

10. Eric Hoffer, *The Temper of Our Time*, Harper & Row, 1967, p. 20.

11. Typical of such reintrusion of quasireligious symbols is the argument of Paul M. van Buren, *The Secular Meaning of the Gospel*, Macmillan, 1963.

12. These accents are treated in summary fashion in Ronald Gregor Smith, *Secular Christianity*, Harper & Row, 1966.

13. Franklin Littell traces this history in *From State Church to Pluralism*, Doubleday, 1962.

14. Readings on this subject appear in Adrienne Koch, *The American Enlightenment*, Braziller, 1965.

15. See Chs. II and III in Sidney E. Mead, *The Lively Experiment*, Harper & Row, 1963.

16. Mead, op. cit., Ch. VII.

17. University of Nebraska Press, 1964.

18. Robin M. Williams, Jr., *American Society*, Knopf, 1951.

19. The point is developed in Ch. V of their *Religion and Society in Tension*, Rand McNally, 1965.

20. Ch. III in his *The Political Community: A Study of Anomie*, University of Chicago Press, 1948.

21. Numbers of findings in Charles Y. Glock and Rodney Stark, *Christian Beliefs and Anti-Semitism*, Harper & Row, 1966 demonstrate this.

22. J. Marcellus Kik works with this distinction in his polemical *Ecumenism and the Evangelical*, Presbyterian and Reformed, 1958.

23. Samuel S. Hill, Jr., *Southern Churches in Crisis*, Holt, Rinehart & Winston, 1967, develops these themes on a Southern basis, but they are generally applicable.

24. Joseph T. Klapper, *The Effects of Mass Communication*, The Free Press, 1960, and William Stephenson, *The Play Theory of Mass Communication*, University of Chicago Press, 1967.

FOUR, A: SISTER ANN PATRICK WARE, S. L.

1. "The habit of calling every meeting 'ecumenical' in which there are representatives of more than one church is a misuse of the term. The basic concept of the term implies universality." William A. Norgren, "Ecumenism and Catholic Education: A Protestant Perspective," *Educating for Ecumenism*, Anti-Defamation League of B'nai B'rith, n.d., p. 8.

2. *Institutes* 4, 18, 1.

3. Ibid. 4, 18, 18.

4. Ibid. 4, 19, 25.

5. Quoted by James F. McCue, "Luther and Roman Catholicism on the Mass as

Sacrifice," *Journal of Ecumenical Studies*, 2, Spring 1965, p. 208.

6. Jaroslav Pelikan, *The Riddle of Roman Catholicism*, Abingdon, 1959, p. 51.

7. *The Mystical Body of Christ*, Catholic Truth Society, 1943, nn. 12, 39.

8. *Instruction on the Ecumenical Movement, Commentary by William Conway*, Unity Studies Number One, Graymoor Press, 1952.

9. Ibid., 15.

10. Hans Küng, Yves Congar, Daniel O'Hanlon, eds., *Council Speeches of Vatican II*, Paulist 1964, p. 146.

11. *Decree on Ecumenism*, in Walter Abbott, ed., *The Documents of Vatican II*, America, 1966, pp. 341ff.

12. Ibid., nn. 3, 6.

13. Ibid., n. 4.

14. Ibid., n. 21.

15. Samuel McCrea Cavert, "Response to the Decree on Ecumenism," *Documents of Vatican II*, op. cit., p. 369.

16. The whole notion of religious education on the American Catholic scene is undergoing serious re-evaluation. Some readers may remember the storm of controversy triggered by Mary Perkins Ryan's *Are Parochial Schools the Answer?*, Holt, Rinehart & Winston, 1964, a book which many were more ready to refute than read.

17. Eugene Bianchi, "The Ecumenical Plateau," in *American Catholic Exodus*, Corpus, 1968, pp. 25–26.

18. *Decree on Ecumenism*, op. cit., n. 3.

19. It is true that for many the validity of ministry and sacraments does present a serious doctrinal problem but not an insuperable one. Cf. the recent speculation of Franz Jozef van Beeck, "Towards an Ecumenical Understanding of the Sacraments," *Journal of Ecumenical Studies*, 3, Winter 1966, pp. 57–112.

20. Paul Verghese, "Will Dialogue Do?" *Ecumenical Review*, 18, January 1966, p. 28.

21. "Report of a Consultation on Christian Education in an Ecumenical Age," *Risk*, 2, 1966, p. 9.

22. Yves Congar, *Ecumenism and the Future of the Church*, Priory, 1967, pp. 130–31.

23. Several articles have been written to show that there is no anti-Jew bias in the gospels: Bruce Vawter, "Are the Gospels Anti-Semitic?", *Journal of Ecumenical Studies*, 5, Summer 1968, pp. 473–87; Gregory Baum, *Is the New Testament Anti-Semitic?*, Paulist, 1965.

24. Jack Epstein, "Roots of Religious Prejudice," *Journal of Ecumenical Studies*, 5, Fall 1968, p. 714.

25. Carl Pfeifer, S. J., in eds. R. Shaw and R. J. Hurley, *Trends and Issues in Catholic Education*, Citation, 1969, pp. 138–40.

26. "Report of a Consultation on Christian Education in an Ecumenical Age," loc. cit., p. 11.

27. Ibid., pp. 12–15.

28. For an indication of how anti-Semitism can creep into Christian teaching and how it can be eliminated, see Bernard Olsen, *Faith and Prejudice*, Yale, 1962.

29. "Consultation on Christian Education," loc. cit., p. 15.

30. According to H. Richard Niebuhr's thesis the forces of social, economic, political, and national difference contribute largely to the birth of denominations and serve to reinforce the divisions created even long after the original reason for schism disappears. Cf. his classic study, *The Social Sources of Denominationalism*, World, 1963 (original ed., 1929). A more recent study, *The Social Sources of Church Unity*, Abingdon, 1960, by Robert Lee, attempts to identify a countertrend in American Protestantism in the era following the publication of Niebuhr's book.

31. Gordon W. Allport, *The Nature of Prejudice*, Doubleday, 1958, pp. 41–42.

32. Ibid., p. 44.

33. Ibid., pp. 176–77.

34. Ibid., p. 267.

35. J. C. Hoekendijk, *The Church Inside Out*, Westminster, 1966, pp. 157ff.

36. Ibid., p. 159.

37. *Study Encounter*, 1, 1965, p. 175.

38. W. A. Visser 't Hooft, *The Meaning of Ecumenical*, SCM, 1952, p. 28.

39. Allport, op. cit., p. 422.

40. For a hard look at confessional loyalties cf. J. C. Dekkers' article "Confessional Loyalty at All Costs?", *Risk*, 2, 1966, pp. 77–91.

41. Max Thurian, *The One Bread*, Sheed and Ward, 1969, p. 97.

FOUR, B: HOWARD GRIMES

1. See *The Social Sources of Denominationalism*, Living Age Books, 1929, 1957.

2. See *Institutionalism and Church Unity*, Nils Ehrenstrom and Walter G. Muelder, eds., Association, 1963; also Robert Lee, *The Social Sources of Church Unity*, Abingdon, 1960.

3. *The Shaping of Protestant Education*, Association, 1966.

4. Information for the history of the Sunday school movement may be found in such sources as the following: Robert T. Handy, "Sunday School Movement," *The Westminster Dictionary of Christian Education*, ed., Kendig Brubaker Cully, Westminster, 1963, pp. 640–43; Frank Glenn Lankard, *A History of the American Sunday School Curriculum*, Abingdon, 1927; William Clayton Bower and Percy Roy Hayward, *Protestantism Faces Its Educational Task Together*, C. C. Nelson, 1949; and Kennedy, op. cit.

5. I find very little in the ecumenical histories in recognition of the early non-denominational and later interdenominational character of the Sunday school movement. Only passing references occur in *A History of the Ecumenical Movement: 1517—1948*, Ruth Rouse and Stephen Charles Neill, eds., Second Edition, Westminster Press, 1967; see pp. 235 and 612. It is true that the Sunday school movement was not in the mainstream of ecumenical development, which is more closely related to the world mission of the church, first, and later to theological discussion and social outreach. The lack of reference does not quite seem justified, however.

6. Op. cit., pp. 69ff.

7. The principal documents emerging from this interdenominational study are *The Church's Educational Ministry: A Curriculum Plan*, Bethany, 1965; *Tools of Curriculum Development for the Church's Educational Ministry*, Warner, 1967; and *Design for Teaching-Learning: The Work of CCP*, Bethany, 1967.

8. "Young Men's Christian Association," in *The Westminster Dictionary of Christian Education*, op. cit., p. 735.

9. Paul H. Vieth, "Editorial," *Religious Education*, LXII:82, March–April 1967.

10. I served as chairman of the Division of Christian Education of the Texas Council of Churches from 1961–67, and the comments in this section are based on my experience with this agency.

11. "A Call for Ecumenical Polemics," *Religious Education*, LXII:107, March–April 1967.

12. "What We Might Do Together," *Religious Education*, LXII:145, March–April 1967.

13. *Faith and Prejudice: Intergroup Problems in Protestant Curricula*, Yale, 1963, Ch. 2.

14. Ibid., p. 297.

15. Cf. Philip Scharper, "What We Might Do Together," op. cit., pp. 141–42.

16. "Secular Ecumenicity and the Teaching of the Faith," *Religious Education*, LXII:124, March–April 1967.

17. The Consultation on Church Union (COCU), now consisting of ten churches, began its deliberations in 1962 with four churches involved. See *Consultation on Church Union: Principles of Church Union, Guidelines for Structure, and a Study Guide*, Forward Movement Publications, 1967. A bibliography may be found on pp. 140–42.

FIVE, A: JAMES J. MEGIVERN, C.M.

1. *Decree on Ecumenism*, par. 4.

2. *Constitution on the Church in the Modern World*, par. 19.

3. Ibid., par. 6.

4. Ibid., par. 5.

5. Ibid., par. 7.

6. Ibid., par. 8.

7. Ibid., par. 9.

8. Ibid.

9. Jaroslav Pelikan, *The Riddle of Roman Catholicism*, Abingdon, 1959, p. 212.

10. Robert Adolfs, *The Church is Different*, Harper & Row, 1966, p. 18.

11. *Decree on Ecumenism*, par. 11.

12. Bernard Leeming, ed., *Towards Christian Unity*, Chapman, 1966, p. 298.

13. *IDO-C Dossier*, n. 66-1, p. 3.

14. *Decree on Ecumenism*, par. 3.

15. Ibid., par. 24.

FIVE, B: GERALD E. KNOFF

1. *Ecumenical Review,* October 1950, p. 52.
2. *National Catholic Almanac,* Doubleday, 1965, p. 586.
3. Ibid., p. 550.
4. *Encyclopedia of Associations,* Gale, Fifth Edition, p. 427.
5. Cf. Herbert G. May, "The Revised Standard Version after Twenty Years," *McCormick Quarterly,* Vol. 19, May 1966, pp. 301–8, and the Introduction, Revised Standard Version of the Bible, Catholic Edition. The full history has yet to be written. Other narrations are to be found in yearbooks of the Division of Christian Education, National Council of the Churches of Christ in the U.S.A.: 1964, pp. 64f., 84, 92; 1965, pp. 54f.; 1966, pp. 45f., 51–54, 100–2. See also articles by Luther A. Weigle in Yearbook of American Churches: 1964, pp. 290–93; 1965, pp. 291–94; 1966, pp. 226–31; 1967, pp. 57f., 62–64, 230–33; 1968, pp. 237f.
6. General Board, National Council of the Churches of Christ in the U.S.A., *Special Order on Crisis in the Nation,* February 21, 1968.
7. There were some exceptions. Some Orthodox Jewish leaders claimed a share of public money, and the Citizens for Educational Freedom, a national organization pressing the cause of such support, had Protestant members, some of whom were members of the Christian Reformed Church.
8. *Religious Education,* LXII, March–April, 1967, p. 129.

SIX, A: GEOFFREY I. KEATING, S.S.E.

1. Herder & Herder, 1968, pp. 200–1.
2. Compare, for example, Chs. 2 and 3 of *"The Dogmatic Constitution on the Church"* in W. Abbott, S.J., ed., *Documents of Vatican II,* Herder and Herder and Association, 1966, pp. 24ff. Henceforth we shall refer to this simply as *Documents.*
3. Two excellent books are examples of this perspective: Bernard Cooke, *Christian Sacraments and Christian Personality,* Image, 1968; and E. Schillebeeckx, *Christ, the Sacrament of the Encounter with God,* Sheed & Ward, 1963.
4. *Documents,* pp. 137ff.
5. Cf. especially the *Decree on Ecumenism, Documents,* pp. 341ff.
6. For the significance of this expression as used in the *Decree on Ecumenism,* see Avery Dulles, *The Dimensions of the Church,* Newman, 1967, pp. 31ff.
7. Sheed & Ward, 1967, p. 319.
8. Cf. R. Campbell, ed., *Spectrum of Catholic Attitudes,* Bruce, 1969. This attitude is hinted at in some of the essays in Ch. 22, "The Ecumenical Movement," pp. 134ff.
9. This is the position of Vatican I. It is also the position of Vatican II, *mutatis*

mutandis. Cf. *The Dogmatic Constitution on the Church,* Ch. 3 in *Documents,* pp. 37ff.

10. *The Credibility of the Church Today,* op. cit., p. 128.

11. Cf., e.g., G. Tavard, *The Church Tomorrow,* especially Ch. 2, "The End of the Counter-Reformation," Image, 1966, pp. 23ff.

12. W. McNamara, "The Heart of Ecumenism," an essay found in *Ecumenism, the Spirit and Worship,* L. Swidler, ed., Duquesne, 1967, p. 85.

13. *The Church,* op. cit., p. 275.

14. Gabriel Moran and Maria Harris, *Experiences in Community,* Herder & Herder, 1968, p. 204.

15. Ibid., pp. 186–87.

16. *Spectrum of Catholic Attitudes,* Bruce, 1969, p. 142.

17. *Constitution on Sacred Liturgy,* No. 10; *Documents,* p. 142. This statement is made within the context of an explanation that "the sacred liturgy does not exhaust the entire activity of the Church" (No. 9). Another very strong statement on the importance of liturgy is found in No. 7: "No other action of the Church can match its claim to efficacy, nor equal the degree of it."

18. In making the following points I have drawn especially from Nos. 2 through 7 of the *Constitution.*

19. Bernard Bro, *The Spirituality of the Sacraments,* Sheed & Ward, 1968, pp. 218ff.

20. Daniel Callahan, in *Spectrum of Catholic Attitudes,* op. cit., pp. 142–43.

21. This expression is found in *Pastoral Constitution on the Church in the Modern World,* No. 19; *Documents,* p. 216.

22. *Spectrum of Catholic Attitudes,* op. cit., p. 143.

23. Ibid., p. 147.

24. For a penetrating analysis of the underground church, see L. Cunningham, "Some Reflections on the Underground Church," in *The Homiletic and Pastoral Review,* March 1969, pp. 443ff.

25. "Toward a People's Liturgy", *Worship,* May 1968, pp. 258ff. The quoted passage is on pp. 261–62.

26. D. Buttrick, "Renewal of Worship—a Source of Unity?," in *Ecumenism, the Spirit and Worship,* op. cit., p. 236.

Additional Bibliography

Yves Congar, *A Gospel Priesthood,* Herder & Herder, 1967.

———, *Ecumenism and the Future of the Church,* Priory, 1967.

F. Houtart, *The Eleventh-Hour Explosion of a Church,* Sheed & Ward, 1968.

R. Marshall and M. Taylor, *Liturgy and Christian Unity,* Prentice-Hall, 1965.

———, *Catechesis of Revelation,* Herder & Herder, 1966.

Gabriel Moran, *Visions and Tactics,* Herder & Herder, 1968.

SIX, B: IRIS V. CULLY

1. *Christian Nurture and the Church*, Scribner's, 1961, p. 1.
2. Quoted in Massey H. Shepherd, Jr., *Liturgy and Education*, Seabury, 1965, pp. 56f., from a pamphlet, *Family Corporate Worship*, published by the Department of Christian Education, Protestant Episcopal Church.
3. *Jacob's Ladder: the Meaning of Worship*, John Knox, 1958, p. 42.
4. *Worship: Its Theology and Practice*, Oxford, 1965, p. 119.
5. In *The Episcopalian*, letter by Mrs. Charles C. Rettew, Vol. 133, No. 4, May 1968, p. 4.
6. *Worship in the New Testament*, John Knox, 1961, p. 82.
7. *Worship and Mission*, Association, 1967, p. 111.

Additional Bibliography:
Hervé Carrier, *The Sociology of Religious Belonging*, Herder & Herder, 1965.
Iris V. Cully, *Christian Worship and Church Education*, Westminster, 1967.
Gerhard Delling, *Worship in the New Testament*, Westminster, 1962.
Douglas Rhymes, *Prayer in the Secular City*, Westminster, 1968.
Eric Routley, *Hymns Today and Tomorrow*, Abingdon, 1964.
Everett M. Stowe, *Communicating Reality Through Symbols* (Westminster Studies in Christian Communication, ed. Kendig Brubaker Cully), Westminster, 1966.
Bard M. Thompson, ed., *Liturgies of the Western Church*, Meridian, 1961.

SEVEN, A: BENEDICT M. ASHLEY, O.P.

1. See *The Sixteen Documents of Vatican II*, St. Paul's Editions, pp. 315–22. All references to Vatican II documents in this paper are from this translation. This basic document is being implemented for the United States by the National Bishops' Conference in a series of documents, two of which have already appeared: *Interim Guidelines for Seminary Renewal*, Part 1, May 1968, and Part 2, December 1968, published by Bishops' Committee on Priestly Formation.
   The term "formation" is sometimes used by Protestants, e.g. Ernest T. Campbell, "The Formation of Ministers for the late 20th Century: Community on Campus," Theological Education, Autumn 1965, pp. 3–8.
2. See Karl Herman Shelke, *Discipleship and Priesthood*, Herder & Herder, 1965.
3. "Let them [priests], as fathers in Christ, take care of the faithful whom they have begotten by baptism and their teaching. Becoming from the heart a pattern to the flock, let them so lead and serve their local community that it may worthily be called by that name, by which the one and entire people of God is signed, namely, the Church of God." (Vatican II, *Constitution on the Church*, 28).

4. The best surveys of this history are to be found in *Seminaria Ecclesiae Catholicae,* published by the Sacred Congregation of Seminaries and University Studies, 1968, section entitled *Breviarium Historiae Institutionis Clericorum,* pp. 25–172, and in John Tracy Ellis, *Essays in Seminary Education,* Fides, 1967. The latter was originally published in James Michael Lee and Louis J. Putz, *Seminary Education in a Time of Change,* Fides, 1965, pp. 1–81.

5. Henri-Irénée Marrou, *Saint Augustin et la fin de la culture antique,* Éditions E. De Boccard, 1958, C. 3, pp. 387ff.

6. Louis Bouyer, *The Meaning of the Monastic Life* (Burns and Oates, 1955, Part II, C.V. "Lectio Divina," pp. 168ff.

7. Marrou, op. cit., "Conclusion," pp. 541ff.

8. F. Van Der Meer, *Augustine the Bishop,* Sheed & Ward, 1961, Part 1, 8, pp. 199–234. Also Eugene Kevane, *Augustine the Educator: A Study in the Fundamentals of Christian Formation,* Newman, 1964.

9. M. H. Vicaire, *The Apostolic Life,* Priory, 1966.

10. The Dominicans were founded by a canon and had strictly canonical structure. The Franciscans, however, were not originally a priestly order, but their university communities took on this character.

11. Charles A. Briggs, *History of the Study of Theology,* Duckworth, 1916, pp. 105–83.

12. For the sake of typology I exaggerate. Undoubtedly the Pietistic tradition also contains elements of an ecclesiology of a more communal emphasis. In Methodism, the issue of a charismatic vs. an ordained ministry illustrates the problem. See Eomer T. Clark, *The Small Sects of America,* Revised Edition, Abingdon-Cokesbury, 1937, pp. 56–66.

13. See S. A. Witmer, *The Bible College Story: Education with Dimension,* Channel, 1962. Witmer writes of these schools: "They represent a pietistic reaction to secularism, a theistic reaction to humanism and agnosticism, a restoration of Biblical authority and direction in education, and a return to the central concern of Christian education—the implementation of Christ's Great Commission: 'Go ye into all the world . . .'." (p. 30) "From the time of Moody and Simpson, Bible schools have had formal arrangements for worship, meditation and missionary challenge. Daily quiet periods for private devotions, regular chapel periods given to worship, spiritual emphasis weeks, missionary conferences, special days of prayer—are the kinds of events that are found in nearly all Bible colleges. Then there are many informal occasions for prayer in meetings of dormitory and activities groups." (p. 174)

14. See M. Papa, "Pentecostals: Wave of the Future?", *National Catholic Reporter,* 4:1, June 5, 1968.

15. J. A. O'Donahoe, *Tridentine Seminary Legislation: Its Sources and Its Formation,* Louvain, 1957, and his article "Seminary," in *New Catholic Encyclopedia,* McGraw-Hill, Vol. 13, pp. 72–73, with its bibliography.

16. H. J. Schroeder, O.P., *Canons and Decrees of the Council of Trent,* B. Herder, 1941, XXIII Session, c. xviii. p. 176.

17. J. T. Ellis, *Essays in Seminary Education,* Fides, 1967, pp. 41–59.

18. For the development of the Jesuit colleges which so much influenced the seminary pattern, as well as the Catholic colleges for the laity, see George E. Ganss, S.J., *St. Ignatius' Idea of a Jesuit University,* Marquette, 1954, espe-

cially Ch. 8, "Ignatius' Appropriations and Adaptations," pp. 153ff.

19. Maurice A. Roche, C.M., *Saint Vincent de Paul and the Formation of Clerics*, Fribourg, 1964.

20. See J. A. Weisheipl, O.P., "Scholasticism Part 3" in *New Catholic Encyclopedia*, Vol. 12, pp. 1165–70, for history of this revival.

21. See P. Pourrat, *Christian Spirituality*, Burns, Oates and Washbourne, 1927, Vol. 3 Ch. XIII, 1, "Berullian Abnegation," pp. 346–55.

22. CF. in Lee and Putz, op. cit., Lee's discussion of this problem, pp. 154–69, and J. T. Ellis, op. cit., pp. 206–8.

23. "In summary, we reiterate our fundamental conviction that there is no truly viable alternative to cooperative action between seminaries as a means of making the profound changes which are required in theological education. However, we believe that substantial additional financial resources will be required by seminaries to mount the required new programs, even though seminaries undertake such programs cooperatively. Denominations need to appropriate vastly larger funds for theological education." "Resource Planning in Theological Education," *Theological Education*, Summer 1968, p. 810.

24. *The Official Catholic College Guide* (Rockville Centre, N. Y.).

25. See "Protestant Seminary Education in America," in Lee and Putz, op. cit., pp. 533–56. Littell says, "It has been said of the Mennonites and Friends, for example, that they have no trained clergy. A more accurate statement would be that they have no laity, at least none of the traditional type. What they sought was a 'group ministry' of all the Christians. Their hostility to a special professional education for the clergy derived in part from the reaction to the intellectual style of the state-church clergy, but even more from their determination that all of the baptized should be thoroughly schooled in the Bible and in Christian apologetics." (p. 539) An interesting aspect of the same attitude is the development of ministries for women (see pp. 539f).

26. *Constitution on the Church*, Ch. 4. "The supreme and eternal Priest, Christ Jesus, since he wills to continue his witness and service also through the laity, vivifies them in this Spirit and increasingly urges on to every good and perfect work. For besides linking them to His life and His mission, He also gives them a sharing in His priestly function of offering spiritual worship for the glory of God and the salvation of men. . . . Christ the great Prophet . . . . continually fulfills His prophetic office until the complete manifestation of glory. He does this not only through the hierarchy who teach in His name and with His authority, but also through the laity whom He made His witnesses and to whom He gave understanding of the faith and an attractiveness of speech so that the power of the Gospel might shine forth in their daily social and family life. . . . Let the spiritual shepherd's recognize and promote the dignity as well as the responsibility of the laity in the Church. Let them willingly employ their prudent advice. Let them confidently assign duties to them in the service of the Church, allowing them freedom and room for action. Further, let them encourage lay people so

that they may undertake tasks on their own initiative." (34, 35, 37)

27. Reginald Masterson, O.P., ed., *Theology in the Catholic College*, Priory, 1961, and J. Barry McGannon, S.J., et al., *Christian Wisdom and Christian Formation: Theology, Philosophy and the Catholic College Student*, Sheed & Ward, 1964.

28. Richard Butler, O.P., *God on the Secular Campus*, Doubleday, 1963.

29. On a possible model for an integration of an academic program in theology with clinical training to be taken in pastoral centers see "A Theological Curriculum for the 1970s," *Theological Education*, May 1968.

30. Charles L. Taylor summarizes the situation in Protestant theological schools at present as follows: "The relation of school to church is sometimes close, sometimes distant; the pattern of life may approach Catholic discipline and practice on the one hand, or be highly permissive and individualistic on the other. Worship may range from chapel services twice a day to almost no corporate observance at all." "Theological Education, Protestant," in *New Catholic Encyclopedia*, Vol. 14, pp. 32-34.

31. *Constitution on the Church*, Ch. 2, 9-11.

32. *Constitution on the Church*, Ch. 3, 18-24.

33. *Constitution on the Church*, Ch. 3. "In the bishops, therefore, for whom the priests are assistants, Our Lord Jesus Christ, the Supreme High Priest, is present in the midst of those who believe." (21) "The Sacred Council teaches that by episcopal consecration the fullness of the sacrament of Orders is conferred, that fullness of power, namely, which both the Church's liturgical practice and in the language of the Fathers of the Church is called the high priesthood, the supreme power of the sacred ministry." (21)

34. On the ontological character of the priesthood resulting from the "sacramental character" conferred by ordination see Clement Dillenschneider C.SS.R., *The Holy Spirit and the Priest*, B. Herder, 1965, Ch. 2 and 11-13. Against exaggerations on this point see Karl Rahner, S.J., "The Meaning of Ecclesiastical Office," in *Servants of the Lord*, Herder & Herder, 1968, pp. 13-46.

35. Vatican II, *Dogmatic Constitution on Divine Revelation*, Ch. 2, 7-10, and *The Church in the Modern World*, Ch. 4, 40-45.

36. A very balanced treatment of the relation of active and contemplative lives will be found in Henri Petitot, O.P., *An Introduction to Holiness*, Mercier Press, 1949.

37. See note 29.

38. Littell, op. cit., p. 540. "For three centuries, in those areas where universities and theological faculties functioned under church auspices, the seminary was a kind of Protestant monastery. The common life was featured, i.e. common worship in chapel, common meals in the refectory, common living quarters in the dormitory: indeed the earlier generations also enforced common labor . . . and a strict daily regimen for all students. The professors were spiritual directors as well as academic instructors, and censored mail and social habits of the students as well as encouraged private and public direction to the religious as well as intellectual life . . . Wives and children were to join the parade later, after the men had prepared for their work as ministers." It was

World War II and the married students that changed the structures; Cf. n. 541.

39. A very interesting example of an apostolic and pastoral center based on a permanent community involving both married couples and celibates is the Ecumenical Institute in Chicago.

40. See Bouyer, op. cit. for a synthesis of the elements of this formation.

41. Ibid., pp. 130–145.

42. The anthology of Maurus Wolter, O.S.B., *The Principles of Monasticism*, B. Herder, 1962, gives a view of this rich heritage.

SEVEN, B: RANDOLPH CRUMP MILLER

1. See Milton D. McLean, ed., *Religious Studies in Public Universities*, Central Publications, Southern Illinois University, 1967.

2. See Robert A. Spivey, "Modest Messiah: The Study of Religion in State Universities," *Religious Education*, LXIII, January–February 1968, p. 6.

3. See Clyde A. Holbrook, *Religion, a Humanistic Field*, Prentice-Hall, 1963, p. 36.

4. See E. Thomas Lawson, "A Rationale for a Department of Religion in a State University," in McLean, ed., op. cit., p. 40.

5. See Claude Welch, "The Function of the Study of Religion," in Karl D. Hartzell and Harrison Sasscer, eds., *The Study of Religion on the Campus of Today*, Association of American Colleges, 1967, p. 10.

6. Holbrook, op. cit., p. 36.

7. Cf. Hartzell and Sasscer, eds., op. cit., pp. 10f., 22, 39. "Anyone who sees the nature of the horse or the ass in a mule will find himself in difficulties; anyone who tries to find out what a Christian is by studying a man who can't really decide to be one . . . is working on inadequate evidence." (Hans Urs von Balthasar, *Who is a Christian?*, Newman, 1968, p. 51.)

8. Cf. Welch, in Hartzell and Sasscer, eds., op. cit., p. 12.

9. Cf. Lawson, in McLean, ed., op. cit., p. 41; Donald Evans, *The Logic of Self-Involvement*, SCM, 1963; Ian T. Ramsey, *Religious Language*, SCM, 1957, and Macmillan paperback, 1963.

10. See McLean, ed., op. cit., pp. 61–191 for lists of courses at 135 public universities, and pp. 193–260 for the programs of eleven private colleges.

11. Cf. Herman E. Wornom, "Critical Issues," *Religious Education*, LIV, March–April 1959, p. 107.

12. Holbrook, op. cit., p. 71.

13. Ibid., pp. 81–85.

14. Nevitt Sanford, "Aims of College Education," in Charles W. Havice, ed., *Campus Values*, Scribner's, 1968, p. 16; see pp. 1–16.

15. In McLean, ed., op. cit., p. 48.

16. Ibid., p. 48.

17. Cf. McLean, ed., op. cit., pp. 51f., 152–57.

18. Cf. Holbrook, op. cit., p. 33; Hartzell and Sasscer, eds., op. cit., p. 72.

19. Marvin Fox writes: "George Foote Moore was a scholar of Judaism of the first rank, though he himself was a Christian. Ignaz Goldziher, a Jew, was a distinguished student of Islam. Joseph Klausner was a Jew who produced outstanding studies of early Christianity. Harry A. Wolfson of Harvard is a Jew who has written one of the most important studies of the church fathers. . . . Why should we demand of teachers of religion something unique? . . . If it is because the subject-matter is peculiar, then perhaps this is an indication that the subject-matter has no proper place in the university curriculum. If the subject-matter is not peculiar, then I see no argument in favor of this demand." (Who Is Competent to Teach Religion?," *Religious Education*, LIV, March–April, 1959, p. 113)

20. William Temple, *Nature, Man and God*, Macmillan, 1934, p. 35.

21. Ibid., p. 45.

22. Ibid., p. 315.

23. Ramsey, op. cit., p. 28.

24. Temple, op. cit., p. 306.

25. *On Being Sure in Religion*, Athlone, 1963, p. 47; see *Christian Discourse*, Oxford, 1965, p. 89.

26. Bernard E. Meland, *Higher Education and the Human Spirit*, University of Chicago Press, 1953, p. 57.

27. Ibid., pp. 63f.

28. Vol. I, University of Chicago Press, 1951, p. 9.

29. See H. Richard Niebuhr, *Radical Monotheism and Western Culture*, Harper & Row, 1960, pp. 14f.

30. See John Wisdom, "Gods," in *Logic and Language*, First Series, Anthony Flew, ed., Blackwell, 1951, p. 192.

31. See Alec Vidler, ed., *Soundings*, Cambridge, 1962, pp. x–xii.

32. David Jenkins, "Oxford—the Anglican Position," in John Coulson, ed., *Theology and the University*, Helicon, 1964, p. 152.

33. Op. cit., pp. 82f.

34. Ibid., p. 108.

35. Ibid., p. 138.

36. See Jaroslav Pelikan, *Religion and the University*, University of Toronto Press for York University, 1964, pp. 1–19.

37. In Vidler, ed., op. cit., p. 19.

38. John Cobb, *A Christian Natural Theology*, Westminster, 1965; Schubert Ogden, *The Reality of God*, Harper & Row, 1966; Charles Hartshorne, *A Natural Theology for Our Time*, Open Court, 1967.

39. Wornom, op. cit., pp. 99–101.

40. G. E. Hutchinson, "Religion and the Natural Sciences," in Erich A. Walter, ed., *Religion and the State University*, University of Michigan Press, 1958, pp. 170f. Cf. John A. Hutchison, "Language Analysis and Theology: Present and Future," *Journal of the American Academy of Religion*, XXXV, December 1967, pp. 323–36.

41. Cf. Philip Scharper, "The Relevance of Theology to the University," in

Katharine T. Hargrove, ed., *On the Other Side*, Prentice-Hall, 1967, pp. 12f.

42. Spivey, op. cit., p. 12.
43. Cf. Nathan M. Pusey and Charles L. Taylor, *Ministry for Tomorrow*, Seabury, 1967, p. 71.
44. "Theological Curriculum for the 1970's," *Theological Education*, IV, Spring 1968, pp. 675-76.
45. H. Richard Niebuhr, *The Purpose of the Church and Its Ministry*, Harper & Row, 1956, pp. 110, 117. See Randolph Crump Miller, "For the World of Tomorrow," *The Christian Century*, LXXXI, April 29, 1964, pp. 544-46.
46. See Paul F. D'Arcy and Eugene C. Kennedy, *The Genius of the Apostolate*, Sheed & Ward, 1965.
47. See Keith R. Bridston, "Form and Function in the Education of Ministers," *Theological Education*, IV, Autumn 1967, p. 552; "Theological Curriculum for the 1970's," *Theological Education*, IV, Spring 1968, p. 680; Pusey and Taylor, op. cit., pp. 75-77.
48. See E. Thomas Lawson, "Implications for Theological Education in Seminaries of the Study of Religion in the University," *Theological Education*, III, Spring, 1967, pp. 400f.
49. H. Richard Niebuhr, op. cit., p. 118.
50. Ibid., pp. 113f.
51. Charles R. Feilding, et al., "Education for Ministry," in *Theological Education*, III, Autumn 1966, p. 9.
52. *Theological Education*, II, Spring 1966, p. 175.
53. Op. cit., pp. 30f.
54. Ibid., p. 47.
55. See Keith R. Bridston, op. cit., pp. 554f.
56. Op. cit., p. 25.
57. *Language, Persons, and Belief*, Oxford, 1967, p. 207.
58. Cf. ibid., pp. 210f.
59. Edited by Martin E. Marty and Dean G. Peerman, World, 1965.
60. By John Macquarrie, Harper & Row, 1963.
61. Edited by Martin E. Marty and Dean G. Peerman, Macmillan: No. 1, 1964; No. 2, 1965; No. 3, 1966; No. 4, 1967; No. 5, 1968.
62. H. Richard Niebuhr, Daniel Day Williams, and James M. Gustafson, *The Advancement of Theological Education*, Harper & Row, 1957, p. 87.
63. See the full-fledged description of how this might be worked out in "Theological Curriculum for the 1970's," op. cit., pp. 692-709.

Additional Bibliography:

Keith R. Bridston and Dwight W. Culver, *Pre-seminary Education*, Augsburg Publishing House, 1965.

Lawrence Bright, ed., *Theology in Modern Education*, Darton, Longman & Todd, 1965.

Robert Clyde Johnson, ed., *The Church and Its Changing Ministry*, The General

Assembly of the United Presbyterian Church, 1961.

Robert Michaelsen, *The Study of Religion in American Universities,* The Society for Religion in Higher Education, 1965.

Allen C. Moore "Education for the Practice of Ministry," *Religious Education,* LXIII, July–August 1968, pp. 294–300.

Walter D. Wagoner, *Bachelor of Divinity: Uncertain Servants in Seminary and Ministry,* Association, 1963.

EIGHT, C: KENDIG BRUBAKER CULLY

1. Martin Buber, *I and Thou,* trans. by Ronald Gregor Smith, Clark, 1937.
2. Cf. Iris V. Cully, *The Dynamics of Christian Education,* Westminster, 1958, p. 84.
3. Kendig Brubaker Cully, ed., *The Westminster Dictionary of Christian Education,* Westminster, 1963, p. 563. See the discussion of *I and Thou* in relation to religious education theory in Kendig Brubaker Cully, *The Search for a Christian Education—Since 1940.* Westminster, 1965, Ch. 4, especially with reference to the thought of Randolph Crump Miller and David R. Hunter.
4. Cf. ibid., especially Ch. II, "Historical Dimensions for Christian Education." See also two articles in *Religious Education,* Vol. LXIV, No. 2 (March–April 1969): Iris V. Cully, "Teaching History in Church Curriculum," pp. 133–137, and Kendig Brubaker Cully, "The Uses of History in Religious Education," pp. 139–44.
5. *Christian Faith and Action: Designs for an Educational System* (approved by the 179th General Assembly, The United Presbyterian Church in the U.S.A., May 22, 1967, Portland, Oregon), Board of Christian Education, The United Presbyterian Church in the U.S.A., 1967, pp. 5–7.
6. Gabriel Moran, F.S.C., *Vision and Tactics,* Herder & Herder, 1968. "Ch. I, in which the suggestion occurs, appeared in *The Living Light,* V, Spring 1968. It has met with contagious interest in the same periodical. See V, Summer 1968, pp. 62–70, 125–29, 138f." (Cited by Father Schaefer in his communication to the editor.)
7. Macmillan Paperback edition, 1961.
8. George Herbert Betts, *The Curriculum of Religious Education,* Abingdon, 1924.
9. William Clayton Bower, *The Curriculum of Religious Education,* Scribner's, 1925.
10. E. Schillebeeckx, *Christ, The Sacrament of the Encounter with God,* Sheed and Ward, 1963.
11. Cf. *The Teachings of the Second Vatican Council,* Newman, 1966, pp. 13–58.
12. At the time of publication, students of some other theological schools were becoming involved also.
13. Dr. Shuster called the editor's attention to *The Idea of the Catholic University,* a statement growing out of the deliberations of a group of Catholic educators who met under the auspices of the North American region of the International Federation of Catholic Universities July 20–23, 1967. The paper was preliminary to other discussions prepared for an international meeting of the

Federation at Lovanium University, Kinshasa, Congo, 1968. He also cited the report on the educational program of the Boston Theological Institute, prepared by Charles E. Sheedy, S.C.S., and issued by Walter D. Wagoner, Director of the Institute, in January 1969.

CONTRIBUTORS

BENEDICT M. ASHLEY, O.P., Dean, Aquinas Institute of Philosophy and Theology.

IRIS V. CULLY, Associate Professor of Christian Education, The Divinity School, Yale University.

KENDIG BRUBAKER CULLY, Dean and Professor of Christian Education, New York Theological Seminary.

HOWARD GRIMES, Professor of Christian Education, Perkins School of Theology, Southern Methodist University.

GEOFFREY I. KEATING, S.S.E., Chairman, Department of Theology, St. Michael's College.

GERALD E. KNOFF, Associate General Secretary for Christian Education, National Council of the Churches of Christ in the U.S.A.

JAMES MICHAEL LEE, Chairman, Department of Education, University of Notre Dame.

ROY S. LEE, Chaplain, Nuffield and St. Catherine's Colleges, Oxford, England.

MARTIN E. MARTY, Professor of Church History, The Divinity School, The University of Chicago.

JAMES J. MEGIVERN, C.M., Chairman, Graduate Department of Theology, St. John's University.

RANDOLPH CRUMP MILLER, Horace Bushnell Professor of Christian Nurture, The Divinity School, Yale University.

ROBERT P. O'NEIL, Assistant Professor of Psychology and Associate Director of the Psychological Clinic, University of Detroit.

ROSEMARY R. RUETHER, Lecturer in Sociology, Howard University.

SISTER ANN PATRICK WARE, S.L., Staff Member, Faith and Order Department, National Council of the Churches of Christ in the U.S.A.

D. CAMPBELL WYCKOFF, Professor of Christian Education, Princeton Theological Seminary.

INDEX

Index

Abbott, W., 195
Academic freedom, 17
Accrediting associations, 192
Administration, 14, 34, 193, 204
Adolescence, 51ff, 54, 61ff, 68ff, 147
Adults, 23f, 42f, 61ff, 67, 200, 235ff, 327, 92f
Advent, 91, 237, 255
Affluence, 209
Africans, 94
Age groups, 199f, 253, 348
Aggiornamento, 177
Aggression, 50, 71ff, 343
Akron plan, 35
Alaska, 27
Allport, G., 142
American Association of Colleges of Teacher Education, 10
American Association of School Administrators, 10
American Council on Education, 192
American Federation of Teachers, 16
American Independent Party, 91
American Protestant Association, 5

American Sunday School Union, 157ff
Anabaptists, 96, 252
Anglicans, 25, 93, 128, 156, 309
Animism, 67ff
Anomie, 117
Anselm, 308
Anthropology, 54, 104f, 290
Anticlericalism, 109
Anti-Semitism, 137
Apocrypha, 196ff
Apollo, 264
Apologetics, 182
Apostolic succession, 117, 223
Appalachia, 27
Appenticeship, 22, 32, 277ff
Aquinas T., 266, 270, 274, 295, 327
Armed Forces, 152, 167
Arts, 18, 29, 92, 102ff, 193, 308, 336
Asceticism, 269
Association of American Colleges, 192
Atheism, 179, 338
Athletics, 33, 35
Atonement, 236, 250
Attendance, 42f, 52

377

Attitudes, 42ff, 56, 71f, 127, 134, 181, 247
Audio-visual media, 8, 171
Augustine, 263ff, 280, 308
Augustinians, 270
Authority, 43f, 48, 53, 55f, 232, 292, 308

Baltimore Catechism, 348
Baltzell, E., 102
Baptism, 93ff, 117, 181ff, 251ff, 278f, 321
Baptist Record, 5
Baptists, 25, 119
Barth, K., 182, 295, 298, 306
Basil, 264
Baum, G., 216f, 223
Bea, A., 183
Behavior, 20, 41ff, 50f, 56ff, 65f, 71f
Behavioral sciences, 20, 44ff, 47, 54
Belford, L., 247
Beliefs, 42ff, 56, 253, 297
Bennett, J., 206ff
Benz, E., 106
Berkeley, 273, 346
Berkeley, Bishop, 25
Bermuda, 27
Berry, C., 8
Betts, G., 348
Bianchi, E., 133, 135
Bible, 27, 34f, 41ff, 55f, 92ff, 133, 151ff, 194ff, 243ff, 263ff, 290ff, 345ff
Bible reading, 29, 110, 170, 241ff
Bible schools, 268
Bill of Rights, 156
Bishops, 7, 14, 16, 81, 129, 183, 191f, 218f, 263ff, 272ff, 177ff
Black Liberation Army, 88
Blacks, 26, 79, 86ff, 92f, 106ff, 134, 199, 208
Boethius, 264

Bonhoeffer, D., 113, 182
Borowitz, E., 165
Borromeo, C., 268
Boston Theological Union, 273, 346
Bower, W., 348
Brethren of the Common Life, 83
Brotherhood, 54, 65
Bruner, J., 34
Brunner, E., 182
Buber, M., 101, 112, 298, 342
Buckley, W., 228, 233
Bultmann, R., 182
Burns, J., 4
Bushnell, H., 28
Buttrick, D., 24

Callahan, D., 231
Calvin, J., 115, 128, 267
Calvinists, 25f, 114
Camping, 25
Camp meetings, 25
Campus ministry, 26, 117, 192f, 275
Camus, A., 142
Canisianum, 347
Canon law, 7, 134, 217
Canterbury, Archbishop of, 196
Cappadocian Fathers, 263
Catechetics, 50, 177, 216, 323f
Catechism, 18
Cathedral school 265, 268
Catholic Biblical Association, 195f
Catholic Council for Youth and Oikoumene, 146
Catholic University of America, 273
Cavert, S., 132
Celebration, 100, 113ff, 216, 247, 351
Celibacy, 84, 264, 282f
Cenobites, 284
Chamberlin, J., 347

Change, 37, 44, 75, 80, 86, 89, 136, 148f, 177ff, 246, 293

Character education, 23, 29, 269

Charity, 11, 181, 264, 326

Charters, W., 34

Chautauqua Institution, 23

Chesterton, G., 127

Chicago, 91, 273, 347

Children, 4, 12f, 33, 35, 42, 45ff, 49ff, 59ff, 75f, 95f, 191, 207, 235ff, 320ff

Christian endeavor, 24

Christian Reformed Church, 203

Christology, 93

Church Women United, 210

Citizenship education, 29

Civil War, 25f, 115

Clark, T., 170

Clergy, 14, 16, 25, 27, 36, 81ff, 88ff, 96, 128ff, 191ff, 237ff, 261ff, 329f, 338ff, 349

Closely Graded Series, 160

Cobb, J., 301

Coe, G., 30

Cognitive development, 45ff, 59ff

Cohen, J., 10

Colonial period, 4f, 22ff, 109

Columbia University, 347

Commitment, 93ff, 293

Commonweal, 81

Communication, 59f, 82, 143, 233, 271, 281, 297f, 323, 335ff

Communion, 43, 91, 95ff, 242ff

Community, 8, 22, 33, 215-257, 279ff, 290, 303, 320

Concrete operations, 46

Conditioning, 52, 243

Conduct, 55, 74

Confession, 50, 230

Confirmation, 95f, 253

Conflict, 35, 155

Confraternity of Christian Doctrine, 11, 20, 42, 45, 167, 191

Congar, Y., 136

Congregationalists, 103, 114, 119, 156, 242

Conscience, 41, 73f, 321

Conservatives, 6, 119, 226, 350

Constitution, 203ff

Constitution on the Church, 180ff

Constitution on Sacred Liturgy, 219ff

Consultation on Church Union, 169ff

Conversion, 119, 181

Conway, W., 130

Cooperative Curriculum Project, 170

Cooperative Publishing Association, 159

Council of Trent, 18, 263, 268ff

Councils of Baltimore, 4, 6f

Councils of churches, 172, 189ff

Counter-Reformation, 128, 189, 223

Covenant, 85ff, 95

Creeds, 139, 251ff, 255

Cully, I., 2

Culture, 29, 97f, 103ff, 271f, 285, 323, 336

Culture-Protestantism, 29, 93

Curriculum, 27ff, 32ff, 93, 139, 158ff, 170ff, 199ff, 208, 253, 310f, 348

Cushing, R., 197

D'Amour, O., 204

Darwin, C., 106

Deardon, J., 200

Declaration on Christian Education, 8, 319-330, 345

Decree on Ecumenism, 130ff, 179ff

Decree on Priestly Formation, 261, 270f

De Grazia, S., 118

Deism, 115
Democracy, 10, 22, 84
Democratic Party, 91f,
Denominationalism, 36, 117ff
Department of Health, Education
and Welfare, 192
De Smedt, Bishop, 179
Dewey, J., 9, 28, 31, 152, 348
Dialogue, 87, 92, 190, 282, 331ff
Dialogue with Non-believers, 331-
341
Diffley, J., 3
Disciples of Christ, 251f
Divini ilius magistri, 7f
Divino afflante spiritu, 195
Doctrine, 41ff, 50, 55ff, 80ff, 116ff,
241, 227, 332f
Dominic, 285
Dominicans, 274
Dorchester, D., 5
Dostoievsky, F., 136
Drama, 33
Dual school enrollment, 205ff
Dubuque, 273, 346
Dutch Catechism, 81, 181

Easter, 93, 153
Eastern Orthodox, 83, 102, 128f,
147, 162, 183, 188ff, 309
Ecclesiology, 187, 219ff
Economics, 72, 117, 152, 209, 336
Ecumenical Institute, 152
Ecumenical movement, 178, 188ff,
209, 220, 275
Ecumenical youth councils, 162ff
Ecumenicity, 94, 178ff
Ecumenism, 36, 84f, 93, 127-173,
179ff
Edinburgh, 152, 196
Ego, 70ff, 74ff
Electronic media, 35
Elementary schools, 4, 15, 19, 26,
191, 293

Elson, R., 116
Emmaus House, 87
Emotions, 48ff, 69ff
England, 76, 157, 195, 256
Englewood, 204
Enlightenment, 115ff
Environment, 72, 304, 348
Episcopalians, 118, 237ff, 249ff
Epstein, J., 137
Erie, 14
Ethics, 37, 96, 293, 336
Eucharist, 81ff, 243ff, 254
Evangelicals, 118f, 239, 248
Evans, D., 298
Evolution, 30
Experimentation, 37f, 256f, 348

Fairy tales, 51
Faith, 11, 87, 96, 153, 218, 249,
297, 321ff
Faith and Order, 190, 206f
Family, 13, 22f, 35, 43, 54, 62, 149,
154, 235, 245, 252ff
Fantasy, 44, 48, 51f, 62, 65ff
Farrell, W., 274f
Federal Council of Churches, 208
Feilding, C., 304f
Finance, 15, 42, 240, 272
Fiske, J., 104
Fixation, 50, 70
Flavell, J., 46
Flemming, A., 199f
Folklore, 102ff
Folk singers, 102
Fordham University, 273
Forgiveness, 49, 86, 93
Formation, 87ff, 95f, 212, 215,
261ff, 325ff, 351
Forums, 89
Franciscans, 83
Franklin, B., 115
Fraternization, 44

Freedom, 88, 99, 155, 247, 320ff, 340
Free churches, 85ff, 251, 309
Freud, S., 61f
Froebel, F., 34
Fundamentalists, 151, 308

Gallup Poll, 110
Georgia, 5
Germany, 155
Glock, C., 117
Godfrey, W., 196
Gogarten, F., 113
Gospel, 98, 119, 139, 223, 236, 252, 257, 332f, 338
Grace, 54, 86, 93f
Grading, 33, 253
Graduate Theological Union, 273
Gray, G., 196
Greeley, A., 13, 42f, 52
Griffin, B., 196
Grimes, H., 343
Group dynamics, 162, 286
Guilt, 44, 238
Gustafson, J., 311

Habits, 49, 53, 246
Haines, G., 208
Hallinan, Bishop, 232
Hampton Institute, 106f
Harris, M., 226
Harris, W., 9
Hawthorne, N., 110
Heenan, J., 196
Herbart, J., 34
Hierarchy, 4, 13ff, 43, 80ff, 192, 232, 279, 337
High, D., 298, 307f
High School, 26, 191, 274
Higher education, 23, 26, 35, 37, 192
Hinduism, 262
Hippies, 100f

History, 3ff, 12, 22f, 34, 84, 97ff, 107, 148f, 171, 218, 240, 294, 301, 308, 343ff
Hobson, J., 91
Hochwalt, F., 203
Hoekendijk, H., 144ff
Hoffer, E., 111f
Hofinger, J., 349
Holbrook, C., 290ff
Holy Thursday, 92f
Homework, 33
Hope, 93, 218, 249
House churches, 254
Houses of study, 269
Houston, 6
Humanae vitae, 82f
Humanism, 269, 275
Humanitarianism, 22
Hunt, R., 204
Hymns, 133, 226, 236, 239, 254f

Iakovos, Archbishop, 200
I Ching, 110
Idealism, 62
Ideals, 59, 264
Identification, 70f, 74, 262
Identity, 62, 70f, 75, 82, 211
Image, 66ff, 74, 98, 121f
Imperialism, 79, 86
Indians, American, 26
Individualism, 67, 282
Industrialization, 22, 25
Infallibility, 218
Institut catholique, 347
Instruction, 18, 35, 56, 70, 75f, 326
Internalization, 41, 44, 73ff
International Council of Religious Education, 159
International Lesson Series, 160f
International Sunday School Association, 158
Interseminary Movement, 161, 167

Iowa Association of Theological Schools, 273
Irenism, 334, 339
Islam, 92, 238, 291, 299, 339
Italy, 185

James, W., 296
Jefferson, T., 115
Jerome, 195, 263
Jesuits, 5, 268f
Jesus Christ, 4, 21, 43, 59, 68, 75, 113, 131, 215ff, 233f, 236ff, 256, 261ff, 278ff, 307, 345
John XXIII, 130, 177ff, 188
Judaism, 30, 88, 92, 101ff, 107, 137, 151ff, 155ff, 201, 238, 339, 346
Justice, 49f, 84, 199, 206, 321
Justification, 84

Kennedy, J., 6
Kennedy, W., 157f
King, M., Jr., 107
Klapper, J., 122
Knowledge, 68, 75, 245, 292, 329f
Kohlbrenner, B., 4
Ku Klux Klan, 5
Küng, H., 219f, 298

Laity, 15, 25, 27, 81, 90ff, 120, 159ff, 194 278ff, 287ff, 329f, 337
Lambeth Palace, 196
Language, 59, 63ff, 95f, 143, 207, 247ff, 291
Latin America, 106
Lawson, T., 294
Lay trusteeism, 16
Leadership education, 25, 164
Learning, 41-76, 172
Lecture, 19, 41
Lee, J. O., 208
Liberal arts, 22f, 27, 263f, 265
Liberalism, 6, 81, 119, 218, 251ff
Life and Work, 188

Life-styles, 90, 97, 245, 308
Limbert, P., 160
Link, M., 347
Literature, 29, 171
Liturgy, 91ff, 215-257, 323
Liverpool, 196
Living Room Dialogues, 167
Logic, 64, 85
Lombard, P., 267
London, 160, 196
Lord's Prayer, 239, 251
Lord's Supper, 94, 151, 225, 237ff, 248ff, 254
Louisville, 2
Love, 49ff, 69ff, 181, 218, 249
Loyola University, 273
Lumen Vitae, 347
Lund, 144
Luther, M., 84, 128, 181, 218, 241ff
Lutheran Church–Missouri Synod, 26, 156, 166, 203
Lutherans, 25f, 119, 134, 237, 251ff, 308

Madden, W., 31
Madison, J., 115
Majority-minority relations, 102ff, 104f, 144
Mann, H., 8f, 29
Maritain, J., 274
Marquette University, 273
Marx, K., 86, 88
Marxism, 165, 336
Maryknoll Seminary, 348
Maryland, 5
Mass, 128, 230ff
Massachusetts, 5, 8
Mathematics, 12, 48, 57
Maturity, 61, 65, 71, 87, 95f
McCluskey, N., 8
Meland, B., 296, 299f
Melville, H., 110
Mendicant orders, 266

Methodists, 82, 118, 242, 251, 266
Methodology, 19, 141, 239, 290, 305, 344f
Mexican War, 105
Middle Ages, 113, 265, 272, 291
Middle Colonies, 4f, 156
Miller, R., 1, 235f, 340
Mission, 27, 93, 103, 119, 194, 256, 345, 350
Mobility, 121
Models, 33, 36, 292, 298
Moore, A., 351
Moral education, 9ff, 29, 49ff, 60f, 72ff
Moralism, 30, 74, 160
Morality, 41f, 44, 47ff, 53ff, 74f
Moral theology 266
Moran, G., 226, 348
Moule, C., 255
Mount Sinai School of Medicine, 137
Music, 29, 33, 250ff
Myers, J., 209
Mystery, 180, 321f, 345
Mystical Body of Christ, The, 129
Myth, 48ff, 58ff, 65, 102ff

National Association of Evangelicals, 162
National Catholic Education Association, 14ff, 191, 202
National Catholic Reporter, 81
National Catholic Welfare Conference, 203
National Conference of Christians and Jews, 162
National Council of the Churches of Christ in the U.S.A., 2, 159, 188ff, 199, 206ff, 348
National Education Association, 8, 16

National Federation of Catholic College Students, 193
National Home and School Service, 15f
National Newman Student Federation, 193, 275
National Student Christian Federation, 193
Native American Party, 5
Natural theology, 306
Neo-orthodoxy, 160
Netherlands, The 81, 347
New Brunswick, 161
New Deal, 274
New England, 4f, 103, 114, 156
Newman, J., 28
Newport, 26
New Testament, 49, 196ff, 263, 276
New York City, 87, 92, 107, 204
New York Theological Seminary, 350
Nicholls, E., 242
Niebuhr, H., 151, 304, 310f
Nijmegen, 347
Nursery school, 122

Obedience, 44, 53
O'Boyle, Cardinal, 81
Ockham's razor, 12
O'Donahoe, J., 268
Oedipus complex, 61f, 70, 73f
Offertory, 90, 239, 246ff
Ogden, S., 301
Old Testament, 49, 196ff
Olson, B., 166
Oral tradition, 22, 32
Oriental peoples, 26
Original sin, 45
Oxford, 152, 266
Oxford Annotated Bible, 197

Pacifism, 211

Pangrazio, Archbishop, 185
Papacy, 7, 15, 84, 133, 136, 192, 266
Paraparochial ministries, 38
Parents, 8, 15f, 43, 48, 53f, 74, 92, 122, 322ff
Parent-teacher associations, 15
Paris, 136, 347
Parishes, 15ff, 23ff, 38, 211f
Parochial school system, 29, 42ff, 103, 143
Participation, 43, 95, 167, 236, 245ff, 253, 262
Past, 3, 12, 54, 149, 221, 225, 304
Paternalism, 136
Paul, 262
Paul VI, 130ff, 178ff, 188f, 197
Peace, 86, 88, 193, 206
Peace and Freedom Party, 91f
Pelikan, J., 128
Pennsylvania, 170
Pentecost, 22, 255
People of God, 15, 17f, 322ff
Perception, 48, 58, 66ff
Personalism, 229
Pestalozzi, J., 34
Peter, 132, 222f
Philadelphia Sunday and Adult School Union, 157
Philosophy, 35, 64, 265ff, 291ff
Piaget, J., 46f
Pietism, 267
Pike, J., 298
Pius IX, 7
Pius X, 191
Pius XI, 7f
Pius XII, 195
Playboy, 103
Pluralism, 11, 28, 30, 83ff, 88, 104ff, 116ff, 222ff, 278, 289ff, 324, 335f
Politics, 72, 93, 102ff, 110, 152
Political science, 153

Poverty, 206, 209, 288, 313
Power, 48, 68, 82, 96, 117, 201
Practical theology, 37, 309f
Prayer, 236, 263ff, 284f
Preaching, 89, 142, 179, 236ff, 338f
Preadolescence, 51ff
Presbyterians, 118, 166, 241, 251ff
Preschool nursery, 25, 253
Press, 81, 121, 202
Priesthood of believers, 84, 273
Professionals, 4, 16ff, 27, 99, 233, 313, 323
Programmed instruction, 171
Projection, 57, 74, 290
Projects, 37f
Prophecy, 93, 268
Protest, 82, 193
Protestant Banner, 5
Psalms, 239, 253
Psychology, 19, 41-76, 199, 218, 238, 262, 285, 240, 311, 320
Psychoanalysis, 62, 286
Public schools, 6f, 8ff, 22ff, 31f, 38, 163, 170, 202ff
Publishing, 27, 120, 169, 343
Punishment, 41, 49, 73f
Puritan ethic, 103
Pusey, N., 307

Quakers, 25
Qumran, 280

Racism, 82, 103
Radical theology, 113
Radio, 121, 245
Ramsey, I., 296, 308
Readiness, 51ff
Reconciliation, 86f, 278, 288, 345
Redemption, 49, 233
Reform, 81f, 131, 266
Reformation, 93, 127ff, 224, 278, 291, 308
Reformed, 251

Reformers, 83ff, 113, 279
Reinforcement, 244ff
Relationship, 50, 59, 70, 236
Released time, 31, 164
Religiosity, 36
Religious, 13f, 83, 191, 266, 274ff, 329f
Religious Education Association, 1, 152, 165, 168, 206
Renaissance, 267, 269
Renewal, 131, 177, 285
Republican Party, 91
Research, 272, 328
Responsibility, 50ff, 320
Resurrection, 238
Retreats, 25, 123
Revised Standard Version (Bible), 195ff, 248, 345
Revivals, 109, 157, 239, 254
Revolution, 79, 86ff, 93
Rhode Island, 115
Rituals, 226
Romanticism, 62
Rome, 81, 185, 222, 269
Rooney, P., 20
Root, H., 300
Rossi, P., 13, 42f, 52

Sacraments, 43, 96, 134ff, 217, 229ff, 232, 268, 290
Sacred Congregation of the Propagation of the Faith, 7
St. Stephen and the Incarnation Church, 87ff
Salvation, 41, 45, 49f, 87, 119, 140, 185, 219ff, 321ff, 345
San Diego, 199
Schaefer, J., 349
Scharper, P., 165
Schillebeeckx, E., 185, 349
Schleiermacher, F., 308
Scholastic theology, 266f, 274
Schools, 3ff, 22ff, 33, 35

Science, 18, 27, 35, 97, 193, 267, 327
Scripture Press, 166
Scrupulosity, 52
Secondary schools, 4, 15, 18, 26, 293
Secretariat for Non-believers, 339
Secretariat for Promoting Christian Unity, 130
Secularity, 28, 89, 101, 108ff, 166ff, 230ff, 269
Seminaries, 26f, 96, 113, 120, 128, 161, 184, 261-313
Sensitivity training, 162
Sentiments, 59, 64
Separatism, 83ff
Sermons, 89, 108, 236ff
Seventh-Day Adventists, 156, 203
Sex, 62, 320
Shalom communities, 81
Shared time, 32, 284ff
Sheed, F., 231
Shepherd, H., 240ff
Shuster, G., 350
Sigel, I., 46
Sin, 41, 49f, 74, 182
Sloyan, G., 2, 20
Social action, 19, 23, 30, 193, 199
Social workers, 27
Sociology, 54, 79-123, 187, 199, 218, 238, 285, 290, 311, 336
South, 5, 104ff, 114
South America, 274
Southwest, 26
Spanish-speaking people, 26
Spelling, 12
Standard Bible Committee, 194ff
Stanford-Binet Intelligence Scale, 47
Stark, R., 117
State, church and, 29f, 32, 93, 156
Stearns, H., 204
Stephenson, W., 122

Structure, 37, 82ff, 95, 132, 190, 263ff
Student Volunteer Movement, 161
Subsidiarity, 322ff
Sulpicians, 269
Sunday school, 24ff, 92, 103, 157ff, 207, 235, 348
Superego, 41, 50, 74ff
Superintendents, 34
Supreme Court, 29, 109, 170
Switzerland, 183
Syllabus of Errors, 7
Symbol, 30, 65, 102ff, 114f, 229ff, 239, 245ff, 271f
Syncretism, 339

Talmudic studies, 30
Taxation, 30
Taylor, C., 307
Teachers, 26, 43, 48, 76
Teacher training schools, 23, 26
Teaching, 20, 76, 154, 162, 183, 235ff, 310ff, 320ff
Team teaching, 310
Technological society, 32, 86, 301
Teilhard de Chardin, Pierre, 106
Television, 121, 245
Temple, W., 295f
Tennessee, 30
Textbooks, 8, 11, 33, 45, 48, 141, 266
Thanksgiving Day, 117
Theology, 19, 23, 34ff, 41, 96ff, 151ff, 177ff, 187ff, 207, 261-313
Thomism, 260, 274
Thurian, M., 149
Tillich, P., 182, 296
Toolen, T., 7
Toronto, 190
Triumphalism, 179, 184, 234

Underground church, 82, 231f

Union Theological Seminary, 206f, 350
Unitarians-Universalists, 29, 153, 166
United Bible Societies, 195
United Church of Christ, 241
United Presbyterians, 252
United States Catholic Conference, 20
Unity, 131, 173, 180ff, 207, 215ff, 279
University, 4, 19, 22ff, 32, 35ff, 143f, 191, 261-313, 327ff
University Christian Movement, 193
University of Fribourg, 183
University of Iowa, 294
University of Notre Dame, 20, 207, 350

Vacation church school, 24
Vahanian, G., 98
Values, 35, 41, 59, 104, 122, 271, 287, 321
Van Allmen, J., 249
Van Buren, P., 297
Van den Heuvel, A., 168
Vatican Council II, 1, 8, 19, 43f, 80, 130ff, 164, 177ff, 195, 216ff, 234, 268, 273ff, 291, 345, 351
Vernacular liturgy, 84, 244
Vietnam, 93, 211
Vincentians, 269
Virginia, 107
Visser 't Hooft, W., 147
Vocational education, 33, 261ff
Voluntarism, 191ff
Volunteers, 35

Waldensians, 83
Walker, A., 9
Walther League, 142
War, 95, 212

Washington, G., 115
Washington, D.C., 81, 87ff, 93ff, 204
Washington Priests Association, 81
Wayne State University, 45
Webber, G., 350
Wechsler Intelligence Scale for Children, 47
Weekday church school, 24f, 238
West Indies, 26
Whitehead, A., 67
Whites, 92, 134, 203, 208
Williams, D., 311
Williams, R., 116
Witness, 255, 262
Women's societies, 200
Worcester, 234
World Council of Christian Edu-cation and Sunday School Association, 158, 187
World Council of Churches, 129, 139ff, 190f
Wornom, H., 301
Worship, 10, 35, 55, 123, 139, 154, 215-257, 278ff, 345

Yale University, 25
Young adults, 228
Young Men's Christian Association, 25, 160f
Young people, 25, 27, 33, 86, 92, 121f, 207, 320ff
Young Women's Christian Association, 25, 161

Zen Buddhism, 110
Zwingli, H., 128